Lynnette Widder

Year Zero to Economic Miracle Hans Schwippert and Sep Ruf in Postwar West German Building Culture

Table of Contents

Introduction

The present has no need for the language of imagination to convey a world in which millions of refugees have been set in motion, cities reduced to rubble. War is, tragically, as much a constant in this century as it was in the prior. But among the countless military conflagrations with which the twenty-first century has begun, not one has a name that records its implications beyond its immediate territory. Not so the two wars at the start of the twentieth century. "World War" conveys the hubris of empires. And by contrast to the political motivations that now constrain the names of wars to geography, itself often a product of mid-twentieth-century carve-ups, the designation "World War" was always intended to imply a dimension of historic destiny. The scale of destruction the World Wars left behind was likewise vast and all-encompassing.

Germany's historic destiny was the pretext for the World War instigated by the Third Reich. After Hitler's unconditional surrender, this destiny was utterly recast by the victor nations. The two new German states were conceived to embody ideals that would, so it was believed, result from a recalibrated balance between individual ethics and shared responsibility. Economic certitude, coupled with moral education and equal opportunity, would ensure peace. This aspiration, if realized in very different manners, held true in Western and Soviet sectors alike. Both the (western) Federal Republic and the (eastern) Democratic Republic were inventions that served as proxies for a new world order. The facts of private everyday life on the ground, although quite different in the two Germanies, were inextricable from that order.

But before this everyday life and the society it was meant to yield could come into being, Germany had to be rebuilt one building at a time. The devastation of cities, transportation, infrastructure, industry and agriculture was near complete. The number of displaced persons in 1945 / 1946 hovers between eight and twelve million; by 1950, when more accurate counts could be made, some 20 percent of West Germany's citizens reported having arrived in the aftermath of the war. In East Germany, that number was closer to 25 percent.[01] Rebuilding had to begin without standard construction material or equipment, without an adequately skilled workforce, without reprieve from harsh winter weather and, no less detrimental than physical hardship, without any way to address the utter disorientation of living amidst rubble.[02] To consider architecture in Germany in the aftermath of the war is to consider a discipline bereft. Charged with responding to homelessness and physical destruction, the discipline was still coming to terms with its own contributions to the regime that had instigated disaster.

Photographs, journals, and news reports from the mid- and late 1940s register what citizens, including the architects among them, would have seen.[03] But such documents, whether text, film, or photograph, cannot explain what architects understood to be their role or their purpose under such conditions. Between ruin and rubble lies a boundary that is difficult to locate but unequivocal in its meaning. "The ruined building is a remnant of, and portal to the past," essayist Brian Dillon points out in his introduction to an anthology of texts on ruin (2011), "and yet by definition, it survives after a fashion: there must be a certain (perhaps indeterminate) amount of a built structure still standing for us to refer to it as a ruin and not merely a heap of rubble."[04] In the late 1940s and in some cases, even later, German cities more closely resembled rubble than ruins. "Year zero" is the term that recurs in descriptions of the time. It was also the title of Roberto Rossellini's 1948 film shot in Berlin. The fields of weeds, stones and dirt through which Rossellini's characters move are not, by any definition, a city. They are barely recognizable as human settlement. The emotional, moral, and social void in which his characters hover bears the imprint of their city's erasure.

Architecture had more to account for than physical destruction. The discipline was set adrift from its ethical and aesthetic grounding in technical and moral progress, a grounding upon which modern architecture as credo was predicated. The rupture was as unequivocal as it was distressing. It extended, for many, beyond vocation to individual

01   Eric Solsten, "Germany: A Country Study," (Washington: GPO for the Library of Congress, 1995). http://countrystudies.us /germany/ and http://countrystudies.us/ germany/84.htm, accessed May 27, 2021.
02   Returning to Frankfurt in the late fall of 1949, Theodor Adorno wrote, "the world has ended but I still recognized, as I had in childhood, the difference between the tram lines 1 and 4 by the fact that the former had two green lights and the latter, one grey and one white. That has remained. Regression." Theodor W. Adorno and Theodor W. Adorno Archiv, *Adorno: Eine Bildmonographie*, 2nd ed. (Frankfurt am Main: Suhrkamp Verlag, 2003), 213.
03   To name only one: Max Frisch, *Tagebuch, 1946–1949* (Frankfurt am Main: Suhrkamp Verlag, 1965).
04   Brian Dillon, *Ruins*, Whitechapel: Documents of Contemporary Art (London; Cambridge, MA: Whitechapel Gallery, MIT Press, 2011), 11.

sense of self. Architects, like all private citizens during the National Socialist regime, had been under duress to choose some degree of acquiescence to political demands. Very few had embraced "internal emigration," full withdrawal from professional life. More, although not a majority, had worked as party loyalists with Albert Speer, Hitler's architect and quartermaster general, the logistics genius who ensured reliable delivery of war materiel. Many in this group were nonetheless quickly de-Nazified after the war, especially in the American-occupied zone and then installed in offices of city planning throughout West Germany.[05] Their expertise was simply too valuable to forego. Most architects, however, had found a path somewhere in between the extremes of collusion and refusal. Several of those who would define postwar discourse had found refuge in the branch of the official building ministry that specialized in industrial buildings. There, they could realize buildings in a modernist language, which they imagined as a kind of exculpation by virtue of style. Others quietly worked as professors, industrial designers, city planning employees or church architects. Some continued independent practice and designed small residential projects, without actively drawing notice to their political convictions. And of course, the most famous Weimar protagonists simply left the country. Many ended up in the United States, a fact that would have important implications for the American-occupied sector, its architecture, and its building industry.

The ambiguities—in the best case—and recriminations provoked by these architects' choices were debated during the late 1940s into the early 1950s in magazine articles and public conferences, in private venues, meetings, and letters, and in the architectural works that were produced. Style was no longer a touchstone, as it might have been in the past. There was no way to rely upon the "comfortable simplification: modern, democratic; traditional, national socialist."[06] With the emigration of Walter Gropius and his Bauhaus cohort, championed in architectural history writing as the originators of modern architecture, the architectural achievements of the Weimar era could no longer be claimed as exclusively German. That legacy had emigrated along with its most famous practitioners. And of course, Weimar, Dessau, and the historical center of Berlin, the wellsprings of the German architectural avant-garde, now sat within the German Democratic Republic, on the "wrong side" of the border, at least from a West German perspective. From an East German perspective, the modernist legacy of these cities presented an inappropriate architectural heritage for a country obligated to the official neoclassical Stalinist style.

This, then, is the world in which architects attempted to find their bearings again. Their challenges were ones of both material and conviction: how to address the devastation that war had left behind, the drastic shortage of housing, the utter lack of means to compensate for it; but also how to represent a new, anti-totalitarian, anti-National Socialist Germany. The subdivision of Germany, a young nation-state by European standards, produced competing answers. This book addresses developments in West Germany; or specifically, developments in the material, theoretical, and stylistic aspects of West German architecture as practiced and realized by two important figures of the postwar period, Hans Schwippert and Sep Ruf.

This framing of subject matter correlates to the period between Year Zero and its resolution in the *Wirtschaftswunder*, the Economic Miracle. It considers the broader narrative in terms of the imprint it left in these two architects' oeuvre. It offers an analysis that draws on material that is broader in scope than architectural history's usual domain. It attends to all the ways in which architecture comes into being: the ideas that motivate it; the many authors who contribute to it; the diverse materials, techniques, and industries at play; the different ways in which architecture is represented and in which it represents. Schwippert and Ruf were close colleagues if not close friends, advocates for each other's careers if not regular collaborators, modern architects albeit of a different stripe.

05   See Werner Durth, *Deutsche Architekten: Biographische Verflechtungen 1900–1970*, rev. ed. (Stuttgart: K. Krämer, 2001).
06   Durth, *Deutsche Architekten: Biographische Verflechtungen 1900–1970*, 212.

They also shared a similar fate in the way posterity has received them. Despite their importance to the manner in which the Bundesrepublik would represent itself in architecture and design, despite the importance of the buildings they realized, neither was the subject of comprehensive monographs until the twenty-first century. The leading roles they assumed after the war contrast with their relatively quiet status as fellow travelers amidst the vibrant architectural scene of the Weimar Republic. Their wartime careers, well documented in research, did not distinguish them in the way that it did others. The job of this book is not to adjudicate discussions, despite their importance, about the legacy of the Third Reich in architectural practice after the war. It is also not to valorize or demonize a specific version of the modernist architectural aesthetic. Instead, it considers the parallel and reciprocal developments between an architectural language and a country guided by ideals of participatory democracy within a social market economy. The two architects whose work provides the specific instances for analysis were not selected per se for their design finesse, their charisma, or their success, although they both had all these assets. Instead, their work is studied as a way to reflect on what can be learned about society and about architecture in this period from documents of a kind not always available or legible to architectural history: construction drawings, catalogues, telephone notes, letters, job books, site photographs, and other ephemera. Such documents have much to contribute.

A photograph from the late 1950s, when Sep Ruf and Hans Schwippert were both at work on the West German pavilion for the Brussels World's Fair, is preserved in Schwippert's bequest at the German National Museum in Nuremberg. **[0.1]** It shows Ruf at a buffet table, smiling. Ruf's collaborating architect on the project, the debonair Egon Eiermann, is grinning in the background. The scene is a testament to good humor and relaxed bonhomie. It is easy to imagine that Schwippert saved this photo as evidence of the friendship and commonalities he and Ruf shared over the course of the 1950s. Like Ruf, Schwippert left a largely unwinnowed archive that permits the writing of an architectural history with reference to ephemera that in other cases remain inaccessible. Although they were friends, occasional collaborators, and postwar German Werkbund colleagues, the two men nonetheless represent distinct tendencies during the period in question. Sep Ruf, a prolific Bavarian architect, became famous for large corporate and public sector clients. Hans Schwippert, heady and articulate, was as an architect who remained fascinated by the one-off, despite his savvy in connecting industry to product design on behalf of the German Werkbund.

In the late 1940s and early 1950s, Schwippert and Ruf produced architecture that was still similar in style. In the course of the following decade, however, the thin window mullions, attenuated glazing proportions, and simple white stuccoed surfaces of Ruf's earlier postwar work **[0.2]** gave way to a far more robustly dimensioned and varied palette of elements. By contrast, Schwippert's work remained closer to the interests and spatial sensibility that characterize even his first postwar projects in Bonn, then the new West German capital. **[0.3]** His late-career renovation of St. Hedwig's Cathedral, a public project completed after nearly a decade of work across the division of Berlin, bears out his love of subtlety, for example, in the careful instructions he gave for the different sand and marble dust additives in the plaster applied to the cathedral's different surfaces. The changes undergone by Ruf's work in the mid-1950s correspond to stylistic shifts seen elsewhere in West German architecture; but Ruf's stylistic evolution is particularly intriguing because of his direct access to the construction techniques, contractors, and design language that were introduced to West Germany by the American architecture firm Skidmore, Owings, and Merrill (SOM) for their US consular projects. With their specific version of architectural modernism, SOM fostered a material culture and construction palette new to West Germany. Ruf gained access to these in advance of other German architects. The study of changes in architectural form relative to construction

0.1 Sep Ruf with Egon Eiermann during preparations for the 1958 Brussels World's Fair

processes provides greater nuance in understanding this period than can derive from standard formal analysis alone.

Architecture places huge demands on capital, material, and labor for its making; its technologies of communication and realization are specialized and difficult to coordinate. Changes in industry and society thus often overtake architecture as it moves from ideation to completion. West Germany's postwar period was unusual in its near parity between these discrepant rates of change. The building industry leveraged postwar rebuilding efforts to regain the very high levels of precision manufacturing that had been purveyed before (and in many cases, during) the war. Over time, companies also differentiated their trades and products to find increasingly niche market share. In the course of rebuilding their businesses in the late 1940s or early 1950s, many manufacturers made concessions to realize architectural details that were bespoke, in other words, were dictated by architects rather than being driven by economies of scale. The result was a context in which decisions about architectural expression were more fully in the hands of a designing, construction-literate architect. As the economy surged, business models demanded greater standardization. This in turn meant more systematic, reproducible approaches towards architectural detailing, especially in facade construction and interior finishes. Logically, these changes in manufacturing and product development capacity meant changes in architectural design and style. It is unimportant whether stylistic or manufacturing priorities motivated changes in clients' taste or vice versa. The reciprocity among industry, design, and taste during this period is unequivocal.

Close reciprocity between industry and architecture had already existed in Germany during the interwar period. By the time war mobilization was underway in the 1930s, both building technology and manufacturing capacity had more than caught up with the aesthetic and spatial demands of modernist architecture. Two handbooks on windows and doors by Adolf Schneck, published in 1932 and 1933, respectively,[07] are among the popular guides that attest to the sophistication of the available hardware, and the large number of fabricators. There was, it seems, proprietary hardware for every conceivable size, configuration, and movement of any imaginable door, gate, or window. The images Schneck included record the still-famous and now lesser-known architects who availed themselves of these possibilities.

After the war, the monopolies that had facilitated production and stockpiling of war material were split apart and Germany was forced to rebuild from a fragmented industry. Despite shortages and hardships, the know-how in machining that had produced the technical efflores-cence of the 1920s and 1930s in the building trades remained.[08] Collaboration with modernist architects, struggling amidst the dearth of appropriate products and components in the late 1940s and early 1950s, was an ideal outlet for this ingenuity. The survival and success rate of West German companies involved in significant early postwar projects is remarkable—in many cases, such companies have persisted into the present.[09] This evidence of business savvy speaks again to the potentials of modern architecture in this era, not only as a stylistic choice, but also as a business model, as is attested in construction drawings, catalogues, and advertisements.

The postwar symbiosis between modern architecture and advances in business management and manufacturing was not unique to West Germany. The trajectory of curtain wall fabrication from bespoke to systematic as it occurred in Germany after 1949 mirrors a trend that occurred slightly earlier in the United States, if under completely different economic and socio-cultural conditions. American architects and builders benefited from an expanded wartime industrial base, particularly as the capacities of wartime industry were redirected to building construction. The accelerated optimization in the US building industry provided an example to West German companies. American architects working in Germany, accustomed to designing for an American construction culture already predicated on economies of scale, transposed their expectations to German associate architects and suppliers, who responded with accelerated development. As American models were adopted, West German construction shifted. In this way, not only through appearance and taste-making, American architecture impacted the way West Germany built. Within this competitive, transforming construction envi-ronment, companies working on projects sponsored under Consular and America House program of the US High Commissioner in Germany had advance insight. [0.4] In almost all cases, their businesses flourished.

Although the need for housing dominated construction activity during the 1950s, public buildings were conceived to represent the ideals of a still emergent society. In this moment, a new balance was sought between a public sphere characterized by mutuality and distinct from the mass culture associated with the national socialist regime, and a private life that was secure at the same time as it cultivated the social engagement required by participatory democracy. Much effort went into creating pari-ty between public and private, both in social structures and in design. The practices cultivated in the domestic realm were conceived to support responsible participation in public life. Transparency, modesty, and thoroughness were the values inherent in both. Architects were challenged to represent these values in exhibitions, model homes, schools, public buildings, and consumer products. Spaces and artifacts were implicated

07   Adolf G. Schneck, *Die Bauelemente Bände I und II: Fenster und Türen* (Stuttgart: Julius Hoffmann, 1932/3).
08   For example, Josef Gartner, Gundelfingen.
09   Many steel window and door firms that bid on Sep Ruf's Akademie der Bildenden Künste still exist, i.e., Brehm GmbH (originally a glazer, now a window manufacturer), Klöckner Stahl- und Metallhandel (door frames), Vögel GmbH (steel doors), and Jucho (steel windows; later, a large-scale metalworking company).

10   Richard M. Brickner, *Is Germany
Incurable?* (Philadelphia: J. B. Lippincott, 1943).
Brickner's was a popular thesis in the United
States during the 1940s.

in large-scale social reeducation, which from the very beginning
included everyday life.

There is a hilarious and telling scene in Billy Wilder's *A Foreign
Affair* (1948, Paramount Pictures), filmed on site in the ruined German
capital of Berlin not long after Rossellini's *Germania: Anno Zero* (1947/8).
The difference between Wilder's comedy and Rossellini's drama could not
be starker. Wilder's film includes an early scene at a US Army reeducation
center. One of the boys playing baseball, a sport that Hollywood audiences
would likely have agreed is foundational to democratic values, has
accidentally broken a window. The boy, roughly the same age as the suicide
in Rossellini's film, has been brought to see the army officer in charge.
The boy's father, a heel-clicking underling, has also been summoned.
Despite best efforts, the father cannot be made to understand what
the officer is trying to teach him: that although his son has made an error,
boys will be boys, rambunctiousness builds character, and Germans
need to relearn how to color outside the lines. The difference between
responsibility and obedience, the importance of mistake-making for
learning: such experiences in daily life were meant to turn Germans away
from the so-called psychology of Fascism.[10] In schools, in recreation,
in street life, but above all in the activities organized by and around the
two German Churches, Protestant and Catholic, the practices of this
daily life were cultivated as a way out of and forward from a generation
of Fascist socialization. Public architecture supported this transformation by imagining and embodying it in a lightness and transparency that
corresponded to a way of life that had nothing to hide.

Housing had to be built quickly. It was not a field for experimentation.
In fact, the plentiful experimentation with construction practices and
housing typologies that had taken place in the Weimar period now proved
to have real utility, allowing emphasis on production, not reinvention,
of housing types. Public spaces enabled the exercise of architectural
imagination in a way that housing could not. This was especially
true for the churches and chapels built in response to the needs not only
of a bereft and largely devout population but also of the Allied forces in
West Germany, for whom the two primary Christian churches were ideal
partners in the reconstruction effort. At the same time, architects
found space for experimentation at the small scale, in the consumer object.

**0.2 Akademie der Bildenden Künste,
Nuremberg, upon completion in
1958, from *Baukunst und Werkform 4***

0.3 Hans Schwippert, Bundeshaus, terrace to plenary, ca. 1949

They designed furniture, doorknobs, candlesticks. The benefit of strong consumer goods production to the West German economy was clear early on, and the Werkbund, West Germany's assembly of artists, designers, and architects reestablished in 1947, worked hand-in-glove with economic advisors, officers, and their cohort. The utopian visions first articulated in the interwar period, of a just society realized by means of architectural design, resurfaced in the hope that well-designed everyday objects could uplift the public spirit. The connection of these intertwining mandates to design—the public and the private, the ethical and the consumerist—was a recurrent motif. It appears in 1951 during Schwippert's explanation of his concept of *Wohnwollen*, or the will to dwell, in the Darmstädter Gespräch. It is epitomized in Ruf's model house at West Germany's pavilion for the 1958 World's Fair. Embedded almost surreptitiously within the large, involuted brick retaining wall upon which the better-known glass exhibition halls rested, Ruf's house was both sheltering and transparent. It captured the era's *Wohnwollen*.

Likewise, Schwippert imagined his 1949 Bundeshaus in Bonn as "the lightest parliament in the world,"[11] its transparency and clarity an embodiment of Germany's new democratic soul. Built only a short time later, the Akademie der Bildenden Künste in Nuremberg by Sep Ruf (1950–1954) shares the same lightness and transparency. Both buildings were also realized during a time of material and product shortages. Because the job books and working drawings for Ruf's building survive, and because Schwippert's project was well-photographed during construction, these projects can be used to characterize the interplay between construction practice and architectural expression in the early years of the Bundesrepublik.

The Akademie der Bildenden Künste was completed in 1954 at an important moment of transition. Architectural language was changing, partly in response to discussions within the professional press that critiqued the perceived stylistic monotony resulting from the first wave of rebuilding. The gridded elevation, a direct expression of structural and functional logics, was dismissed in favor of a new facade strategy that could allow the architect greater expressive discretion while maintaining the basic tenets of modern architecture. This new facade was epitomized by the curtain wall, based largely upon American precedent. The solidifying West German construction industry, no longer

11 Will Grohmann, "Das hellste Parlamentsgebäude der Welt" *Die Neue Zeitung* (Munich), March 4, 1951, 53.

0.4 Sep Ruf, American Consulate, late 1950s

plagued by the shortages and inadequacies of the early 1950s, was a keen partner in systematizing facade construction. This confluence of taste and material culture is unmistakable in the buildings of this period: the American Consulate in Munich (1956–1959), the West German Pavilion at the Brussels World's Fair (1956–1958), and finally, Ruf's Hochschule für Verwaltungswissenschaften in Speyer (1957–1960). **[0.5] [0.6]**

Schwippert's St. Hedwig's Cathedral in East Berlin (1956–1963) is a poignant but important outlier to this tendency. Schwippert's patience and care, his embrace of material shortages and political struggle, are unmistakable in the project, which occupied a near decade of his professional life and compelled him to work across the political divide that rent his country. Especially by comparison with Ruf's roughly contemporaneous Hochschule in Speyer, the Hedwigskathedrale in East Berlin feels like a remnant of material culture circa 1949 or '50. As a study in construction practice and collaboration between blue collar and white, the cathedral is a rare and moving instance of what it means to rely upon native knowledge rather than technological progress.

The choice to end this book with the Hedwigskathedrale is not only dictated by chronology. The conditions under which the project was realized were extraordinarily complicated. The dearth of materials available for the project in the German Democratic Republic contrasts starkly with Ruf's contemporaneous Hochschule in Speyer. But the building also provides a telling counterpoint to Schwippert's own Bundeshaus. The Bundeshaus could be realized with unheard-of speed in a time of material scarcity only because the project was inextricable from the goal of establishing the new Federal Republic as a political entity. Ruf's Hochschule was likewise essential to stabilizing West Germany's government because it was to be the primary site at which a new cadre of bureaucrats could be trained. In both cases, architectural design was called upon to represent a new postwar state that was both appropriately modest and reliably stable. As much as these two buildings differ in appearance, both represent dominant cultural moments. The situation was quite different for the Hedwigskathedrale. Berlin had traditionally been Protestant, though historically religiously tolerant; after 1949 it became the capital of the programmatically atheistic German Democratic Republic. The Catholic cathedral was treated as a stepchild, more closely tied to the physically remote and politically constrained Vatican than to local jurisdiction. Realized at a distance by an architect who was deeply invested in the materialization of his work—and who would have relished time on the job site—St. Hedwig's is a fascinating document of ingenuity and trust. The extended time required for its construction bespeaks the difficulties that were encountered. If one reads the Hedwigskathedrale in relation to the ideas about material, spirit, and expression that Schwippert articulated at Darmstadt in 1951, more than ten years before its completion, the cathedral's stark spaces and modest palette answer many of the questions inherent to the idea of *Wohnwollen*.

Neither of the two protagonists in this book are well known to English-speaking audiences. An excellent and charismatic practitioner, Sep Ruf (1908–1982) is singular in Bavaria, a region of more traditional tastes, for having achieved an exceptionally prolific body of work without compromising his commitment to modern architecture. Ruf's daughters, one of whom worked with him, have maintained his office archives in nearly undisturbed condition. Those archives include original construction documents in versions from initial sketches to approved shop drawings. Project correspondence, time sheets, disputes, contractor negotiations, product specifications, and selected product brochures have also survived, in exception to the general tendency to discard such things as soon as a project's statute of limitations has expired. The generosity of Elisabeth and Notburga Ruf in sharing their archive was invaluable to understanding Ruf and his office staff as practitioners in reciprocity with specific material and labor conditions. Ruf's contact with American architects building in Germany during the 1950s could only be reconstructed by recourse to these archival documents. Assistance from the SOM Archives and the US Department of State provided documentation vital to understanding SOM's position in this period, when the firm was responsible for four of the five consulates built in West Germany under the US Consular and America House program through a site office managed by German architect Otto Apel, at the time a frequent collaborator of Ruf's.

The quality of Ruf's work, its architectural expression, and the availability of vital project documents are in themselves compelling. His work also provides insight into how influence was transmitted and change occurred, and thereby contributes to deciphering the stylistic shifts of the period. Ruf did not subscribe to American architectural publications,[12] nor was he in regular correspondence with German émigré architects in the United States before a three-week trip there in 1963, during which he met Ludwig Mies van der Rohe in Chicago. His professional contact to American architecture came, at least initially, through the process by which he received and completed the commission for the American Consulate in Munich. Ruf's earlier contact with American culture was in a completely different context: the bloodless takeover of the region where he lived in Germany left a favorable impression on him of American culture that served him well in his dealings with the occupying army. His affinity registered in both family lore[13] and in professional opportunity, beginning with housing projects and other studies he completed in collaboration with other architects during the 1940s.[14]

The wealth of documentation in the Ruf family archive was the exception, however, in the effort to track the interplay of design and construction in the exchange between American and German architectural traditions through construction-related documents. The remnants of Apel's archive mostly originated with his subsequent firm ABB and include nothing from his work with SOM. Even after the consulates were completed, security dictated that all the documents used for their construction remain in the possession of the US High Commissioner for Germany,[15] whose record keeping was meticulous and centralized, a fact that ultimately doomed their preservation. Until the US Embassy in Bonn was closed after German reunification, the records were in the embassy's Consulting Engineers Office. Harald Nethe, the architect who supervised the archive in its last permutation, described its fate:

"As long as the American Embassy was in Bonn (where I still live), it had what was called the Consulting Engineers' Office. When I started working for that office (1984), Richard Neumann was the (German) boss. [...]

12   Elisabeth and Notburga Ruf in conversation with the author, July 20, 2011. In 1963, Ruf visited the United States, where he met Ludwig Mies van der Rohe and visited the offices of SOM. He briefly corresponded with Richard Neutra, whom he invited to lecture in Munich.
13   Elisabeth and Notburga Ruf in conversation with the author, July 20, 2011.
14   Ruf was singled out as an "architect of particular status" for projects in Bonn by Minister Director Wandersleb. Letter from Wandersleb to Schwippert, May 18, 1949. Architekturmuseum der Technischen Universität München (AM TUM), schwi-92-209.
15   Email from Oliver Elser of DAM, November 9, 2011.

What I will now tell you will bring tears to your eyes. When Bonn was closed down, the question was what was to become of the drawings in the archive? Since I was being transferred to Frankfurt, I took the Frankfurt plans with me. The plans of Bonn and anything else we had were to remain where they were. We left them in our office and closed the door. I'm sure the new owner threw them all away."[16] Of course, loss of material evidence is the condition with which any attempt at history writing must contend. Construction documents, specifications, catalogues, and other records related to the realization of buildings are particularly susceptible because of the way they are perceived. For their authors, their value ends when the information they communicate has been realized in built work. Once legal demands on architect, builder, or manufacturer liability expire, there is little reason to keep them. They are not seen as intrinsically valuable or of art historical interest, as design development or presentation overview drawings traditionally are. Architecture history, through close attention to nuanced systems of authorship, labor, and material culture, has the capacity to change this perspective, if it chooses. Until such a change occurs, the passage of time that transforms the detritus of a finished project into a bearer of cultural significance may prove too long for an architecture office's patience with the by-products of its own production, and the space demanded may seem unjustified when an archivist needs to make room for additional files.

The construction documents still intact are conclusive, however. Ruf's buildings register the tight control he maintained over design and construction. Details drawn to millimeter precision, receipts for on-site labor that have been checked and double-checked: these are the hallmarks of Ruf's office. The greater precision and control gained through collaboration with the building product industry was an appropriate, if not synergistic, extension to Ruf's values. His changing architectural idiom relates directly to the way in which his projects were built and the industry that provided the necessary products and semi-products. His prolific career would not have been the same without developments in building construction, which allowed him to remain exacting while realizing numerous, sizable projects.

Schwippert's archives are as prodigious as Ruf's, including material from years of architectural and design practice, teaching, writing, and postwar German Werkbund orchestration.[17] His copious collection of newspaper clippings and letters reveal the intrigue and politics that make up the intensive reception history of the Bundeshaus. The candid group shots that he retained of Ruf, Eiermann and himself at a round table in front of the site plan for the Brussels World's Fair have the cigarette smoke-tinged fashion flare of an early James Bond film. Schwippert's ability to navigate volatile situations, to judge from his correspondence, seems to have resulted from persistence rather than slickness, at least by comparison to some of his contemporaries. A less prolific although important practicing architect, he exerted his primary influence as the first head of the postwar German Werkbund (1950–1963) and as a leading figure in pedagogic and theoretical discourse during the period in which the Wirtschaftswunder gained momentum.

Schwippert's architectural practice reflects the attitude that architecture is only one component within a larger design culture. His projects actively involved product design, lighting design, interior architecture, artisanal production, and exhibitions. Although this kind of all-encompassing practice was not uncommon in the postwar period, as the examples of Ruf and SOM can also attest, Schwippert's approach is different. Detail drawings are conceived to cede some control to the fabricator during realization. Both the Bundeshaus and the Hedwigskathedrale were realized with barely annotated or dimensioned construction details. This reticence speaks to his implicit trust in the people who realized his intentions. They were his collaborators, not merely his workforce. The ground-up design of furniture, hardware, lighting and architectural environment in these two projects allowed

16   Email from Harald Nethe, June 30, 2010.
17   There are eleven Schwippert job books at the AM TUM. Thanks to Dr. Anja Schmidt, I viewed them briefly in December 2021. One binder details the first phase of the Bundeshaus but contains no drawings. Binders on the Brussels pavilion are concerned only with the curation that Schwippert oversaw, not with the architectural project.

0.5 Sep Ruf, College of Public Administration, Speyer, ca. 1960

him to reflect both on the material limitations under which the projects were realized and on his practical relationship to the industrially produced designs he championed via the Werkbund.

Amidst the massive changes in building industry, construction products, and even taste that were occurring around him, Schwippert's architectural style remained largely consistent over the 1950s and into the 1960s. Bespoke, labor intensive, filigree: by the time the Hedwigskathedrale was being built, this manner of building ran counter to the material culture of the post-Wirtschaftswunder building economy. However, Schwippert's interest in construction as a negotiation between the replicable and the unique was appropriate to the context of East German material frugality and skilled, committed labor. Like an "Art by Telephone"[18] painting, in which the artist's verbal directives were transmitted without visual referent to the site where the art was made, everything at spatial and temporal remove, Schwippert's cathedral plans were executed through a considerable network. This network connected his Düsseldorf office by post to a contact architect in East Berlin, the diocese in West Berlin, and a host of fabricators and manufacturers distributed throughout both Germanies. In addition to the geographic difficulties exacerbated by Cold War politics, the lack of materials and technology in East Berlin was comparable to the conditions he had known in the late 1940s, when ingenuity and making-due had to compensate for such inadequacies.

It is fair to say that Schwippert's influence exceeded that of his built work. As Werkbund president, Schwippert worked with an array of architects and designers to redefine a version of German style that could acknowledge the complex historical moment at which he assumed leadership. As a measure of his success, the West German pavilion at the 1958 Brussels World's Fair was internationally celebrated as perfectly appropriate to the new German Republic.

The writing in this book began conventionally, as an academic undertaking. Academic books often have recourse to methodology in order to explain choices of inclusion or omission. The important influence of personal experience and discretion is repressed. I have chosen a different approach, through which I explain my impetus to tell this particular story. By presenting my personal relationship to the material of study, I emphasize that insight can come from the most unexpected quarters. I am reminded of an article I once read in a long-lost issue of the German newspaper *Frankfurter Allgemeine*.[19] The paper had interviewed Marron Curtis Fort,

18   Museum of Contemporary Art Chicago bulletin, undated. https://mcachicago.org /Exhibitions/1969/Art-By-Telephone, accessed January 22, 2022.
19   Edo Reents, "Der Letzte Frisist," *Frankfurter Allgemeine Zeitung Feuilleton* (October 24, 2018). https://www.faz.net /aktuell/feuilleton/dem-frisisten-marron-curtis -fort-zum-80-15852907.html, accessed December 18, 2021.

0.6 Hans Schwippert, St. Hedwig's Cathedral, Berlin, 1962

the world expert on Northern Germany's *Plattdeutsch* dialect. Born in Boston to emigrated Creole-speaking parents, Fort's choice of subject matter, and his superlative mastery of it, seemed as unlikely as it was remarkable. My investment in this era and its architecture is, by comparison to Fort's in a language so far from home, much closer at hand, but it still bears explanation.

Interleaved with chapters written in accordance with academic tradition are texts of another sort, essays in which I speak directly to the experiences and affinities that converged in the writing of this book. Taken together, the academic chapters and essays expand the narrative to include the importance of distributed authorship, as much in the making of buildings as in the writing of histories. Both scholarly and personal draw heavily upon ephemera that has, sometimes by chance and sometimes by design, survived long enough to suggest a narrative that otherwise might be repressed. The book opens and closes with accounts of two buildings, one each by Schwippert and Ruf, which capture the conditions and spirits of the conditions under which they were conceived and realized. The two middle sections consider the period between these two pairings through theoretical debates among architects, architectural journalism, advertising and industry standards, and the monumental influence of American architects practicing in West Germany under the auspices of the European Recovery Program (known as the Marshall Plan). Each of these four sections is punctuated by an essay that considers the circumstances under which I conducted my research, the people under whose influence the work came into existence, the peculiarities of the research documents I favor and, comingled with all of this, some elements of my own biography that have underpinned my scholarship. Consider this an alternative to the more usual account of methodology. Consider this a way to recognize what otherwise remains in the background of much scholarship.

Conversations with generous mentors and friends, considerations both analytical and serendipitous, led to my decision to structure this book around exemplary works by two architects, who should be appreciated not only for their specific contributions but also for the paradigmatic way in which they represent distinct approaches to a modern architecture appropriate to the Bundesrepublik Deutschland in its initial decades. This book is a document of their trajectories and mine. It speaks, both historically and personally, to one of my favorite German compound words: *Werdegang*. The word, as applicable to this book in itself as to the material it considers, combines two root words, "trajectory" (*gang*) and the verb for becoming (*werden*), to denote the process of coming into one's own.

Architectures of Lesser Means, 1949–1954

Hans Schwippert's Bundeshaus, Bonn

Two men stand at the top of a laddered column. **[1.1]** The steel truss they are positioning, one that will span the thirty-meter-wide plenary hall of the new German Federal Republic's parliament, is as high as they are tall. There is no doubt that the men, each one secure in his stance, have done work like this before: both look towards the come-along at the truss's center span as their hands guide the suspended truss into position at the column's top. The far bank of the Rhine lies just below the horizon line marked by eye level; the two men's feet, planted stably on the thin edge of a steel strut, hold them high above the ground. Both column and truss type are typical of bridge building, the primary business of their company since its inception in the mid-nineteenth century. Lengths of steel pipe nearly as thick in diameter as the men's legs form the trusses' up-sloping top and bottom chords, which meet at a shallow peak at the center of the span. This peak, which will be invisible to the ground-level visitor when the building is complete, corresponds to the angle selected by the architect Hans Schwippert from among numerous, careful bird's eye-view studies. Through these studies, which were, for the most part, completed over the course of a single week in January 1949, Schwippert developed the subtle, illusory tricks that underpin the perceptual ambiguities in the building's spatial, surface, and volumetric syntax. These tricks and the resulting ambiguities compensate for stringent limitations: they permit transparency although there is little steel or glass. They create the non-hierarchical

1.1 Installation of the steel pipe trusses for the Bundeshaus plenary, Bonn 1949

"DER BAU" 7/1950   Seite 159

Bild 3: Montage der Stahlrohr-Dachbinder

spaces that connote democracy while nevertheless retaining an inherent sense of sequence and decorum.

The trusses in the photograph conform to a common structural principle. Their web forms a so-called Pratt truss, in which the diagonal connective members begin at the top corner of the upper chord and run towards the lower corner of the first vertical element in the web. The Pratt truss was patented in 1844 in the United States, although its principle had long been intuited and was known elsewhere by other names. The steel bearing structure in this photograph is technologically no different than the tens of thousands of rail, road, and pedestrian bridges that connected Germany, or had, before its disastrous war. Still, this particular iteration of the structure merits a special insert in the July 14, 1950, issue of the widely-read industry publication *Handelsblatt*.[01] Certainly the attention the new parliament building receives is appropriate to its symbolic importance. But the two steel trusses also signify an industry resurgent from the rubble in the midst of which Germans had lived for the past half-decade. Most worthy of note is the speed with which the building was completed: five months from initial design to occupancy for the plenary hall and restaurant, only three for the office tract.[02] **[1.2]**

At the end of the 1940s, conditions in Bonn were no less dire than elsewhere in Germany, in terms of both available labor and construction materials. An October 1944 bombing raid had entirely destroyed Bonn's university, the city's most famous landmark, which had been founded in 1818 upon Wilhelm von Humboldt's principles for modern education. As early as March 1945, its faculty returned to the site, not to teach but in an attempt to rebuild their campus. A few months later, construction work became a requirement for university matriculation. The so-called *Bautrupp*, led by an art history professor and the head of campus facilities, comprised younger students and returning soldiers. Beginning in August 1945, these students, with or without prior construction knowledge, acted as masons and carpenters, rebuilding walls, forming rough openings for windows and doors, and securing roofs.[03] In the winter of 1945–46, these same students were sent out to fell trees for firewood. Numerous reports made in 1946 and 1947 describe the problems that arose from their lack of skill, physical strength, and maturity; nonetheless, the students' contribution to reconstruction was so central to the city's rebuilding that the Bautrupp was later reassigned to rebuild the town hall and the Poppelsdorf palace.

With construction material no easier to come by than skilled labor, the shortfall was compensated by recovered brick from the debris of ruined buildings. In Bonn as in other cities, between the end of the war and the currency reform of June 1948, organized groups as well as resourceful individuals devoted their days to salvage. The situation was still extreme less than a year before construction began on Schwippert's parliament, as eyewitness accounts document:

> "While an army of 'rubble-seekers' were out […] people who searched through the ruins for useful objects for their own building projects […] there were already transport groups in the old city who brought hand-cleaned bricks to trucks and brick fragments to a facility that made new blocks from milled brick and a cement mixture."[04]

Other eyewitnesses in Bonn recall the near-impossibility of finding cement to reinforce the Rhine bank, or the grueling work of breaking basalt for the revetments, which masons brought to the site by hand in wheelbarrows. Conditions were similar throughout the country: not until 1950 was there a uniform national act to provide funding for new residential building.[05] There were few apparent resources upon which the construction of the new parliament could draw, either locally or nationally.

Schwippert's design for the plenary hall's long-span structure and large-scale glazing, the sources of the "transparency" that would come to dominate the building's reception, would have been inconceivable without structural and detail metalwork. **[1.3]** The decision to use steel

01   "Das Bundeshaus in Bonn." Handels-blatt: Deutschlands Wirtschafts- und Finanz-zeitung, Die technische Linie 3, no. 13 (Friday, July 14, 1950), 1–2.
02   Wera Meyer-Waldeck, "Das Bundes-parlament in Bonn," *Architektur und Werkform* 58, no. 5 (1950), 99–109, here 99.
03   Christian George, "Studieren in Ruinen: Die Studenten der Universität Bonn in der Nachkriegszeit (1945–1955)" (Diss., University of Bonn, 2008–2009, V&R unipress, 2010), 100–105. Hans Döllgast tells a similar story about students in Munich. See Hans Döllgast, *Journal Retour*, vol. 1 (Salzburg: Anton Pustet, 2003) 12–13.
04   Reiner Pommerin, ed. *Bonn zwischen Kriegsende und Währungsreform: Erinnerungs-berichte von Zeitzeugen* (Bonn: Bouvier, 1991), 183–84.
05   Dirk Dorsemagen, *"Büro und Geschäfts-häuser der 50er Jahre konservatorische Probleme am Beispiel West-Berlin,"* vol. I (Diss., Berlin Technical University, 2004), 6.

**1.2 The Bundeshaus across the
Rhine, Bonn, ca. 1949**

in the building was more than a design preference: although the industry
was at best emergent in 1948–49, metalwork was connected directly
to the new republic's aspirations and its revitalized capacities. Steel was
also faster than either concrete or masonry. Moreover, Bonn was located
near Germany's mining and steel industry in the Ruhr and Saarland
areas. This proximity was meaningful to both identity and economics.
The construction industry was seen as an engine of the rebuilding effort,
which began in earnest with currency reform. The synergy between
cultural and industrial identity in the new *Bundesrepublik* in general,
and in Bonn specifically, found expression in everyday life. It was even
the subject of a 1949 postage stamp series printed in France, the Allied
power that occupied Bonn. Evidently popular, the series remained
in circulation through 1957. Entitled "Industrie, Handel, Landwirtschaft
und Kultur" (industry, trade, agriculture, and culture), the stamps
included one of Beethoven, born in Bonn, alongside others with iconography
associated with mining, smelting, and industrial labor. Several stamps
bear the words *"unsere Wirtschaft in Wiederaufbau"* (our economy in reconstruction).[06] One shows molten steel and a smelter flanked by two
figures, one holding a sheet of drawings. Its caption identifies the group
as representing "the building arts."

The structural steel for the Bundeshaus was furnished by the
Rheinische Röhrenstahlwerke in Mülheim, due north along the Rhine
from Bonn. The company had been part of the conglomerated Vereinigte
Stahlwerke AG. Consolidated in 1934, the conglomerate had spread
across the entire Ruhr valley. It had been the source of the fuel (coal), ore,
and steel that supplied the Third Reich's war. In June 1948, after the
war, the occupying forces subdivided the conglomerate's remnants into
smaller, less dominating companies. The Rheinische Röhrenwerke was
one of the several intact operations to emerge.[07] Only a few years later,
these small, independent steel companies, like the Rheinische, would
again be combined under the directorship of some of the same firms that
had led the industry before the war: Mannesmann and Thyssen. Over time,
these companies would redefine themselves via specialization and scales
of operation. This had not yet occurred in 1949. Anticipating that the
building industry would lead steel manufacturing to renewed economic

06   For images of these stamps, see http://
de.wikipedia.org/wiki/Briefmarken
-Jahrgang_1949_des_Saarprotektorats,
accessed January 22, 2022.
07   "Vereinigte Stahlwerke," https://
de-academic.com/dic.nsf/dewiki/1454888,
accessed December 19, 2021.

08   This is true of Josef Gartner and of the Georgsmarienhütte, later owned by Klöckner. See *Glückauf—Die Zeitung für Freunde, Kunden und Mitarbeiter der Georgsmarienhütte Unternehmensgruppe*, no. 2 (2005), 13.
09   Josef Gartner, a provider of steelwork and steel hardware, marketed aluminum facades as of 1951 following fabrication work for the 1950 Stuttgart *Gartenschau*. Josef Gartner Facades, Gundelfingen.

stability, as it had in the United States, all manner of steel manufacturers and metalworking firms offered structural steel[08] to the construction market.

As described in the *Handelsblatt* insert, the Bundeshaus trusses were purpose-made of welded standard steel pipes. The same technique was used elsewhere that same year for long-span public buildings, including the Apollo Theater in Düsseldorf (1949–1950) and the restored convention center in Cologne, as well as in generic industrial buildings. For the fabricator of the truss, the universality of its component members was a virtue: the round, hollow sections could be manufactured and stocked, then used for any number of purposes. Exactly such sections had formed both conduits and struts in a bridge built for Ruhrgas AG completed that same year. Across the industry, from the late 1940s through 1951 or '52, it was standard practice to adapt generic steel sections as needed rather than to create specialized sections for particular usage. This practice only began to change after 1952, as companies began to specialize in particular market niches,[09] and the construction market was able to support this specificity.

While the use of interchangeable, standard steel sections was good business practice for the steel industry as it emerged from reconstruction, it created difficulty for architects. Steel and aluminum window and facade elements or systems were difficult to source, and in most cases were not yet commercially available in the early 1950s. The trusses were, in some ways, the least of it: they vanished from view entirely. Built around and supported by the trusses was a structural steel cage, within which sat Schwippert's refracting, gill-like glass facades. In the finished wall, structure and glazing elided; the distinction between rough and finish construction was moot. To understand the immensity of the undertaking that the Bundeshaus represented—the sophistication of its aura, the speed of its realization, the modulation of its limited material palette—is to accept that its construction was makeshift.

The material constraints to the building's realization and the ways that its architects dealt with them correspond to the dichotomy between ambition and capacity that preoccupied West German architects as their country emerged from its initial, existential rebuilding. This challenge gave

1.3 The Bundeshaus, plenary under construction, Bonn, May 1949

rise to Schwippert's doubts, verbalized publicly in 1951, that the modernist bond between material and expression was absolute; he foresaw that the lack of proper materials would bring "the end of spatial building."[10] The Bundeshaus was a nationally significant project for which all available building resources were mobilized despite shortages, and for which participating construction firms developed unique products and solutions. Structural steel, lighting elements, dropped ceilings, and window details were only a few of the products developed in collaboration with Schwippert's office and that of his engineer. In some cases, these proved to be singular solutions, in others, prototypes developed towards mass production. But in each case, the products used to construct the Bundeshaus were bespoke combinations of available parts, guided by ingenuity and given meaning by careful calibration.

Schwippert's prior career had groomed him to address the challenges that arose from the mandate to complete the new parliament building more or less *ex nihilo* in record time. The construction drawings his office issued over the course of the following decades express his willingness to entrust his ideas to the skills and judgment of those on site. Schwippert stayed true to this trust in skilled construction and continued to demonstrate ingenuity despite material lack even as the construction market transformed, even as he helped to proselytize the quality manufacturing and high design for which West Germany became known. Both traits would again serve him well during the near-decade of remote work renovating the Hedwigskathedrale in East Berlin, amid material limitations of a very different nature.

Schwippert's knowledge of how things were built came first hand. As a student, he worked in cabinet and interior millwork shops.[11] That work aligned well with the curriculum of his architectural studies. After a year of military service on the Western front at the end of World War I, he began studies in engineering and attended two different technical universities in the course of a year. Ultimately, he enrolled in architecture at the Technische Hochschule Stuttgart, where he studied under Professor for Building Construction and Design Paul Schmitthenner and graduated in 1924.[12]

Schmitthenner's professional biography is inextricable from the architectural styles and cultural policies of the Third Reich, especially in housing. His houses and urban master plans, no less than his publications on building during the new Reich, epitomized an architecturally facile *Heimatstil*.[13] He insisted on a typological approach to architecture that prized variation of traditional forms more highly than invention. This approach extended to construction, as is apparent in his book *Baugestaltung: Erste Folge, Das deutsche Wohnhaus*, first published in 1932.[14] In contrast to modernist claims about the unified, singular correspondence between form and material, Schmitthenner argued for "the meaning of a material in its transformability."[15] As an example, he presented a series of six variations on Johann Wolfgang von Goethe's garden house in Weimar, the city that all architects would identify with the foundations of modern architecture education, at Walter Gropius's Bauhaus and Otto Bartning's subsequent Staatliche Bauhochschule. Schmitthenner understood polemic.[16]

The text describes his engagement in the contemporary discourses of construction, progress, and expression. He advocates for construction based in both craft and technological advancement, although ultimately independent of architecture's formal language; this conviction also underpinned Schmitthenner's pedagogy. Using a motif of "theme and variations," illustrated plates depict how traditional carpentry and masonry building techniques can be adapted to give the same basic volume different appearances. This variability, he writes, is "nothing new, but perhaps something forgotten;" it demonstrates "the meaning of material in its transformability and the significance of the measure as placid and constant."[17] The plates juxtapose precisely drawn details with elevations of houses in the manner of anatomical books in which human bodies,

10   Ulrich Conrads and Peter Neitzke, eds., *Mensch und Raum: Das Darmstädter Gespräch 1951* (Braunschweig: Vieweg, 1991), 106.

11   Agatha Buslei-Wuppermann, "Hans Schwippert 1899–1973: Von der Werkkunst zum Design," (Diss., Bergische Universität Wuppertal, 2006, Utz Verlag, 2007), 19 and 37.

12   Agatha Buslei-Wuppermann and Andreas Zeising, *Das Bundeshaus von Hans Schwippert in Bonn: Architektonische Moderne und demokratischer Geist*, 1st ed. (Düsseldorf: Grupello, 2009), 30.

13   Hartmut Frank, "Dächerkrieg?" in Barbara Burren, Martin Tschanz, and Christa Vogt, eds. *Das schräge Dach: Ein Architektur-handbuch* (Sulgen: Niggli, 2008).

14   Paul Schmitthenner, Baugestaltung: Erste Folge, *Das Deutsche Wohnhaus*, 3rd ed. (reprint) (Stuttgart: Deutsche Verlags-Anstalt, 1984), 13. Wolfgang Pehnt argues convincingly that Schmitthenner used Goethe's canonical garden house as the template for the illustrations in this book. See Wolfgang Pehnt, *Die Regel und die Ausnahme: Essays zu Bauen, Planen und Ähnlichem* (Ostfildern: Hatje Cantz Verlag, 2001), 138.

15   Schmitthenner, *Baugestaltung*, 13.

16   Pehnt, *Die Regel und die Ausnahme*, 139.

17   Pehnt, *Die Regel und die Ausnahme*, 9.

18   Pehnt, *Die Regel und die Ausnahme*, 9.
19   Pehnt, *Die Regel und die Ausnahme*, 11.
Schmitthenner's 1930s buildings for the
Reichspost use high-precision hardware for
monumental doors, gates, and locks; clearly
he was invested in modern construction (and
an example of how cutting-edge technology
could have various expressions).
20   Buslei-Wuppermann and Zeising,
Das Bundeshaus, 38.

flayed and sectioned along their axis of symmetry, reveal internal organs. Schmitthenner argued that architectural abstraction was embodied through material: "all building is the conjoining of material to mass [*Körper*] and space."[18]

The act of construction, Schmitthenner also seemed to imply, limits the architect's claim to authorship and reminds him that craft has primacy over invention: "Technology in building is always craft, even today with machines, cranes, and bulldozers. [...] The building art is always an impersonal art form."[19] The architect and the act of construction exist in reciprocity. Materials are the *sine qua non* of architecture as its embodiment, and at the same time, matter is subordinate to architecture's formal predilection. Schwippert chose political and architectural positions entirely different from Schmitthenner's. Still, the loose fit that his drawings offered between architect's intention and craftsman's best practice seems to owe something to Schmitthenner's ideas.

Following graduation in 1924, Schwippert went to work in Erich Mendelsohn's large and prolific Berlin office. There, he would have learned directly the dictates of realizing modern architecture. During his employment, Schwippert was responsible for the renovation of a villa, from design to construction drawings to construction supervision.[20] The difficulty translating modern architectural ideas into the variety of available building technologies would have been most conspicuous in the context of a renovation, but the challenge was evident even in the offices most iconic projects. Mendelsohn's Einsteinturm in Potsdam (1924), for example, was actually a masonry building plastered to look like cast concrete. Although it was a central to modernist rhetoric and design, material expression in interwar modern architecture was, of course, not necessarily "true" to its construction. By the late 1920s, however, the German building industry had caught up with architects' desires. The famous retractable windows in Ludwig Mies van der Rohe's Haus Tugendhat (1929–1930), for example, relied upon high-precision window hardware available as a standard catalogue product. **[1.4]**

1.4 Commercially available German window hardware, pre-war period

Schwippert met Mies van der Rohe during his time in Berlin, and the two maintained a lifelong friendship. Vicissitudes of architectural expression

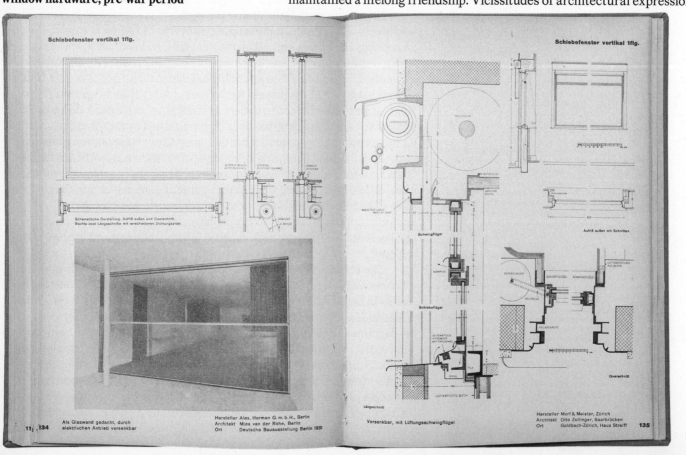

that outstripped the simplistic dictates of "truth in materials" were certainly part of Mies van der Rohe's practice in the mid-to late 1920s as well, as can be seen in his Krefeld villas from 1927 / 1928.[21] Schwippert's undogmatic attitude towards the construction site might well date to that period. His unerring sense of delicacy and near-illusory lightness in design developed over the course of the years that followed.

Schwippert returned to his family in Duisburg after his time in Berlin and tried with modest success to work independently, relying upon family commissions. In 1927, he accepted a teaching position in Aachen at the Handwerker- und Kunstgewerbeschule at which Rudolf Schwarz was director. Schwippert's architecture curriculum integrated representation, theory, construction, and design. During this period, he also began to catalogue domestic furniture and to generate speculative furniture designs that were both generic in form and subtly adaptable in the way they might be executed. His furniture research, which translated directly into the work he did during the war, reveals much about his character as a *constructeur*, as he integrated both industrial and craft production modalities and sought to negotiate between serial and bespoke design.

In 1930, the Aachen Kunstgewerbeschule published the first iteration of Schwippert's furniture research in a catalogue entitled *Neuer Hausrat* (new home furnishings).[22] The furnishings include a series of tables, chairs, and cabinets, each of which combines solid rectilinear wood sections as structural support with plywood or textile to form usable surfaces. In each of the objects' designs, the differentiation between support and surface is explicit. Connections between elements are concealed by means of slots or intercuts. Independent of structure, however, all the furniture shares formal characteristics and was intended to be combinable. As Schwippert explained,

> "Although I was concerned about a rational and useful form for each individual piece, I still did not neglect to think about the fact that these individual pieces should have a good familial relationship among themselves. They should be able to stand together in ever new combinations and get along well, in addition to facilitating as many types of furnishings as possible."[23]

It is worth noting how Schwippert tempered the mandates of use and rationality with specific formal ambitions.

The catalogue's title page featured six photographs that emphasized the collection's serial, component-based construction: at the top of the page are photographs of completed and partially completed chairs and side tables, lined up in precise, equally spaced rows so as to emphasize the repetition of identical pieces. The lower band of photographs depicts components, stacked and ready for assembly by means of the long vertical slots visible in the central photograph. In the lower right-hand photograph, three identically dressed men, apparently assembling side tables, look up at the camera. The emphasis on standardization in these photographs belies that each component was differently dimensioned, so the components were not interchangeable. Instead, each piece of furniture was conceived proportionately, in terms of its appearance and structure. For example, the catalogue included two similar hard-backed, plywood seat chairs, one with a vertical back for dining or use at a desk (Stuhl 2), the other with an angled back for a more relaxed posture (Stuhl 4). The two chairs differ in seat height, overall width, and depth, as would be expected on the basis of their different purposes. The solid wood frame they share, however, is similar enough to justify the expectation that it would be standardized to facilitate serial production. Instead, Schwippert subtly varied the dimension of the wood frame elements, using 2.5 × 3.5 cm hardwood for the frame of Stuhl 2 but 3 × 3 cm components in Stuhl 4. An armchair in the same series has structural components of 5 × 5 cm. These subtle differences, made on the basis of appearance rather than bearing capacity or serial production, indicate Schwippert's shifting value system within his design process, which dealt selectively with the repetitive, production efficiency-based values the title page images represented. Instead, repetition and construction logic is subverted in

21   Kent Kleinman and Leslie Van Duzer, *Mies van der Rohe: The Krefeld Villas* (New York: Princeton Architectural Press, 2005).
22   Hans Schwippert, *Neuer Hausrat* (Aachen: Kunstgewerbeschule, 1932) as cited in Buslei-Wuppermann and Zeising, *Das Bundeshaus*, 54–68.
23   Gerda Breuer, Pia Mingels, and Christopher Oestereich, eds., *Hans Schwippert 1899–1973: Moderation des Wiederaufbaus* (Berlin: Jovis, 2010), 213.

favor of a differentiated design sensibility. This is borne out in Schwippert's preface to the catalogue's second edition. There he wrote, "The fact that this furniture is not produced serially in large quantity but rather piece by piece or in small series through a crafts-based process spontaneously gave rise, over time, to multiple changes of the same basic form, and it offers the possibility to choose at will."[24]

This same sensibility reemerged in a more systematic form in the furniture Schwippert designed during the early 1940s. As part of the government agency commissioned by Heinrich Himmler's Ministry of the Interior in the context of the *Festigung deutschen Volkstums* (stabilization of German nationhood), he spent the war developing the architectural systems to facilitate new German settlements in occupied Eastern Europe. This furniture continues a tendency already visible in his 1938 edition of *Neuer Hausrat*, in which solid wood in heavier dimensions replaces the lighter, more modern materials, such as plywood and visible textile webbing, used in his earlier designs. The slotted connections are visible in the later designs, giving the furniture a more rustic, heavier sensibility, aligned with the conservative stylistic dictates of the time. Photos show a child's crib made from woven willow and unmilled logs stripped of bark. Because the building material was not standardized, the design could be replicated only in construction technique and general appearance. The specific configuration and dimensions would be unique each time the crib was executed. Schwippert's "design" was more akin to how-to instructions rather than rigorous specifications.

This approach to standardized furniture, which was rustic in appearance and realized using a set of instructions for variable reproduction, is the foundation for the furniture designs Schwippert made available to the public in 1943[25] for the new German settlers to take along and, in the pioneer spirit, build for themselves in their new homes. As Schwippert noted, both traditional techniques and "contemporary practices"[26] had been combined so that both skilled and unskilled builders could reproduce the designs despite variable access to materials and tools. The publication was intended as both pattern book and building primer. Variability was to be embraced:

> "And even if we believe that many will receive useful guidelines, if not instruction, in the form of these patterns, then at the same time, we also expect that some of their users, inspired by these precedents, will recall appropriate forms and means as were practiced earlier; or that one person or another will invent something better that did not occur to us."[27]

Here, and throughout his career as an architect, Schwippert moved comfortably in the terrain between forms determined only by the architect and those found in the process of construction. Although his construction documents bespeak a decisive, knowledgeable designer with full understanding of the construction implications of his decisions, the architectural expression that characterizes his buildings offers evidence of his interest in the assembly of each element, the expression of that assembly, and the latitude to be found between the repetitive and the unique.

The photograph on the cover of this book is part of a collection numbering more than four hundred photographs commissioned by the regional government of North Rhine-Westphalia, the state in which Bonn is located. It is the work of Erna Wagner-Hehmke, a commercial photographer who ran her own small studio in Düsseldorf. She had come to her profession traditionally, through an apprenticeship rather than by studying at art school or university,[28] and prior to 1949 received commissions from local industry, photographing blast furnaces, steel works, and metal rollers, as well as from private clients, particularly for portraits of children. Her photographs show her to be intrepid, shooting from high up on scaffolding she shared with her subjects. They also demonstrate her clear understanding of the transparency Schwippert valued: her architectural photographs skillfully balance the reflective qualities of the glazed facades

24　Buslei-Wuppermann, "Hans Schwippert 1899–1973," 73.
25　Buslei-Wuppermann, "Hans Schwippert 1899–1973," 79.
26　Breuer et al., *Schwippert: Moderation*, 236.
27　Breuer et al., *Schwippert: Moderation*, 239.
28　Benedikt Wintgens, "Neues Parlament, neue Bilder? Die Fotografin Erna Wagner-Hehmke und ihr Blick auf den Bundestag," in Marij Leenders and Andreas Biefang, eds., *Das ideale Parlament: Erich Salomon als Fotograf in Berlin und Den Haag, 1928–1940* (Düsseldorf: Droste Verlag, 2014), 293–314.

1.5 The plenary in session, Bundeshaus, Bonn, Fall 1949

29   Wintgens, "Neues Parlament, Neue Bilder?" 300.

30   Werner Durth and Paul Sigel, *Baukultur: Spiegel gesellschaftlichen Wandels*, 2. rev. and enl. ed. (Berlin: Jovis, 2010), 421–22.

31   Adenauer and Schwippert did not see eye to eye; a standard tour of the Palais Schaumberg includes the story that Adenauer said the Schwippert-designed porte-cochère looked like a gas station.

32   Buslei-Wuppermann and Zeising, *Das Bundeshaus*, 44.

33   Hans Eckstein, "Ist das Bonner Bundeshaus zu schlecht gebaut? Zu den Angriffen gegen die Schlichtheit der neuen Architektur," *Die Neue Zeitung* (1950).

against the depth and clarity of the space on the far side of the glass. Still, despite best efforts in research, there is no documentation of how she was chosen for this important commission.[29] A number of explanations seem plausible: that a former industry client with good political connections recommended her; that her architect husband was involved; or simply, that her work caught the eye of the right person, who like the rest was scrambling to accomplish what had been demanded.

Likewise, there is no definitive documentation that explains exactly how Schwippert received the Bundeshaus commission, except that he received it directly, to some extent because of his professional status and to some extent by virtue of his good relationship with Hermann Wandersleb, head of the State Chancellery, who would be running the project for the new government.[30] The apparent ease with which he acceded to the commission would be evenly matched by the difficulty he encountered while completing it and, thereafter, in defending his work against critics no less powerful than Bundespräsident Konrad Adenauer.[31] At stake were both his design and the caliber of its realization.

Schwippert had been involved in designing the parliament during Bonn's competition with Frankfurt to become the new capital. He had completed preliminary designs even before the decision to move to Bonn was finalized.[32] Although his office successfully navigated a breakneck design and construction schedule, support for the project flagged immediately following its completion and, eventually, turned to political strife. As early as the summer of 1950, only a year after its inauguration, the German parliament was forced to allocate an additional DM 290,000 for repairs to its brand-new building. The debate made waves in the press. Public opinion centered not only on the quality of the building's construction, but also on the architect and his architecture.[33]

The attacks on Schwippert's design continued into the 1960s, in debates over the geometry of seating in the plenary hall. The pain all this caused Schwippert is easily inferred from the letters he wrote in the weeks before Christmas 1962 to Konrad Rühl, who had been the director of the Reconstruction Ministry and a fellow postwar German Werkbund member, and to Wandersleb. Fifteen years after the completion of the Bundeshaus, Schwippert found himself asking Wandersleb

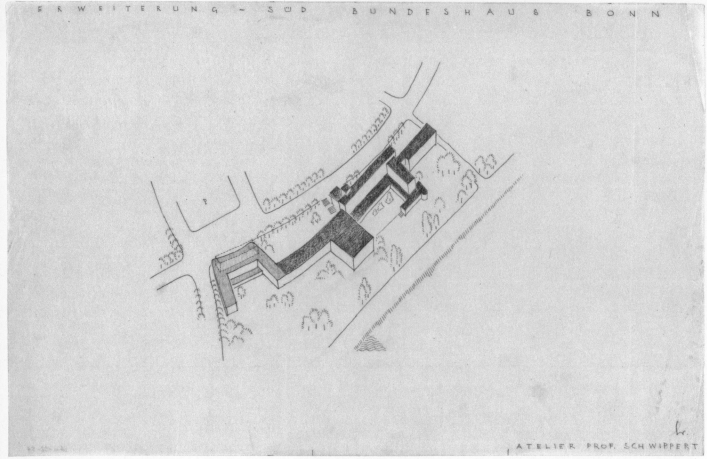

ERWEITERUNG - SÜD   BUNDESHAUS   BONN

ATELIER PROF. SCHWIPPERT

1.6 Hans Schwippert, volumetric study, Bundeshaus, early 1949

to confirm that the balance his design had achieved between spatial and political representation had been hard-fought but ultimately successful. Wandersleb wrote in tepid response, regarding the design of the plenary hall interior, "Herr Dr. Adenauer proved very open to your argumentation and judged your respective sketches to be excellent. However, he opined that one should not immediately seize upon such radical novelty for the beginning of parliamentary work."[34] **[1.5]**

The complex was an addition to an existing building in the *Neue Sachlichkeit* tradition, the Bonn Pedagogic Academy, completed from 1930 to 1933 after a design by Martin Witte. To a casual viewer, Schwippert's light-colored volumes suit that context. Even from the standpoint of Adenauer's decidedly conservative architectural taste, the putative radicality of Schwippert's design is hard to see. Its simple volumetrics and repetitive facades seem to plant it firmly in the genre of administrative buildings in a general modern tradition. Indeed, in the architectural exhibition accompanying the Darmstädter Gespräch of 1951, it was displayed among other "spaces of work," without any particular recognition of its distinct representative or symbolic attributes. Nonetheless, the building's apparent simplicity belies both the enormous efforts that went into its materialization and the sophistication behind the design strategies that allowed it to be understood, for generations to come, as largely transparent.

From the start, and in no small part thanks to the phrases Schwippert selected for his inaugural address, the ideal of transparency dominated the project's reception. The building was interpreted as a literal representation of the new, democratic West German government's political transparency, exemplified by the glazed walls on either side of the plenary hall.[35] Certainly, as he claimed, Schwippert's building embodies "an architecture of encounter and conversation,"[36] but not only by virtue of the plenary hall's generous glazing. The facade articulation and the treatment of interior spaces contribute to this impression. A more careful assessment might see the Bundeshaus not as a radical glass structure but as a carefully fenestrated and articulated complex of buildings. Its aura of transparency, much like the orchestration of the plenary

34   Hermann Wandersleb to Hans Schwippert, January 14, 1963, Germanisches Nationalmuseum, Deutsches Kunstarchiv, Nachlass, Schwippert GNM, DKA, NL, Schwippert.
35   Deborah Ascher Barnstone, *The Transparent State: Architecture and Politics in Postwar Germany* (London: Routledge, 2005), chapters 5 and 6.
36   Typescript of Schwippert's speech at the inauguration of the Bundeshaus, GNM, DKA, NL, Schwippert, binder marked "Bundeshaus Adenauer Finanzierung."

37   Buslei-Wuppermann and Zeising, *Das Bundeshaus*, 44; see also Barnstone, *The Transparent State*; and Durth and Sigel, *Baukultur*.
38   Buslei-Wuppermann and Zeising, *Das Bundeshaus*, 309–312.
39   Buslei-Wuppermann and Zeising, *Das Bundeshaus*, 52.
40   The plenary hall was to sit on the foundations of a former air raid shelter. Buslei-Wuppermann and Zeising, *Das Bundeshaus*, 48.
41   All drawings referenced are at the Architekturmuseum der Technischen Universität München (AM TUM).

hall's curvilinear interior and its seating, its most salient spatial gesture, owed as much to the church architecture Schwippert developed with his mentor and colleague Rudolf Schwarz as it did to the glazing technology of the curtain wall, a facade type already burgeoning in the United States, which would soon come to dominate West German drafting boards.

Schwippert's first design studies were part of Bonn's successful bid to wrest the seat of the federal government from Frankfurt am Main.[37] These date to November 1948 and depict a series of additions and changes to the academy where the Parlamentarischer Rat, from which the Bundestag emerged, was already meeting provisionally. Over the next several months, Schwippert produced numerous sketches of the complex, many of them developed via axonometrics or bird's eye perspectives, to depict the massing and fenestration of the plenary hall and new adjoining tracts. Ground was broken for the plenary hall in April 1949, and the hall was inaugurated to great fanfare[38] on September 7 that same year.[39] The pressure to design, detail, source, schedule, and oversee construction on the building is hard to imagine. In this context, the luxury of drawing and redrawing aerial views, sketched and drafted, in ink and pencil, is almost impossible to reconcile with the scale of this challenge. As such, this series of drawings deserves careful consideration to understand what Schwippert was seeking to accomplish. They enabled him to resolve the problem posed by the need to represent the building's parliamentary role while balancing its administrative function. Finally, these design studies depict how Schwippert developed a means to create a "transparent" building despite material limitations.

The initial design for the complex was much more expansive than what was ultimately realized.[40] **[1.6]** Early sketches in pencil,[41] dated to late January 1949, show the existing pedagogic academy connected via an administrative office bar to the plenary hall, located on the foundations of an existing air raid shelter. In this series of three sketches, the plenary hall sits like a fulcrum between two wings of office buildings. In all three, the building has a low-pitched gabled roof, with its primary glazing on the gable side. **[1.7]** The sketches show two versions of a similar scheme, which can be associated with orthographic drawings dated from January 27 to 31, 1949. In one scheme, the gable side faces the river and is on axis with the entry, whereas in the other two sketches, the roof ridge runs parallel to the Rhine. The former scheme shows a basilica-like massing, with two lower wings as side aisles on either side of the main hall. In the alternate scheme, the massing does not call out the side aisles, although they still appear in the plan of the plenary hall. In both versions, the directional massing of the overall volume does not register the centralized, square floor plan below the gabled roof.

As he worked through different massing studies, while clearly keeping in mind the need to add office area in successive phases, Schwippert also rendered the facades of his complex with detail far greater than would be expected from initial massing studies sketched in soft pencil. Each drawing tests and develops fenestration strategies, many intended to relate the large plenary hall building to the office wings. Schwippert's design intends to represent, if not the integration of, then at least a balance between bureaucratic and parliamentary functions.

In these early sketches, Schwippert identifies two separate strategies for facade articulation, both of which he continued to develop in subsequent three-dimensional drawings. The first is to find a window format and dimension that could be applied to both the plenary hall and office wing. Schwippert seems to have decided quite quickly that the primary glazing on the plenary building should cover its gabled sides and occupy a large, consolidated portion of these two walls. But for the version in which the glazing faces the Rhine, he renders this glazing as sixteen tightly spaced, individual windows that share the same format with those in the adjoining office tract. This same sketch proposes continuing the two aisle-like wings that flank the plenary hall with two thinner office bars running perpendicular to the Rhine. Both aisles and office bars share similarly formatted

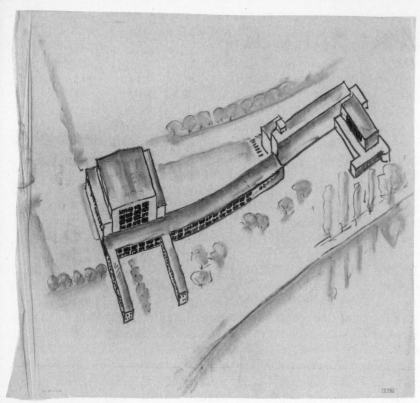

**1.7a Hans Schwippert,
axonometrics, January 1949**

1.7b

small windows. In the sketch that maintains the same plan configuration with slightly different massing, Schwippert simply embeds one of these "aisles" into the office building. He distinguishes this part of the office volume from the rest by its height and by its fenestration, which picks up the rhythm and width of the office windows but conjoins them into a single, vertical window element. In another sketch, Schwippert abandons the gabled, basilica-like massing for the plenary building in favor of a flat pyramidal roof on a cubic volume, a version of which he would ultimately realize. Vertical windows at the plenary hall's base continue the horizontal line struck by a lower, adjacent office wing; the plenary hall's large glazing is shown as five vertical windows of similar format, which are then picked up by another, taller office wing.

The second facade strategy, which Schwippert would continue to study throughout his various versions of the complex's massing, foresaw a surface grid on the long facade of the plenary hall and between the windows that comprise the primary glazed area on the gable side. Light pencil lines imply that Schwippert first drew this grid across the wall surfaces to guide his placement of windows. In one early version, the windows on the plenary hall's long side maintain the rhythm and format of those in the office building wing it adjoins. In later drawings, however, these grids became elements in themselves. Applied in low relief, the gridded skeleton implied an open infill facade, despite the fact that the grid was laid on a primarily opaque wall surface.

Once Schwippert had settled on a parti, with the square plenary hall between two office wings running parallel to the Rhine, his office generated three more detailed, drafted axonometric drawings of the

1.7c

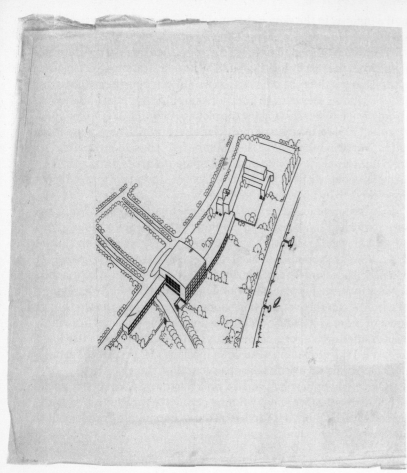

**1.8a Hans Schwippert,
inked axonometrics, January 1949**

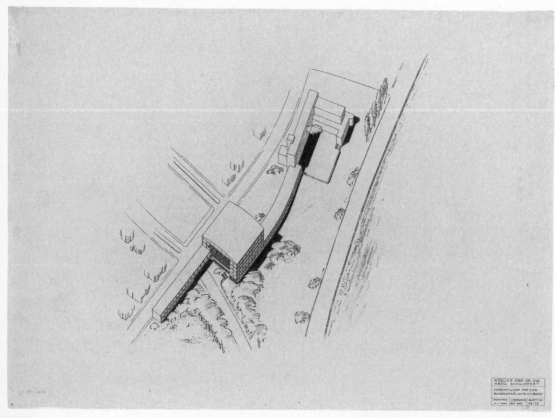

1.8b

scheme, two as viewed from the river **[1.8]** and one from the street side, to accompany plans dated January 31, 1949. These drawings depict more precisely a strategy for entry on two sides of the plenary hall, one facing the street and the other perpendicular to it, accessed by driving beneath a portion of the office wing raised on columns. A transitional horizontal band is used on the facade to integrate the height of the adjoining office wings into the plenary hall building. Moreover, the expression of the building complex is significantly different from the earlier sketches. A slightly bowed roof running parallel to the Rhine lends an implied axial orientation to the square plenary hall below it. In the pencil perspectives, a surface grid that surrounds three smaller windows in the plenary building continues across the two office wings. On the gable sides, the grid is omitted on the building's corners, but again brackets the five bays of glazing at the center of the facade. Brise-soleil tops the central windows. The grid, which also appears to a lesser extent in the ink perspective, does more than simply unify the disparate buildings. It gives the appearance of larger-scale glazing, and the semblance of skeleton construction, to all the buildings without requiring the detailing, manufacture, and installation of a construction typology—curtain wall—that might well have interfered with the construction schedule or been simply unavailable.

In late February 1949, the project budget was reduced and the complex reconceived as only an addition to the original building, meant to use as much of the existing building infrastructure as possible.[42] A delicate pencil sketch dating to February describes Schwippert's revised design intention, balancing the expression of a gabled plenary hall against a grid that subsumes it among the adjacent buildings and their subordinate functions. **[1.9]** The thumbnail axonometric indicates gridded pavers on the terrace and tiny figures standing between the plenary building and the river's edge. A plan sketch below shows centralized seating within a square plenary hall, although the axonometric above it seems to indicate a rectangular plenary hall with a roof ridge parallel to the river. The tension between centralized hall and directional hall evocative of a basilica is evident throughout the design process.

One last pre-construction drafted perspective, showing Schwippert's signature and dated March 1949, shows the most relentless use of surface grid and fenestration as a strategy to unify the parts of the new complex. **[1.10]** This is one of the few surviving perspectives taken from eye level rather than from above, a viewpoint that makes it even more difficult to identify component building forms. Except for the slightly peaked roof receding towards the drawing's left edge, there is no indication that the plenary building in the foreground is in any way exceptional as compared to the administrative office buildings around it. The river facade of the new buildings appears small in comparison to the existing academy, which had been dwarfed by the complex rendered in Schwippert's earlier designs. It is subdivided into an unequal grid of two shorter stories. To the right of the image, a flatter building—designated as a restaurant in two diagrammatic drawings from the spring of 1949—abuts the existing building but does not pick up its horizontals. The lower floor of the restaurant building shows small, square windows in the lower portion of the grid, with a set of four large doors near the building's center; above, filling the total height of the larger portion of the grid, are bays of what appear to be four windows, rendered so dark that the lines between window elements are hardly visible. The plenary building is rendered with the same four dark windows in each of the four central grid bays. It is almost impossible to differentiate the spaces behind the grid, or even to know what is intended as glazed or what is intended to be only surface articulation.

The realized complex, as shown in an axonometric of November 1949, dealt differently with the problems Schwippert studied in all his earlier design drawings, in that it finds more subtle means of creating affinities among the buildings, including window formats, shared horizontals, and wall surface articulation. **[1.11]** The plenary building's river facade is blank, closer in expression to the *Sachlichkeit* of the original building than to Schwippert's earlier design studies. Its relationship to the adjacent

42   Buslei-Wuppermann and Zeising,
Das Bundeshaus, 48.

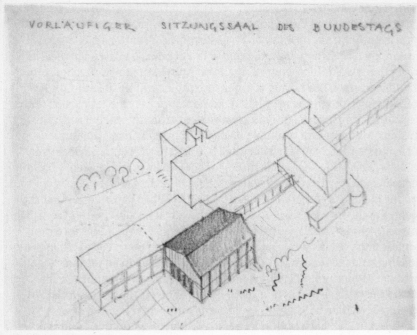

VORLÄUFIGER   SITZUNGSSAAL   DES   BUNDESTAGS

**1.9a Hans Schwippert,
sketched axonometric and plan,
February 1949**

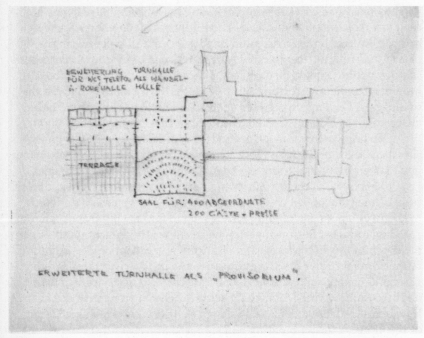

ERWEITERUNG TURNHALLE
FÜR WCS TELEFON ALS WANDEL-
Ú. ROUEHALLE HALLE

TERRASSE

SAAL FÜR 400 ABGEORDNETE
200 GÄSTE + PRESSE

ERWEITERTE TURNHALLE ALS „PROVISORIUM".

1.9b

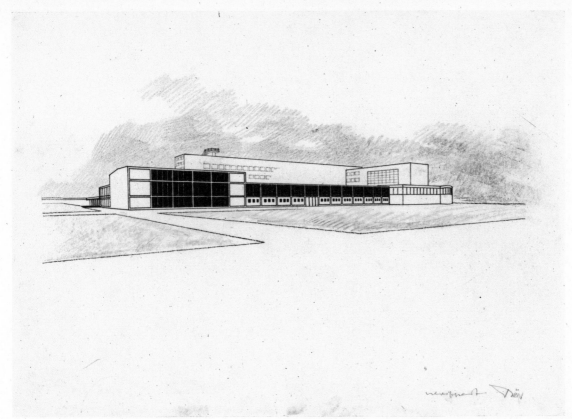

1.10 Hans Schwippert, hand-colored axonometric on diazo paper, March 1949

restaurant is asserted by aligned window mullion heights and in the mullion details. The corner between the two building elements is treated as if the glazed surface had simply turned the corner. The office wings, however, reflect Schwippert's studies of the implied skeleton-and-infill represented by the surface grid. Although, from the inside, the relatively small offices had high sill heights and relatively standard-sized windows, the building's exterior is read in relief: a white foreground grid with gray basalt cladding as infill alternating with bronze and aluminum framed windows gives the impression of a larger-scale facade treatment commensurate with the scale of the plenary hall. By carefully calibrating glazing and facade articulation, Schwippert was able to convey the sense of much greater glazing and "transparency" than in fact was present.

When Schwippert speculated that it was possible to satisfy the contemporary "yearning for light housing, for brightness, for openness"[43] even without the material means that could most directly achieve it, he envisioned more than the tricks of surface articulation tested in his axonometric sketches. Even before he had conceived the new complex as a whole, he had begun to study the space and orientation of the plenary hall in a series of sketches completed in November 1948, for which he worked through a progression of lighting conditions and seating geometries. Of these sketches, the simplest represented the situation in the temporary plenary housed in the gymnasium of the pedagogic academy. More complex variations included concentric circular arrangements, both symmetrical and asymmetrical to their lighting sources. The series' geometric exploration recalls Schwarz's *Vom Bau der Kirche* (published in translation in Chicago with the assistance of Ludwig Mies van der Rohe under the title *The Church Incarnate*[44]) which depicted a series of spatial typologies relative to their different liturgical virtues and ultimately envisioned one type that could unify both directional and centralized organizations. Schwippert's early axonometric sketches of massing and fenestration may therefore also be seen in the context of a "transcendental" transparency, conceived in analogy to the churches he and Schwarz designed together.[45] As had been the case in the churches, transparency, as a corollary of light, literally and metaphorically embodied the light of the world and the light of God. The conviction, shared by Schwarz and Schwippert, about the physical relationship of the building's occupants to one another and to carefully orchestrated natural light informed both

43   Conrads and Neitzke, *Mensch und Raum*, 106–7.
44   Rudolf Schwarz, *The Church Incarnate: The Sacred Function of Christian Architecture* (Chicago: H. Regnery, 1958).
45   Schwippert and Schwarz's collaboration extended beyond the date usually given, 1934: in December, 1949, they bid unsuccessfully on the reconstruction of the Maria-Himmelfahrt Kirche in Wesel. Correspondence, Rudolf Schwarz and Hans Schwippert, December 7–31, 1949, and January 1–February 22, 1950, GNM, DKA, NL, Schwippert.

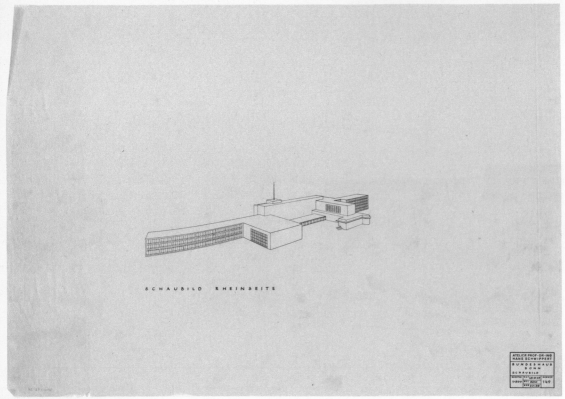

1.11 Hans Schwippert,
inked axonometric, November 1949

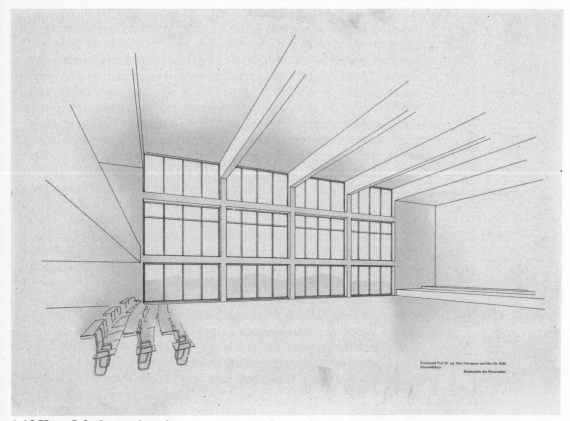

1.12 Hans Schwippert, interior
perspective, Bundesrat plenary,
Bonn, 1948

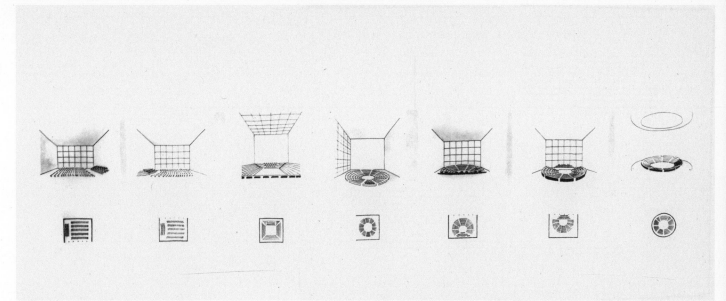

1.13 Hans Schwippert, sketches for plenary layout, 1948

the design and the spiritual meaning in Schwippert's plenary studies. Both the seating configuration and daylighting offered means to transcend materials such as glass and steel, and thereby achieve transparency despite the physical limitations around the building's construction.

The earliest interior perspective drawn by Schwippert's office to support Bonn's initial capitol bid depicts a simple long-span hall analogous to the gymnasium that the parliament used provisionally in 1948/1949. **[1.12]** In this scheme, the original gymnasium would have been reused as an entry hall, with the new plenary hall adjacent at a slightly higher level. The plenary hall is a rectangle with plan proportions evoking the golden section; it featured a traditional dais on its western end, perpendicular to a large glazed wall overlooking the Rhine. Although the reference to the original gymnasium was evident in the glazing—three-by-four bays of four windows located in a generously dimensioned structural grid that corresponded to the depth of the ceiling beams—the orientation of this new glazing was more appropriate to a view out rather than, as in the original gymnasium, a view in. A light gray wash in the inked perspective indicates the landscape outside these windows, counterpoised to a subtle indication of light entering the room on the floor in front of the windows. Seats are positioned in rows, as in a lecture hall or classroom. The hall would have been entered in two ways: either on the south, to afford a view towards the window wall, or on the east, from a side corridor, on axis with the dais. The two entries and the side-lighting defuse the otherwise hierarchical plan, but the perpendicular geometries of dais and seating are completely distinct from each other.

An abstract rendering of exactly this layout is the first of the seven diagrams Schwippert produced in his typological progression. **[1.13]** Each variation, like those proposed by Schwarz, seems to consider an appropriate balance between hierarchical or directional space and centered space. In *The Church Incarnate*, Schwarz designated the long, directional plan 'the sacred journey' in which 'sheltering space turns into the path leading toward the goal which lies 'ahead.'"[46] With respect to the centralized plan, he writes,

> "sacred inwardness [...] Through the unending chain of hands the ring links human being into human being. Through their hands the individuals exchange themselves for the higher form and in doing so, they grow stronger. When people know they are at one they form the ring in accordance with an inner law. [...] Ring is inviolability."[47]

For each of these different liturgical spatial types, Schwarz also ascribes a specific relationship to light. His final church type conjoins his processional, internalized, and extraverted typologies. By means of the bird's eye view, Schwippert tested the roof's low peaks and curves, the walls' surface articulation, and the way in which glazing was placed;

46   Schwarz, *The Church Incarnate*, 114.
47   Schwarz, *The Church Incarnate*, 33–34.

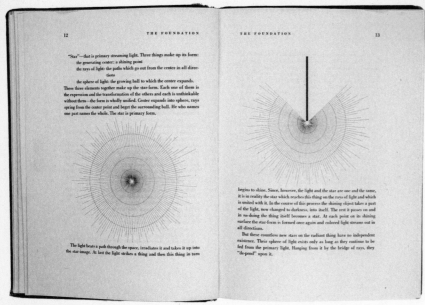

**1.14a Rudolf Schwarz, 1947,
"Open Ring"**

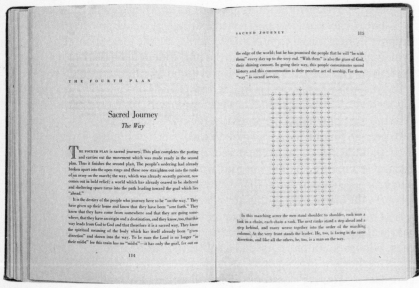

1.14b "Sacred Journey"

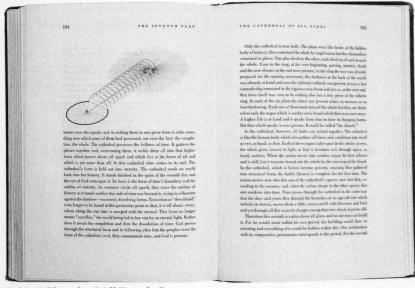

1.14c "Church of All Epochs"

but in these same drawings, his design development acknowledged its debt to Schwarz and Schwippert's Fronleichnam Church in Aachen (1930), and to Schwarz's contemporary articulated concrete frame and infill facades, such as St. Mechtern (1946–1954) or the eastern facade of the Gürzenich in Cologne (1949–1955), among others. **[1.14]**

Schwippert's studies **[1.13, from left to right]**, depicted in perspective and parti sketch, also vary the relationship among dais, seats, and glazed wall. The first scheme replicating the situation as it existed in the provisional plenary hall would have been useful as a known baseline to everyone involved in the design process. The second scheme retains the position of the glazing perpendicular to the hall's orientation, but introduces concentric curves to dais and seating. This geometry, shared between speaker and audience, mitigates the implicitly hierarchical distinction between dais and seating in the first scheme. The third scheme integrates the dais into the seating, organized as a series of concentric squares within the square room, and punctuated by aisles on the corners at 45 degrees. Underscoring the centralized organization in this study, daylight enters evenly from above.

In the fourth scheme, the dais has almost disappeared into the circular seating, which is sectioned into wedges. It is distinguished only when compared to the long benches depicted in the other wedges of seating. The large, glazed facade is perpendicular to the dais, but this relationship is reconfigured in the next two sketches. Both schemes revert to a linear dais, distinguished from the surrounding banked, circular seating, but each sketch presents a different glazing orientation: the first seems to depict the view from the dais toward backlit seating, whereas the second shows glazing behind the dais. A final sketch depicts concentric seating in a round room with a centralized, round skylight above. Dais and seating are only differentiated by the proportion of the wedges allocated to each, and both are steeply banked so that they read as a single object in the surrounding space.

Elements derived from these studies appear in Schwippert's design proposals. These show that he remained intent on the problem of locating circular seating in an asymmetrically glazed, orthogonal space. One variation appears in a large charcoal and pastel perspective from 1948, in which the curved, banked seating appears to cantilever above the floor. Human figures, red forms collaged into the sketch, dwarf the floating seating, which seems as reduced in scale as children's furniture. Another, more realistically rendered ink sketch from November 1948 shows Schwippert's skill as both delineator and designer: stepped platforms accommodate banks of upholstered swivel chairs and fixed desks, which are rendered using a soft pencil to describe the way the light from the large glazed wall would accentuate the curvature of the seating. Another tiny sketch, no more than marginalia, shows him working in plan on the idea of two perpendicular entries, as he had planned for the plenary hall in his first rendition.

Two large charcoal drawings directly precede the plenary hall design that would ultimately find its way into the two earliest drafted plan sets and axonometrics: one shows a peaked roof on the plenary hall, the other a bowed roof. **[1.15]** The first sketch retains the geometry of the early study sketches. In it, the plenary hall is a square room edged in meander-like entry vestibules and occupied by concentric seating subdivided in wedges. The second sketch resolves the tension between centralized and directional organizations by placing the interior circle figure off-center within the larger circle of seating. The intersection of the two radial geometries would allow those in the seating to see one another as in an amphitheater while simultaneously giving a spatial cue about where to focus attention. The balance between the seating and dais was a central topic for Schwippert; he sought to avoid the traditional hierarchy. As he explained to his consulting engineer,

> "At that, with your help [...] I tried to organize the assembly space of the new Bonn Bundestag in a circle, and to designate a section of this circle for the government, to avoid a dais and to allow all

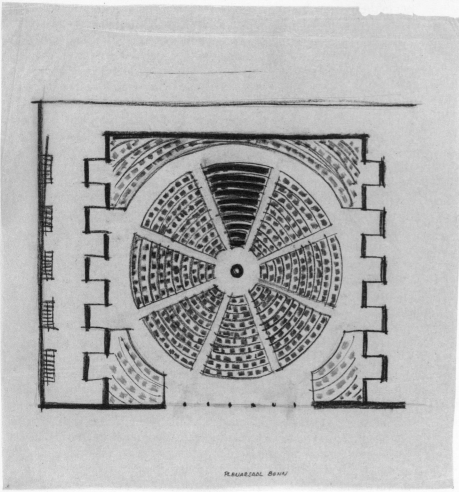

PLENARSAAL BONN

**1.15a Hans Schwippert,
Bundeshaus, plan studies for the
plenary, 1948**

speakers of all types the opportunity to speak from their seats. [...]
He [Adenauer] decided to my chagrin in favor of a traditional form
[...] which confronted the parliamentarians on one side, the ruling
party, government, etc. on the other in the 'style of a school room'
(my argument!)."[48]

The marginalia on this sheet of drawings also reveals Schwippert's
thoughts on lighting. It shows three different approaches to the plenary
hall's glazing and wall articulation: a large glazed area within a solid
wall flanked by vertically articulated sidewalls; a glazed area in the lower
half of a wall flanked by sidewalls with high clerestory glazing; and two
hybrid versions showing different ideas for the larger glazed area and the
articulation of the sidewalls, either vertically or with a clerestory.
Large glazed areas would have created glare, whereas clerestory lighting
could illuminate the space more evenly and indirectly. Interior studies
such as these allowed Schwippert to balance the symbolic dissolution
of the wall against appropriate illumination.

Schwippert's innovations in the form of the seating were to falter
on resistance from Adenauer, among others. In February 1949, as he
undertook a new set of designs for the complex that would be commensurate
with a reduced budget, he returned to the initial sketches that show
a linear dais surrounded by curved, banked seating. Versions of this strategy
appear in plan, axonometric, and interior perspective sketches at that
time. A corresponding interior perspective is also the earliest of the surviving drawings in which Schwippert depicted glazing on both sides
of the plenary hall, perpendicular to the dais. A version of this bilaterally
symmetrical glazing was ultimately realized. Nonetheless, until quite
late in the process, Schwippert continued to draw a roof ridge perpendicular
to the hall's interior line of symmetry, implying directionality on the
building's exterior and tempering the interior hierarchy of the central
podium framed by symmetrical glass walls. To realize the glazed walls
that were central to his design, Schwippert arrived at innovations in the
act of construction, which he developed while still engaged in defining

48   Schwippert to Konrad Rühl, December 12,
1962, GNM, DKA, NL, Schwippert.

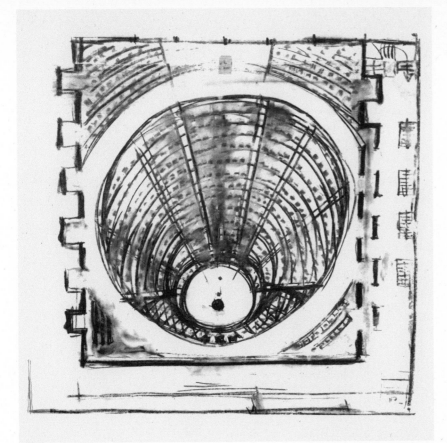

1.15b

the building's form. **[1.16] [1.17]**

In February 1949, Schwippert took time from his breakneck commission to make a special trip to a film synchronization studio in Calmuth for the purpose of "acoustical studies."[49] This particular studio, Internationale Film-Union, founded in the spring of 1947, had been built into a late nineteenth-century country estate in the French sector of occupied Germany. Retrofitting an existing building as soundproof studios was then, and remains, particularly difficult because of sound waves carried on vibrations that move through walls, floors, structure, and other materials. This problem had been addressed by building new linings into the existing shell with the fewest possible points of contact, so as to minimize material bridges along which vibrations might move.[50] Although the plenary hall was a new building rather than a retrofit, the construction techniques at the Internationale Film-Union offered an important precedent. By doubling the building's surfaces, it was possible to ensure acoustic separation without recourse to specialized acoustical building products, which would not have been readily available.

Every surface in the plenary hall is consequently doubled, with an air gap between exterior and interior surfaces. Along the length of the masonry walls, an extra layer only one masonry unit thick runs parallel to the bearing steel structure and its exterior masonry cladding. In the window walls, a clever solution allowed the double construction to be integrated with the deeper structural mullions necessary to resist wind loads on the large glazed surface: working as a double shell, the ruffled, saw-tooth surface of windows angled within the thickness of the mullions also provided some acoustic benefit.[51] **[1.18]**

To ensure audibility of the spoken word, Schwippert, working with an engineer and the appropriate manufacturers, developed a suspended ceiling system. As described by Schwippert's employee Wera Meyer-Waldeck, the result cleverly integrated function and design:

"The dropped ceiling in the hall is independent of the sound-absorbing ceiling above and carries the required acoustic panels differentiated by low, middle and high frequency. The square acoustical elements are simultaneously the housing for fluorescent tube lighting. The design resolution is clearly derived from the technical and acoustic demands;

49   This excursion was listed as a reimbursable travel cost on February 26, 1949. GNM, DKA, NL, Schwippert.

50   Rathausverein Oberwinterthur, http://www.rathausverein-oberwinter.de/Pdf/Calmuth4.pdf, accessed December 19, 2021.

51   See Meyer-Waldeck, "Das Bundesparlament," 102. A letter dated June 27, 1949 from the acoustical engineer Karl Kaus confirms this assertion. AM TUM, schwi-92-209.

52   Meyer-Waldeck, "Das Bundesparlament," 102.

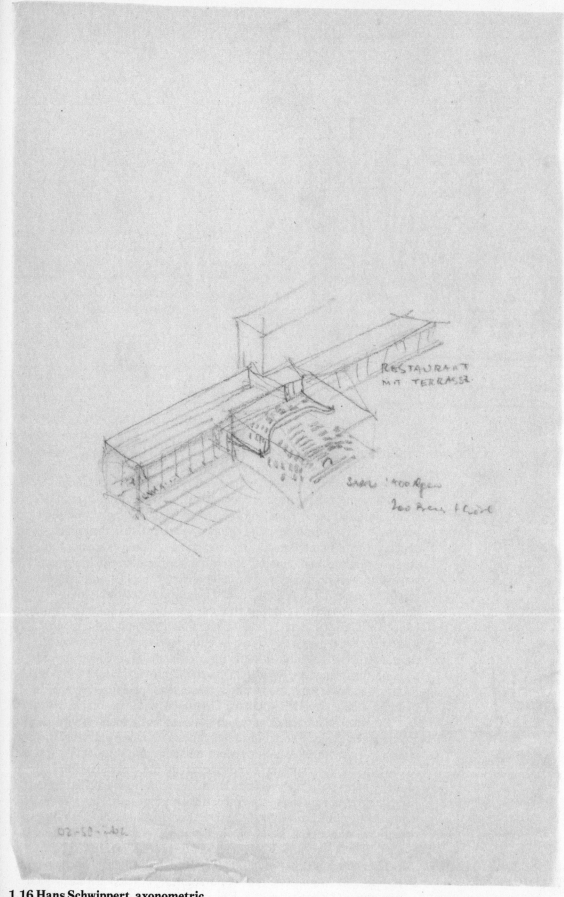

1.16 Hans Schwippert, axonometric
with plenary

53   Schwippert's balance of bespoke and standardized manufacturing is clear by comparison to the acoustic ceiling in Paul Baumgarten's Concert Hall for the Music Academy in Berlin (1949–1954). Baumgarten's ceiling is suspended from a rough board shell by threaded rods and pieced together from ash-veneered plywood, frosted wire glass, acoustic insulation and standard OSRAM spotlights. Everything is ad hoc. See "The Architects' Journal," (London: Architectural Press, 1957), 25–58.

still, a harmonic rhythm and coherence was achieved."[52] The need to design a component-based ceiling that optimized technical performance was a challenge well suited to Schwippert's interest in finding design solutions that engaged both replicable and unique aspects of production.

    Aligning with the 2.25 meter on-center measurement between the primary structure of the window wall, the ceiling reads as a series of squares set corner to corner rather than as a grid. The flush squares of the checkerboard ceiling, though not the recessed panels, were outlined by surface-mounted fluorescent light bulbs. To accommodate the standard length, the fluorescent tubes were offset from the centerline of each square, toward the center, and their corners did not abut. This negotiation between standard industrial and site-specific measurements created a geometry that underpinned the space's overall rhythm, although its unassuming appearance could easily have been mistaken for a standard dropped ceiling system suitable to any number of applications. Manufactured by OSRAM, the ceiling is emblematic of the special relationship between the architect and a reemergent building industry, eager to develop economies of scale through singular, collaborative projects.[53]

    As is evident in his facade studies, with their relentless search for an appropriate window format, Schwippert never intended the plenary

1.17 Hans Schwippert, sketch of plenary interior

hall glazing as a curtain wall or self-supporting glazed structure. Instead, it is without exception rendered as groups of windows, usually four in a row, set into a horizontal opening. As realized, the window walls have two sets of windows. On the exterior, the windows lie flat within a steel grid. On the interior, they are angled, with one edge coplanar with the innermost point of the structural steel flange and the other coplanar with the exterior glazing. The steel grid in which the windows sit is part of the building's structure: each primary vertical and horizontal mullion supports the roof and each intermediary mullion, equally deep, resists horizontal loading. To keep the structural steel as thin-seeming as possible, its rigidity results from its depth in plan rather than its thickness in profile. This thinness permits a conflation between window frame, window structure, and bearing structure, so that these large glazed areas appear as independent, unified structures. The gap between exterior and interior glazing served as both acoustic separation and thermal insulation. The fixed frames in which the hinged windows operated were detailed inside and out to overlap the structural fin, so as to conceal the structure and create the optical illusion of a continuous glazing on both sides.

The window frames themselves were elegantly but simply constructed. Repeating similar details for interior and exterior glazed doors and windows created an economy of scale and, presumably, contained costs

1.18 Paste-up for an unrealized publication on the Bundeshaus, plenary glazing, "Windows" chapter

and complications for the manufacturers who were, apparently, not specialized in window building: according to a list provided by Schwippert's office to the federal government upon the building's completion, all the windows were built by two metalworking shops in Cologne that also provided steel furniture.[54] The frames comprised two components, one that held the hinging mechanism and one that held the glass. The former was executed in natural aluminum and the latter, gold anodized. A reveal was left between the two frames, with the interior frame slightly proud of the hinged frame. This created the appearance of even greater thinness and delicacy on the front of the windows. The operable frame was significantly deeper, employing structural principles similar to those used in the plenary hall fins. Hinges were standard in execution, simple band or butt hinges with none of the finesse seen in interwar German architectural hardware. Glazing was inset to create yet another plane of relief in the relationship of fixed frame, operable plane, glass stop, and glass.

The bas-relief of grid, infill, and windows corresponds to the strategy used in the office tract facade. Each element, as thinly dimensioned as possible, overlays to form a network of gridded, minimally sculptural surfaces, whether glazed, as in the restaurant and plenary hall, or mostly opaque, as in the office tract. Schwippert was thus able to translate the unifying pencil lines in his sketches to the Bundeshaus facades, in aluminum and basalt, in steel and stucco. The overall impression was one of lightness and transparency.

In the year following the inauguration of the Bundeshaus, Schwippert began to plan a monograph about the building, both in its empty state, as architectural photos tend to be, and full of legislative life. The chapter titles are clearly addressed to a lay audience with their humorous tone—among them, "Heads," showing politician mug shots [1.19], immediately followed by "… and Chairs," illustrating seating throughout the building. Even the restaurant menu was to have been reproduced. The book's concept seems to take cues from reports on the Bundeshaus and its occupants, filed in the so-called boulevard press beginning with the inauguration, which emphasized the comparative luxury and bonhomie of life in the capitol.[55] However, by positioning parliamentary life firmly within its architectural and design context, Schwippert's monograph would have corrected the tendency of the popular press to misinterpret, or even worse, to ignore, his architecture and its symbolism. Notes in Schwippert's script on the pasted-up galleys are evidence of his investment in the project, on which he worked during the spring of 1951 in collaboration with a graphic designer.[56] It is unclear why the project was discontinued. Perhaps its purpose was diminished amid ongoing strife that ultimately led to the redesign of the plenary hall in 1953. Had it been completed, the book would have addressed many remaining questions about how Schwippert imagined and understood the project. It would have done justice to both the better and the lesser-known contributors to its realization, from craftsmen on the construction site, to unidentified government administrators, to top-level politicians. The extant galleys capture what Schwippert described as "the dignity of a building of today, which attempts to earn the love of people with the economical and stringent means of a technical era. A small push towards openness and friendliness, a frontal attack against what we call bitterly seriousness."[57]

The book's introductory text would have been an expanded version of an article entitled "Das hellste Parlament der Welt" (the lightest parliament in the world) by journalist Will Grohmann, published in March 1951 in *Die Neue Zeitung* Berlin.[58] The rest of the book was primarily photographic. Grohmann's title emphasized the building's character as "the most modern government building in the world, although it might also be the most modest":

"The first impression is that work is done here, and that the human being is the measure of all things. […] We rejoice in this solution since even countries with architectural culture embarrass themselves

54   "Liste der am Bau Bundesparlament beteiligten Firmen," 3. AM TUM, schwi-92-209.
55   Wintgens, "Neues Parlament, Neue Bilder?" 310–12. On March 3, 1950, both major parties voted for a commission to investigate "luxurious" spending. As SPD representative Graf von Spreti expressed it, "we have no interest in garden design when we can't even offer others a bed to sleep in. […] We don't need to hunt for easter eggs in the garden!" AM TUM, schwi-92-209.
56   A four-page letter and layout preserved in GNM, DKA, NL, Schwippert is signed only "ch." I have not been able to identify the designer, although Schwippert was in contact at the time with both Hans Leistikow and Otl Aicher.
57   Address at the inauguration of the Bundeshaus, GNM, DKA, NL, Schwippert.
58   Will Grohmann, "Das hellste Parlament der Welt," *Die Neue Zeitung* 3 (1951).

when they build for the government: one need only think of the
awful palaces of the past. [...] The Bundeshaus does not stand alone,
from an artistic standpoint; but this connection between function
and beauty is rare in Germany, although it is found internationally
in the Scandinavian states, and in America especially since the
emigration of numerous excellent architects such as Mies, Gropius,
Neutra, Saarinen, Mendelsohn. The most recent architecture
exhibition to come from the United States to Europe in 1951 showed
exemplary governmental buildings: even the United Nations
Secretariat Building is a functional building. Beauty resides everywhere in the balance of materials, proportion and spatial sense,
in the organization of needs, the desires of people, and the landscape.

In the case of Schwippert's building, comparison is made
to a university. This is good: what do we wish to represent here if not
our reason, and a bit, too, our instinct for the situation. [...] Hans
Schwippert has built using all the technical means at his disposal
but without seeing technical achievement as an aim. The consequence
was inexpensiveness, functionality, and extreme formal cleanliness.
Although planning and construction occurred simultaneously
because of the tight schedule, things were handled so rationally and
work was executed so effectively with the construction companies
that there were no failures."[59]

Grohmann praises the handling of construction and asserts that the
building's modesty is integral to its architectural value. "Modest" is not
a euphemism for poorly handled on-site exigencies or professional
incompetence, as critics claimed who faulted the building's almost
immediate need for repairs, to Schwippert's lasting anger.[60] Giving the
measure of its well-calibrated tone, Grohmann ranks the complex
internationally among important recent modernist public buildings,
most pointedly, those by newly emigrated Germans in the United States.
He praises its beauty, its "balance of materials, proportion, and spatial
sense, in the organization of needs, the desires of people, and the landscape."
Competent construction, representational capacity, and aesthetic
balance, all attributes noted in the opening paragraphs of Grohmann's
text, correspond directly to what Schwippert wanted the photographs
to convey, as a register of everything he valued most in his building.

Grohmann's mention of the United Nations Headquarters in New
York is an indication of the position it held as a model for the cultivation
of a new governmental architecture free from traditional iconography.
The United Nations figured, if only briefly, in the 1951 Darmstädter Gespräch
in a series of podium and audience discussions, which even now offer rare
insight into architectural theory and thought in that era. Philosopher
Alfred Weber, who, by his own admission, had "nothing to say as a specialist
in architecture," introduced the United Nations into the discussion.
His self-admitted ignorance did not prevent Weber from using the United
Nations to exemplify modern architecture's failure to capture what
he termed "collective experience":

"If architecture wishes to be more than building, if architecture wishes
to become monumental and representative [...] then it must form
a space from the spiritual collective. [...] What has happened to the
palace, to the place of occupation of the United Nations in New
York? If one imagines the collective content which the United Nations
should represent, what has happened? Do you believe that a cigar
box on its side should have been the result, which by the way has
ruined the New York skyline, as far as I can tell?"[61]

The response from the architects in his audience was telling. Otto Bartning,
head of the Bund Deutscher Architekten and a co-organizer of the
conference, was also critical of the building's sleek, administrative patina,
but was quick to shift the blame from architecture per se to the client,
claiming that it was the United Nations "which did not understand how
to formulate its needs in terms of [...] its entire thought." Bartning character-

59   Grohman, "Das hellste Parlament."
60   Only months after its completion, the
press began to criticize the Bundeshaus as
poorly built. Defenders saw these as attacks on
modern architecture per se. As late as 1963,
Schwippert was still defending the integrity of
his building. See Eckstein, "Ist das Bonner
Bundeshaus zu schlecht gebaut?" and letters
from Gerstenmeier from April 5, 1963, and
Dr. Heinrich König from March 20, 1961, in
GNM, DKA, NL, Schwippert.
61   Alfred Weber quoted in Conrads and
Neitzke, *Mensch und Raum*, 117–118.

1.19 Paste-up for an unrealized publication on the Bundeshaus, "Heads" chapter

ized the building's architecture as emblematic of the organization's pitfalls, and as "a clear signal of the bureaucracy of the entire UN Organization."[62] Hermann Mäckler, a Frankfurt architect who would enjoy a prolific career, defended the building and its position among the other Manhattan skyscrapers. He reminded his colleagues, "It is merely an administration building, and I ask you, independent of the position you may take on architecture, what is this at its core other than the true production of space for the bureaucracy? Of course. It is in fact a bureaucracy that needs its space."[63] Expressing a very different concept from the "collective content" invoked by Weber, Mäckler's words presage the impending era of the "man in the gray flannel suit" and welcome a well-functioning, transparent bureaucracy as the antidote to *Kaiser, Führer*, and the cult of personality.

Despite the obvious differences in scope, the Bundeshaus bears comparison with the United Nations headquarters, which was designed in 1947 and likewise completed at breakneck speed. The comparison is also instructive in understanding the way in which building construction operated during postwar economic recovery. As an industry, it accelerated innovation in the market viability of products and services; at the same time, it fueled the rise of international modernist architecture. Although the American construction industry had been highly developed and diversified before World War II, its resources had been directed to technical rather than stylistic modernization. The limited resources expended on building during the war effort had not helped to advance the development of prod-

62   Conrads and Neitzke, *Mensch und Raum*, 118.
63   Conrads and Neitzke, *Mensch und Raum*, 119.

64   In a public lecture staged with the exhibition "Kevin Roche: Architecture as Environment," Roche described working on the UN Secretariat detailing: "There was no Sweet's Catalogue, but there were lots of Mom and Pop shops. You could get anything made that you wanted [...] The development from that to the curtain wall industry was natural, because someone in a backyard shop gets a commission to do a few window frames, sees the potential and then the real industry picks it up. Prefabrication and the factory-built take over." The Museum of the City of New York, January 17, 2012.

65   Robert A. M. Stern, Thomas Mellins, and David Fishman, *New York 1960: Architecture and Urbanism between the Second World War and the Bicentennial* (New York: Monacelli Press, 1995), 606–7.

ucts for the construction of modern architecture. In terms of the products offered, Germany's interwar building industry was more amenable to modern architecture. As US manufacturers retooled for the postwar economy, modern architects found ample opportunity to direct the industry toward their stylistic preferences.[64] The glass wall, especially as a self-structuring curtain wall system, was a locus of this development.

There is high drama in the design history of the United Nations complex, negotiated by the young Oscar Niemeyer on behalf of Le Corbusier to allay the objections made by the original design team. But it pales in comparison to the force of the New York real estate smarts behind its construction. Although the complex was originally to be located outside the city, its midtown site was strategically acquired through a barter brokered by Nelson Rockefeller with William Zeckendorf for the land along the East River.[65] Rockefeller's architect of choice, Wallace K. Harrison, was retained to translate the design into working drawings and construction documents; his partner Max Abramovitz was named Deputy Director of Planning for the United Nations headquarters. With the involvement of Turner Construction, the largest construction management company in the United States, the consortium of New York City architectural power brokers was complete.

Harrison's core business was residential construction. New York's building trades, in the housing boom years of the 1920s, had refined a variety of fireproof steel construction methods in which variously sized

1.20 Paste-up for an unrealized publication on the Bundeshaus, office corridor, "Unbureaucratic" chapter

steel beams were connected to make a structural skeleton, which was then encased in cast concrete. This type of method was not only extremely fast to construct; in allowing the structural engineer to tailor the structural height of each steel beam to its specific span, it minimized the cost of structural steel. Harrison's office applied a variant of this construction technique at the United Nations with particular effectiveness in the General Assembly, the most public and expressive building in the complex. The building's long spans and non-rectilinear geometry were framed in steel, in direct analogy to both fireproof residential construction and to the ship construction in which the US steel industry excelled during the war. The transposition of familiar methods to the General Assembly allowed Harrison to take advantage of the available know-how and materials on hand, and to ensure that the strong, unionized trades on site were comfortable with the techniques.[66]

The Secretariat building, on the other hand, followed the construction model of the office towers then rising in Midtown Manhattan. Skidmore, Owings and Merrill's Lever House, built only one year earlier, is the best-known example: steel frame, metal decking with cast concrete flooring, a systematized suspended ceiling with integrated ventilation and lighting, and an equally systematized glass and aluminum facade. Here, too, the choices of materials, products, and construction techniques were in lock-step with the prevailing practices of New York City construction at the time. The contrast with Bonn in 1949 could not be clearer. Schwippert found a way to associate his building's appearance with a larger, international movement despite the limited means at his disposal.

Haltung der Zurückhaltung,[67] a posture of restraint, was the phrase that Schwippert would apply a few years later to the atmosphere for which he strove in his design for the Bundeshaus. It not only rejected the excesses of monumentality and pomp exemplified by the governmental and civic architecture of the Third Reich. It also demanded a specific architectural language that avoided banality or might trivialize the new German Republic as mindless bureaucracy, a danger exemplified by Weber's "cigar box on its side." Instead, it required something discrete but still honorific enough to represent the fledging democracy's egalitarian ideals, close in spirit to the "mere" administrative building Mäckler extolled. Schwippert envisioned an architecture in which civil servants would act efficiently and conscionably, in which they would take pleasure in their day-to-day, in which they would remain "unbureaucratic" despite being part of a high-functioning bureaucracy. [1.20]

As conceived by Schwippert, the Bundeshaus monograph would have described the way in which people used the building and the social environment it supported, not only the architecture he had produced. For that reason, images of architecture, design objects, and occupants were interspersed throughout the nine sections in which the book was laid out. Two early sections, "Doors and Windows" and "Honest Columns," were laid out with only traditional architectural photos. The chapter entitled "Heads" followed the elected politicians and civil servants at work in their offices, while the chapter "… and Chairs" documented the plenary hall in session as well as its furniture. The book's final chapter, "What do you want to eat?" included images of the restaurant filled with diners as well as shots of its tablecloths, the abstract floral-patterned curtains on the windows that faced the Rhine, and chairs for dining and lounging designed by Marcel Breuer and Johannes Krahn, respectively. [1.21]

The formal architectural photos in the paste-up are primarily by Albert Renger-Patzsch, long-standing collaborator of Rudolf Schwarz and the photographer with whom Schwippert preferred to work. Architectural plan and elevation drawings adjacent to these photographs in the book's first pages helped to orient the reader. For the pages that followed, however, the right images must have been harder to come by. The paste-ups use random stand-ins or tiny photographs clipped from 35mm or medium-format film contact sheets. Among these tiny images are those of delegates in the plenary hall; Adenauer in a

66   Construction photographs and the original 1:50 drawings of the complex show typical fireproof steel construction. The UN office of facilities management and construction granted the author access to these drawings in 2002.
67   Buslei-Wuppermann and Zeising, *Das Bundeshaus,* 29.

1.21 Paste-up for an unrealized publication on the Bundeshaus, view from the restaurant. The pencil lines represent the patterns in the curtain fabric.

top hat departing from the main entrance; or three men and a woman walking across the terrace. Elsewhere, the layout includes stand-ins for a grid of portraits or for candid images of people caught in their daily routines. In a letter to Schwippert, the graphic designer[68] recommended using snapshots ("*knipsen*") to explain the exemplary openness and lack of formality in the complex, as Schwippert had written, "a building of today, which attempts to earn the love of people." In Grohmann's words, the building was "light" because it is "simple, human and friendly."[69] The surviving paste-up borrows cleverly from both conventional architectural monographs and the newly burgeoning illustrated weekly press. It successfully depicts the socio-spatial rewards of Schwippert's calibrated transparency and modest, well-handled construction: an unbureaucratic bureaucracy inside the "lightest parliament in the world."

Because of the way the Bundeshaus was photographed, it requires some imagination to recreate its spatial sequence. Schwippert's original plenary hall, terrace, and restaurant were all demolished and replaced by a larger, modernized hall completed just before German reunification. For those—I am included here—who never bothered to visit Bonn for its capitol architecture before history more or less mothballed it, all that remains are several rows of original, green leather-upholstered seating and a fragment of the office tract. And even for those trained to envision architecture from technical drawings, it remains hard to imagine the

68   In a letter to Hans Wandersleb dated September 10, 1949, Schwippert advocated for the publication, citing the positive response it had elicited from the architectural press. AM TUM, schwi-92-209.
69   Letter, April 8, 1951, GNM, DKA, NL, Schwippert.

experience of Schwippert's building.

Its primary entrance led from the street up four flights of stairs, less wide in dimension than even the smaller offices inside. Steps and entry door seem radically under-dimensioned, narrower than the interior doors that gave onto the plenary hall. The rare published photographs shot along an entry facade show the building's white stuccoed surface, continuous with the original building, punctured by a few, normative-seeming windows. In these photos, Schwippert's addition is entirely indistinguishable from the 1920s building to which it was adjacent. **[1.22]**

Upon entry, the visitor stood in one corner of an elongated room and opposite a solid wall. To her or his left, stretching perpendicular to the entry and more or less the same in its dimensions, was a space that connected to the corridor of the older building. Furnished with small groups of seating, and with access to coat check and bathrooms, this was the so-called *Ruhehalle,* or lounge. Both initial spaces were defined by heavy walls, which were also the structural support for the buildings above. Neither the entrance nor the adjacent transitional space provided the visitor any view to the outdoors. The only daylight came from the entry doors at the visitor's back.

Only as the visitor proceeded toward the entrance space's rear wall did two sets of glass doors, one to the right and one to the left, provide a sense of what was to come. On the left, the doors opened onto the restaurant, its ceiling supported on narrow steel columns and its Rhine-facing glass facade eliciting the impression that its space simply elided with the enormous outdoor terrace in front of it. Expansive, flooded with natural light, dominated by the Rhine view, the restaurant was a dramatic contrast to the entry sequence. On the right was the foyer, or *Wandelhalle,* in what had been the original gymnasium, where the parliament had met prior to Schwippert's renovation. The oft-photographed *Wandelhalle* was two stories high, with three large windows that faced the street and a concrete staircase that floated without visible support from a U-shaped balcony to the dark, rectangularly gridded stone floor. The main entrance to the plenary hall sat asymmetrically in this foyer, on the wall opposite the windows. Only upon entering the plenary hall was the visitor positioned on axis; every other element of the sequence, from entry point onwards, was organized on the oblique. Even the symmetrical plenary hall, in the experience of its users, would rarely be entirely balanced: the two glass walls, facing east and west, would have produced variable lighting conditions over the course of a day. The shadows and lighting effects Schwippert's office had been careful to render in his perspective drawing of the plenary hall seating underlined these changing effects.

Color and surface finish, central to Schwippert's atmosphere of levity, can only be reconstructed from description. A long article published in 1950 in the German interior architectural journal *Architektur und Werkform* goes into great detail.[70] Its author was the remarkable Wera Meyer-Waldeck, one of the very few women to graduate the Bauhaus with a degree in architecture, for which she studied under all three of the school's directors. She herself briefly taught interior architecture, thanks to a recommendation from Grohmann, author of the text Schwippert had intended for his Bundeshaus monograph. Although scholarship on Meyer-Waldeck is still emergent,[71] it seems possible that Grohmann introduced her to Schwippert. By 1949, she was living in Bonn and freelancing on the parliament project. She is listed as a project collaborator in numerous publications for her work on the interior fit-out. Perhaps it was she who authored the rendered drawing of the plenary hall seating. Her article describes the surface finishes, including color, texture, and materiality, that must, somehow, be mapped mentally onto the sequence in which each space revealed itself:

> "In the [plenary] hall [...] the closed wall behind the lectern demands concentrated work. The gold-green vinyl curtain, which hangs in deep folds and in its neutral position covers the wall behind the lectern, can be drawn across both window walls to create near-total darkness. The same is true of the neutral-colored sun shades with their

70　　Meyer-Waldeck, "Das Bundesparlament."
71　　Josenia Hérvas y Heras, "Eine Bauhaus-Architektin in der BRD: Wera Meyer-Waldeck/ A Bauhaus Architect in West Germany: Wera Meyer-Waldeck," in Christina Budde, Mary Pepchinski, Peter Cachola Schmal, and Wolfgang Voigt, eds., *Frau Architekt. Seit mehr als 100 Jahren: Frauen im Architekturberuf* (Tübingen: Wasmuth, 2017).

green sunburst figures. A white velour curtain hangs in front of the dark vinyl curtain. On the white curtain are the crests of all twelve states in gold […] The seating comprises specially developed folding seats, painted in flawless black, with seat and back upholstered in green leather; the moveable desk is black. […]

[In the *Wandelhalle*] a straight cantilevered stair with white vinyl flooring leads from the foyer to the gallery, also in tones of white. The only contrasting color is the glowing red vinyl floor and the sparing use of gold anodized aluminum, as well as the tasteful blue-gray-green curtains, produced using a silk screen technique based upon designs by Margret Hildebrand. The seriousness of the room makes for a pleasant contrast to the celebratory atmosphere of the plenary hall.

North of the *Wandelhalle* […] is the large restaurant. […] This room is characterized by a joyous levity and happiness with its 65 m long glass facade, whose doors open onto the terrace, facing towards the Rhine's banks. The well-designed garden solutions by Professor Hermann Mattern transition discretely and organically to the natural landscape. Large-format colorful print curtains (design Margret Hildebrand) emphasize the space's cheerfulness. The alternation between Thonet steel tubular seating and black oak chairs (upholstery alternating red and green vinyl) by the architect Johannes Krahn, the white-painted columns with sparing gold trim in anodized aluminum and not least, the hundreds of simple light bulbs in elegant brass fittings, complete the unified, celebratory impression. […]

The *Ruhehalle* […] in delicate light green and brown tones is reserved for relaxation and intimate conversation."[72]

The *Ruhehalle*, the first space on the left after entry, would have been diffuse in atmosphere: indirectly lit, furnished in pale, earthy tones. The *Wandelhalle* and restaurant would have been utterly different: the former, stark white except for its glossy red vinyl floor, and the latter, sun-flooded and dominated, if not by the landscape, then by the bright, patterned curtains, which the magazine *Der Spiegel* compared, condescendingly, to "the colorful style of an American girl's blouse."[73] The color scheme culminated in the plenary hall, with the gold and white curtain recalling the gold-accented columns, the green seating an intensification of the lighter colors in the lounge, and the sunburst pattern a subtle play on the curtains of Hildebrandt's design in the other rooms.

As in his use of grid and low relief in the facades, Schwippert's orchestration of the interior spatial sequence remarkably calibrates daylighting, dimension, controlled view, color, texture, asymmetry, and orienting movement to establish drama and hierarchy without recourse to the typical architectural language of civic buildings.

Transparency—the view through, the view out, the view across— is tightly controlled, almost stingy throughout the entry sequence. Once the visitor is in the building, however, and is able to move across its open terrace with its dramatic vistas towards the Rhine, the plenary hall, and the restaurant, then she or he indeed experiences these spaces as expansive, accessible—quite plausibly the "lightest parliament in the world."

Schwippert's approach to the design and construction of his Bundeshaus challenges any simple claim that the technical means unique to an era and the expression of those means is the only legitimate basis for modern architecture. It is possible that, as Schwippert himself claimed,[74] he struggled intellectually to extrapolate from his own experience in order to recognize the ethical validity of transcending material determinacy. As a designer of furniture and other everyday items, Schwippert showed an abiding interest in the balance between what was replicable—a technique, a geometric relationship—and what was more variable, whether the tree branches he had foreseen in his furniture designs for new settlers or the final interior fit-out of the spaces that

72 Meyer-Waldeck, "Das Bundes-parlament," 100–109.
73 "Die Weihe des Hauses," in *Der Spiegel* (September 8, 1949), 5, and Meyer-Waldeck, "Das Bundesparlament."
74 Wolfgang Pehnt, "Die Würde des Werks: In Erinnerung an Hans Schwippert," in Buslei-Wuppermann and Zeising, *Das Bundeshaus*, 8.

would include his "family" of standardized furniture.

The architectural idiom advocated by Schwippert in his design for the Bundeshaus as a rejection of "seriousness" could, in various permutations, be found throughout West Germany in new buildings constructed between the war's end and the early 1950s. Over time, however, this idiom began to shift, in accordance with ideas about architectural expression as much as with the new possibilities offered by a revitalized construction industry and an increasingly affluent society. In Schwippert's case, however, the architecture and detailing of the Bundeshaus not only represented an idiom tied to a particular moment in his career and his country's history; he cleaved to this modality even as his colleagues' work began to change within a year or two after the Bundeshaus was completed.

Rather than avail himself of the glut in available commissions as the country rebuilt, Schwippert chose to invest his energies in teaching and in revitalizing the Werkbund. The fewer than twenty buildings he completed after 1952 develop many of the themes already evident in the plenary hall and office wings of the Bundeshaus: the effect of a surface grid on a facade, the manipulation of glazing and interior spaces to create perceived transparency, the finesse of thinly dimensioned window mullions, the balance between a bespoke element and the capacity for standardized reproduction. His last building in particular, the Pädagogische Hochschule Rheinland in Neuss (1964–1970), offers some particularly beautiful examples of the latter: subtly varied ceramic floor tiles; bricks inscribed with circular patterns in low relief and burned to different hues of cream,

1.22 Paste-up for an unrealized publication on the Bundeshaus, street side entrance

75   Breuer et al., *Schwippert: Moderation*, 398.

orange, brown, and black. In general, however, to achieve this balance of bespoke and reproducible required a particular building economy, one in which labor was less costly and materials were less refined. The ideal construction economy for Schwippert's sensibilities was quite different than the one towards which the building industry was moving in the 1950s, which favored building products over semi-products that the architect could then assemble and reassemble for a slightly different expression each time.

Just as this construction economy was disappearing in West Germany with the rise of the *Wirtschaftswunder*, Schwippert acquired the commission to renovate the most important Catholic church in East Germany, St. Hedwig's Cathedral in Berlin. During the project's seven-year span, Schwippert produced and transmitted numerous sketches to compensate for the fact that he was unable to make frequent site visits. As he had in the 1920s he solicited designs for the ecclesiastical instruments from colleagues, including his brother, the sculptor Kurt Schwippert.[75] By the time the cathedral was inaugurated in November 1963, Cold War politics had inserted an immense spatial cleft between Schwippert and his project. It is fair to say that the passage of time, and the cultural and economic developments to which Schwippert's Werkbund efforts contributed, had inserted a different kind of cleft between West German architecture and the way Schwippert liked to practice. The difficulties inherent in East Germany's planned economy, with its supply chain oddities and anachronisms, suited him. At the Hedwigskathedrale, as in the Bundeshaus, Schwippert found his way to lightness and transparency, more transcendent than literal, again in the face of material scarcity and tenuous cultural grounding.

The chapter title quotes a 1933 speech
by Eduard Brill, then director of the school,
as cited in Vera Lose, " 'Unser Sinn steht
nach der Werkstatt [...]': Von der Königlichen
Kunstgewerbeschule in Nürnberg zur Staats-
schule für angewandte Kunst," in Jana
Stolzenberger, ed., *350: Festschrift der Akademie
der Bildenden Künste Nürnberg* (Nuremberg:
Verlag für modernen Kunst Nürnberg, 2012), 104.

"A Yearning for the Workshop, the Construction Site, the Finished Work"

Akademie der Bildenden Künste, Nuremberg

Even the earliest photographs taken of the Akademie der Bildenden Künste in Nuremberg include plant life. In the ones shot upon the building's completion, the walls are unblemished and the only signs of occupation are white curtains pulled to the windows' edges or barely discernable reflections of figurative sculptures in the windowpanes. The dark, crooked trunks of mature birches stand at irregular intervals, juxtaposed to the precisely spaced, white-painted steel columns that support the covered walkway as it threads the complex. Leaves and meadow plants texture the surfaces on and against which the buildings stand. The trees, miracu-lously, have escaped the woodstoves and bonfires of the desperate years at the war's end. Miraculously, too, they have escaped construction unscathed. It is as though the new buildings arose, perfect and complete, inside a perimeter drawn and maintained precisely so as not to disturb a single living root structure. [2.1]

Of course, this cannot be true. Pristine white stucco and glass buildings do not simply arise. The act of building is destructive. Construction inevitably scars the ground. Foundation trenches extend beyond the buildings' edge. Trucks drive in and out. Cranes swing. Backhoes pile soil. Materials are stacked, awaiting use. Tree and plant life suffers. Any exception to these givens demands vigilant, relentless supervision; necessitates meticulous planning; gives preference to the precision of human labor over the swift messiness of machinery.

Sep Ruf, the Akademie's architect, and all those working for him brought this precision to bear on the project. Their relentlessness is clear in every drawing made and every project document preserved. The care lavished on the birches equals the care lavished on the window sashes, the floorboards, the roof overhangs, and, not least of all, the building's design as an embodiment of collaborative, fluid art pedagogy. The birch trees' remarkable preservation is, part for whole, a perfect metonymy of Ruf's approach to making architecture.

The birches are, however, much more than a rhetorical trope. Represented as figure and texture, as counterpoint to hard-edged geometry, plant life appears in even the earliest drawings for the school complex. It is integral to the architecture. Several formal inked drawings go so far

2.1 Akademie der Bildenden Künste, Nuremberg, walkway and fir tree

as to omit entirely the line of glazing that would, during seasons when snow obscures the grass spanning between pavilions, keep the weather out. And although the drawings were likely authored by different hands, plants and trees are rendered consistently, from an early site plan dated May 1951 to the elevation of a small residential building dated February 1954, with attention to species-differentiated shapes captured in a palette of line types, weights, and stipples.

"Nature" in its more abstract usage, as counterpoint to "built," also belongs to the project's conceptual vocabulary. To relocate this particular art school, whose history went as far back as Albrecht Dürer, to a site outside the city in which it had always resided was to provide it with a fresh start, its own Year Zero. To configure it as an open campus, an architectural type adapted from Anglo-American tradition and associated in Germany with widely-published Weimar-era schools by Bauhaus directors Walter Gropius and Hannes Meyer, was to indicate a new trajectory. Its new site on the forested outskirts of Nuremberg evoked all of this. In the process of planning and construction, however, abstract "nature" has to become specific. In Ruf's case, the "nature" represented so lovingly in the drawings was not merely symbolic. It was translated into botanical genus. Several annotated invoices in the project job books issued by the local landscape gardener Ernst Merkel document this specificity. An invoice dated September 6, 1956, at the end of a growing season for seeds or grasses and the start of the tree-planting season, has two sets of pencil annotations, one in graphite and one in green. [2.2] Like all the other

2.2 Invoice for plants for the Akademie der Bildenden Künste, twice corrected by Ruf's office, 1956

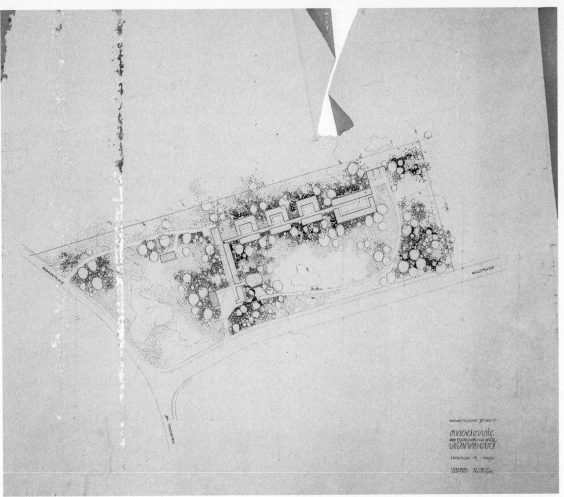

2.3 Site plan, May 1951

Merkel invoices, this one is addressed to the supervisory office at Ruf's construction site. Green pencil appears to supersede graphite, adding more of one item and correcting the final costs. The invoice lists each species of tree and flower delivered: Japanese larch, red oak, decorative cherry, lilac, quince, decorative apple, sour cherry bush, clematis, lupine, digitalis. Few architects would know one from the other. The architects who wielded the black and green pencils knew enough to check and double check the list. Other invoices confirm: the architects on site knew when to add more meadow flower mix, when to strike an order of privet. This precision also suggests that for the Akademie's architects, the plants were another means at their disposal, not an afterthought. One species at a time, they constructed the "nature" within which the Akademie der Bildenden Künste sat.

Sep Ruf was awarded the first prize in a competition for the Nuremberg Akademie der Bildenden Künste campus in 1950. The school had a remarkable history, beginning with its founding just after the Thirty Years' War. It had been in continuous existence since 1662, when it became the first art academy in German-speaking Europe.[01] Under the Third Reich, the school enjoyed new status: its faculty was responsible for the design and fit-out for several projects planned after Nuremberg became "city of the Reichspartei." After an aerial bomb damaged the school's building, instruction moved to a castle on Nuremberg's outskirts. Upon the American army's arrival, the school was closed and its former facilities repurposed.

In the spring of 1946, the occupying forces reopened the academy. Ruf became professor of architecture in 1947. Even more so than other cultural institutions, the school represented a dilemma typical of the era. A desire for continuity with its deep cultural history was in conflict with the imperative to divest its National Socialist legacy. The appointment of a new director, Fritz Griebel, an artist whose work the National Socialists had been deemed *entartet* (degenerate), offered an initial resolution.[02] The new campus in the woods was intended in the same spirit, although

01   "Akademie der Bildenden Künste in Nürnberg," Historisches Lexikon Bayerns, https://www.historisches-lexikon-bayerns.de /Lexikon/Akademie_der_Bildenden_Künste _in_Nürnberg#9, accessed July 18, 2014.
02   Irene Meissner, *Sep Ruf 1908–1982, Kunstwissenschaftliche Studien* (Berlin: Deutscher Kunstverlag, 2013), 106.

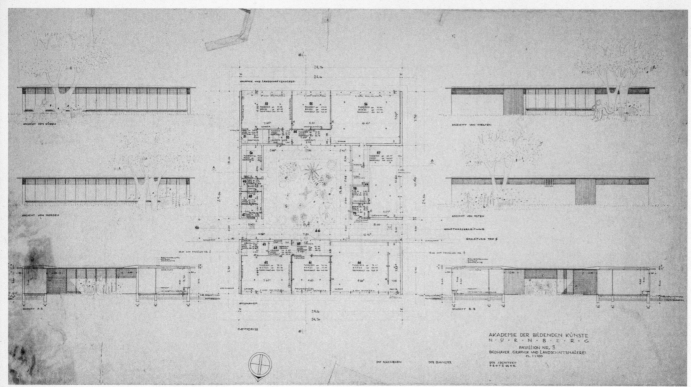

2.4 Pavilion and courtyard, plan and
elevations, undated, with corrections
from 1955

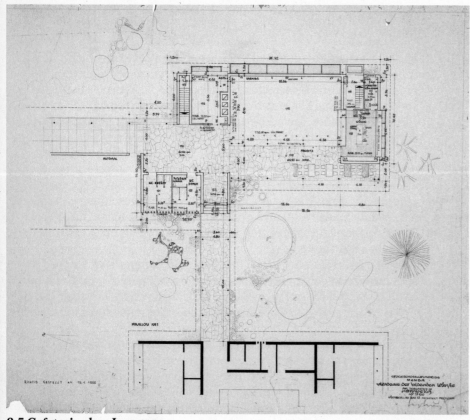

2,5 Cafeteria plan, June 1953

its realization required several years. After the cornerstone was laid in 1950, construction stalled as material prices rose during the Korean War, when the US occupying forces requisitioned German steel. Construction resumed in summer 1952 and the building opened for use in July 1954, although Ruf's office continued to amend the project for two more years. By 1954, however, Ruf had departed the faculty for a professorship at the Academy of Fine Arts in Munich.[03] The long period of project development and construction supervision meant that the project overlapped with different phases in Ruf's rapidly changing postwar practice. Still, in its realization and idiom, it remained something of a time capsule, preserving the attitudes, values, and interests of the moment in which it was conceived.

An inked site plan drawn from 1951, generated in the process of reworking the competition project, demonstrates how plant life participated in establishing the relationship between interior and exterior, bounded and expansive. [2.3] Unbroken and broken lines, dots indicating columns, gray tones and a full array of points, squiggles, kidney shapes, and blackened figures express the proximate landscape. The depiction of plant life is painstaking and luxuriant. Thinly drawn contour lines indicate the gentle slope of the site, two meters across the building's length. Stipples indicate the edges of footpaths and the complex entry; condensed into tighter, irregular patterns, they indicate the edges at which the plantings that belong to the school complex give way to uncultivated meadow and forest. Circles of varying size—bushes? ground cover? hedgerows? small trees?—edge the open colonnade along the administration building, running north to south, and complete the second edge of exterior corridor, running east to west, which connects the studios. Finally, at six specific points, blackened squiggles seem to indicate denser vegetation, perhaps a strategic obstruction to shield the building's entry from the main street and to reinforce the fiction that the campus stood remote within its wooded clearing.

The L-shaped building complex looks as if it had been carved from dense vegetation or perhaps, as if tangles of plants had caught on the reef-like building. Its ruled lines also elide inside and outside. The elongated administration building that runs vertically at the plan's left, like the narrow perpendicular passage that connects it to the fan-shaped auditorium, are enclosed spaces. Still, they are drawn no differently than the covered exterior porticos that ring the enfilade courtyards along the cross axis. The covered walkway between courtyards is rendered in a single, solid line, equal in weight to the walls of the buildings, although the walkway line registers the roof's edge rather than a boundary between inside and out. Consistently, however, the ruled edges distinguish sharply between built and growing environments. The built stands out in relief against the foliage that shifts against it. Unlike, for example, Joseph Gandy's spectacular renderings of Soane's Bank of England or Schinkel's landscape oils of ruined Gothic churches, eerily similar to the architecture on his own drawing board, Ruf's building gently resists renaturalization. It maintains discipline. This is not a site of future archeology.

This sensibility, which expresses the built and the vegetative as equals in the definition of space, recurs. An early plan carefully represents fieldstone pavers and, in plan as well as in elevation, small trees, bushes, and flowers. [2.4] It seems likely that this drawing was used for cost estimate take-offs, deduced from the notation in each room of the square footage of its surfaces. Exterior pavers are drawn, although no take-off information is provided for them. The extensive elaboration of landscape elements is an unusual flourish for a technical drawing. Only if these elements were considered integral to the building's conception would the draftsman's work have been incomplete without them. In fact, they appear in most of the drawings produced in the course of the project's execution.

An early, simplified plan for the cafeteria explains how spaces and their boundaries were to be defined, by always allowing for elements that slip across those boundaries. [2.5, 2.8] An asymmetrical U-shaped masonry-wall at its rear encompasses the dining area. On the right, the U ends at

2.6 Chain-link fence, elevation, and plan, undated

2.7 Workshop pavilion, 2019

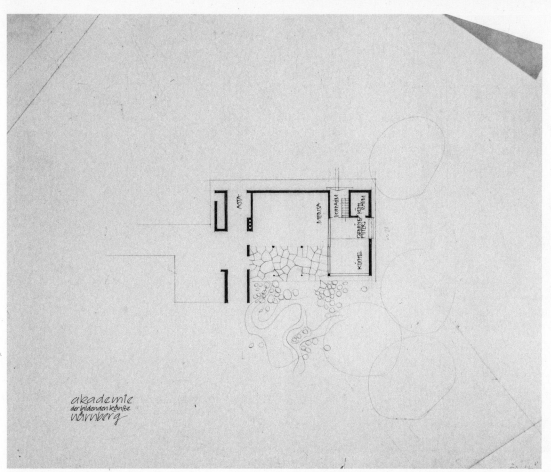

2.8 Initial design for the cafeteria, undated

the kitchen pass-through, and on the left, at a break in a long wall that continues past the outside wall of the cafeteria into an irregularly paved garden. The cafeteria's fourth edge is marked by two columns, which sit on the dividing line between the main dining area, its floor left unpatterned, and an area that appears to be paved in fitted flagstone. Two thinner mullions, aligned with the columns, mark another boundary—perhaps a glazed facade—beyond which the paving stones, now round and irregularly placed, ultimately give way to a swirling garden path. The drawing gives little definitive information on what is inside or out, what is architecture or landscape architecture. It certainly references a modernist space-making tradition, in which boundaries are implied by the alignments of elements rather than unequivocally drawn. Still, the variety among those elements—the volume of a utility space, a flat wall, the U-shaped element already described, round columns, and square mullions—is unorthodox, especially in this otherwise stripped-down drawing. A much more detailed drawing of the same spaces from 1953 reveals the additional work needed to translate these early spatial ideas into a functioning architecture with all its technical exigencies. But notably, nothing of the ambiguity of interior, exterior, and something in between has been lost in translation.

It is almost inconceivable that an architect would be asked, or would volunteer, to draw a chain link fence, but that is exactly what Ruf's office did on June 24, 1952. **[2.6]** This drawing attests, among other things, to the meticulousness and thoroughness with which Ruf approached the project, at the same time as it raises questions about what otherwise banal-seeming products might have been so scarce that architects were required to provide specifications. In a discussion of landscape and boundary, however, the drawing reinforces the value ascribed to plant life. For the craftsman receiving the drawing, the elevation is of little use, except for the thread of dimensions that skirts the leaves and branches obscuring the fence he is supposed to be building. The small sectional sketch shows the basic height and centerline measurements for the metal verticals as well as the dimensions and desired shape of its foundations; but the drawing's real subject are trees, shrubs, grasses, flowers, and meadow. Some of the

2.9 Workshop pavilion with donkey, 2019

plants are rendered naturalistically, while others resemble Calder mobiles. As in the fluid boundary described in the cafeteria's garden-facing edge, the fence was designed to merge with the larger landscape and leave the visitor to wonder: what is inside, what is out?

Summer is the season in which most published images of the Akademie der Bildenden Künste were shot. They evince what Ruf's drawings correctly foresaw: a lush background within which the sharp-edged white buildings stand in relief. The photos here were taken during two days of light snowfall. There were puddles to navigate along the covered walkway that spans the pavilions. Messy remnants of snow edging the buildings had frozen overnight into gray clumps where thick-soled shoes had churned the ground. Art students, no longer limited to the genres originally registered in the design of the pavilions, had taken their work out of doors: ramshackle structures from the end-of-semester party, ad hoc graffiti, warping stretched canvases, imprecisely nailed two-by-fours, even a coin-op donkey ride more at home on a sidewalk than in an art academy. [2.9] Behind the single-glazed windows, plaster casts of *Gründerzeit* busts seemed oblivious to change. [2.7]

There are two bus stops at walking distance from the Akademie. One is on the corner of a well-trafficked high street. The other is in the middle of the woods. Seek out the latter. A short walk down a road lined on both sides with trees and underbrush, then a right turn: the entrance to the school lies between two established hedgerows. It gives onto a long rectangular forecourt paved in the same dark gray flagstone that appears in all the building's exterior spaces. On one side of the courtyard is a small residential building intended for the on-site caretaker. [2.10] On its opposite side is the long, glazed facade that follows the entire length of the main building, in which the school's communal spaces are housed: library, auditorium, and cafeteria. There is a short stretch of plastered wall at the building's head. In it, to the right of the main doors, a glass vitrine cantilevers out from the concierge's small office. A porte-cochère balanced on white steel columns emphatically marks the entrance. [2.11] It corresponds exactly to the width of the foyer inside the glass doors. [2.12]

2.10 Caretaker's house and garden, 2019

Directly opposite the entry doors is the auditorium's convex end wall. [2.13] Its doors are on either side of a blue-tone mosaic, believed perhaps to be the design of the Akademie's first president Fritz Griebel.[04] Sunlight strikes the bowed wall through the glazed walls of the element that joins the auditorium to the main building. Inside the auditorium, the side-walls are also glazed, although they can be darkened by drawing heavy, full-height curtains. The entry wall at the space's rear is faced in perforated wood acoustic panels, into which the two doors vanish when closed. The planks in the wood floor align with the rows of seating. This is no trick of the camera lens: it is difficult to judge the space's length and depth, especially with the curtains open, when the entire complex of surrounding buildings appears within the space. If, instead of walking toward the blue mosaic, however, the visitor turns left upon entry, he or she will enter a corridor wide enough to double as an exhibition space, for which Ruf's office designed custom, removable steel-framed panels. [2.14] It is a space envisioned to be full of people, but when empty, its extent is stunning. The boundary between entry foyer and corridor is sharply drawn by the change in flooring from limestone to durable red tile, meant to withstand constant traffic.

The building's two primary perpendicular axes cross on the cafeteria, at the end of the long, glazed corridor. Looking back from that juncture along the administration building, the modulation in shape and depth signals the building's public functions. The auditorium, the only non-rectilinear form in the entire complex, sits on slightly higher ground. It marks the edge of the central green spaces of the campus and presides over them, an independent volume in its own right. Looking ahead along the line of pavilions, the line of sight crosses the courtyards, three square and one rectangular, which organize each studio. [2.15] [2.16]

The roof that runs through all of them attenuates in perspective. The shaded ground below the roof registers the alternation between light and shadow that is produced by the rhythm of building to courtyard to interval between courtyard buildings. And across these intervals is a clear view back to the forest. [2.17] [2.18] [2.19]

The colleagues to whom Ruf was closest in the late 1940s and 1950s thought deeply about architectural theory. Many of them wrote extensively.

05   Meissner, *Sep Ruf*, 95–96.
06   Johannes Busmann, *Die revidierte Moderne: Der Architekt Alfons Leitl 1909–1975*, (Wuppertal: Müller und Busmann, 1995), "Im Freundeskreis 1945–54," 54–69.
07   Meissner, *Sep Ruf*, 91.
08   Alfons Leitl, "… keine Zeit, eine verlorene Generation zu sein," *Baukunst und Werkform* 4 (1958), 183–84.

Ruf wrote little, if at all, although he was part of the conversations those colleagues held privately and in print. In 1946 and 1948,[05] he was present at two round-table discussions that were organized by Alfons Leitl, journalist, architect, and later, editor-in-chief of the postwar German Werkbund periodical *Baukunst und Werkform*, in Aulendorf. The Aulendorf meeting included some of the most prominent modern architects of both the Weimar and postwar eras: Otto Bartning, Hugo Häring, Egon Eiermann, Rudolf Schwarz, and Hans Schwippert. In its efforts to define the trajectory for architecture after the Third Reich, the circle was juxtaposed politically and philosophically to a similar gathering organized by Rudolf Wolters and Friedrich Tamms, two powerful, "de-Nazified" figures whose realpolitik had gained them good standing in the new planning agencies set up by the Allied occupying forces.[06] As an act of continuity with the politically progressive modern tradition, those who met in Aulendorf chose to reconvene the German Werkbund. In doing so, they took pains to contrast the implied continuity against their rejection of an immediate Fascist past, which Wolters and Tamms personified. In the opening pages of the first 1947 issue of *Baukunst und Werkform*, they demanded that architecture come to terms with the country's ruptured history rather than simply moving on, a tendency that Tamms and Wolter's success exemplified. Many of those who met at Aulendorf would later curate the 1951 Darmstädter Gespräch, at which Ruf would make the most public and explicit of his very rare statements on architecture. At the time of the Aulendorf meetings, Ruf was already an established postwar practitioner who had authored more than forty projects between 1945 and 1949.[07] In 1958, in an open letter that introduced an issue of *Baukunst und Werkform* exclusively on Ruf, Leitl recalled that, during the "unheroic" work of reconstruction, those early meetings enabled the participating architects to "turn and transform things."[08]

His professorship at the Nuremberg Akademie der Bildenden Künste would have given Ruf occasion to engage in debates on art, which were especially active in an era preoccupied with redefining the ethical role

2.11 Main entrance with porte-cochère, 2019

2.12 Corridor looking towards main entrance, 2019

of culture in German society. His colleagues included significant representation of the Münchner Bildhauerschule, a group that traced its roots to Adolf von Hildebrand's writings on form, and that was known for positioning sculpture between representation and abstraction, particularly in depicting the human figure. Hans Wimmer, professor of sculpture beginning in 1949, and Ruf had worked simultaneously on restoring the Church of Christ the King in Munich, where Ruf directed reconstruction from 1947 to 1950 and Wimmer installed bronze reliefs depicting the stations of the cross in 1950 and 1951. Wimmer also maintained contact with Martin Heidegger, who collected Wimmer's work, including the mask-like portrait of himself completed in 1958. Heidegger's 1950 article "The Origin of the Work of Art"[09] resonated with Wimmer's thoughts on the relationship between figuration and abstraction, which Wimmer would articulate some ten years later. His writing frames the role of the object, the perceiving subject, the artist as author, and the relationship between art and the natural world in ways that also resonate with Ruf's word choice and ideas, so unlike the statements of others at the 1951 Darmstädter Gespräch.

Ruf's participation in the Darmstädter Gespräch took place several weeks after he completed the Bavarian State Bank in Nuremberg, and during the hiatus between the laying of the cornerstone and resumed construction at the Akademie der Bildenden Künste. Hans Schwippert, head of the German Werkbund, framed the discussion to which Ruf would respond. Schwippert questioned the plausibility of a modern architecture that, in contrast to early modernist paradigms, did *not* depend on using exclusively the technologies and materials of its era. Ruf seemed predestined to respond, at least based upon his empirical knowledge. Since 1945, he had sold building supplies for a time and had developed a proprietary system for building prefabricated housing,[10] both tasks requiring that he deal immediately with the situation on the ground. Instead, when given the floor, Ruf began by asking that he not be "compelled to speak about construction and its application."[11] Construction and its truthfulness

09   See Martin Heidegger, *Basic Writings*, ed. David Farrell Krell (San Francisco: Harper Collins, 1977), 139–212.
10   Meissner, *Sep Ruf*, 92.
11   Ulrich Conrads and Peter Neitzke, eds., *Mensch und Raum: Das Darmstädter Gespräch 1951* (Braunschweig: Vieweg, 1991), 106.

2.13 Auditorium entry wall, 2019

2.14 Auditorium entrance with
mosaics, 2019

or lack thereof seemed a banality, he implied. "If the spatial form and that which today is necessary is clear in my mind—the open building, which binds itself to nature," he replied, "then I can express it, too, with the means from which earlier forms were made, with the old building elements such as wood and stone."[12] Of course, this answer belied the effort Ruf himself had expended in detailing the elegant facades and interiors of his recently completed Nuremberg bank.

Ruf had no interest in the conventional modernist teleology of technology as a driver of progress in architectural expression. He was much more invested in the progress made by architectural expression itself, which could then be realized in whatever way necessary. His hope, it seems, is that the desire for spatial openness would grow. As it did, the architectural means used to realize it was justified because of the spaces it could make, not because it represented technological advancement. The historians of the modern movement might have located its origins in technologies such as concrete or steel, which facilitated spaces that were harbingers of "the open building which binds itself to nature." But Ruf argued quite differently, imagining that architecture would liberate itself from material constraints to

> "move forward into the spheres of the purely artistic. [...] We must achieve the same creative freedom with these building elements as other creative human beings who use words, color, and sound to achieve the artistic expression of their spiritual world in order to move in the same plane of formal creation. In architecture, this involves cognition of the essential form-defining elements: the pure metric, the vertical, the horizontal, in other words, roof and column or wall, the opening that spans space. [...] The decisive aspect, I think, is that we know how to form the atmosphere, the spirit's atmosphere, and then we will find the form, too. Because architecture has to create a specific spatial feeling."[13]

It is striking to read his enumeration of the "essential form-defining elements" in relation to the Akademie der Bildenden Künste, a building couched in the reduced tectonic language of "the vertical, the horizontal, in other words, roof and column or wall, the opening that spans space." The desire to approximate the means of those who use "color and sound" connects directly to the copious vegetation integrated into his architecture from the start. Finally, his regular interactions with artists and art students resound in his desire for formal exploration not limited to direct, causal relationships between material, function, and expression.

The audience held its applause after Ruf spoke. It seems he was not happy with that response. Later the same day, Bartning, who was acting as discussion moderator, "made good on his debt of the morning,"[14] and Ruf again took the floor. This time, he tried to address directly the question Schwippert had asked him:

> "If contemporary building makes use of steel and glass, then [it does so] not for formal reasons but out of the need to represent an originary and undeniably new sense of life. [...] And if these were no longer available to us—as Schwippert speculated at the beginning— then we would do it with wood. It is really not formal preconditions, but decisively spiritual ones under which we exist, and if you had let me say one more sentence earlier, I would have said that we must not only live, act, and create using these means from this sense of life. We must also achieve the functional solutions that are required, and represent them so simply and clearly. We must do so in order to know what the fundamental element of building is, the element with which we wish to create, not only in drawing and design, but actually, in what we realize. Assuming that we have already understood that the purely functional will itself no longer suffices, you will deduce that we also desire the artistic. We have already stated that claim."[15]

Ruf had not changed his position between the morning and afternoon. At least, he expressed himself in a subtly different way: it was not that material selection was no more than a technical issue. Instead, the impulse

12   Conrads and Neitzke, *Mensch und Raum*, 108.
13   Conrads and Neitzke, *Mensch und Raum*, 107.
14   Conrads and Neitzke, *Mensch und Raum*, 126.
15   Conrads and Neitzke, *Mensch und Raum*, 126–27.

2.15 Auditorium and administrative wing, night, 2019

to prefer materials with the greatest affinity for "open" architecture was more than mere formal preference. It had a higher calling, motivated by the need to represent a "new sense of life." In elevating this "new sense of life," Ruf used the terms "form" and "function" pejoratively. Schwippert, addressing modernist orthodoxy only obliquely, had largely eschewed both.

To illustrate his "new sense of life," Ruf selected an unimpeachable example, one that would resonate with the conference's organizers and which would embody the potentials of both new and old materials to hold "the spirit's atmosphere": Rudolf Schwarz's Gürzenich. Schwarz had inserted a new sequence of public space between the shell of a former medieval guildhall and the remains of St. Alban's Church, left in its bombed condition. Compared to the project with which Schwarz and his collaborator Bernhard had shared first prize in the competition, the project was radical: it left intact effects of bombing, the gap between guildhall and church stretching along the building's entire length. This gap became an unobstructed foyer, as deep as the entire city block, behind a modest street-front entry building. New, freely cantilevering stairs, which brought the visitor up to a gallery level, plumbed its length. To the left were the entry doors punctuating the long wall of the reconceived event hall, built within the stabilized walls of the old guildhall. On the left was the retained perimeter wall of St. Alban's, its geometry traced by a line of refracting glass pendant lights. Throughout the building were integral elements produced by collaborating artists and artisans—murals, stained glass, carved wood handrails, hand-cast doorknobs, each unique—which laid out a new iconographic program in the old medieval craft tradition. This, in Ruf's words, exemplified a building "which expresses directly the celebratory and the joyful. [...] One forgets that it is a functional form that represents this expression. And we call this art, we aspire to it."[16] To drive his point home, he referenced Schwarz's lecture from the preceding day, then continued:

"We want more than only a place of gathering, a hall spanned only by technical means: a steel frame and trusses. We will be inspired to know that it is technically possible. But no, we want, here again, to create a place to inhabit in which even the over-stimulated modern human being can, and must, pray once again. We want to create this atmosphere. It is truly something spiritual that moves us to do these things, not only for formal reasons, of which some might accuse us."[17]

16   Conrads and Neitzke, *Mensch und Raum*, 127.
17   Conrads and Neitzke, *Mensch und Raum*, 127–29.

18   Ruf used the word *Atmosphäre*, not *Stimmung*. Despite current interest in the term, there is little research on how and when it entered architectural discourse.
19   Conrads and Neitzke, *Mensch und Raum*, 107.

Ruf's use of the term "atmosphere" was unique at the time and indeed rare, if not singular, in contemporary writing about architecture.[18] There is no way to trace how he arrived at it. In his short statement, he used the term almost transcendentally: it is not the technologically-founded spirit of an era, and not space per se, but rather the "spirit's atmosphere" to which an architecture appropriate to its time aspires. Ruf's desire to deflect attention from the technical manipulations at which he was so gifted and toward an ineffable, intangible quality vaguely captured in the word "atmosphere" was more than a desire not to be pigeonholed as a technician. "Atmosphere" is by its nature a quality dependent on subjective perception. In describing the effect of an architectural environment upon its user, it focuses on affect rather than on the indisputable qualities of an architectural object. It highlights perception as an emotive act. The term would gain currency during the 1950s and 1960s in a development that has yet to be consistently traced. As a concept, it would come to encompass not only architectural space, but also its interior and exterior environments—the contributions of design objects, landscaping, and subjectivity.

Schwippert's question was meant to interrogate one of modern architecture's central tenets, the era's defining unity of material and spatial expression. This unity seemed predicated upon material conditions that would elude West Germany for the foreseeable future. For a true believer in the modernist credo, this was a catastrophe. For Ruf, however, the "many technical and economic problems and needs [...] required to complete a building"[19] comprised nothing more than a quotidian baseline. Material choice was just a problem that could be solved differently. The coat of stucco and white paint at the Akademie made its subcutaneous construction more or less moot. Ruf argued that architecture's value was its capacity to transcend material and functional concerns. By contrast, for Schwippert, architecture and space became transcendent by negotiating dissonant material and spiritual impulses, not by finding a work-around.

2.16 Auditorium and administrative wing, day, 2019

**2.17 Forest beyond the
walkway, 2019**

2.18 One of the linked courtyards and pavilions, 2019

2.19 Walkway connecting pavilions, 2019

20   Conrads and Neitzke, *Mensch und Raum*, 107.
21   Conrads and Neitzke, *Mensch und Raum*, 107.
22   Conrads and Neitzke, *Mensch und Raum*, 126–27.

Ruf connected his aspiration to "advance into the spheres of the purely artistic" to a hope that formal freedom would allow the architect "fully to do justice to the tasks of our era."[20] Unlike Schwippert, Ruf expressed confidence that material specificity could be overcome, "since we have already understood the means of expression, the construction potentials of steel, concrete, even wood frame, as comprehensively in their essence, and can use them with the same economy and experience as we can earlier building materials."[21] Schwippert still insisted that material is inextricable from expression: material or expression may be appropriate or inappropriate to an era, but neither can be discussed without the other. Ruf made very different assumptions. For him, regardless of whether the medium is "words, color, and sound" or architecture, it is the artist who would give expression to an era.

There is more at stake here. Ruf's conception implies that both a work's author and its recipient is a single individual. The artist as subjective self creates a work purely; its recipient as subjective self perceives space atmospherically. Schwippert, however, characterized his discipline as expressive of societal or collective desire. At Darmstadt, he used the term *Wohnwollen*, or the desire to inhabit. The distinction between individuated and communal also characterizes the ways the two architects practiced. Schwippert's approach to construction recognized the architect as one of many authors involved in the production of the building, and his design process foregrounded the questions of consensual reception, which he studied copiously in his designs for the plenary hall of the Bundeshaus. Ruf's highly disciplined office proved that the architect could actually bring his control to bear in the most exacting ways. Nonetheless, both architects agreed on the spirit of their era. After the dark times of the recent past, it was an era that required openness. Schwippert described what he foresaw as "tent-like" structures. For Ruf, there was "a sense of life that seeks connection to light, air, and sun, not for sport, but because they are elemental."[22]

The Akademie der Bildenden Künste is exemplary of Ruf's immediate postwar idiom. It is an idiom made up of slender white exterior steel structural columns, minimally dimensioned roof overhangs that continuously

2.20 Porte-cochère construction details, 1955

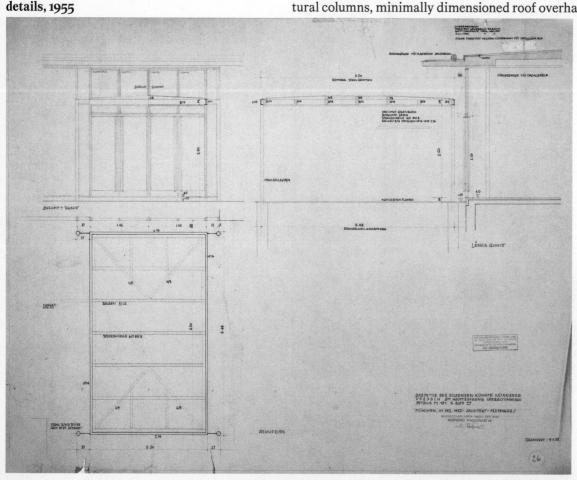

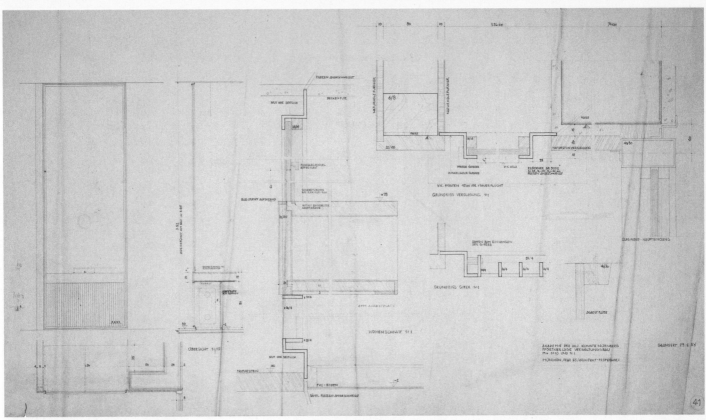

2.21 Elevation and construction details, concierge window, undated

shade glass facades, narrow steel mullions pieced from steel L-angles, and flush-detailed stuccoed walls. Because the shaded glass beneath the roof overhang is always transparent, the facade helps to elide indoors and outdoors. In the Akademie, everything refers the view to the broader landscape, both proximate and beyond, in the forested park.

This architectural language is dependent upon detailing expertise, which achieved the greatest possible slenderness in all its leading edges, but did so without being overly precious or obtrusive. Rather than being drawn to the way the building is materialized, attention is deflected from it. All architectural elements are sleekly profiled and the material palette is minimized so that the emphasis falls on the resulting spaces rather than on the component elements or constituent parts that define them. The building's finished state offers little specific information about its genesis or even about the way it carries loads. The columns are dimensioned to appear almost too thin to carry the weight of the roof at which they end. No indication is given of how the juncture between vertical and horizontal spanning members is negotiated. The facade is kept stringently in plane. Plaster and white paint conceal differences in subcutaneous construction, which, as the drawings attest, alternates between masonry, wood, and steel. The plain appearance is deceptive. No less skill is required in its execution than in more luxurious, materially expressive buildings. Sleekness requires thorough planning and precise execution to integrate the heterogeneous material properties, divergent dimensions, and multiple trades involved. At the same time, it would be inaccurate to characterize the Akademie as abstract or dematerialized. Each element's essential tectonic role can be identified as support, shelter, or enclosure. This approach to tectonic expression, neither didactically explicit nor laconically suppressed, is illustrated by the detail between the porte-cochère and its supporting steel column. **[2.20]**

Even as his idiom and architectural interests changed and developed, Ruf would repeat this particular detail in other projects. Its challenge was the juncture between the round steel column and the rectilinear edge of the entry roof. The roof edge of the porte-cochère was originally designed to correspond in depth to the roof edge of the building behind it, although the two elements responded to completely different structural demands. The span between supporting columns is attenuated beyond what the thinly dimensioned porte-cochère roof would seem able to withstand.

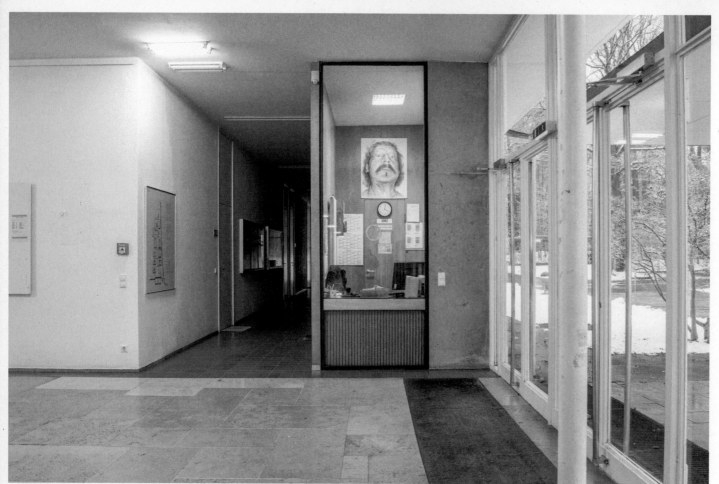

2.22 Concierge window and entrance, 2019

Ruf's solution at the vertical-to-horizontal meeting point subtly explains how the structure works, but keeps the explanation vague, so that the spatial effect of the long, thin, tenuously held roof remains dominant. Welded to the top of the two supporting columns is a flat profile, painted white to match the columns. The dimension of the flat steel is exactly that of the porte-cochère's edge. This correspondence suggests to an attentive observer that the roof's internal structure is also steel. Without consulting the drawing, no one would guess that the roof's interior structure is conventionally framed in dimensioned lumber.

As a rule, the building's tectonic language is careful to denote steel only as a bearing material, as in the round columns. These steel columns are juxtaposed to the white-edged planes of roof, porte-cochère, and exterior canopies, which connote shelter. By allowing this small piece of white-painted steel to mediate between bearing and sheltering elements, Ruf's detail resolves a formal problem in a way that suggests a consistent tectonic syntax. The welded flat steel is a simple element, but it accomplishes multiple, complex architectural purposes: a transition between two unlike geometries, a reveal and offset that makes the horizontal roof plane appear to float, and a subtle indication of the "magic" behind the lightness of construction.

The detail drawing of the porte-cochère is only one in the remarkably intact array of construction documents. These include drawings and sketches ranging in scale from detail to site studies, along with product brochures, specifications, and correspondence. In all, they attest to the enormous effort invested in realizing the building, and to the still-limited palette of materials and methods at the architect's disposal in the early 1950s. They indicate how Ruf and his office negotiated standard construction, and the very high level of standard skill that was expected for execution. This is most obvious in instances where a simple written specification might have sufficed, but Ruf's office instead provided a drawing with millimeter tolerances. This intensity certainly drew on the knowledge Ruf had gathered selling building materials.[23] Whatever its basis, his detail drawings often pre-empt what otherwise

23   Conrads and Neitzke, *Mensch und Raum*, 91.

2.23 Concierge window, detail view showing alignments, 2019

might have been on-site construction decisions made more routinely or casually by the worker or foreman.

Such drawings must have required time. There was indeed a hiatus between the cornerstone ceremony in 1950 and the start of construction two years later, a long and luxurious amount of time to consider how to put together a building. However, most of the construction drawings date to 1952 or later. Ruf and his office were both precise and efficient: the construction detailing of the Bavarian State Bank, which went into construction only three months after the competition was decided and was completed in only nine months' time, is no less exacting. Their exactitude was strategically considered and well communicated.

In realizing the Akademie, Ruf availed himself of nearly all possible means of construction in various combinations: steel for bearing and framing, cast concrete of varying capacity, masonry, finish-grade and carpentry-grade wood, veneered plywood, and natural stone finishes. The complexity involved in conjoining these subsurface and surface structures is everywhere. It was undertaken in even as small a moment as the glass partition to concierge's office in the entry foyer. **[2.21] [2.22] [2.23]**

A large, fixed glass plane spans from the inner surface of an exterior wall to a thin, wood-clad partition wall. In height, it spans from the wood counter to the ceiling. Each of the surfaces it touches is different in subconstruction, different in tolerances, and probably was completed by members of different trades. The glass is held against a metal angle equidistant on all four sides from adjacent surfaces, regardless of their heterogeneous composition. The element holding the glass, as the drawing annotation communicates, is a standard Z-angle from a Klöckner catalogue, painted dark gray on the leg attached to the wall and white on the

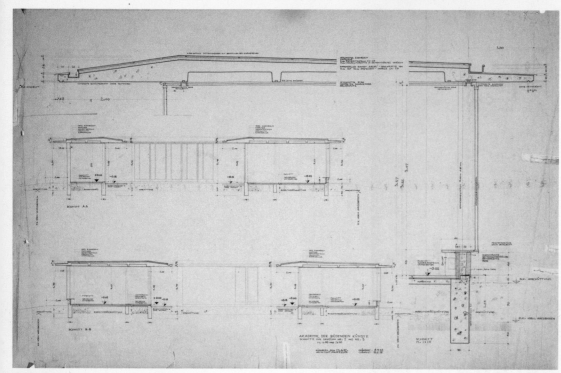

**2.24 Detail and overall section
through a typical workshop pavilion,
1952**

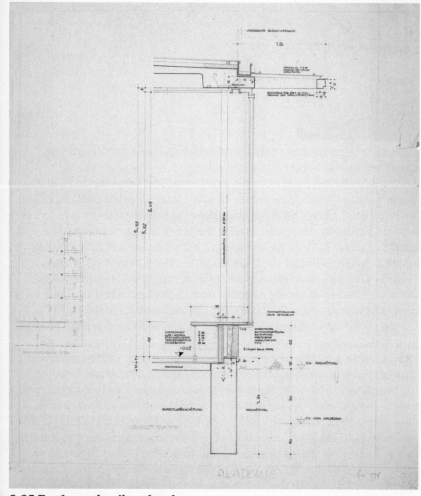

2.25 Roof eave detail, undated

two other legs that hold the glass. At ceiling and floor, the drawing specifies that the Z be spot-welded to anchors sunk in the concrete floor, the exterior masonry wall, and the ceiling. The glass is in turn secured against the steel with a small sixteen-by-sixteen millimeter wooden glass stop.

Each edge of the steel frame interacts with different construction types but this difference is never allowed to show. In its finished state, the steel frame's offset to each must look exactly the same, with no deviation in plumb and true. On the exterior wall, where the angle was welded to a corner anchor, a fifteen-millimeter finish layer of stucco was applied after installation, and an additional stone panel installed on the wall's leading edge. The drawing dimensions the offset between the surface of the stone and the leading edge of the steel: twelve millimeters exactly. On the other side, the steel is fastened to a framed partition wall clad in wood, a material that can be worked with high precision to pick up alignments and correct small imperfections in truing. Still, the drawing notes give some insight into the order of construction. The notes call for the interior vertical wood support for the partition wall to be positioned fifteen millimeters in front of the unplastered exterior masonry wall. In other words, the partition wall was framed before plastering, and therefore would have had to be at exactly fifteen millimeters offset to align flush with the masonry wall; the partition wall cladding, a solid wood plank, makes up the dimensional difference to align with the stone panel applied on top of the plaster. A floor-to-ceiling long piece of solid wood that would not twist or warp must have been hard to find. Wood this true, slowly and completely dried after milling, would likely have been preserved from the period before the war.[24] The detail is a little more forgiving at plastered ceiling and tile-clad floor, where the drawing notes only "reveal as on the sides," allowing construction on site to negotiate how to match the millimeter precision demanded on the window's two sides.

With no tolerances given in this detail, the negotiation among members of different trades—mason, plasterer, wall framer, metalworker, glazer—would have had to be seamlessly organized. Each of the implicated trades worked to a different level of precision, but the drawing gives no indication of how imprecision is to be adjusted. As realized and as conceived, it is a beautifully executed detail, and one that hints, by virtue of the stone and wood cladding, at the underlying differences between interior and exterior walls. But it never betrays the materials beneath any of its surfaces.

Another construction detail that demonstrates the immense effort and finesse that Ruf demanded is the roof edge. The deep eaves on all the buildings mark a continuous, attenuated datum. This continuity, as well as the interstice the eaves define between building interior and proximate landscape, and the shade they cast on the glass walls, are all fundamental to the elision between inside and out that is so essential to the building's character. The thin edge of the cantilevering eaves comes from offsetting the gutter to the point of support, at the column line, and extending a much thinner plane of concrete beyond that point. The deep eaves thus conceal from eye-level view both the integrated rain gutters and the much thicker bearing slab of the building. In addition, the flat eaves maintain a true horizontal line and belie the slope of the primary roof behind, necessary to shed rain and melting snow. As a result of this clever solution, even careful observers have characterized the building as having a flat roof.[25] [2.24] [2.25]

But not all the roofs were concrete, nor were all the windows and doors steel. Drawings for the caretaker's house opposite the main entrance as well as those for a small storage building specify a gently sloped, deeply overhanging roof in traditional *Zimmermann*-framed wood construction. [2.26] [2.27] These smaller, more utilitarian buildings also have windows and doors made of wood, which was easier to procure than steel. The detail drawings offer numerous angles and tapers for the window frames and glass stops to achieve the most slender sightlines possible. Nothing in the literature on the Akademie to date

24   In 1995/96 I visited the cabinetry shop of Richard Fahnkow in Berlin-Kreuzberg. Located in a building miraculously spared from bombs, the space had already been a cabinetry shop before the war. In the cellar were whole milled trees harvested in the late nineteenth century. Such material caches are, of course, rare.

25   Meissner, *Sep Ruf*, 126.

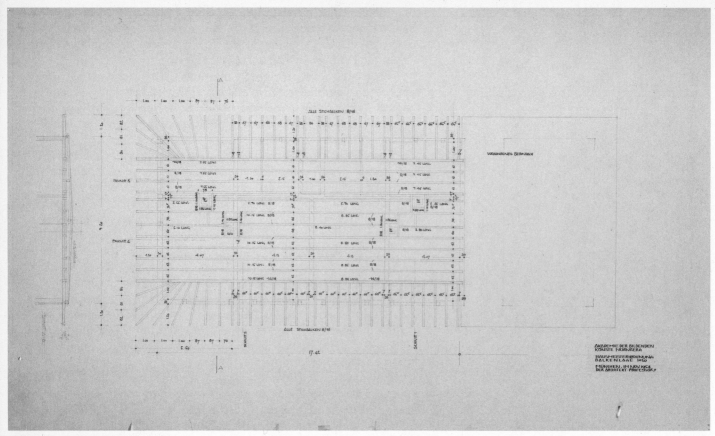

2.26 Caretaker's house, roof
framing, 1954

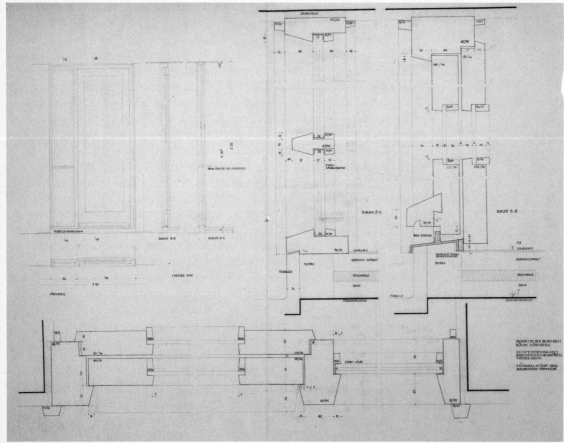

2.27 Caretaker's house, wood
window construction details, 1954

26   All references to the correspondence, brochures, and other documents related to the building of the Akademie der Bildenden Künste in Nuremberg are from the collection of Notburga and Elisabeth Ruf.

would indicate that this difference in material application or subconstruction was ever even noticed.

The ratio between labor and material required to realize a building is a good barometer of construction practice in the late 1940s and 1950s. A change in idiom accompanied the increasing availability and sophistication of factory-made products. Initially, industry sought economies of scale in more generic elements that had multiple applications. The market was still developing for highly specific building systems or larger-scale components. In a sense, this meant that steel construction, regardless of its application as facade, light-gauge structure, truss, or other context, was pieced together using sections that all bore close family resemblances to generic rolled L, Z, U, and tube sections. Those generic sections were differentiated for specific applications in a second step, sometimes in the small workshop of a window manufacturer and sometimes on site, but in both cases, through skilled labor rather than through tooling. The balance between work in the shop and on site, between specific trades and a more flexible workforce, permitted adaptability and customization. The architect who specified the assembly determined how materials were transformed from generic to specific. If he (or rarely she) knew the workforce and their capacities, there was little that could not be imagined. The hierarchy among architect, construction firm, and building product provider was steeply vertical, with the architect at its apex. The various steel windows, doors, and fixed glazing at the Akademie attest to this. The job books, all of which are in the possession of Ruf's heirs, add even more nuance to an understanding of the process.[26] Such minutia as the time sheets submitted by the glazers, and the correspondence in which Ruf and one window contractor contest payments, are time capsules of standard practice.

In one job book are brief minutes from a telephone conversation held on June 25, 1954, between Ruf and his Nuremberg office. Based on the call's outcome, payment to the window manufacturer Jucho was withheld. The minutes are stapled to a time sheet dated May 20, 1954, which listed hours worked to repair windows. The disagreement about payment continued for some time. A letter from Jucho dated March 16, 1955 references the fact that the 196 individual steel windows had "16 different widths" and were ordered in several batches, which created "additional costs to the total amount of DM 4,725.30." There is much that would be familiar to twenty-first century architects in this exchange: the architect's responsibility to defend his client's budget, the contractor's need to remind the architect that post-contract changes must be billed. This series of documents indicates a different distribution of responsibilities

2.28 Typical steel window construction detail, 1951

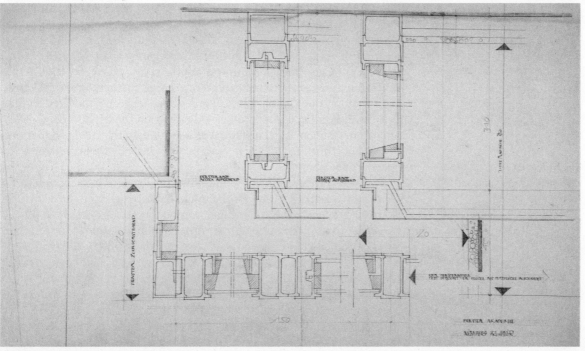

accruing to architect and fabricator, as well as specific aspects of the means of production that are different from current practice. For example, it is hard to imagine a case in which an additional order for window elements would translate into lost revenue. Jucho's complaint suggests that suppliers maintained an at best tenuous business model of building products as the German construction boom accelerated.

Ruf's site office was apparently charged with managing construction in the most immediate and intimate way. In order to judge the veracity of a time sheet, of which there are many in the archived job book in addition to countless corrected invoices for the purchases of plants, trees, and other landscaping materials, Ruf and his employees must have had a constant, near-omniscient presence on the construction site. Trade foremen would have had to accept the architect in this role; and the architect's contract would have had to include this phase of work explicitly. In this supervisory role the architect's responsibility is immense, and the kind of knowledge required is very different from that needed in the daily life of an architecture office. This powerful position also explains how drawings requiring millimeter precision could have been executed.

Jucho, the window company, apparently received the contract both to factory-produce and to site-install the units. The separation of expertise between supplier and builder had not yet become standard. The claim that executing the window order in several stages (*Nachbestellung*) caused such substantial budget overruns offers another insight into the company's operations. The cost of the window frame products had been agreed upon in advance. It is fair to assume that the cost of production should have been factored into that cost. But these windows were not standard catalogue items. They were produced on demand, through an assembly of generic elements rather than specialized, standardized window components. Rather than increasing profit, the subsequent order caused the producer to work at a loss after the first batch of windows had been produced and, presumably, templates and lay-ups had been dismantled. These were bespoke, not assembly-line, products.

Detail drawings for the windows support this presumption. **[2.28]** An early drawing depicts painstakingly rendered steel angles combined with wood glass stops. A later shop drawing dated September 1954 reduces the number of steel angles required. The drawing includes a sectional drawing of fixed glazing with a hopper window above and, in plan, two fixed units flanking an operable unit. The fixed glazing is built up from exactly drawn tubular steel sections and steel angles, glazed with fifteen-by-fifteen-millimeter tubular steel stops. In the operable window, only the glass stop is dimensioned, also fifteen by fifteen millimeters, to match the fixed glazing. It seems that the given dimensions were manufacturer-determined, with the glass stop as the only variable. The operable window's constitutive components are only slightly less generic than those in the fixed frame, and significantly less varied than the ones drawn in the 1951 sketch. Variation occurs only in the Z-shaped steel section in the lower frame, configured to integrate a drip edge, and in the vertical leg of the T-shaped frame, bent ninety degrees to nest against the fixed frame. The use of these simple steel profiles indicates that the window components had been chosen from standards used across the steel production industry, not from specially developed profiles intended especially for window production.

The 1951 and 1954 drawings offer different levels of information for the windows' production than for their installation. Although the drawings are extremely specific about the dimensions and types of steel sections, there is next to no information on the order of construction, connections, or installation. No fasteners or welds are indicated and, aside from an anchor shown in dashed lines that connects into walls and floor, no notes are made on how the subconstruction is to be prepared. Presumably, installation would have required a combination of welding to connect to the anchor, and bolts, which could be screwed into place by making threaded holes in the eighty-by-forty-millimeter tube section. These are drawings made for discussion with three different areas of competence:

a fabricator, who would determine the best way to conjoin the steel sections to make a frame; a glazer, who would verify the sizing of the glass stop and the location of its connections; and an installer, who could determine provisions needed for the anchorage. Jucho appears to have been all three: fabricator, glazer, and installer. The drawing expresses both the architect's insistence on the exact outcome of the building process and full confidence in the workers' ability to understand the desired outcome. Given the complexity of configuring the frames themselves and the lack of adjustment on site to make up tolerances, it is no wonder that Jucho feared losing money on the commission.

The intensity of the demand that Ruf's working drawings placed on construction precision is evident. It is most pronounced in cases where dimensions are given in millimeters for trades whose margin of error is traditionally much larger. This was the case in the details for the concierge's window. Another excellent example appears in drawings for the cafeteria. This space is extremely important to the building's architectural integrity. It marks the point of intersection between the two primary axes, north–south from the entry and east–west along the pavilions. Because of its position, it also offers the only point from which views open across the rising, open meadow that culminates at the auditorium; the experience of this view is an important counterpoint to the strong axial views that organize the complex. Finally, as is evident in the early plan drawing of the space, its threshold to the outside is deep, gradual, and ambiguous. This threshold speaks volumes about the continuity of inside and outside in which the building engages.

A February 1955 drawing depicts the glazing at exactly this critical threshold, between inside dining area, adjacent exterior terrace, and stone pavers that belong to the proximate landscape. The full-scale section is taken through a heating vent set level with the solid wood floor on the left and the terrace, paved in stone from the Jura region, on the right. To execute this detail, the architect needed to provide information on the order of construction. This is registered in the millimeter precision with

2.29 Cafeteria, symmetrically milled floor boards at the column and flush wooden heating vent, 2019

which the floorboards are dimensioned. The tight fit of glass to floor allows no margin of error. The drawing's information is almost anatomical: on the right, an anchor angle is cast into the concrete subconstruction; to it is attached a standard steel L-angle whose legs are slightly longer than the depth of the 20-millimeter floorboards. The first floorboard on the right is shown as carefully routed to accommodate the L-angle's depth and to bypass the regularly spaced anchor angles. This board would have been slipped into place first, with the other floorboards subsequently. Still, each tongue-and-groove floorboard would have to be specially milled in width, either to 65 or 72 millimeters, in order to allow the seam between the two 72-millimeter boards to sit symmetrically to the 133-millimeter diameter steel column. On the left-hand side, a C-channel, stabilized in the concrete using another anchor angle, supports the heating grille.

The only concession to imprecision is the thin plywood shim resting on that C-channel. This shim would permit adjustments in height between the top of the angle and the bottom of the floorboards and adjustments in length, just in case the improbably precise measurements in the floorboards could not be maintained. It is hard not to shudder at the responsibility that the site office would have assumed in order to ensure that the steel column and concrete angles were perfectly positioned to conform to such precisely dimensioned finish assemblies. Yet because all the materials arrived on site in a more or less generic state, the architect was in a position to stipulate their installation with incredible precision. Had the floorboards, for example, been pre-milled by a larger fabricator rather than by the

2.30 Fabricator's shop drawing, door jamb, 1956

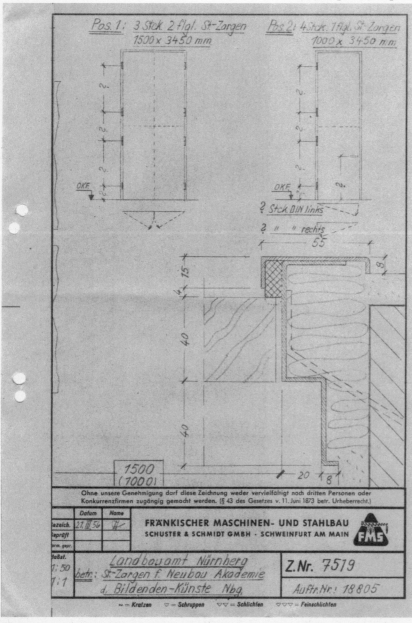

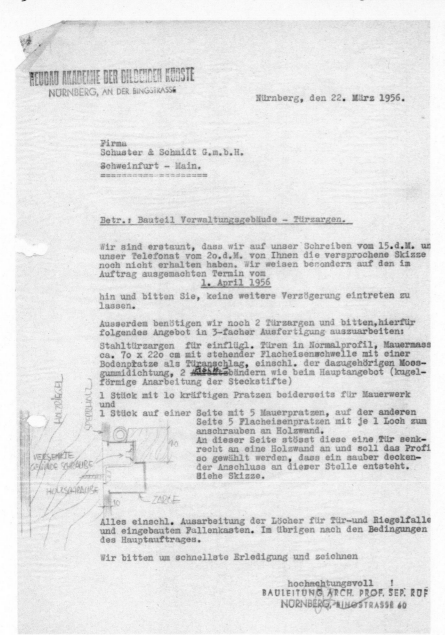

NEUBAU AKADEMIE DER BILDENDEN KÜNSTE
NÜRNBERG, AN DER BINGSTRASSE

Nürnberg, den 22. März 1956.

Firma
Schuster & Schmidt G.m.b.H.
Schweinfurt – Main.
==========–=========

Betr.: Bauteil Verwaltungsgebäude – Türzargen.

Wir sind erstaunt, dass wir auf unser Schreiben vom 15.d.M. un
unser Telefonat vom 2o.d.M. von Ihnen die versprochene Skizze
noch nicht erhalten haben. Wir weisen besonders auf den im
Auftrag ausgemachten Termin vom
               1. April 1956
hin und bitten Sie, keine weitere Verzögerung eintreten zu
lassen.

Ausserdem benötigen wir noch 2 Türzargen und bitten, hierfür
folgendes Angebot in 3-facher Ausfertigung auszuarbeiten:

Stahltürzargen für einflügl. Türen in Normalprofil, Mauermass
ca. 7o x 22o cm mit stehender Flacheisenschwelle mit einer
Bodenplatte als Türanschlag, einschl. der dazugehörigen Moos-
gummidichtung, 2 Stahlbändern wie beim Hauptangebot (kugel-
förmige Anarbeitung der Steckstifte)

1 Stück mit 1o kräftigen Pratzen beiderseits für Mauerwerk
und
1 Stück auf einer Seite mit 5 Mauerpratzen, auf der anderen
           Seite 5 Flacheisenpratzen mit je 1 Loch zum
           anschrauben an Holzwand.
           An dieser Seite stösst diese eine Tür senk-
           recht an eine Holzwand an und soll das Profil
           so gewählt werden, dass ein sauber decken-
           der Anschluss an dieser Stelle entsteht.
           Siehe Skizze.

Alles einschl. Ausarbeitung der Löcher für Tür-und Riegelfalle
und eingebautem Fallenkasten. Im übrigen nach den Bedingungen
des Hauptauftrages.

Wir bitten um schnellste Erledigung und zeichnen

               hochachtungsvoll !
        BAULEITUNG ARCH. PROF. SEP. RUF
        NÜRNBERG, RINGSTRASSE 6o

2.31 Correspondence with a door jamb fabricator including sketch, March 1956

installer, it would hardly have been viable to order both 65 and 72 millimeter boards and to keep them in order on the job site. **[2.29]**

The conflation of fabricator and installer, the relatively generic nature of available building materials, and the capacity of the architect to stipulate such exactitude—and to assume responsibility for it during construction supervision—produced a very specific architecture. The continuity of the floor plane across different elements installed flush to each other (the heating grille, the wood floorboards) is central to the desired continuity between interior and exterior. The L-angle to which the fixed glazing is anchored makes a precise, minimal edge while providing a daringly brief height differential of only three centimeters between interior and exterior. The glazing profile itself is little more than a C-channel with canted legs and an additional flange, which acts as a glass stop. The cant in the legs, which creates a shadow line where the profile meets the floor, minimizes the frame's apparent height. Finally, the glass itself, all that separates interior and exterior, is held in place against the steel by a tapered wood stop whose strength comes from its depth and not from its height, which would have reduced the glazing's sight lines. The stop, the detailer might presume, would blend visually with the floorboards. This detail remained in near-perfect condition in 2019, when the photograph here was made. All the dimensional precision, and all the careful selection of building materials, serves a spatial idea that, in true modernist fashion, holds true from site planning down to the details.

**2.32 Cafeteria and vestibule with
door and window hardware, 2019**

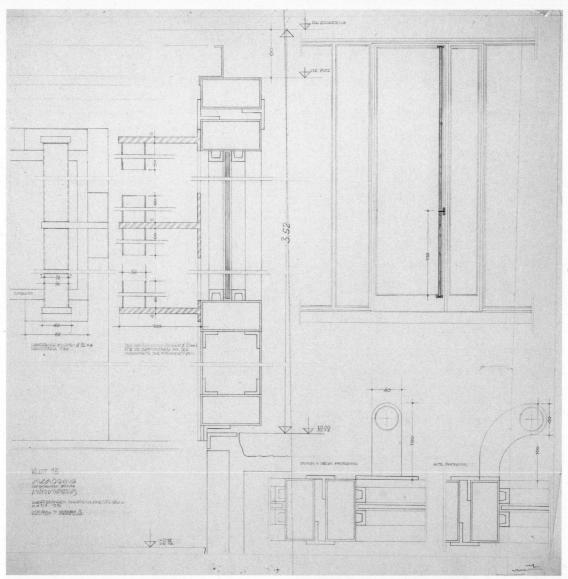

2.33 Main entrance door handle fabrication details, 1953

The bronzed door pulls, the flush-mounted door frames, and the zigzag stair rails are among the details that help to periodize the Akademie der Bildenden Künste as an exemplar of 1950s architecture. These details are familiar, recurring in shop fronts, apartment houses, and public buildings from the era. Objects of everyday life, they speak to a common sensibility or taste. Near-ubiquitous standard products, they stand in for a shared design culture. Of course, they were designed at some point, but the specifics of that point have mostly been treated as largely irrelevant. The Akademie der Bildenden Künste precedes that moment. Its working drawings include precisely those pulls, jambs, and stair rails. The demarcating line between bespoke and standard, already immanent in the window frame details, is anything but clear in the cases of these elements.

In West Germany as in the United States, the immediate postwar period was characterized by competition among many smaller fabricators whose workmanship and skills were needed to adapt anonymous elements to an architectural purpose. As opposed to the situation in the United States, many of the smaller firms in West Germany had much deeper historical roots in machining and metalworking. At the war's end, many were devastated. For them, the construction industry was a means through which to regain market share. Others were new, leveraging the postwar building boom. The firms under contract at the Akademie der Bildenden Künste are among those that were best able to navigate this competition and prevail. [2.30] [2.31] Several still in exist. Jucho had been founded as a bridge-building firm in 1877[27] and continued as a window manufacturer into the 1970s. Other newer firms, such as the glazier Brehm, now a window manufacturer, and Schuster & Schmidt, which supplied the steel door frames and now focuses on prefabricated steel buildings and

27   John Martin Kleeberg, "The Disconto-Gesellschaft and German Industrialization: A Critical Reexamination of the Career of a German Universal Bank, 1851–1914," (Diss., St. Catherine's College: Oxford, 1988), 186.

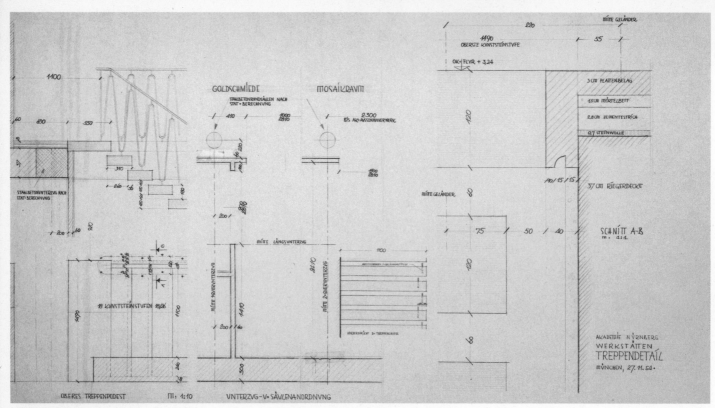

2.34 Workshop stair construction detail, 1954

2.35 Workshop stair, handrail detail, 2019

their installation, were able to leverage their modest beginnings as subcontractors within a much larger network of building trades.

As with every other detail, the effort invested in the design of the doors, including frames and handles, was in the service of architectural qualities: flush, unbroken trajectories; elision of interior and exterior; views defined along the primary axes, or, intriguingly, at their intersection. [2.32] Ruf's office drew every possible door hardware type, each for a different application: the locks, the rosettes, the handles and knobs, the long pulls. [2.33] There are several ways to interpret this intensity. The opportunity to design even the hardware would seem irresistible, especially to an architect as detail-oriented and controlling as Ruf. The products available on the market were limited, making design a necessity. The need to harmonize all these different hardware types demanded design coordination. This last assumption corresponds to a moment in the cafeteria, which, as noted, is spatially the building's point of greatest intensity at the crossing of the primary axes. There, seen through layers of interior glass partitions and exterior glazed walls, all the different hardware types appear together. The effect is spectacular. At this moment, each element is a custom piece. Soon, though, similar elements would be catalogue items. The migration of design from specific case to general product characterizes the period and is in part responsible for its consistent "period" look.

The stair rails in the only two-story portion of the complex, originally designed as a workshop, are another instance of this design migration from bespoke to standard and typical. The splined, zigzag motif used in the uprights appears in no fewer than four drawings, including several enormous 1:50 elevations that specify its exact geometric derivation. The drawing here provides primarily information on the stairs themselves, prefabricated cast stone planks cantilevered from the abutting masonry wall. [2.34] On the side furthest from the supporting wall, each step includes a sleeve, either fifty millimeters on center or one hundred millimeters on center from the edge. The rail was to be slipped into these sleeves and mortared into place, the hole then covered by a brass rosette. [2.35] Here, too, enormous precision was needed to install these stairs plumb and in perfect alignment to accommodate the rail, which also would have been made off site. There is perfect continuity in the elements, even at the hairpin turn at the top of the stair. Components would have been welded together on site, then ground and covered in white enamel paint. It looks simple when finished, an expected 1950s element. Once it had been piloted here, the handrail configuration, like the door handles, could be applied elsewhere. In fact, Ruf's Maxburg renovation in Munich (1952–1957) makes copious use of the design. The zigzag design, in different variations, would ultimately become identified with the architecture of West Germany in the 1950s. What had been bespoke became standard. The rail's reproduction makes clear: economies of scale were much easier to achieve with products than with site and use-specific architectural detail.

Even the most basic elements were subject to design. One example is the steel grating located both directly outside and inside the glass doors. On the exterior, the grates indicate which bays of the facade are operable. The grates are both foot-scrapers and secondary rainwater catchments. On the interior, they are heating grilles above invisible sub-floor radiators, so that the floor can continue uninterrupted to the glass wall. Nothing about the grates seems unusual. The sheer number of drawings depicting this grate, of which three have survived, says otherwise. [2.36] [2.37] One, a 1:20 detail, [2.38] makes clear the degree of customization required even for this seemingly standard product: height and grid dimensions are given; welded mounting tabs are specified. The carefully shaded drawing evidences a degree of care in execution and interest in visual effect that exceeds a standard construction document. It certainly seems to exceed the standard building material depicted. In this case, the "standard" grate was actually made to specifications. Although no drawing's title block notes its author's name, the Sütterlin lettering on this drawing matches that on the drawing for

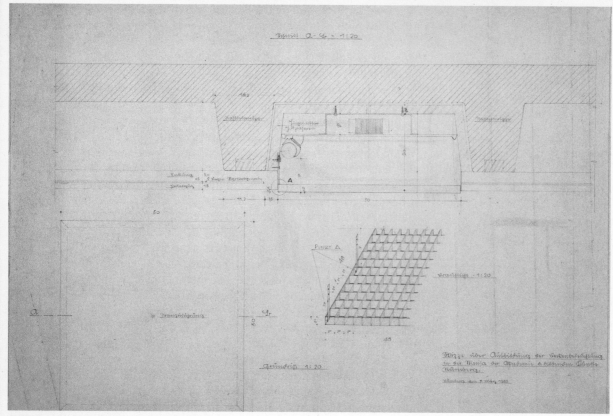

**2.36 Welded steel grate construction
and installation details, 1955**

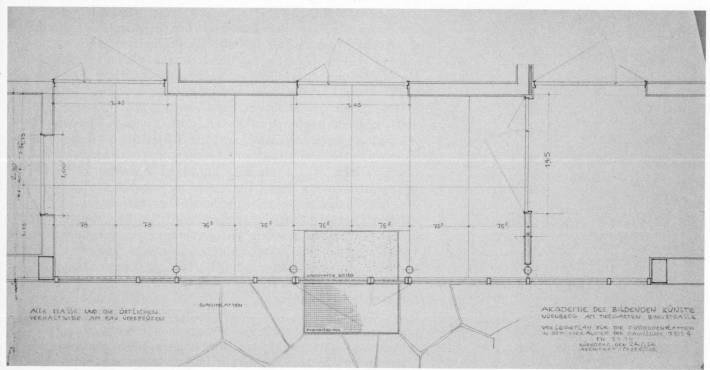

**2.37 Exterior (metal) and interior
(coco fiber) doormats, 1954**

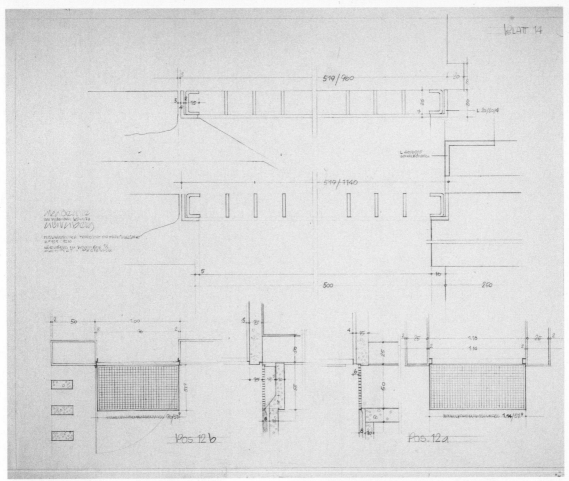

2.38 Welded steel grate, fabrication drawing, 1953

the millimeter-dimensioned floorboards at the cafeteria column. The drawings share an assumption that tolerances would be minimal; that specificity could be demanded from such standard products as floorboards and metal grilles; and that every element that reinforces continuity between interior and exterior deserves study. **[2.39]** These seemingly quotidian (but secretly customized) components are essential to the building's spatial continuity with its immediate environment.

In his open letter that prefaced the 1958 issue of *Baukunst und Werkform*, devoted to Ruf, Leitl wrote,

> "Those returning from the First World War, who during the decade of their 20s or 30s had been cast out of the orbit of secure, bourgeois daily life, felt after all the horror was over that they were a lost generation. [...] A similar age group after the Second World War did not even have the opportunity or the time to perceive themselves as a lost generation. [...]
>
> In the meantime, we no longer speak about [architectural] training or the educational system, since many of those with whom we gathered earlier for discussion are now professors, and the practice of architecture has hopefully given them the possibility to develop those methods about which we had then only tried to think forward."[28]

The letter was as much a meditation on the path taken by the generation of architects to which the two men belonged as it was a specific reflection on Ruf. This was a generation called to action, as Leitl said, with time to reflect only for a brief moment. That brief moment, which they had shared, was the basis for their future architectural development. Beginning with his early realized projects in Nuremberg, Ruf's career proceeded apace, producing demanding modern architecture in a stylistically conservative region. Despite the exigencies of professional practice, as Leitl noted, the quality of Ruf's buildings was undisputed. Richard Neutra had visited and photographed the spaces of Ruf's own home, a fact that prompted Leitl to remark that he, too, found an echo of Neutra's work, whether conscious or subconscious, in Ruf's buildings. Overall, however, Leitl did

2.39a Administration building corridor with welded steel grate as doormat (exterior) and radiator cover (interior), 2019

2.39b

not introduce the issue by explaining the importance of Ruf's career, one that paralleled the timeline of *Baukunst und Werkform*, the magazine Leitl had founded and led for more than a decade as editor-in-chief. Instead, Leitl positioned the architect's career in the context of a moment at which modern architecture was characterized by expressive heterogeneity. It was not a moment led by geniuses, Leitl contended. It was a moment determined by the need "to refine the basic intentions of the founding fathers in their full array and to realize them with consistency."[29]

Leitl saw the absence of a singular, identifiable West German modernist style as a virtue. Elsewhere it was framed as critique. Beyond the West German architectural press, the emigration of Mies van der Rohe, Gropius, Mendelsohn, and other significant figures from Germany's interwar modern movement became an explanation for the "merely" competent work emerging from the Bundesrepublik. A typical instance of this reception of West German architecture was offered by Patwant Singh, editor of the CIAM-connected Indian journal *Design*. His article was no marginal event. It was important enough to be clipped and preserved in the archive of prominent Berlin architect Paul Baumgarten, whose work was included in Singh's condescending catalogue of "competent" work. After returning from a tour sponsored in early 1960 by the German cultural ambassador in New Delhi, Singh wrote in resumé,

"Contemporary architecture in Germany reflects functional competence, technical skill, and meticulous detailing; in addition, some of the buildings reach a high aesthetic standard. But what is lacking is a powerful, creative, original expression. If one might put it this way: there are no trail-blazers in architecture there at the

30　　Patwant Singh, "Design in Deutschland," in *Design* (New Delhi, 1960), 13–20, here 15.

moment. [...] Their understanding of the materials of construction is equally impressive: there is no question of any hit and miss methods. A great deal of research and analysis goes into determining the behavior of different materials under different conditions, before they are incorporated in a design. The detailing reflects precision and thoroughness, with the result that the efficiency of buildings is at their peak."[30]

The virtuosity of Ruf's construction at the Akademie der Bildenden Künste, as in his other project, certainly created the circumstances that Singh would disparage for the "hit and miss methods" of customization rather than an embrace of standardization. This easy formulation overlooks the fact that Ruf's adaptation of available materials in the building constituted invention, or an experiment conducted on the basis of deep knowledge. For this experiment to succeed, Ruf and his office undertook the enormous responsibility of overseeing all the outcomes of their exacting drawings. They took seriously their decision to develop architectural ideas in the context of practice. Leitl characterized the outcome positively as the modesty of a generation called to action; Singh dismissed it as mere competence without brilliance. These themes would recur in public evaluation of the generally well-received West German pavilion at the Brussels World's Fair of 1958.

As Ruf made clear in his words at Darmstadt, he did not wish to be considered a technician. After declining to speak about construction, he offered the audience a fact on the ground, based on his first-hand experience: construction was no longer a primary challenge or primary form-giver for modern architecture because the previously new, transformational materials had been understood and mastered. As his oeuvre developed through the 1950s, Ruf expanded his modernist vocabulary to express his interest in the elision of interior and exterior spaces and in the relationship between the occupants of his buildings and their non-built environments. His controlled experiments in building construction, realized so skillfully at Nuremberg, gave way to more complex experiments in his later work. Throughout his career, he found ways to deploy elegantly everything that the developing West German building industry had to offer. Over time, he would translate this approach into a new, more robust architectural syntax.

JOB BOOKS

During my first summer internship in an architecture office, I stopped at the remainder table of a Madison Avenue bookstore and bought a copy of *Oppositions* magazine. Published in 1982, a moment at which architecture's fascination with the past was displacing modernist enthusiasm for the future, its theme was monument and memory. It included the first English translation of Alois Riegl's "The Modern Cult of Monuments: Its Character and Its Origin."[1] I read that particular text with rapt attention, in one sitting, on the Long Island Railroad. When I finished, it was after midnight and my train was on a siding in Montauk.

Riegl is a hard read, even now when I reread it under more ideal conditions. But the focus required to read it that first time, amidst the raucous Friday nighters who'd been sharing canned beer even before the train left Queens, has meant that I've never forgotten it. Riegl recognized the residues of anonymous lives captured in otherwise undistinguished objects, and he asserted validity on behalf of both the objects and the lives embodied. He argued in favor of monuments that emerged over time. "Monuments," he wrote, "are nothing other than indispensable catalysts which trigger in the beholder a sense of the life cycle, of the emergence of the particular from the general and its gradual but inevitable dissolution back into the general."[2] These catalysts, he insisted, were no less decisive than those that came about by force of will.

The Riegl text was more important than I could have imagined upon that first reading. It is fair to say that all contemporary interest in the everyday artifact is beholden, whether unknowingly or by design, to Riegl, Viennese art historian, curator, and philosopher *um 1900*. Riegl gave standing to history writ small. His argument, which remains as radical as it must have been when the essay was first published in 1903, made the designation of a monument communal and consensual. He offered three criteria for that designation: intentionality, materiality, and, the

---

1 Alois Riegl, "The Modern Cult of Monuments: Its Character and Its Origin." Kurt W. Forster and D. Ghirardo, trans. *Oppositions* 25 (Fall 1982), 21–51.

2 Alois Riegl, *Stilfragen: Grundlegungen zu einer Geschichte der Ornamentik* (Berlin: n.p., 1893), 24. As translated in Margaret Iverson, *Alois Riegl: Art History and Theory* (Cambridge, MA: MIT Press, 1993), 33.

most quotidian but least possible to ensure, age. Any artifact, not only those intended to recall a person or event deemed important, could come to be considered a monument once enough time passed to allow it to be seen as witness to part of a larger history: a monument not produced but instead granted that status through reception. The unintended monument obviated genius, connoisseurship, usefulness, and most definitively, the singular author. Survival was enough, plus the right audience.

Riegl's theory proved its personal value to me years later in a new, more intimate context as I cleaned out my deceased mother's orderly file cabinets. There, I found she had preserved a stack of unused parents' association stationery from the elementary school I attended circa 1971. Some forty years thereafter, what kind of monument had the paper become? Its textured surface and offset-print gothic-type letterhead had been designed for the typewriter, for an era in which each piece of correspondence was an original. The rough-textured paper provided for correction: a coarse rubber typewriter eraser could lift an inked word, leaving only trace abrasion on the high-rag-content page. The address on the stationery captured a salient detail of New York City history: when its university opened enrollment to everyone (a policy far ahead of its time in acknowledging encoded systemic bias in public education), the expanded number of admittees forced my tiny elementary school, also housed in a university building, to vacate its spaces. Third and fourth grade were spent at protest marches in front of City Hall, carrying hand-lettered oak-tag signs and yelling slogans copped from union strikes. The stationery proved Riegl's point. It invoked personal recollections, of course, but it also captured the material facts of New York City life in the early 1970s. I held in my hands that "indispensable catalyst" for a moment, then slid it into the recycle bin, allowing the specific to return to generality.

To interpret Riegl's ideas as I do gives credence to my affinity for the detritus of architectural practice. What is collected in job books—the binders that hold all paperwork accruing to an ongoing project (lists of supplies, specifications, take-offs, cut sheets, invoices)—has no intrinsic value, no evidence of craft or hand. Unlike the construction drawing, the basis for discussion between architect and builder over the long course of realization, the documents in job books are not part of productive negotiations. Quite the contrary: they are a hedge against unforeseen

96

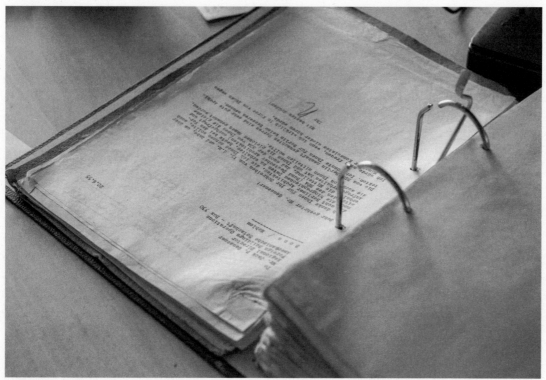

Office of Sep Ruf, Job Book for the Akademie der Künste in Nuremberg

costs, errors in execution, denials of responsibility. They anticipate the job site's ugliest moments, born of the rule that dictates never to admit error or ignorance. They record variances in allowable margins of error, from the mason's centimeter to the millworker's millimeter. They support the architect in all the frustratingly difficult attempts to adjudicate disputes between laborers who are loathe—*you're going to pay me to do his work for him?*—to negotiate the gaps in precision that separate what is respectively sold as finished work. They also address the distrust between labor and capital, the two fronts whose wrath converges on the architect. They are a heavy and unrewarding burden on a discipline that would prefer to imagine itself as, simply, good.

If job books survive, however, their aspect changes as time passes. They come to represent the concerns of an era, the values of those involved, the state of technology, what preoccupied the person who collected them. In this way, they compare to my mother's hoarded stationery. Perhaps even more so than the construction drawing, which often bears the initials of its drafter, job book documents are a monument to the anonymous history from which architecture always emerges. In the 1950s, letters trafficked almost daily among architects, site supervisors, and foremen of job sites. Those letters make unmistakably clear the extent of respective dependencies and mutual responsibilities. Consider a letter from Hedwigskathedrale foreman Horst Poller to bedridden site architect Theodor Blümel. After providing a litany of requests for additional spackle, the precise location of a handrail, and various outstanding items for completion before an inspection two days later, Poller ends his letter with a question that might apply to construction sites everywhere: "Perhaps you are, upon receiving my letter, so much improved that you can have my back."[3]

It is no small thing to tell the story of architecture by tracing provenance: creator, client, chronology, cultural and symbolic context, history of reception. But it is no less small, Riegl seems to imply, to expand provenance so that it includes the multiple daily acts of negotiation, compromise, acrimony, or resistance that result in a building. There is a footnote in Irene Meissner's impeccable monograph on Sep Ruf that makes clear

---

3   Letter from Horst Poller to Theodor Blümel, October 3, 1962. Archive St. Hedwigs-Kathedrale Berlin.

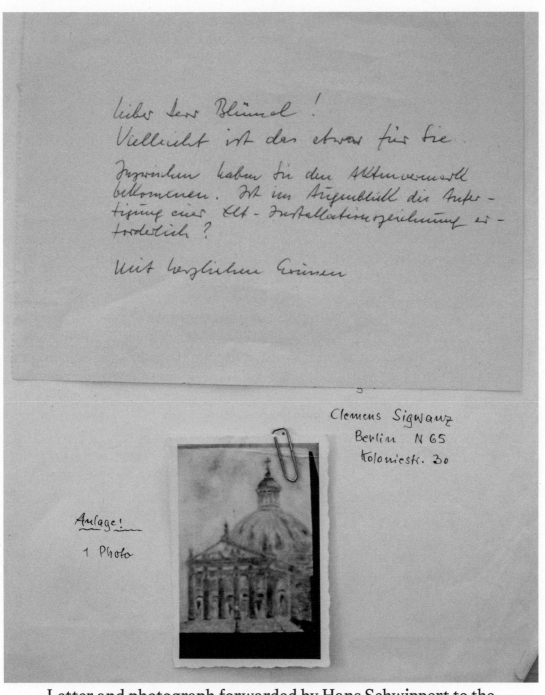

Letter and photograph forwarded by Hans Schwippert to the
Hedwigskathedrale Berlin site foreman

this distinction. "In Ruf's bequest," she notes, "despite intensive research, no written records on the Akademie der Bildenden Künste were found except for company invoices."[4] I read those same documents differently. Annotations in green pencil to bills of lading, recalculations of hours spent on site by painters and plasterers, negotiations of the cost to fabricate additional steel windows: each captured a different facet of architectural history, whether the building product industry, labor relations, or architectural practice so vigilant that a project architect was expected to count each boxwood plant delivered. These are documents I am perversely well equipped to read. Because of my years practicing architecture, I am able to gauge what they communicate.

Job book ephemera are only infrequently part of architectural history. Like the working drawings to which they are sometimes addenda, these documents, expedient and instrumental in the act of making a building, are the ones usually jettisoned as soon as liability concerns permit—seven years' time, as I learned while practicing architecture on and off for a decade in Germany. The intact job books I found in my research had survived ten times their intended lifespan. They had escaped file purges endemic to efficient office practice. Chance, oversight, inertia, sentimentality, even love: the reasons for their existence were as varied as the documents themselves. But without them there would be no way to know that, for example, the white interior of Schwippert's Hedwigskathedrale comprised no fewer than four distinct plaster formulations and application techniques, selected over the course of eleven months, three on-site meetings, and many mock-ups. Or, that these plaster techniques were uniquely appropriate to the limited means and materials of a difficult job site pinioned between Cold War fronts.

It may also be that my fascination with these documents comes from admiration. During my decades in architectural practice, I was forced to exercise discretion in strategically choosing documents to serve as a bulwark against cut corners, chimerical clients, or stupid oversights. I almost inevitably lost track of the most contentious documents. Maybe my advocacy for job books comes from empathy for future researchers

---

4 Irene Meissner, *Sep Ruf 1908–1982*, Kunstwissenschaftliche Studien (Berlin: Deutscher Kunstverlag, 2013), 116, fn. 33.

who will need to sift through endless emails and CAD files to experience what I have found in unabridged caches of old Leitz-brand two-ring binders.

There is no obvious place for job books in the acquisition practices standard at most institutions. To a museum, drawings may have value as art objects, but a job book—unless one of Thomas Demand's fakes—has none. To a library or archive, documents with clear narrative value, such as correspondence and notes, may have worth, but the readymade and the quantitative, such as cut sheets and invoices, likely do not. An intact job binder might, in the best case, be culled during accession, sparing only items signed by someone deemed important. More likely, a job binder becomes landfill. Few institutions are equipped to preserve everything wholesale.

Exceptions occur. I was fortunate to find the archives of Ira Rakatansky[5] and Kaneji Domoto[6] complete, in their families' possession, now acquired by Harvard University and the University of California, Berkeley, respectively. Stored in old metal flat files or second-home attics, their drawings, photographs, newspaper clippings, sketches, notes, even Christmas cards survived. It was the entirety of these archives that made them exceptional. In both cases, the libraries that acquired them unabridged were associated with schools of architecture. These accessions will, I hope, expand the use of past practice in training future architects. Perhaps they also reflect a shift in the way scholarship values the documents used to realize architecture. Riegl might be pleased.

Other exceptions occur unintentionally, as Riegl also recognized, simply by eluding change. I saw this first hand in Berlin on an impromptu research trip to the Hedwigskathedrale. The cathedral was at a contentious juncture about which I had known little before my trip. With German reunification had come the reunification of Berlin's divided Catholic

---

5 Rakatansky studied at Harvard's Graduate School of Design during World War Two, then became Marcel Breuer's first American employee. See Lynnette Widder and John Caserta, *Ira Rakatansky: As Modern as Tomorrow* (San Francisco: William Stout Books, 2010).

6 Domoto grew up in a family of immigrant Japanese landscapers and, before wartime internment, was part of Frank Lloyd Wright's Taliesin West project. He went on to practice as an architect and landscape architect in the New York area from the late 1940s through the 2000s.

bishopric. The congregation, at least during holiday services, had out-grown its space. In 2014, the cathedral as rebuilt by Schwippert, the design I had arrived to study, was about to be undone; since then (despite a sequence of lawsuits) it is gone. New construction has erased Schwippert's radical spatial move: a circular cut in the floor at the circular cathedral's altar to connect crypt and sanctuary and to memorialize damage from wartime bombings. It was a design concept that at its very heart embodied Riegl's definitions of the monument. On the day of my visit, however, the impending renovation proved to have some benefit to my work. A study by an expert in historic preservation had recently been completed. "*Hier haben Sie alles,*" said Mr. Schenk, whose job is to maintain the building in good repair: "here you have everything." He passed me a USB drive onto which he had thoughtfully copied the preservationist's report. A thorough accounting of the building's history, well-illustrated and digitized, it was indeed a useful document.

But it was absolutely not everything that Mr. Schenk had set aside for me. At the center of the long wooden table in the conference room where I was to work stood two binders. Both their spines were labeled with a reduced photograph of the cathedral in its prewar state and carefully hand-lettered titles: "Correspondence—Prof. Schwippert;" "Construction Documents—Designs, Sketches." They had been retrieved from a filing cabinet in the parish house. Recently rediscovered, the binders were quint-essential job books for an inconceivably complicated project, conducted over seven years during which Schwippert ran the renovation in East Berlin from Düsseldorf, across an ideologically fractured country.

Over the next four hours, I photographed every page in those binders: the ones on which Schwippert had written to Blümel, his beloved East German site architect, who died unexpectedly during the building process; the ones on which the Bishop of Berlin expressed his doubts and preferences and financial limitations; and the ones by which metal scaffolding had been requisitioned, glass samples delivered, and a water heater (still not on site almost a year after being ordered from an East German company) desperately sought. As I fingered the onionskin carbon copies, feeling the depressions and punctures made by vanished typewriters, the thrill I sensed came not only from what the documents told me. Here they were, physical witnesses to the past, of value for what

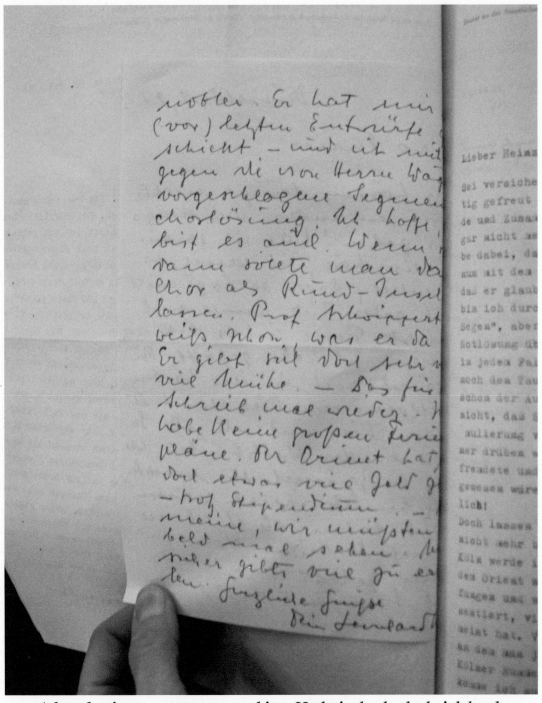

A handwritten note preserved in a Hedwigskathedrale job book

they communicated and of value for the fact of their survival. It was a sensation I had known before, as I momentarily paused at the parents' association stationery in the untenanted apartment where I had been a child. Each page a catalyst.

Theories and Ethics, 1951 and 1953

01   Ulrich Conrads in conversation,
February 3, 2004.
02   Johannes Busmann, *Die revidierte
Moderne: Der Architekt Alfons Leitl 1909–1975*
(Wuppertal: Müller und Busmann, 1995), 54–58.
03   To listen to Martin Heidegger's lecture,
see https://www.youtube.com/watch?v
=mqSSzgg5eio, accessed August 9, 2020.

The Second of the Darmstädter Gespräche

Over the course of three unusually hot days at the beginning of August 1951, an audience of journalists, architects, and lay people filled the town hall in the Hessian court city of Darmstadt. Despite sweltering temperatures and poor acoustics, they listened raptly to the debate and discussion at the podium.[01] A live radio broadcast of the proceedings reached an even larger audience in their homes. The "conversation" that held this audience in its spell addressed the "human being and space," *Mensch und Raum*. It was the second in a series of conversations meant to reestablish Darmstadt as a center of culture following the city's complete destruction in the Second World War; its architectural theme extended to an accompanying exhibition that celebrated the fiftieth anniversary of Darmstadt's Mathildenhöhe artists' colony of the Jugendstil era. Otto Bartning, then head of West Germany's trade association of licensed architects (Bund deutscher Architektinnen und Architekten, or BDA) and a resident of Darmstadt, had enlisted his inner circle to organize the event.[02] With invitations accepted by the country's most prominent architects and by two internationally admired philosophers, the event promised nothing less than a chance to redefine "space" after the erasures of the country's recent past.

The event was planned to demonstrate symmetry between past and future. On the one hand, it was meant to evince cultural continuity between 1901 and 1951 by returning to a place where the cause of modern architecture had been advanced, in order to reconsider where things now stood. The first group of works shown in the exhibition and the categories into which they were organized described an architectural pre-history of current discourse and practice. [3.1] On display in the last room of the exhibition halls was the future: twelve *Meisterbauten* in drawings and models, all of them publicly funded buildings to be commissioned by the city of Darmstadt. The event organizers and city administrators had selected their architects to represent the best of what was possible in 1951. A fulcrum between what had come before and what lay ahead, the three-day discussion set out to establish the conceptual basis for both selective continuity with the past and open-minded visions for the future. The collective cultural ambition of the era, to strike a balance between a celebrated but fraught tradition and an existentially stressed but forward-looking present, was taken up whole-heartedly at Darmstadt.

Ultimately, frustratingly, the event's ambitions outpaced its impact. The discussion's participants were the period's most prolific and publicly visible West German architects and architectural thinkers. To provide intellectual grounding, two internationally recognized philosophers were given the floor: Martin Heidegger and Jose Ortega y Gasset.[03]

3.1 Gallery plan, with each room dedicated to a different space of everyday life, *Mensch und Raum* exhibition, Darmstadt 1951

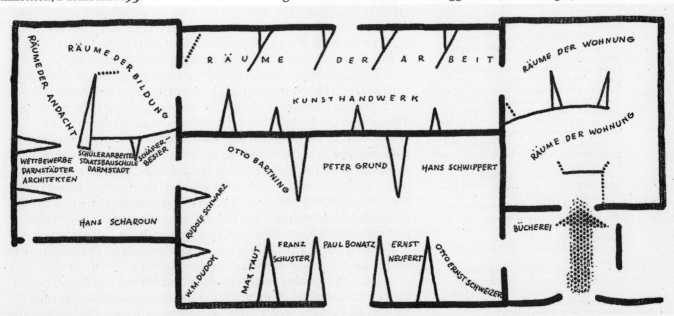

04   I have Ulrich Conrads to thank for
introducing me to the Darmstädter Gespräche.
He first piqued my interest by telling me that
"everything to be said about space" had been
said there. In a later conversation, in February
2004, he said the event had had "no effect on
the postwar period."
05   Ulrich Conrads and Peter Neitzke, eds.,
*Mensch und Raum: Das Darmstädter Gespräch
1951* (Braunschweig: Vieweg, 1991), 7–10.
06   Werner Durth and Paul Sigel, *Baukultur:
Spiegel gesellschaftlichen Wandels*, 2nd rev.
and enl. ed. (Berlin: Jovis, 2010) covers the event
but it is barely known outside the German-
speaking world.
07   The topic was the primacy of representational and abstract art, respectively.
08   See the reprinted articles by Otto
Bartning ("Entscheidung zwischen Wahrheit
und Lüge") and Hugo Häring ("Neues Bauen")
in Ulrich Conrads, *Die Städte himmeloffen: Reden
und Reflexionen über den Wiederaufbau des
Untergegangenen und die Wiederkehr des Neuen
Bauens 1948 / 49*, Bauwelt Fundamente (Basel:
Birkhäuser, 2003), 159–61 and 48–64.
09   Greg Castillo, in conversation on April
21, 2005, made reference to communications
with Herwin Schaefer, a US administrator for
cultural affairs who attended on behalf of the
US administration.
10   Even in professional publications,
coverage was limited. *Baukunst und Werkform*,
whose editorial board included several
participants, covered the exhibition and
presentations separately in issues 8 and 9 from
1951. Leitl's exhibition review in *Baukunst und
Werkform 8* (1951) discussed only Scharoun's
Meisterbau as "an attempt to understand
education [...] as a spatial problem beyond the
specific givens of the Darmstadt commission."
Franz Meunier's review of the conference in
Baukunst und Werkform 9 was dismissive: "It [...]
seems that the active and passive participants
in the Darmstädter Gespräch had hoped,
despite the abstract subject, for something
relevant and concrete, whether in the form
of assertion and conclusion, or in that of
program or polemic. None of them got their
money's worth." The article "We Build Because
We Are Discontent" in the newspaper *Die Zeit*
noted wryly that "most of the participants
belonged to the generation that, exactly half a
century ago [...] were addressed as 'youthful,'
[and] already had grey hair." *Die Zeit* August,
1951, no. 32. http://www.zeit.de/1951/32
/wir-bauenweil-wir-unzufrieden-sind, accessed
January 2, 2015.
11   Conrads and Neitzke, *Mensch und
Raum*, 134.
12   See Ulrich Conrads, Magdalena Droste,
Winfried Nerdinger, and Hilde Strohl, eds.,
*Die Bauhaus-Debatte 1953: Dokumente einer
verdrängten Kontroverse*, Bauwelt Fundamente
(Braunschweig: Vieweg, 1994).

Thousands visited the exhibition over the course of the summer. But few found occasion to translate their thoughts into practice. Architecture was a rapidly transforming field, both in technical and aesthetic terms. Caution, self-doubt, and the return to first principles could not compete with the immediate demands of the Marshall Plan-facilitated economy. The discrepancy between the fundamentally idealistic impulse behind the conference and its comparatively limited effect continued to haunt no less a figure than Ulrich Conrads, who attended the event. Several months later, he became an editor of the Werkbund publication *Baukunst und Werkform*, the periodical that—unsurprisingly, given its editorial board's overlap with the conference organizers—most thoroughly covered *Mensch und Raum*. Conrads thereafter went on to become the highly influential editor-in-chief of the magazine *Bauwelt* and a tastemaker in German architecture through the 1990s. His assessment of the architectural work that emerged from *Mensch und Raum*: "enormously banal."[04] He felt very differently about the accompanying discourse, which remained relevant to Conrads for decades on account of its intellectual merit.[05]

There is no obvious explanation for the disappearance, until relatively recently, of *Mensch und Raum* from accounts of postwar architectural history.[06] The drama around the 1951 event was not as high as it had been at the first Darmstädter Gespräch the preceding year, when the debate about "the image of the human being in our time"[07] had culminated in acrimony between Willi Baumeister and Hans Sedlmayr, each of whom was unable to accept the other's conviction about the status of representational art in the aftermath of *entartete Kunst*. There was no such controversy in 1951. Despite the pivotal position of Germany between East and West,[08] a geopolitical locus whose propagandistic architectural and cultural potential was lost on no one, the US occupying agencies did little more than send an observer to the event.[09] There was no coverage of the debate in the American press, and its transcription has yet to be fully translated. Although covered widely, if not extensively, by the German architectural media,[10] it received no attention in the contemporary international press. Perhaps its conceptual focus was to blame for its marginality: as one of the audience respondents said, "we are discussing philosophical concepts while outside, there are burning problems."[11]

This disregard in no way detracts from its value as a means to assess the intellectual impact of wartime experience on the proponents of modern German architecture and to gauge the nature of their concerns. There are many viable ways to consider *Mensch und Raum*. The ideas under consideration in this book give priority to two aspects of the discussion: The first is the way the conceptual legacy of early modernist architecture was recast. The second, which follows from the first, involves the speakers' attempt to reframe the constituent tenets from which an ethics of modern architecture might be derived. The ethical stakes were high. For all participants, architecture was understood to play a central role in a new, moral, democratic German nation.

The early 1950s saw a more homogeneous modernist architecture emerge around a tidy International Style articulated not least of all by prominent German expatriate architects, many of them Bauhaus denizens, in the United States. The debate on the heritage of the Bauhaus and its legitimacy, which preoccupied several of the major figures at *Mensch und Raum* two years later, brought this essential conflict to a head.[12] Fractures equally deep divided those who had remained in Germany. These fractures were political: the question of National Socialist culpability remained. They were also ideological: a new country demanded a new architecture, for which the trappings of modernist architecture might, or might not, be adequate. In any case, a new way of speaking about architecture was certainly required. Defeated nations did not use the declamatory style of the manifesto.

Thus, the speakers and respondents at *Mensch und Raum* framed their architectural beliefs in complex, if sometimes abstruse, language. Such foundational concepts as the inherent unity in modernist architecture of historical imperative, determinate technology, material truth, and spatial expression played out differently in a defeated Germany, which had no truck with messianic visions and whose technological capacity had been dramatically reduced. This changed climate resonated in the organizing committee's co-authored preamble, posted at the entrance to the *Mensch und Raum* exhibition. It describes the urgent need its authors must have felt to rethink things entirely, based on the metaphysical importance they attributed to architecture:

> "Building is a fundamental activity of the human being—
> The human being builds by structuring spatial constructs and
> thus forming space—Building corresponds to the essence
> of our time—Our time is the time of technology—The exigency of
> our time is homelessness."[13]

On the surface, the preamble corresponds to older modernist tropes. It correlates architectural expression, era, and technology. But the hierarchy among the three is subtly different. The statement implies it is not technology that drives architecture as a cultural expression, but instead space. Space, in turn, is not an expression of an era's particular character as determined by the march of progress. Instead, space is existential and timeless, the product of a fundamental human activity. This basic human activity and the dictates of the particular time in which the authors lived converged in the exigency of homelessness, for which they were bound to offer solutions. Of course, homelessness described the literal state of the country after the war. It also evoked a central leitmotif of German Romanticism reemergent in literary and philosophical discourse in the 1920s. From Novalis's "transzendentale Obdachlosigkeit" to Georg Lukács's *Theory of the Novel*,[14] homelessness was both a physical and a philosophical condition.

By 1951, the urgency of the *Luftkrieg* cityscape had begun to yield to the imminent *Wirtschaftswunder* of the mid- to late 1950s. Homelessness, while still a problem of enormous proportions, was becoming logistical rather than existential in nature. This societal transformation from Year Zero to problem-solving in the fields of architecture and planning had been accomplished in part at the cost of accepting de-Nazification. In practical terms, this allowed the occupying forces to reinstate experts from the toppled regime after a brief period of ideological reprogramming. For many involved in *Mensch und Raum*, this expedience produced a need to distinguish themselves from those who had been permitted to maintain their influence by swapping their Speer-mandated monumentalism for the International Style. The public confrontations between these two camps, both active in postwar reconstruction, would soon also fill the pages of *Baukunst und Werkform*.[15] Those who sought actively to separate themselves from Third Reich architectural culture openly challenged those who were tactically silent about their activities in the 1930s and 1940s. Others simply took advantage of opportunities that arose from the dearth of available expertise. The war, emigration, and German partition had shrunk the cadre of qualified architects and planners. Despite attempts to convince expatriate architects to return from the United States, England, or Palestine,[16] Germany was dependent upon the architects who had remained in practice for the decade of National Socialist rule. These were augmented by the few younger men, and a very few women,[17] who had managed to study architecture and survive the war.[18]

With cities decimated, the occupying forces, citing reasons of expediency, had been fast to reinstate practitioners with urban planning and architectural experience in local government positions. This was true in the case of Peter Grund, the head of Darmstadt's building department in 1951 and a co-organizer of *Mensch und Raum*. At least two others whose names were familiar to participants, Egon Eiermann and Ernst Neufert, had also been subject to de-Nazification. Eiermann offered an object lesson in how modernist language had been used within official Third Reich architecture to glorify progress and industry. His 1937 design for the exhibition entitled *Gebt mir vier Jahre* (give me four years) was only one example of how a monumental machine aesthetic could be adapted

13   Conrads et al., *Die Bauhaus-Debatte 1953*, 33.

14   Georg Lukács, *The Theory of the Novel: A Historico-Philosophical Essay on the Forms of Great Epic Literature* (Cambridge, MA: MIT Press, 1973), 41.

15   See Conrads et al., *Die Bauhaus-Debatte 1953*.

16   Ulrich Conrads in conversation, February 3, 2004.

17   One of the few publications to address directly the importance of women architects in Germany in the postwar period is Nadja Häupl, *Münchner Nachkriegsarchitektinnen: Bea Betz und Edith Horny—Sieben Beiträge zu Leben und Werk nach Begegnungen im Winter 2010* (Munich: Institut für Entwerfen Stadt und Landschaft, TUM, 2010).

18   Conrads stated that only approximately three hundred men who had studied architecture during the war survived. Half of his own graduating class in art history died in the war. Ulrich Conrads in conversation, February 3, 2004.

to express progress and power under the National Socialist dictatorship.[19] Other cases elsewhere in West Germany were much more egregious. The transition from a leading position in Albert Speer's Arbeitsstab für den Wiederaufbau kriegszerstörter Städte (task force for the reconstruction of cities destroyed by war), which began its work in 1942 under the directorship of Rudolf Wolters, to an important role in postwar reconstruction could proceed with little interruption, as had occurred in Hamburg and Düsseldorf.[20] Culpability—by virtue of choice or necessity—was often a matter of degree, a fact of which all were conscious.[21] *Baukunst und Werkform* took up this topic broadly. In its pages, prominent architects acknowledged that their ability to find opportunities during the Third Reich to build modernist architecture was not exculpation: Speer's ministry had been their employer or client.[22]

All of this meant that, by 1951, simple fidelity to modernism as a style was an inadequate political touchstone. As modernism became the official expression of postwar democracy, especially within the cultural context of the Cold War, its political lassitude grew. Indeed, many of Speer's former protégés after the war achieved success by building in an exclusively modernist idiom. Friedrich Tamms, a member of Speer's internal staff (*engerer Arbeitsstab*),[23] summarized the situation in a letter of 1952: "The comfortable simplification: modern, democratic; traditional, national socialist has no credibility. Conceptual discussion crosses political boundaries. It is apolitical."[24] By virtue of its success across political lines, modernism had lost its ethical aura. It needed new rules.

This also dictated a more complex narrative in lieu of one that framed the Third Reich as an architectural aberration within the unbroken trajectory of German modern architecture. The first, 1947 issue of *Baukunst und Werkform*[25] included a statement by its editorial board, which included Rudolf Schwarz, Otto Bartning, Egon Eiermann, Hans Schwippert, and Otto Ernst Schweizer, all official participants and organizers of *Mensch und Raum*. Continuity seemed impossible, rupture unsupportable. The statement's words resonate with the assertions made in the *Mensch und Raum* preamble: that the act of making architecture is endemic to the "essence of our time." Nothing less than a moral imperative demanded a return to architectural work, beginning with first principles:

> "The collapse destroyed the visible world of our lives and work. With a sense of liberation, we thought then that we could return to action. Today, two years later, we recognize the degree to which the visible collapse is only an expression of spiritual erosion and we could lose ourselves in despair. We are left to return to the foundation of things: it is from that point that our responsibility is to be understood."[26]

Mensch und Raum can be understood within the context of the "return to the foundation of things": the objective was to imagine architecture's purpose in a more general story of humanity, to explain space's origins in theology and human perception, to rewrite the founding myths that resonated in interwar manifestoes and pronouncements, many of which had been authored by the *Mensch und Raum* speakers as young avant-gardists.

The architectural work presented at Darmstadt—in the exhibition, in the formal lectures, in the ensuing responses, and in the *Meisterbauten*— is perhaps most accurately understood in relation to the ambitions expressed in the preamble and presaged by the 1947 statement in *Baukunst und Werkform*. This work offers physical evidence that the foundation to which the preamble referred was both spiritual and practical, and that the curators, who in many cases were also authors of the work on exhibit, saw in their architecture the basis for a democratic *Neubeginn*. The public exhibition's organization and content signal the new modernist historiography, including a reconception of such fundamental ideas as function and inhabitation, which they imagined would underpin their efforts.[27]

The city of Darmstadt, and the remarkable Mathildenhöhe artists' colony as its setting, could easily explain the exhibit's predilection

19   Greg Castillo discussed extensively the "retreat into industrial architecture" in his presentation at Columbia University's Collins Kaufman Forum, April 21, 2005.
20   In Werner Durth, *Deutsche Architekten: Biographische Verflechtungen 1900–1970*, Schriften des Deutschen Architekturmuseums zur Architekturgeschichte und Architekturtheorie (Braunschweig: Vieweg, 1986). Durth cites Konstanty Gutschow in Hamburg, Rudolf Wolters in Coesfeld, and Friedrich Tamms in Lübeck, and a scandal after the appointment of Julius Schulte-Frohlinde in Düsseldorf. Peter Grund, the Director of the Building Department in Darmstadt, had been "de-Nazified" before taking his post. See Michael Bender, Roland May, and Kunsthalle Darmstadt, *Architektur der fünfziger Jahre: Die Darmstädter Meisterbauten* (Stuttgart: K. Krämer, 1998).
21   See Durth, *Deutsche Architekten*, 326.
22   Durth, *Deutsche Architekten*. Also see Rudolf Lodders, "Zuflucht im Industriebau," in Conrads, *Die Städte himmeloffen*, 65–75.
23   Durth, *Deutsche Architekten*, 212.
24   Durth, *Deutsche Architekten*, 326.
25   Reproduced in Busmann, *Die revidierte Moderne*, 59.
26   Durth, *Deutsche Architekten*, 59.
27   Otto Bartning, ed., *Mensch und Raum: Das Darmstädter Gespräch 1951* (Darmstadt: Neue Darmstädter Verlagsanstalt, 1951), 33–48.

28   As only one example, see *Baukunst und Werkform* 4, 166–71, in which excerpts from various Henry van de Velde texts were reprinted.
29   Thomas Hasler writes extensively about Schwarz's thinking on architectural history and on form and gestalt in Thomas Hasler, *Architektur als Ausdruck—Rudolf Schwarz*, Studien und Texte zur Geschichte der Architekturtheorie (Zurich: gta Verlag, 2000), 47–92. Schwarz's texts in *Wegweisung der Technik* and elsewhere were collected and reissued by Ulrich Conrads in 1979. See Rudolf Schwarz, *Wegweisung der Technik und andere Schriften zum Neuen Bauen, 1926–1961* (Braunschweig: Vieweg, 1979).
30   Bartning, *Mensch und Raum*, 33.

for German and Jugendstil architecture. Or perhaps it offers an alibi: Jugendstil was central to a historical lineage that had been consistently propagated by Schwarz throughout his career, and one that was evident in the pages of *Baukunst und Werkform*.[28] The focus on Jugendstil as an unnaturally truncated lineage for modern architecture could be traced to the period, before the war, of Bartning's directorship at the Weimar Bauhochschule, which replaced the departed Bauhaus. This focus as well as other aspects of the exhibition's organization recall ideas articulated in an avant-garde tradition distinct from that of the Bauhaus and its circle, which included Schwarz's strange, short-lived periodical, *Wegweisung der Technik*, published with illustrations furnished by photographer Albert Renger-Patzsch beginning in 1926.[29]

The exhibition's underlying revisionist historiography deviates from an otherwise conventional modernist storyline, which might begin with proto-modern works of engineering and include early anti-eclecticism in order to culminate in international modernism by the 1920s. Three points of difference stand out. The first is the clear preference for architects who worked in traditional or solid materials, such as masonry, rather than the transparent or inherently open materials and construction methods, such as steel and glass, which are usually associated with modern architecture. The second is the inclusion of heterogeneous idioms, rather than exclusion of anything not identifiable as "white" modernism. The last, in accordance with the conference name, was the organization of the exhibited projects on the basis of spatial rather than functional typologies.

The typical story of modern architecture as materially and technically driven had repressed the material variation and stylistic efflorescence celebrated in the *Mensch and Raum* exhibition. Much seminal early modernist work was built using traditional wall construction, a fact that was often polemically concealed under a coat of stucco. Here, the weighty, solid architecture of Joseph Maria Olbrich, Peter Behrens, Heinrich Tessenow, Hermann Muthesius, Auguste Perret, Antoni Gaudi, Henry van de Velde, early Frank Lloyd Wright, Otto Bartning, and Paul Bonatz was given most of the wall space in the part of the exhibition devoted to "spaces of inhabitation,"[30] the first room visitors entered. These were

3.2 Visitor's sketches, *Mensch und Raum* exhibition catalogue, Berlin 1951, last page and overleaf

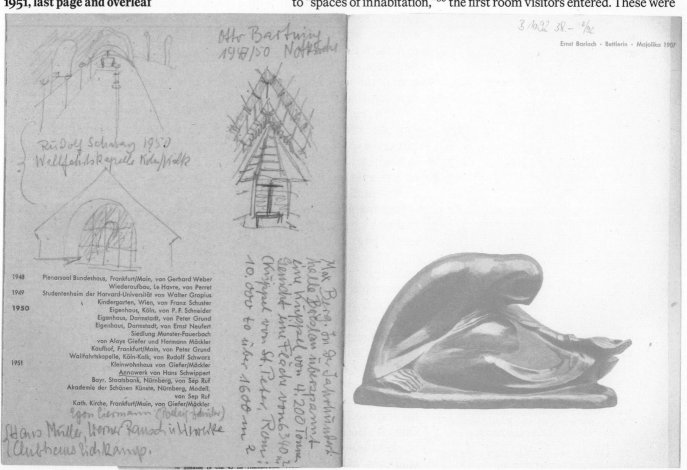

architects whom most modernist histories relegated to the status of "proto-" modern, rather than celebrating them in their own right. Any visitor would have passed houses by Behrens and Olbrich on the way to the exhibition, which was staged in Olbrich's exhibition hall. Outside the exhibition's walls, there was ample evidence of the value this version of modernism ascribed to surface texture, composition, detail, tone, color, and variety.

"White" modernism was not excluded; it was simply sidelined. Only two of Le Corbusier's abstract, painted buildings were included, Villa Savoie and the Pessac complex, and were accompanied by a terse caption: "Le Corbusier designed with an 'aesthetic sense dictated by the civilization of the machine age.'"[31] The knowledge that the curators advocated the turn against the primacy of technology casts this otherwise unexceptional caption in a more subversive light. Walter Gropius received slightly more attention, represented by the Dessau *Meisterbauten*, the Bauhaus, and the Törten complex. His projects were accompanied by direct quotations from texts he had written in the mid-1920s. One judges a successful building by virtue of how "it completely serves the life activities required, and that these life activities are based on both spiritual and material demands." The second quotation insists that "spatial feeling is changing [...] and seeks to maintain the unity of interior space and universal space."[32] Both these assertions would be challenged in the podium discussion, although without specific reference to Gropius, by Hans Schwippert, an active member of the exhibition's curatorial committee.[33]

As described in the catalogue text, the exhibition intended to leave the visitor with a sense of the "different spatial conceptions of the modern master builders"[34] rather than with a singular, consistent image of contemporary space. Irony may well have been intended, then, in a statement attributed to Philip Johnson and posted below an image of the Weissenhof Siedlung: "The Weissenhof Siedlung [...] finally demonstrated that the different architectural elements of the early postwar years had been unified in a single movement."[35] Everything on the walls argued differently.

The representation of modernism as spatially and materially heterogeneous was, by 1951, not unique to this exhibition. Consider, for example, Sigfried Giedion's inclusion of a new chapter dedicated to Alvar Aalto in the second, 1949 edition of *Space, Time and Architecture*.[36] But in the context of the preamble to *Mensch und Raum* and the ambitions of the event's organizers, this reframing was integral to the ambition to accomplish more than mere "return to action."

The exhibition filled four adjoining rooms in Olbrich's building.[37] Angled partition walls further subdivided the rooms but permitted views across the space's entirety. Each room featured buildings that answered to familiar functional categories, but rather than emphasizing use, each function was subordinated prepositionally to the noun "spaces": spaces of inhabitation, spaces of work (incorporating applied arts), spaces of learning, and spaces of contemplation. The last rooms were dedicated to the *Meisterbauten* projects commissioned from prominent architects for the city of Darmstadt.

This nomenclature provided latitude for the curators to create unlikely groupings of projects. Under the heading "spaces of inhabitation," for example, the distinction between public and private, essential to a standard functional approach, was ignored. Villas and housing complexes were shown together to emphasize their shared spatial predilections. "Spaces of work" included functional typologies as diverse as exhibition architecture, factories, hospitals, and artists' studios. Here, too, any distinction between public and private, civic or individual was sidelined. In some cases, spatial affinities seemed to have overshadowed functional ones. For example, Mies van der Rohe's Illinois Institute of Technology was included among "spaces of work," but Olbrich's Hochzeitsturm, adjacent to the exhibition hall where the show was held, was presented among "spaces of education." Defining sports stadiums, movie and stage theaters, schools, libraries, and museums

31   Bartning, *Mensch und Raum*, 39.
32   Bartning, *Mensch und Raum*, 37–38.
33   Bartning, *Mensch und Raum*, frontispiece.
34   Bartning, *Mensch und Raum*, 40.
35   Bartning, *Mensch und Raum*, 38.
36   Giedion's restructuring of his histo-riography in his second edition while in the United States is covered thoroughly in Reto Geiser, *Giedion and America: Repositioning the History of Modern Architecture* (Zurich: gta Verlag, 2018), 139.
37   Bender, May, and Kunsthalle Darmstadt, *Architektur der fünfziger Jahre*, 15.

alike as "spaces of education" ignored any distinction between culture and leisure, or between popular and high culture. A 1920s avant-garde polemic would have affirmed this broadening of the compass of culture to include physical activity, mass events, and popular consumer culture. However, the reluctance to separate public and private would have frustrated that same polemic's political thrust. More importantly, the inclusion of mass spectacles among "spaces of education" downplayed their tendency to political charge in the 1920s and 30s.

Cultural buildings were distributed between spaces of education and those of work, so that any discussion of political representation was completely circumnavigated. Government buildings were subsumed in "spaces of work": one example, Hans Schwippert's Bundeshaus, was captioned with an excerpt from the speech Schwippert held at the building's opening, in which he described its ambience of workaday nonchalance: "an architecture of encounter and conversation."[38] The impulse to forego any differentiation between public and private put particular pressure on the last room through which the visitor passed: "spaces of contemplation." The significance of organized religion in the immediate postwar period was evident in the fact that churches were rebuilt (or temporary churches constructed) even before housing stock. The practice of churchgoing, it was clear, had re-centered communities. It was an immediate and effective way to create a public forum while secular public life was being reinvented.

Building churches provided architects the opportunity to conceive and realize spaces that could assume a representational role, whereas state or work-related commissions at that time only did so with difficulty. Moreover, as Ulrich Conrads recalled "the existential had precedence, no one wanted to live in cellars. [...] Churches were relatively free of purpose, therefore spatial thinking was only possible in church building,"[39] and was materialized in both Catholic and Protestant contexts. Bartning's *Notkirchen* (emergency churches),[40] subsidized by collections from America, proved that spatial invention was possible even when the means of building—rubble, prefabricated wooden trusses, and lime plaster—were primitive. The supposition that traditional masonry construction, a material necessity in the immediate postwar economy, could give rise to progressive spatial constructs is borne out in churches by Bartning as well as those by Schwarz, perhaps the most legitimate heir to the ideas developed at *Mensch und Raum*. **[3.2]**

The title *Mensch und Raum* is attributed to Bartning.[41] Known before the war for his visionary churches, housing projects, and directorship of the Bauhochschule in Weimar, he was the leading church architect for Protestant denominations rebuilding after the war. He also lived in Darmstadt-Mathildenhöhe. Accordingly, he was asked to serve as chairman when plans were made for a second Darmstädter Gespräch. In Bartning's extensive pre- and postwar writing on church architecture, he had focused on the spiritual implications of the space that emerges from modern construction technologies. Written in 1946 about the conditions in postwar German cities, his language presages that of *Baukunst und Werkform*'s founding statement and the Darmstadt preamble in its focus on building as a fundamental, if not the foundational, human act:

> "We have all become well-versed in the desert, externally and
> internally. When two or three people meet in the desert, however,
> and recognize one another by a particular look in their eyes,
> then they remain together. And when there are thirty or forty or four
> hundred of them, then they become a community of silence,
> of hesitant speech, and of sudden prayer and singing. But these
> communities in the desert, they will lay a ring of stones and they
> will build a tent, not only to secure the locus of their communal lives
> but also to make their community of spirit visible and palpable.[42]"

In other words: we emerged from the desert; we form community. We do so first through the act of looking at one another. This act, Bartning explains, is consolidated in the circle of stones and manifested in the tent. Throughout *Mensch und Raum*, the concept "space" was described

38   Hans Schwippert in his 1949 address at the opening of the Bundeshaus. Undated typescript, GNM, DKA, NL, Schwippert, binder labeled "Bundeshaus Adenauer Finanzierung."
39   Ulrich Conrads in conversation, February 3, 2004.
40   The *Notkirchen* were built by anchoring upended wooden trusses between rubble foundation walls. The trusses were paid for by donations from American congregations. Information provided during a visit to a *Notkirche* in Cologne, January 2004.
41   Durth, *Deutsche Architekten*, 361.
42   "Das Zelt in der Wüste" and "Notkirche" [1948] in Otto Bartning, *Spannweite: Aus Schriften und Reden, Ausgewählt und Eingeleitet von Alfred Siemon* (Bramsche bei Osnabrück: Rasch, 1958), 42 and 100. As cited in Joseph Imorde, "Otto Bartning: Spirituality and Modern Building" (unpublished manuscript).

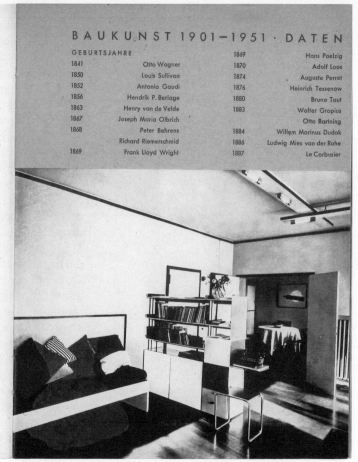

EIN AUFRUF AN DIE ARCHITEKTEN

Es gibt geschichtliche Untersuchungen über Freistil-Ringkämpfe und Kaugummi. Es gibt historische Samm-
lungen von Lippenstiften und Spielkarten. Eine Geschichte der modernen Architektur gibt es dagegen
– zumindest bei uns – noch nicht. Dabei wird heute allgemein anerkannt, daß dieses »Neue Bauen«
in Deutschland geboren wurde. Ganz kurz zusammengefaßt, hat sich folgendes ereignet: 1.) Schon im
19. Jahrhundert entwickelt sich im Ingenieurbau allmählich die neue Raumidee, 2.) der Jugendstil bringt
die Befreiung von den historischen Formen, 3.) in England entsteht aus Handwerk und Baustoff eine
neue Tradition. Das alles wurde bei uns zusammengefaßt, kam unter den Einfluß moderner Malerei und
sozialer Gedanken, und schon 1910 entsteht das Embryo des »Funktionalismus«.

Nach dem ersten Weltkrieg wird dann die neue Architektur geboren. Seit vielen Jahren entsteht zum
erstenmal wieder in Deutschland ein »neuer Stil«. Was Gropius, Mies, Taut und manche andere begonnen
haben, ist heute die Architektur, welche den ganzen Erdball umspannt. Die Bedeutung dieser Frühzeit darf nicht vergessen werden. Sie ist heute schon ein Stück wichtige Baugeschichte.
Das Ausland hat das erkannt. Im Museum für moderne Kunst in New York werden die ersten Stahl-
sessel von Mies van der Rohe, die ersten Skizzen zum Bauhaus, die ersten CIAM-Programme sorgfältig
gesammelt. Es gibt gründliche, umfangreiche ausländische Bücher über den Frühfunktionalismus in Deutschland. Bei uns kümmert sich kein Mensch darum. Noch ist es Zeit, noch gibt es verstreut bei Architekten
und in Bibliotheken wertvolles Material. Dieses Material muß gesammelt werden. Bilder und Modelle
der wichtigsten Bauten, Projekte, auch solche, die nicht gebaut wurden, die ersten Aufrufe und Kampf-
schriften usw., kurz alles, was in dieser fruchtbaren Zeit entstand und sich als Grundlage einer großen,
internationalen Entwicklung erwiesen hat.

Die Ausstellung aus Darmstadt ist ein erster Anfang. Auf der nächsten Bauausstellung könnte sie in
erweiterter Form das historische Rückgrat bilden. Einmal wird es auch bei uns, wie in anderen Ländern,
ein »Bauzentrum« geben, in dem die geschichtliche Abteilung wichtig sein wird. Zunächst gilt es, das
Interesse zu wecken. Bei Vorträgen von Architekten könnte zur Abwechslung außer den ewigen Berufs-
fragen auch einmal ein baugeschichtliches, dabei aber modernes Thema von Interesse sein. Wenn erst
unsere Fachzeitschriften den Gedanken aufgreifen und ihre Leser ansprechen, dann werden wir manche
nette Anekdote zu lesen bekommen, manche Mitteilung wird Zusammenhänge klären, die unbekannt
waren. Mancher deutsche Architekt kennt wichtiges Material zur Quellenforschung des Funktionalismus,
hatte aber bisher weder Gelegenheit, darüber zu reden noch zu schreiben. Dabei keine Lobeshymnen,
nicht die üblichen gegenseitigen Beweihräucherungen, daß alles schön und gut war, was die Herren
damals gebaut haben. Im Gegenteil scharf kritisch absondern, was für die Entwicklung wichtig war,
und was sich als modischer Unsinn herausgestellt hat.

Jetzt ist die richtige Zeit, um das zu sammeln, was die Bomben übriggelassen haben! Schon wieder
melden sich von verschiedenen Seiten Stimmen, die einem öden Klassizismus das Wort reden und uns ein-
reden wollen, die Jahrzehnte hinter uns waren dekadent und krank. Der Gegenbeweis wird nicht schwer
sein. Lieber Herr Kollege, helfen Sie bei dieser Sammlung mit. Retten Sie diesen »wichtigsten Abschnitt
der deutschen Baugeschichte seit 200 Jahren« vor der völligen Vergessenheit. In 50 Jahren kommt
manches davon ins Museum. Die Historiker werden Ihnen dann dankbar sein und Ihren Namen in Gold
fassen.
                                                                    SCHOSZBERGER

BAUKUNST 1901–1951 · DATEN

GEBURTSJAHRE

1841	Otto Wagner	1869	Hans Poelzig
1850	Louis Sullivan	1870	Adolf Loos
1852	Antonio Gaudi	1874	Auguste Perret
1856	Hendrik P. Berlage	1876	Heinrich Tessenow
1863	Henry van de Velde	1880	Bruno Taut
1867	Joseph Maria Olbrich	1883	Walter Gropius
1868	Peter Behrens		Otto Bartning
	Richard Riemerschmid	1884	Willem Marinus Dudok
1869	Frank Lloyd Wright	1886	Ludwig Mies van der Rohe
		1887	Le Corbusier

3.3 "A Call to Architects,"
Mensch und Raum exhibition catalogue, Berlin, Fall 1951

43   Gottfried Semper, *Die vier Elemente der
Baukunst: Ein Beitrag zur vergleichenden Baukunde.*
(Braunschweig: Friedrich Vieweg, 1851).
44   Bettina Köhler, "Architecture History as
the History of Spatial Experience," *Daidalos:
Berlin Architectural Journal* no. 67 (1998), 36–43.
45   Friedrich Ratzel et al., "Der Lebensraum:
Eine biogeographische Studie," in *Festgaben
für Albert Schäffle zur siebzigsten Wiederkehr seines
Geburtstages am 24. Februar 1901* (Tübingen:
H. Laupp, 1901), 101–189. Cited in Woodruff D.
Smith, "Friedrich Ratzel and the Origins
of Lebensraum," *German Studies Review* 3 (1980),
51–68.
46   German History in Documents and
Images, "Hitler's Confidential Memo on Autarky,"
vol. 7. Nazi Germany, 1933–1945 (August 1936)
http://germanhistorydocs.ghi-dc.org/pdf/eng
/English61.pdf, accessed March 31, 2022.
47   Busmann, *Die revidierte Moderne*,
photo p. 34.

as constituent. The act of defining space was understood to be both
transcendental and real, a necessary step in recreating a democratic
society after the zero hour.

The conviction that space—*Raum*—is socially and philosophically
foundational to an imaginary of human culture already appears
in nineteenth-century German architectural theory. A very brief resumé
here will have to suffice: Gottfried Semper's 1851 *Four Elements of
Architecture*[43] describes the first act of architecture as that of demarcating
or bounding by means of a fence, rather than effecting shelter, as was
argued as far back as Vitruvius and had been taken up again in the mid-
eighteenth century by French architectural theorists. Modernist ideas
about dynamic space traced their lineage to the cadre of art historians
who based their work on the scientific theories of Wilhelm Wundt.[44]
Much of Bartning's imagery—the stone circle, the founding of community,
the light roof above—recalls Semper's. Space, in the messianic rhetoric
of interwar German modernism, had drawn upon this longer theoretical
tradition. It was a tradition to which postwar German architects would
have wanted to connect themselves. It was also a way to distance their ideas
from the connotations of the way *Raum* had been used in the 1930s.

The Third Reich had treated space as a commodity, as its manifest
destiny. The term *Raum* argued for Germany's right to expand throughout
Europe and to annex its Eastern neighbors. *Lebensraum*, first coined
in 1901,[45] was the operative term, documented in Hitler's August 1936
"Confidential Memo on Autarchy."[46] Even outside of the compound word
Lebensraum, *Raum* was also perverted for expansionist rhetoric.
It appears in the title *Volk ohne Raum*[47] of a propagandistic 1937 exhibition,
designed by modernist architect Emil Fahrenkamp. Fahrenkamp was
another example of collusion between the National Socialist agenda and
modernist architecture. In the same year, Fahrenkamp designed the
Hermann Göring School for Painting in Kronenberg, a town in the Eifel area
of the *Dreiländereck*. The region was destined to become highly contested
at the end of the war. Fahrenkamp's case was egregious: Joseph Goebbels's
architect of choice, Fahrenkamp was, by his own account, too modern
for Hitler's taste. If not for this, the architectural legacy of National

Socialism might have looked radically different. As he testified in 1947 at his de-Nazification trial, "I was later given exhibition buildings to design so I wouldn't be passed over completely."[48] The 1937 exhibition, staged inside an enormous hangar-like free-span structure, juxtaposed outsized photographic panels of German rural, industrial, and urban landscapes shot at slightly above eye level with encroaching machinery, displays, and models. The deep space depicted in the enormous photographs above the visitors' heads was juxtaposed with the densely occupied space at the level of their bodies. The technology of German productivity, represented in the three-dimensional objects with which visitors vied for space, contrasted with the productive landscapes. The result was to reify space as a tangible, occupiable property—which, as the exhibition title claimed, was apparently in short supply: the masses of workers and factories depicted on the end wall and superimposed with an enormous headshot of Hitler seemed ready to throng into the exhibition space. The space at stake here, far from being constitutive of a reflective community, was a physical commodity subject to a condition of scarcity.

The emphasis on space in *Mensch und Raum* was an act of historical continuity as well as of historical rehabilitation.[3.3] Its usage rejected National Socialist territorial denotations and upheld Semperian traditions. Reconsidering space might also have been seen as a way to stake out territory distinct from the trajectory taken by the German architects who had left during the war, perhaps most prominently Gropius and his Bauhaus lineage. The conference organizers planned for four longer, keynote speeches on space: two by architects and two by philosophers. The first speech, by architect Otto Ernst Schweizer, and the last, by Jose Ortega y Gasset, were well received by their audience. Each considered space relative to technology. Architect Rudolf Schwarz and philosopher Martin Heidegger, whose talks were certainly the most ambitious and complex of the four, argued the socio-spiritual significance of space. Their "space" was of long duration, transcendent. It stood in sharp contrast to the words authored by Gropius and posted on the wall next to images of his Törten Siedlung in the exhibition: "The sense of space changes: whereas in older times of finite cultural developments, the weighty bond to the earth was embodied in solid, monolithic-seeming volumes and individualized interior spaces, the works of today's leading architects [...] reflect the movement, the traffic of our time."[49] Whereas the Darmstadt preamble focused on the timelessness of space-making as the "fundamental activity of the human being," Gropius and the Bauhaus had celebrated an era-dependent spatial sensibility. This temporal sense of space was integral to the story of modern architecture that was fast becoming canon. Giedion's *Space, Time and Architecture*, first published in 1941[50] by Harvard University, resonated with Gropius's courses there on visual culture, which continued the legacy of Bauhaus in its new home.

All podium presentations distinguished the term "space" sharply with either territorial or epochal qualifiers. The first day, a Saturday, began with formal welcomes, then proceeded to talks by the two architects. The next morning began with Heidegger's turgid talk, followed by Heidegger's acolyte Ortega y Gasset. This final talk was welcome comic relief: largely extemporaneous and self-deprecating, it was greeted with laughter and applause from the punch-drunk audience, which then moved on to a lively discussion at least as relevant to the period's architectural theory as any of the prepared talks.

Schweizer, the first speaker, began with a talk entitled "The Architectural Conquest of our Life Space." Technology, also the topic chosen by Ortega y Gasset, operated in Schweizer's thinking as a mechanism with which to measure space, whether in the landscape, in the city, or in a specific building. He illustrated his exposition using historic buildings and towns, all of which he depicted in small sketches that were reproduced in the conference catalogue. Schweizer's propositions were comparatively straightforward. The opposite was true of the next two speakers, Schwarz and after him, Heidegger. Both shared an ambition to define space as

48   See Thomas Friedrich, *Hitler and Berlin: Abused City* (New Haven: Yale University Press, 2012), 416, fn. 119.
49   Bartning *Mensch und Raum*, 38.
50   Sigfried Giedion, *Space, Time and Architecture: The Growth of a New Tradition* (Cambridge, MA: Harvard University Press, 1941).

a manifestation of more transcendental, abstractly historic processes. Both rejected the rhetoric of space exemplified in Gropius's "transformed feeling of space, which reflects the movement, the traffic of our era."[51] In both speeches, space emerges as an expression of the relationship between the infinite (God, whether explicitly identified by the two speakers or not) and human experience; both advocated for the insight that space is an entity produced and lived by human beings in daily life, rather than an abstract or conceptual medium. Despite these similarities in ambition and in complexity of thought, their referents were quite different. In fact, Schwarz had specifically requested the opportunity to speak at *Mensch und Raum* in order to distance himself from Heidegger.[52] Schwarz's concept of space is explicitly theological; Heidegger's, eerily mythic. Both trade in their own historical imaginaries. Although Schwarz modeled their relevance to architectural practice in his own work, his theories registered only negligibly in architecture culture. Heidegger's text remains the only portion of *Mensch und Raum* ever translated into English. Its influence on architectural culture, largely by virtue of its later reception, was, despite its abstractness, great.

Schwarz's text draws upon concepts he developed more thoroughly elsewhere, including his 1947 article "Das Unplanbare" (the unplannable), published in *Baukunst und Werkform*.[53] It also presages arguments he would make as the instigator of the 1953 "Bauhaus debate," his full-throated rejection of the exclusionary technophilia he saw exemplified in the Bauhaus and its culture. His intention seems to have been, by touching on a wide range of topics, to expound his own, unique definition of space.

He began first by praising the movement that produced the venue's architecture and then lamenting its brevity: why had Jugendstil not been longer-lived? Because, he answered, its vitality had been overwhelmed by a "coordinate system of rationality," the same rationality that saw its stock rise with Bauhaus modernism. Schwarz traced this "coordinate system" to the *be-greifen* of nineteenth-century instrumentalism. With the verb's literal sense "to comprehend," the hyphen Schwarz inserted between its prefix and stem underlines the sense of grasping (*greifen*) and hence, rapaciousness in the collection of knowledge. Scientific instrumentalism, he argued, had been able to "place the world in a yoke."[54] He spoke against this objective, in whose service he somewhat idiosyncratically placed architectural photography and art history, both practices that replaced the divine eye and human vision with technology and *be-greifen*.

He offered the alternative of space derived through subjective experience, tactile and visual: "The grasping, gripping [*greifende, packende*] hand only actualizes itself when one internalizes things [...] when the eye joins it, the eye that perceives with astonishment and wonder how the world exists only in forms, of which each form speaks the truth and does so in an irreplaceable way accessible only to the eye."[55] His imagery is that of spatial experience, perceived by vision and touch simultaneously, then ultimately internalized. This was Jugendstil, which, according to Schwarz, believed "it was a world that was beautiful, that burst from its internal force and from its internal intentionality [...] a world that grew entirely from its interior."[56] This world vanished, and was replaced by "all possible erroneous teachings of materialist, functionalist nature."[57] It would have been clear to his audience what architectural culture Schwarz was referencing, and that Gropius was his foil.

For this turn of events, Schwarz did not fault technology or modern life per se. "Technology," he had written in his 1947 article, "an originally high and nobly intended world form, arose in the appropriate continuation of God's work, in the soul of the lonely seeker of God in its love for the sublime, with the single intention of making lighter the stuff of the world."[58] At fault instead was again the same abstract system he faulted for the demise of Jugendstil, the all-encompassing intellectual "abstract system, the web of bars to which the human spirit subjects itself," a kind of Cartesian prison. In its place, he advocated the "unplannable":

"Every era has a particular task to complete: the construction of an economy, the founding of a state, the building of a cathedral

51   Busmann, *Die revidierte Moderne*, 34.
52   "I would be happy to say a few fundamental things about the building arts and what I would have to say is conservative, that is, revolutionary. [...] It is probable that my convictions are contrary to most of the things that one finds in literature and likely, to what Heidegger has to offer. [...] Ten minutes will hardly suffice to put distance between myself and Heidegger." Rudolf Schwarz to Otto Bartning, June 4, 1951, quoted in Hasler, *Architektur als Ausdruck*, 108–9.
53   Rudolf Schwarz, "Das Unplanbare," *Baukunst und Werkform* (1947), 82.
54   Bartning, *Mensch und Raum*, 63.
55   Bartning, *Mensch und Raum*, 63.
56   Bartning, *Mensch und Raum*, 65.
57   Bartning, *Mensch und Raum*, 63.
58   Bartning, *Mensch und Raum*, 63.

or something else. It is called to that task, which is simply its work. Everything else that exists in addition to it or demands to exist is not truly of that time. [...] If one provides space in the soul or in the landscape for any other matter, then it is a free space in the most general sense. [...] Tied to the earth and constricted in body and space, the human found for himself the spiritual way out and broke through the old dimensions knowingly and effectively, and gained breadth, a higher position as well as one with distance from his own center. [...] What can be planned is the beginning, the first decision to take this path and to leave the realm of the plannable in order to do well by the future and to become its fuel, outside, in the realm of the unplanned."[59]

"Free space" in Schwarz's nomenclature was the medium in which the human soul moves in its traffic between the known of the everyday and the unknowable or "unplannable," a concept that seems to contain both God and the simple unknowns of the future. Although an era may have its task, the "spiritual way out" exceeds the measure of that era. This excess is expressed in the space that the era forms, a space that should accommodate the demands of its time. More importantly, implicit in this space is the fact that it, too, will become the "fuel" of the future, just as it has subsumed the past. The dictates of an era are therefore relative, and progress aggregative rather than linear. Planned and unplannable are both components of this space in a world, as Schwarz described it, that depends in equal parts on chaos and order:

"There may be a place where everything that has happened is preserved just as it occurred, an enormous memory of the cosmos; the earth is not this place. What lies on her surface is the rubble of previous eras, themselves barely bringing to completion anything pristine. [...] Between the two possibilities of the earth, crystalline or rubble-heap, are the average things, the half-completed, the resigned, the things that were properly made for a particular purpose or placed in orderly fashion according to a specific consideration as if they belonged together. [...] He who wants to help the earth must know this. He may not overburden himself or the earth with the attempt to eliminate confusion, because the earth and the world require confusion. [...] He must allow space for confusion, enormous free space."[60]

Schwarz's "rubble," in this text written as German cities fell to Allied bombers, was tantamount to chaos. It represented the inherent fallibility of all mankind's attempts on earth. Schwarz juxtaposed rubble to human aspiration, the desire to "bring [...] to completion anything pristine." Rubble and the "crystalline": two extremes between which fell the objects of everyday life, objects that attempted to serve a purpose or reflect a will to order but remained "half completed." This scale, stretching from past to future and from failure to aspiration, was subsumed in what Schwarz termed "space." Space was a continuum, temporal and locational, occupied by rubble but offering a site for the aspirational "crystalline." Schwarz made clear, too, that this "enormous free space" was produced communally and accrued over the entirety of humankind's time on earth. **[3.4]**

Schwarz's *Mensch und Raum* lecture expanded these ideas, which were also elaborated in his monograph *Vom Bau der Kirche*, first published in Germany in 1938[61] and in the United States, with support from Mies van der Rohe, in 1958.[62] In this book, he envisioned the genesis of space as simultaneous with the genesis of a community and its liturgical expression. Space would then arise from perceptual givens that related each community member to both the here and the beyond. At the same time, he stated, the basic forms into which mankind organized itself were historically consistent. He explained,

"You all know that there are two great primary forms with which western architecture has struggled for millennia: the central form and the longitudinal form. The central form is the innermost concentration of a people's community to a unified work, and the

59   Rudolf Schwarz, "Das Unplanbare," in Conrads and Neitzke, *Mensch und Raum*, 91, 102, and 104.
60   Conrads and Neitzke, *Mensch und Raum*, 97–99.
61   Rudolf Schwarz, *Vom Bau der Kirche*, 2nd ed. (Heidelberg: L. Schneider, 1947 [1938]).
62   Rudolf Schwarz, *The Church Incarnate: The Sacred Function of Christian Architecture* (Chicago: H. Regnery, 1958).

63   Bartning, *Mensch und Raum*, 66–67.

longitudinal building is the built transposition of the path taken by a people. Both forms, which are very simple [...] cannot be achieved by an individual. The round form is something that is entirely inaccessible to the individual, since he is not circular in shape. The human being is directional, he has a certain space in front of him and behind him there is no longer anything. The round form [...] arises immediately once many humans join hands, sitting around a table or forming a ring. When they all enter together into something shared, then the round form appears instantaneously. [...] The longitudinal form arises when a community of people, like this one here in this audience, forms rows next to one another, behind one another; then suddenly the longitudinal building appears. [...] Through their sacrifice, the people become part of an entirely different world form, of an entirely new form of existence, which is given back to them again as individuals since they still retain their own personalities."[63]

If the primary forms of buildings simply arise from the two primary spatial forms of creating community—the joining of hands, the path taken—then what remains for architecture? In Schwarz's account, the architect is the bearer of spatial memory. Beholden to the innumerable people whose effort is embedded in these forms, themselves in some ways the "rubble" of earlier efforts that failed to achieve anything "pristine," is the architect who is able to give dimension to these forms and facilitates their realization:

"Architecture has developed its own language, or rather, its own methods [...]: plan, elevation, section. [...] [But] the true achievement of architecture [is]: many individuals sacrifice themselves, give themselves up to a community. [...] The point is not to listen to the 'demands of the hour,' which have nothing to do with architecture. The term 'modern architecture' is nonsense in itself. There is no modern architecture because architecture never calculates in terms of days or years, but in terms of stretches of time. It is essential and inherent to architecture that it is not calculated in terms of the individual, nor by the hour and its so-called demands.

3.4a Rudolf Schwarz and Albert Renger-Patzsch, *Wegweisung der Technik* 1928, affinities among plant life, architecture, and technology

69

73

3.4b

It is rooted in the great community of those who live now and in the other great community across epochs."[64]

Schwarz's "space" was tangible rather than abstract, representative of continuity rather than produced through an architect's will or genius, vessel for both order and disorder, meaningful in the moment of its realization but equally beholden to an imaginary of human community inextricable from Christian liturgy. Although he was effectively written out of mainstream architectural history, Schwarz enjoyed a renaissance in the 1990s in direct correspondence to the spatial interests of a generation of Swiss architects who studied with Aldo Rossi at ETH Zurich. His rejection of canonical modernist architecture and his efforts to realize an alternate trajectory in his buildings and writings finally found an audience.

Heidegger's podium talk, presented on Sunday morning after Schwarz's Saturday afternoon presentation, made equally sweeping claims about history while fastidiously avoiding Schwarz's overtly religious and Christological frame of reference. There are several points of comparison in the topics the two speakers addressed. Heidegger, too, condemned spatial abstraction, which he couched in Latinate words; by contrast, he used German-root words to describe space in its positive manifestations. His linguistic bent was transparent and somewhat stunning, given the context, although despite his association with National Socialist politics, respect for and reception of his philosophic works continued in the late 1940s and 1950s without skipping a beat.[65] Heidegger also addressed a divine force manifested in space, although he took it upon himself to apply his own term: the fourfold. He also addressed technology, a central consideration in modernist architectural theory; he returned it to its root term *techne*. Unlike Schwarz, however, his narrative of space's genesis was individual in nature rather than explicitly communal.

"Building Dwelling Thinking"[66] is too well known and well-studied to merit thorough treatment in a book with so many other interests. Nevertheless, although it has been widely anthologized, little has been said about the essay's context and less still about how it might have been received when it was first made public. A full history of its reception among

64   Bartning, *Mensch und Raum*, 66–67.
65   See for example Walter Schulz, "Über den philosophiegeschichtlichen Ort Martin Heideggers," *Philosophische Rundschau* 1 (1953/54).
66   Martin Heidegger, "Building Dwelling Thinking," in *Poetry, Language, Thought*, trans. Albert Hofstadter (New York: Harper Colophon, 1971).

architects, such as has been suggested at in recent work on phenomenology and architecture, is long overdue. Consider for a moment how the text's original audience might have heard it. The freshly de-Nazified among the crowd might have wondered at Heidegger's instrumentalization of German-root words to prove that his imaginary history, in which human activity began with space-making, was true and righteous. His interest in the boundary as the first act of space-making might have reminded them of concepts learned, earlier in the century, during their architectural studies, although Heidegger left these concepts uncited. Heidegger's resistance to invoking God by name might have irked the many church builders among his hosts and colleagues at the podium. Any or all of these choices could have struck his audience as odd, ill-informed, or objectionable. For a group deeply concerned with expiation of its National Socialist past, the insistence on a mythic German imaginary must have been suspect. For a group well-schooled in architectural theory, his musings on boundary might well have seemed poorly researched. And for his devoutly religious architect-hosts—Bartning, Schwarz, Schwippert—his resistance to admitting his own implicit theology might have seemed even worse. There was no opportunity for questions after his talk, which unlike all the others ran start to finish without any audience interjection, whether laughter, applause, or shouted commentary. Bartning, who spoke immediately after Heidegger, seemed glad to use the metaphor of a bridge to describe his own responsibility to forge connections among ideas, but went no further than that. He also stated it would take "no less than five days" to digest what they had heard. Since time was short, they needed to move on. Whatever the audience thought, it is lost to history.

Raum, in Heidegger's parlance, was the "place that is freed for settlement and lodging."[67] He related the term intimately to the dwelling cited in the *Mensch und Raum* preamble. He juxtaposed *Raum* to the Latinate *spatium* and *extensio*, which referred to spaces of measurement and universality, but not to the spaces inhabited in everyday life. "A space is something that has been made room for, something that has been freed, namely, within a boundary, Greek *peras*. [...] Space is in essence that for which room has been made, that which is let into its bounds. [...] *Accordingly, spaces receive their essential being from locales and not from 'space.'*"[68] Semper's wicker fence, the originary boundary that was the first act of architecture, had suggested a similar genesis. There was an important difference, however: Semper's fence was a gesture that created both separation and inclusion, whereas Heidegger seemed intent upon only what was held within the boundary. With Schwarz's discussion of the plannable and unplannable fresh in their minds, the audience might have noted an important difference here, too: that Schwarz's version of the human being had moved fluidly between plannable and unplannable, between localized and infinite space. The two kinds of spaces were concurrent. Heidegger, instead, insisted on an oppositional relationship between German- and Latin-root spaces, between the space of dwelling and the space of abstract intellectual thought. The tradition of abstraction and rationality, he argued, had come to dominate the space of dwelling, which was implicitly more authentic and valuable than the unbounded space of *extensio*.

Technology as a driver of architectural form, a favored architectural trope dating to the origins of architectural theory, was also upended in Heidegger's text. Returning to the Greek roots of the word "technology," cognate with the German *Technik*, Heidegger argued instead that building as an act of space-making preceded and transcended technology, since building introduced something absolutely new into the world whereas the product of any technology could only ever be a thing among other things already present:

"The Greeks conceive of *techne*, producing, in terms of letting appear. Techne thus conceived has been concealed in the tectonics of architecture since ancient times. Of late, it still remains concealed, and more resolutely, in the technology of power machinery.

67   Jorge Otero-Pailos, *A Polygraph of Architectural Phenomenology: Architecture's Historical Turn* (Minneapolis: University of Minnesota, 2010), 356.
68   Otero-Pailos, *Polygraph*, 356, emphasis in original.

But the essence of the erecting of buildings cannot be understood adequately in terms either of architecture or of engineering construction, nor in terms of a mere combination of the two. The erecting of buildings would not be suitably defined *even if* we were to think of it in the sense of the original Greek techne as *solely* a letting-appear, which brings something made, as something present, among the things that are already present. The essence of building is letting dwell."[69]

Likely obscured to a listener by his acrobatic linguistics, Heidegger's rendition of techne—the root word upon which "architect" itself is built—eliminated the etymological correlation between building and technology. This was a radical counterfeit. It reversed a tenet central to the entirety of architectural theory, and one celebrated in the preamble's assertion that this was indeed an "era of technology." It seems stunning that his listeners would not have objected, especially given the high intellectual caliber maintained during the open discussion that followed. Instead, the unraveling of the technology-building conjunction seemed to open up possibilities, especially among attendant practitioners. They had all dealt in the field with the dearth of technical and material options at their disposal. To be relieved of the burden of technology as determinate might have been liberating.

In his lecture "The Myth of Man behind Technology," Ortega y Gasset returned to the question of technology, bringing the discussion full circle from Schweizer's lecture on the previous day, though Ortega y Gasset's was utterly different in nature from all three preceding talks. His lecture was, by Ortega y Gasset's admission, only incompletely prepared. Downplaying his own impeccable German grammar, which enabled him to poke fun at Heidegger's insistence on language as first-hand evidence, he managed to elicit from the audience nine moments of laughter—Heidegger had earned not one—and five moments of applause. His "myth" translated Heidegger's assertions about techne and building, such as they were, into a more accessible register. Technology, he argued, had no capacity to produce *ex nihilo.* Instead, it created by drawing upon the world around it, *ex aliquo.*[70] This human tendency to produce through technology was linked to the human impulse to create the world anew. This impulse, arising from fundamental dissatisfaction with the world, was proof—he argued as if it were self-evident—that forward-looking mankind was in fact ill-suited to its natural world, which it therefore strove to transform. Mankind's act of refashioning the world to suit itself, he concluded, was in turn evidence of mankind's victory over technology.[71] Victorious over technology, equipped to reinvent the world, the audience was pleased with what Ortega y Gasset had offered them and glad to move on to their own thoughts.

It has been argued that the cultural disarray of the postwar period left a void in the public discussion on the built environment, beyond a crudely understood functional and financial calculation.[72] If this premise is accepted, then the conference organizers' decision to invite Heidegger and Ortega y Gasset was aspirational. Still it seems fair to imagine that Heidegger's "Building Dwelling Thinking" was more demanding than they could have anticipated. For the organizers, Heidegger's ontological story of how the act of dwelling was foundational to social formation might have resonated with the "homelessness" they had included in their preamble. Indeed, despite his difficult language delivered in an evangelical pitch on an impossibly hot day, his speech's immediate impact resounded in the language of those who led and participated in the discussions that followed the formal lectures. Nonetheless, the practicability and relevance of his ideas to German architecture in the accelerating economy of the 1950s is dubious, although his Darmstadt text remains a favorite of twenty-first century architecture students. If Schwarz's concept of space as congregational in nature, created by the joining of hands, is transparently theological, then it seems only appropriate to ask what Heidegger understood to be the activity allowed by architecture in 1951: what did it mean to "let dwell"? Aside from his references to a mythical

69   Otero-Pailos, *Polygraph*, 361.
70   Bartning, *Mensch und Raum*, 133.
71   Bartning, *Mensch und Raum*, 139.
72   Frederic J. Schwartz, "The Disappearing Bauhaus," in Jeffrey Saletnik and Robin Schuldenfrei, eds., *Bauhaus Construct: Fashioning Identity, Discourse and Modernism* (London: Routledge, 2009), 61–82.

German past, his text gives no answers.[73] Schwarz spent his career actualizing the kinds of spaces he foresaw. The renaissance in Schwarz scholarship over the past fifteen years attests to its relevance.

The audio recordings of these lectures make clear that the speakers made few concessions to ensuring that their intellectually demanding convictions were understood. The relentlessly declarative tone would have been even more difficult given conditions in the lecture hall, which Ulrich Conrads recalled was overfilled and swelteringly hot. It is hard to imagine how the audience would have had the capacity to reflect upon and discuss what they had heard over the past two days. Remarkably, the discussion is no less considered and perhaps even more interesting than the prepared speeches.

The role of stimulating an engaged, relevant discussion on space among the audience of largely practicing architects fell to Schwippert, whom Bartning invited to the microphone once applause for Ortega y Gasset faded. Schwippert's charge was to make the discourse of space more immediate. He began in a way that would have been familiar to everyone: with the modernist tenet that correlated an era's spirit, its spatial expression, and its material form. More than a trope, however, this tenet, and specifically the struggle with it, had characterized practice in the lean years between 1945 and 1951. What could spatial expression be when the spirit of an era was defeatist, technology was discredited or destroyed, and materials were scarce?

Because he demanded a direct connection to architectural practice, Schwippert raised the stakes beyond Schwarz's and Heidegger's spiritual and existential rhetoric. Space, Schwippert agreed, was the sine qua non characteristic of architecture by which architecture was to be judged if architecture was to remain meaningful. He spoke from the standpoint of an architect engaged every day in producing meaningful, built work. His brief presentation reframed discussion. Rather than speculating in general, historically vague ways about architectural genesis, he asked specifically how, in West Germany in 1951, space could be meaningfully configured. Schwippert's definition of meaningful space of course related to the fundamental, existential value ascribed to architecture by Schwarz and Heidegger. But it also opened up new questions: What is spatial building anyway? What does it mean to separate space from material when discussing architecture? Which is the sine qua non, if there were friction between these two constituent parts of architecture: the material or the space? Or is it the question of embodying meaning per se? And the question all the speakers had avoided until then: How could positive meaning be found in a collective so recently compromised by Fascism and broken by war?

Schwippert began his brief introduction to the discussion by seeking to describe the reciprocity between an era's spiritual urges and the spaces it inhabits. He coined the term *Wohnwollen*, clearly referencing Alois Riegl's *Kunstwollen*, perhaps also Theo van Doesburg's *Wille zum Stil*[74] to describe an era's spiritual desire for a specific kind of inhabitation. The will to inhabit, he claimed, might well be independent of the era's physical reality, as he hoped would be true in a Germany still deeply pessimistic. The will to inhabit and physical reality might diverge, he proposed; in this case, it would be the architect's role to give *Wohnwollen* expression, regardless of the physical resources at his disposal:

"What does the directive of building look like for us today? How does this dwelling appear to us, if we are to make it into building?
It seems to me that there is something quite peculiar here. In a time characterized by unrest, fear, and threat [...] we sense around the world a directive of building which is anything but a bastion of refuge. [...]
If dwelling precedes building, then we have to ask: is the affinity between the brightness and lightness of our spatial desire, on the one hand, and the technical means of contemporary building, on the other—is this affinity between these two things the only possibility given to us to build concretely in accordance to the internal directive? [...] If we had neither steel nor glass [...] would then spatial building

73   The conference organizers had foreseen Jose Ortega y Gasset as a foil to Heidegger. Ortega y Gasset seems to have captured the popular imagination: the archives of the Darmstädter Gespräch include clippings from at least five newspapers, dating from late fall 1951 through 1952, that reprint his speech: *Der Mittag* from Düsseldorf, which also reprinted Heidegger's speech; the *Stuttgarter Zeitung*; and the *Süddeutsche Zeitung*. His critique of Heidegger in Düsseldorf and Kempton during a speaking tour later that summer was covered in *Das freie Wort* and *Der Allgäuer* in early 1952.

74   Agatha Buslei-Wuppermann, "Hans Schwippert 1899–1973: Von der Werkkunst zum Design," (Diss., Bergische Universität Wuppertal, 2006, Utz Verlag, 2007), 43.

in the sense of the kind of dwelling we desire and require be forever eliminated? In other words, is that spatial being which most precisely bespeaks our dwelling on the earth today tied to the materials of today, or is this 'Wohnwollen' so strong that it can form all simple materials, even all other methods, even all older forms of building—that it can penetrate them?"[75]

To decouple material progress from spatial expression was in some ways analogous to Schwarz's insistence that architecture referenced a long temporal trajectory rather than being a direct expression of the specific time in which it is made. Material progress as a mandate to architecture, as noted, was canon within modernist architecture. To open the question of material appropriateness was certainly also pragmatic. It was difficult to find glass and steel for most building projects in the late 1940s, as Schwippert would have known firsthand. As architect of the new Bundeshaus, which he had aspirationally described as "a building of openness, an architecture of encounter and conversation,"[76] his own struggles with material limitations were legend. The new parliament ratified the desire that West German architecture express a new, light, aspirational postwar republic and its spiritual essence *in spite of* material scarcity. His apparent skepticism about "the technical means of contemporary building" as the "only possibility" may also explain the curatorial concept behind the accompanying exhibition: it presented an alternate modernism, one realized with a much less restrictive material palette. Under the circumstances, a lineage for modern architecture constructed quite literally from bricks and mortar might be advantageous.

Before allowing selected audience members to respond to these first questions, Schwippert added another. The experience of modernist architecture in the Third Reich, and immediately after the war, proved that architectural idiom was no guarantee of its authors' democratic politics. If indeed modernist architecture could be made without modern materials, was it also not the case that modern materials could be perverted? Schwippert's framing asked whether it would be "thinkable that someone could misuse the means of today [...] to make spaces that bear no relation to us?"[77] His words seem to refer to the fact that by 1951, modern architecture had become an official style, employed by architects of all prior political persuasions. They also articulate a larger question: could a former member of Speer's *engerer Arbeitsstab* make spaces that would bespeak the *Wohnwollen* of 1951?

Schwippert's questions cut both ways. If *Wohnwollen* were dependent upon material and architectural style, then either the lack or the misuse of material might be tantamount to "an end to spatial building."[78] Spatial building, in Schwippert's terms and in an echo of both Schwarz's and Heidegger's speeches, was the fundamental community-forming human activity. If it were merely dependent on or, perhaps worse, corruptible by virtue of materials, then there was little that the group assembled at *Mensch und Raum* could do. The complexity and difficulty of the problem Schwippert raised resurfaced again in the discussion of the *Meisterbauten*. Of those, the two projects at the extreme ends of the modernist spectrum—Hans Scharoun's atomized school and Paul Bonatz's symmetrical concert hall—were both the topic of heated debate.

Schwippert's words left the audience to ponder three distinct scenarios: that an affinity between spatial desire and technical means could be "the only possibility given to us to build concretely in accordance with the internal directive;" that spatial desire could be "so strong that it can form all simple materials, even all older forms of construction;" or that someone could "misuse the means of today [...] to make spaces that bear no relation to us."[79] Bartning as moderator invited respondents to the podium. He began with "the architect Sep Ruf." Ruf would not have been seen as a theoretician or rhetorician; his words were at best an oblique answer to Schwippert's challenge. But the way he practiced architecture, as evidenced in the impressive portfolio of projects he had completed between the end of the war and 1951, would have made him particularly well suited to Schwippert's purposes: his contemporaneous

75   Conrads and Neitzke, *Mensch und Raum*, 104–5.
76   Buslei-Wuppermann, "Hans Schwippert 1899–1973," 42.
77   Buslei-Wuppermann, "Hans Schwippert 1899–1973," 104–5.
78   Buslei-Wuppermann, "Hans Schwippert 1899–1973," 106.
79   Bartning, *Mensch und Raum*, 88.

buildings, one of which was included in the exhibition, had required virtuosic, bespoke detailing to attain their open spaces using modest construction means. As was the case with Schwippert, Ruf's practical experience would have equipped him well to discuss the friction between modernist architectural aspirations and the present material challenges to them.

Ruf's initial response, apparently prepared in advance of the event, revealed the ways in which his interests both aligned with and diverged from Schwippert's. Both shared the conviction that the era required open, communicative building, despite its fraught historic moment. As would emerge, however, they thought differently about how an architect should achieve this particular expression. Rather than address the question of material and construction, Ruf asserted the need for the architect to be valued as an artist, not for technical or construction skill. Rather than speaking directly about space as Schwippert, Schwarz, or Heidegger had, he introduced a different idea, that of the "spirit's atmosphere."

Ruf offered only to answer Schwippert's questions "partially at least for now, so as not to be compelled to speak about construction and its application,"[80] even if these did seem to be the topics at hand. On the one hand, his avoidance of the subject of construction belied the effort Ruf and his office expended on detailing. On the other hand, by reducing it to a commonplace, Ruf minimized the teleological force of technology as a driver of progress in architectural expression. He presented a scenario in which the architectural means to achieve openness could be chosen based on amenability, not technological currency. Rather than focus on the problem of means, Ruf instead proposed that contemporary architecture

"move forward into the spheres of the purely artistic. [...] We must achieve the same creative freedom with these building elements as other creative human beings who use words, color, and sound to achieve the artistic expression of their spiritual world in order to move in the same plane of formal creation. In architecture, this involves cognition of the essential form-defining elements: the pure metric, the vertical, the horizontal, in other words roof and column or wall, the opening that spans space. [...] The decisive aspect, I think, is that we know how to form the atmosphere, the spirit's atmosphere, and then we will find the form, too. Because architecture has to create a specific spatial feeling."[81]

His plea for architecture as an art form might well have been intended to rebuff the idea that architecture was technically motivated.[82] He proposed instead that architectural creation was not an independent art object, but rather that the built environment that could generate "atmosphere." Ruf was the only speaker at Darmstadt to use this term; it was not space per se, nor technology, but rather the "spirit's atmosphere" that he believed could produce an architecture appropriate to its time. Although it seemingly led him far afield from the given topic of *Mensch und Raum*, Ruf's desire to deflect attention from the technical manipulations at which he was so gifted and toward an ineffable, intangible architectural quality embodied in the vague term "atmosphere" suggests more than a wish not to be pigeonholed as a technician.

Ruf repositioned the relationship between spatial expression ("the opening that spans the space") and meaning ("conviction") within the purview of architecture as art and the architect as freely creative. He was also alone among the speakers in emphasizing the architect as singular and individual. Other speakers seemed more concerned with mankind rather than the singular human being—whether in the case of Schwarz's community, Heidegger's mysticism, Ortega y Gasset's culture, or Schwippert's *Wohnwollen*. Unsurprisingly, the position Ruf staked out in these passages found little approbation.

Bartning gave Ruf another opportunity later in the day to address Schwippert's challenge. Still speaking as practitioner, Ruf reframed what he had said in terms more amenable to the occasion:

"If the spatial form and that which today is necessary is clear in my mind—the open building which binds itself to nature—then I can express it, too, with the means from which earlier forms

80   Conrads and Neitzke, *Mensch und Raum*, 107.
81   Conrads and Neitzke, *Mensch und Raum*, 107–8.
82   Ruf accepted a professorship at the Academy of Arts in Nuremberg in 1950. His encounters at the art school may also have influenced his thinking about architecture as an art form.

83   Conrads and Neitzke, *Mensch und Raum*, 127.
84   The terms *Stimmung* and *Atmosphäre* also recur in documents related to the 1958 German pavilion at the Brussels World's Fair. "Atmosphere" is used frequently in the reception of SOM's corporate work, as in a 1957 book on Connecticut General Life published by the Schnelle brothers, founders of the Quickborn consulting group.

were made, with old building elements such as wood and stone. The decisive aspect, I think, is that we know how to form the atmosphere, the spiritual atmosphere, and then we will find the form, too. Because architecture has to create a specific spatial feeling [*Raumgefühl*]. I will always, if I am able to see forms artistically, be in a position to create a place of habitation that corresponds to the idea held of the dwelling today."[83]

Ruf was applauded twice during his second time at the lectern: first, when affirming that he could fashion the spatial forms of his time in older materials and again, when he assured the audience that, given the capacity to see artistically, the architect would be able to realize a place appropriate to habitation. In lieu of the words provided by the conference organizers—*Raum* or *Wohnwollen*—Ruf used words that, like "atmosphere," emphasized subjective response: "spatial feeling" (*Raumgefühl*) and "spatial form" (*Raumform*).

"Atmosphere" qualifies the impact of an architectural environment upon a subject, describing affect rather than the architectural object. In its evolving usage throughout the 1950s into the 1960s, the concept, in both its German language synonyms *Stimmung* and *Atmosphäre*, would encompass not only the architectural work, but its interior and exterior environment: design objects, landscaping, and cultivated subjectivity.[84] Ruf's use of "atmosphere" at *Mensch und Raum* presaged the discourse around *die gute Form* as framed by the German Werkbund. His inclination to base the architect's ability to calibrate space and

3.5 Ernst Neufert, interior perspective, home for single men, Darmstadt 1951

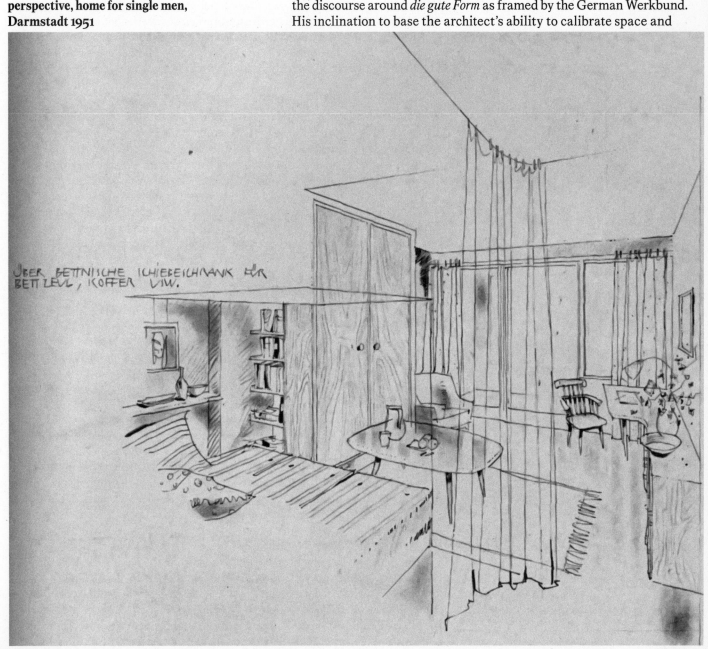

expression not upon technological or historical imperatives, but upon a specific kind of subjective response, was a novel answer to Schwippert's questions. This inclination, and the reinforcement it found in the emerging high modernist idiom exemplified by American firms abroad in the mid- to late 1950s, would also register in his changing construction practices in those transitional years.

There seems to have been general audience consensus that contemporary architecture could be characterized by the desire for openness and lightness, despite other differences. How, then, to account for Conrads's valid critique that the *Gespräch* did not succeed in defining an agenda that could translate its rhetoric into architectural practice for the decade to come? An answer might be found in the *Meisterbauten*. These projected buildings and their varying architectural idioms were hotly debated during the proceedings, particularly in reference to two projects, neither realized, by Hans Scharoun and Paul Bonatz. It was easy to contrast the splayed, irregular forms of Scharoun's school against the symmetrical, typologically referential ones of Bonatz's concert hall.[85] This contrast added little precision to the conception of a new architecture. As was already becoming evident internationally, the heterogeneity of postwar modernism, far from undermining its cultural relevance, would in fact grow to become its hallmark. Another tendency, signaled during *Mensch und Raum* by Ruf's interest in "atmosphere," might more subtly capture the architectural response to Schwippert's challenge of *Wohnwollen* in ways otherwise unforeseen during the podium discussion. That tendency asserted itself, as Schwippert predicted, in the domestic realm.

Indeed, the conference preamble declared homelessness to be "the exigency of our time," but only one of the *Meisterbauten* accommodated a residential program, a single-room-occupancy dormitory for single men by Ernst Neufert. [3.5] Neufert's building as drawn and as ultimately realized eloquently described a shift of architectural focus from communal space to individuated lifestyle and its objects. His success in securing the commission and realizing it also reflect the realpolitik of architectural practice, regardless of the aspirations to a greater ethics of architecture on display at *Mensch und Raum*. Neufert's biography offers ample evidence for the political non-alignment of modernist architecture as a style. He had studied at the Bauhaus in Weimar and been Gropius's technical collaborator, overseeing the building of the Bauhaus and the Masters' Houses in Dessau. He was later a professor at the Bauhochschule in Weimar under Otto Bartning. There, he had studied the normative dimensions and configurations on which he based his reference book *Bauentwurfslehre*, which was first published in 1936 and has been published uninterruptedly ever since. By 1936, however, Neufert's political allegiances belonged to the National Socialist party. In addition to freelance commissions in industrial architecture, Neufert established the norms for the design of hostels for the Hitler Youth, and by 1938 he was working directly for Albert Speer.[86] He regularly attended Rudolf Wolter's gatherings of former Speer associates in Coesfeld from 1947 to 1948 while enjoying a comparatively high standard of living provided by royalties on his *Bauentwurfslehre*.[87]

In Darmstadt, a local Christian Democratic Union party head intervened to secure an invitation for Neufert to author a *Meisterbau*. Neufert attended as a representative of the Technische Universität Darmstadt's architecture department, of which he was a prominent member. During the *Mensch und Raum* proceedings, Neufert was inclined to discretion. Unlike the other architects of the *Meisterbauten* in attendance, he did not participate in any public debate. His project presentation, given on the last day of the proceedings, described only his project's formal and problem-solving proposition. He omitted any speculation on the nature of its spaces or the larger principles governing its design.

There is at least small irony in the programmatic similarity between Neufert's *Meisterbau*, a single room occupancy for single working men, and the mid-1930s designs he produced under Speer for hostels in rural locations. The parallelism was underlined by Neufert's describing his

85   See Durth and Sigel, *Baukultur*, 477–78, for a discussion of the conflict between Scharoun and Bonatz. Conrads, in his introduction to his reprint of *Mensch und Raum*, laments that Scharoun's school was not realized. Conrads and Neitzke, *Mensch und Raum*, 9.

86   Durth, *Deutsche Architekten*, 115 and 150–55. Neufert's design for a housing block included a bomb shelter, peopled with the standard figures he used in his divide as *Bauentwurfslehre*.

87   Durth, *Deutsche Architekten*, 270.

Meisterbau as an "urban vacation home: near to the woods, with a row of cells next to one another."[88] Although Neufert's prominence makes his building a significant case study, it is of greater interest for the way it represents his attempt to apply a revised modernist vocabulary to the problem of inhabitation. Neufert described his building as a volumetric response to its urban context: rising topography, a line of remaining three-story buildings, proximity to the villa structure of the Mathildenhöhe. Certain design strategies recall Gropius and Meyer's Bauhaus on and in which he had worked: the use of ascending volumes, the central bridging element across an open axis, the expressive use of each individual room's balconies, the column grid's significance for the public spaces. The facade is, however, entirely different from the Bauhaus's industrial glazing and abstract white stucco. Neufert chose to face his building with dark-burnt clinker brick and intentionally integrated distended blocks into the bond, just as Aalto had done in his Baker House of 1947 as well as in other projects popularized in Giedion's revised history. The deeply colored, variegated bricks emphasized the building's sculptural qualities. Clearly it fell within a postwar modernist genre and was quite unlike the stuccoed "white" modernism that characterized both Schwippert's and Ruf's contemporary work.

The building's interior adapted early modernist *Existenzminimum* housing to suit a developing sense of lifestyle. The human figures for which Neufert's *Bauentwurfslehre* was famous did not appear in the orthographic and perspectival drawings produced for the exhibition, but were implicit in the most revealing drawing, a perspective. Rendered without a hard frame, the edges of its one-point perspective dissipating across the page, the drawing depicts one of the tiny one-room standard units. It is filled with signs of its occupation, although the contours of its spatial boundaries are left ambiguous. A vase and painting decorate the headboard–night stand, the bookshelf is full, a pitcher and glass stand next to a full fruit bowl on the low, rounded-corner table, and flowers decorate the sideboard. Few of these items seem compatible with the building's program of a men's single room occupancy meant for a displaced working bachelor with minimal income. Instead, they address a design-sensitized 1950s audience such as the one in attendance at the *Mensch und Raum* exhibition.

Like the curtain at the room's entry and the walled balcony intended as a gesture to privacy, the plethora of domestic design objects shown also described the tension between communal living (here, by necessity) and a growing desire for individuality. Unlike the balconies or terraces used as a unifying gesture in the Weimar housing projects of Bruno Taut or Ernst May, each balcony asserted the presence of an individual to "produce a rhythm that describes the interior purpose." Imagining the ground floor public rooms, Neufert described "late afternoon and evening sun, advantageous resting places in the open air for people who are usually at work outside of the home from morning to afternoon."[89] And when would the weary bachelor find time to sit there? With its "open and unobstructed view to the outside,"[90] celebrating continuity between interior and exterior, Neufert's building retained standard modernist gestures. But its vision of community neglected to address the implications of cohabitation by necessity and remained in tension with its architecture's emphasis on individual expression.

"The exigency of our time is homelessness," the organizers of *Mensch und Raum* had proclaimed. By 1951, the accelerating pace of rebuilding, combined with a cultural shift that would produce the consumer culture of the *Wirtschaftswunder*, had already taken hold of the genre that had best embodied the utopian impulse of early modernist architecture: housing. The sheer physical need for accommodation took precedence over what the preamble had foreseen: an architectural discourse for which dwelling has political or ethical potential. Those architects who, in *Mensch und Raum*, strove to anchor "space" in a fundamental conceptual lineage—not coincidentally, architects whose works and thoughts have attracted increasing architecture-historical interest in the past ten

88   Durth, *Deutsche Architekten*, 185.
89   Durth, *Deutsche Architekten*, 184 and 189.
90   Durth, *Deutsche Architekten*, 189.

91   Werner Durth describes Helmut
Hentrich and Hubert Petschnigg's first visit to
the United States and the way in which SOM's
buildings became their models. Durth, *Deutsche
Architekten*, 371.

years—were instead compelled to realize their ambitions in other building types. Expedience prevailed and the attempt to create a new, distinct lineage of modern architecture was subsumed in a more generic modernist idiom. Although none of *Mensch und Raum*'s important participants can be considered marginal, their combined influence on the stylistic turn taken by West German architecture in the 1950s was less than that of other models.[91] Neufert's perspective rendering proved prescient. Stuff, not space, was quickly becoming the medium in which *Wohnwollen* left its imprint. Stuff, in turn, became the focus of Hans Schwippert's work as well, as it would culminate in his curation of the German Federal Republic's pavilion at the Brussels World's Fair in 1958.

The quotation in the chapter title is taken from Hermann Mäckler to Walter Gropius, July 21, 1950 (carbon copy), Series III, file 1153, Walter Gropius Papers, 1925–1969 (MS Ger 208), Houghton Library, Harvard University.

"Harassed by Worldview"

The Bauhaus Debate

A contemporary visitor to the museum that was once Walter and Ise Gropius's house in Lincoln, Massachusetts, could be forgiven for thinking that life there was at least a bit of a come-down. The compass of the couple's world was small by comparison to their prior lives: how, after the glamor of their years at the Bauhaus and in Berlin, could the Gropiuses have been content with their comparatively modest suburban house? In truth, however, the move to Massachusetts marked an expansion in influence. The sway held by the Gropius Bauhaus even today originated in the years Walter Gropius spent at Harvard, without which the Bauhaus might have remained important but undistinguished among the inter-war European avant-garde. Ultimately, he would claim, the stakes were no less than those of democracy itself. He would let nothing dissuade him: an under-discussed debate about the stature of the Bauhaus, staged in 1953 on the pages of a small-run West German magazine, makes this fact clear. By the time the conflict had been resolved, a contentious attempt by a few influential West German architects to write a different Bauhaus history had proved futile.

The reluctance to reevaluate the Bauhaus in its postwar historiography persists. A hundred years after its founding, even as recent scholarship fundamentally reconsiders its claims to social promise, gender equity,[01] and economic transformation, the Bauhaus remains an easy popular shorthand for the modernist imaginary. Much of the credit for this account is due to Gropius and his Cambridge associate, Swiss historian Sigfried Giedion, who was invited to join the teaching staff at Harvard in no small part because of Gropius's advocacy. Two recent studies, which were published to coincide with the Bauhaus centennial, evaluate the impact of American immigration on the two men's identities,[02] both personal and professional. Gropius became a US citizen in 1944. The Bauhaus's American naturalization, as it were, might well be dated even earlier, to Giedion's 1941 *Space, Time and Architecture*, which positioned the Bauhaus at the decisive threshold between the proto-modern—Frank Lloyd Wright, Tony Garnier, and Robert Maillart among others—and everything that followed. The book put modern architecture on the map in the United States. It was, as Philip Johnson said at the time, "the biggest book in this country."[03]

But even as its former masters circulated around the globe, questions of the Bauhaus's true identity remained fraught, as was revealed in an unlikely manner. The Bauhaus debate, as it was called within months of its inception, began with the 1953 issue of the Werkbund journal *Baukunst und Werkform*[04] and its publication of Rudolf Schwarz's damning, if meandering observations on the architect as thinker and maker. Its title turned Johann Wolfgang von Goethe's axiom, "Bilde, Künstler! Rede nicht!" (create, artist, do not speak!) to ironic effect. Schwarz set up his argument simply, in a way that for readers "comfortable with Schwarzian diction," promised "an aperitif not without its own bitter drop [invoking] an appetite for the subsequent menu which, as one may expect of a master chef, would really have something to offer."[05] Schwarz's text was supposed to have introduced the architectural projects of the journal's editor-in-chief Alfons Leitl, but this was merely a canard. [4.1]

Leitl's achievements as an architectural journalist were impressive and his standing untainted by National Socialist Party affiliation. He had begun work as a journalist in 1928 just after high school at the architecture weekly *Bauwelt* in Berlin.[06] Throughout the 1930s and 1940s, he wrote consistently about modernist architecture for both *Bauwelt* and *Wasmuths Monatshefte für Baukunst*. In 1939, drawing upon what he had learned as a journalist and during a yearlong internship for a Berlin architect, Leitl and a partner opened their own architectural practice.

By 1953, Leitl had designed some twenty churches, most of which were realized, in addition to private houses, multifamily dwellings, and school buildings. From 1947 onwards, he served as head of city planning

01　Several excellent studies on women at the Bauhaus were published in celebration of its centennial, building upon the exemplary work of Elizabeth Otto and others. See, for example, Karl Uwe Schierz, Patrick Rössler, Miriam Krautwurst, and Elizabeth Otto, *4 "Bauhausmädels": Getrud Arndt, Marianne Brandt, Margarete Heymann, Margaretha Reichardt* (Dresden: Sandstein, 2019); Elizabeth Otto and Patrick Rössler, *Bauhaus Women: A Global Perspective* (New York: Bloomsbury, 2019); Patrick Rössler, *Bauhausmädels: A Tribute to the Bauhaus's Women Artists* (Cologne: Taschen, 2019). Also see *Wolkenkuckucksheim/Cloud-Cuckoo-Land* 24 no. 39 (2019). These are only a few instances of ways in which Bauhaus history is being constantly rewritten.

02　See, for example, Fiona MacCarthy, *Walter Gropius: The Man Who Built the Bauhaus* (Cambridge, MA: Harvard University Press, 2019) and Reto Geiser, *Giedion and America: Repositioning the History of Modern Architecture* (Zurich: gta Verlag, 2018).

03　Philip Johnson, interview, February 6, 1991, by Sharon Zane. Cited in Geiser, *Giedion and America*, 157.

04　*Baukunst und Werkform* 6 nos. 1, 2/3 (1953).

05　Hermann Mäckler, "Praeceptor Germaniae et Europae?" *Baukunst und Werkform* 6 no. 2/3 (1953), 65.

06　Johannes Busmann, *Die revidierte Moderne: Der Architekt Alfons Leitl 1909–1975* (Wuppertal: Müller und Busmann, 1995), 10–15.

07   Ulrich Conrads, "Aus der Redaktion geplaudert," in Ulrich Conrads et al., *Die Bauhaus-Debatte 1953: Dokumente einer verdrängten Kontroverse*, Bauwelt Fundamente (Braunschweig: Vieweg, 1994).

08   As was well documented in the early issues of *Baukunst und Werkform*, this was not unique to Leitl. See Ulrich Conrads, *Die Städte himmeloffen: Reden und Reflexionen über den Wiederaufbau des Untergegangenen und die Wiederkehr des neuen Bauens 1948/49*, Bauwelt Fundamente (Basel: Birkhäuser, 2003).

09   Conrads et al., *Die Bauhaus-Debatte 1953*, 20.

10   Alfons Leitl to Rudolf Schwarz, December 16, 1952, in *Die Bauhaus-Debatte 1953*, 25.

11   Conrads et al., *Die Bauhaus-Debatte 1953*, 20.

for Rheydt and Wesel, two small Rhineland cities that had suffered near-complete destruction during the bombings directed at German industry. Beginning in 1949, he took responsibility for the reconstruction of the historically significant city of Trier. All the while, he had served as *Baukunst und Werkform*'s editor-in-chief. Certainly the scope and quantity of his architectural production merited journalistic attention; he was tired of being ignored.[07] Perhaps, as Leitl speculated in the text he would ultimately write to accompany the publication of his architectural projects, his work was ignored because, although not a party member, he had spent time during the Third Reich in the office of Hermann Rimpl, the architect and National Socialist party member responsible under Albert Speer for factories, hangars, and other technical buildings in a modernist style.[08] However, he argued, he was not the only architect of his generation to have made this mistake. Rather than relent, Leitl found a fix for the embarrassment of self-publication:[09] Schwarz, an architect of unimpeachable standing, would author a text on "writing and building" to accompany publication of his church buildings. The outcome was disastrous for Leitl. By May of 1954, he resigned his editorial position entirely. He found no pleasure in editorial work after the "discussion on the Bauhaus."[10]

As Ulrich Conrads noted in his introduction to the 1994 reprint of the documents that form the Bauhaus debate, published while Conrads was Leitl's associate editor, he had warned against the dangers to Leitl's journalistic reputation that would accompany self-publication. Leitl was nonetheless driven to proceed. Conrads recalled that "Leitl not only refused to acknowledge the argument [that he would risk his authority and credibility as a critic by publishing his own work] but with annoyance, he reined me back in my role as editor. None other than Rudolf Schwarz would write the commentary on his buildings."[11] True to his word, Leitl published Schwarz's text without any editorial changes

4.1 *Baukunst und Werkform* covers, 1951–1953

although it was in no way the architectural commentary he had asked for, and "rushed and peeved, went about writing the commentary on his buildings himself [...] under the title *A Few Reservations*."[12] It was Schwarz's text, not Leitl's architecture, which drew attention from the architectural community.

Schwarz, whose texts were generally written in a messianic, polemical tone, began in a tactically innocuous manner: upon the request of his friend Leitl, he had agreed to write the forward for a special January 1953 issue on Leitl's built work. His recriminations against the Bauhaus in the text that followed attracted notice well beyond the periodical's relatively small circulation. The January issue was only the beginning. A February / March double issue was dedicated to protests against Schwarz's assertions. Leitl, feeling compelled to print these responses, transformed his magazine into a forum for this "Bauhaus debate." The resulting documents offer a rare but pointed microcosm of the tensions between the German architects who remained in West Germany after the war and their better-known émigré colleagues who had left, many for the United States, in the 1930s and early 1940s. These tensions were in part exacerbated by the US Army-sponsored appointment of expatriate Germans as advisors to reconstruction programs; but as the intensity of the Bauhaus debate shows, there was more at stake than personal affinity or rivalry.

The text Schwarz wrote for the January issue began with a rhetorical question: how could he have resisted his friend Leitl? A chat between the two men over dinner in a Cologne hotel, its clubby atmosphere spilling into Schwarz's initially avuncular tone, provided the pretense for a text that made no reference at all to Leitl's architecture but instead descried a general loss of moral and humanist values in architecture. At the heart of Schwarz's diatribe was an explosive recrimination: he claimed that although this moral vacuum had been exacerbated by National Socialist censorship, it had begun with Bauhaus technocracy. Schwarz's Bauhaus critique was nothing new. He had voiced it in a 1929 essay on the *Neues Bauen*,[13] written as Gropius transitioned from Bauhaus directorship to private architectural practice in Berlin. At that time, there was no response to his critique from Bauhaus circles. This time, the response, carried out publicly with *Baukunst und Werkform*'s readership as audience, was stronger than even a comparison of the Bauhaus and National Socialism could plausibly explain.

The January issue featuring Schwarz's article and the February / March issue dedicated to reader responses reflect the full breadth of national and philosophical tensions at stake in the Bauhaus legacy. For expatriates in the United States, this legacy ensured continuity with their past and relevance within the unfolding story of modern architecture. For West German architects, however, the subsumption of the Bauhaus within historiography of the International Style overshadowed their own Weimar-era work. With many powerful Bauhaus masters in the United States, there was a sense that German modernism was no longer rooted in its country of origin. There was much to contest.

Schwarz's peripatetic article, full of innuendos and references that are often difficult to decode, was nonetheless radical, a shot across the bow. It proposes a counter-lineage to Bauhaus-based modern architecture. The intense controversy to which his assertions led reveals how important the version of Bauhaus history written in the United States during and after the war was both to Gropius and his circle. It was no less important to West German architects as they struggled to envision a new architecture that uniquely reflected their circumstances. But the fact that the entire debate has largely been forgotten makes clear that the more influential side—Gropius's—emerged successful. For Conrads, the affair seems to have revealed something psychological, an aspect to which he alluded in his book's subtitle: "a repressed controversy."[14]

At the time of his article's publication, Schwarz was one of Germany's foremost church architects. [4.2] As the chief urban planner for the reconstruction of Cologne, he would entirely reimagine the historic city. He had co-signed the preface to *Baukunst und Werkform*'s first issue

12   Conrads et al., *Die Bauhaus-Debatte 1953*, 20–22.
13   See Rudolf Schwarz's article "Neues Bauen," originally published in *Die Schildgenossen* in 1927, reprinted in Rudolf Schwarz, *Wegweisung der Technik und andere Schriften zum Neuen Bauen, 1926–1961*, Bauwelt Fundamente (Braunschweig: Vieweg, 1979), 121–31.
14   Conrads et al., *Die Bauhaus-Debatte 1953: Dokumente einer verdrängten Kontroverse*.

in 1947, which described the situation for architects in West Germany as a choice between "desperation" and a "return to the foundation."[15] By 1953, however, desperation had given way to normalcy, and the "return to the foundation" had assumed a different cast. Modernism had become a style shared across the political spectrum during the *Wiederaufbau*. Moreover, the possibility of a uniquely West German modern architecture seemed increasingly remote as America's cultural agenda of export and its hand in rebuilding German industry yielded an increasingly strong influence on the planning, design, and realization of new buildings, especially larger-scale projects.

Schwarz, for his part, felt able to explain why Leitl's work had been ignored. It was not, he claimed, that Leitl's reputation as a journalist overshadowed his ability as an architect. Rather, the generally anti-intellectual environment of architectural practice precluded recognition altogether:

> "[Leitl's readers and fellow architects] apparently cannot imagine that someone can write so well and nonetheless still be an architect who knows how to build as clearly and cleanly as he can write, and they counter with the sentence I have used as a title [*Bilde Künstler, rede nicht*]. [...] They appear to assert a division of labor in the discipline of building, since there are actually quite a few people who can write beautifully and with extraordinary depth. [...] Ill-meaning people misinterpret the words of Goethe and rewrite them as "mess around, artist, don't think." I tried furthermore to console [Leitl] with the observation that it is probably the fault of these "art historians" if so many clever lads in our line of work think so little of the written word."[16]

The press's refusal to recognize Leitl, Schwarz insinuated, was part of a larger problem. It arose, he argued, from a functionalist division of labor within the architectural profession, a division inspiring disbelief that any practicing architect could express himself with intellectual rigor—or even more damning, that an intellectual such as Leitl could ever practice architecture. Schwarz laid out the four primary interrelated points of critique upon which he built his argument: the rise of an "art historical" perspective on architecture; the loss of cultural depth in architectural training; a trend Schwarz called "materialism," his shorthand for technocracy, which he juxtaposed to his theological worldview; and the ruptured relationship to history that these factors produced. He credited the acceleration of all four pernicious tendencies to the Bauhaus and its impact on pedagogy.

Schwarz argued that changes in education had made architects susceptible to what he called an "art historical" perspective:

> "We began to ponder why the architects have allowed themselves to be so bowled over by the art historians without even the quietest of sighs, whereas the physicians have remained the masters of their own homes. It became clear to us that it arose from their inadequate educations—they learn constructive geometry while medical students internalize intellectual discipline. We decided to reconfigure the education of architects. In the future, they would have to complete a basic course in humanities, to include philosophy, theology, sociology, economy, mathematics, natural science, and the German language. This way, no one could intimidate them and, at this glorious moment, we thought of our friend Mies, who openly admitted that he had learned much more from the pictorial orders of Saint Augustine and Thomas than from the whole of functionalism."[17]

In his own undertakings, Schwarz was no more opposed to art history per se than he was to photography, which he also roundly criticized in his article for its role in abstracting and usurping the veracity of vision as part of human consciousness. This seems hard to square with his keen use of both in the 1920s publication *Die Schildgenossen*, one of his collaborations with the photographer Albert Renger-Patzsch.[18] Here, however, he criticized architecture's subjugation to the dual contemporary

15   Werner Durth, *Deutsche Architekten: Biographische Verflechtungen 1900–1970*, Schriften des Deutschen Architekturmuseums zur Architekturgeschichte und Architektur-theorie (Braunschweig: Vieweg, 1986), 59.
16   Durth, *Deutsche Architekten*, 37–38.
17   Rudolf Schwarz in Conrads et al., *Die Bauhaus-Debatte 1953*, 38–39.
18   Schwarz, *Wegweisung der Technik*.

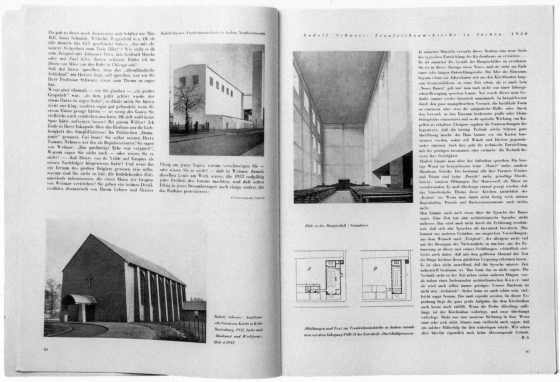

4.2 Two churches by Rudolf Schwarz, *Baukunst und Werkform* 7, 1953

phenomena of art criticism and photographic representation. The Bauhaus, he insisted, was the moving force behind both. Its pedagogical and self-promotional practices were at fault, he claimed, not only during the period of its existence in Germany but also, he implied, thereafter, as its denizens enjoyed successes facilitated by their years together in Weimar and Dessau.[19]

A shift in architectural education away from the humanities and towards exclusively technical matters ceded the leverage that art historians now enjoyed over architects, who had been reduced to learning "constructive geometry while medical students internalize intellectual discipline." Schwarz himself had enjoyed a broad liberal education but had nonetheless interrupted his architecture coursework to study theology in Berlin. Schwarz maintained a long-term relationship with the Catholic theologian Romano Guardini, working with him on *Die Schildgenossen* in the 1920s. Guardini's influence was evident in Schwarz's understanding of technology.[20] Ludwig Mies van der Rohe, another Guardini acolyte with whom Schwarz was befriended, organized a 1958 American edition of *Vom Bau der Kirche* under the title *The Church Incarnate*. It would be Schwarz's only text translated into English. Mies van der Rohe held an unassailable position among West German architects despite his emigration and American naturalization in the same year as Gropius. Recourse to Mies van der Rohe's reliance upon theology as a basis for spatial thinking was strategic and prepared for assertions Schwarz would make later in his article.

In the speech he had delivered at the 1951 Darmstädter Gespräch, Schwarz had described photographic technology as part of the technocratic "cage" that had been imposed on space and had resulted in an architectural practice obsessed with a monocular, dehumanized vision. In its slightly different 1953 permutation for *Baukunst und Werkform*, his critique descried, on the one hand, the glorification of technology over intellect in the Bauhaus's version of "materialization"[21] and on the other, the intellectualization of technology in the photography-dependent practice of art history. The two symbiotic tendencies undermine the genesis of space through the collective, as was also detailed in *Vom Bau der Kirche*.

"Unfortunately, one cannot be angry, since it is really somewhat difficult with art historians. They occupy an aesthetic location and view the world from there. They betray this fact by printing so many photographs in their books, because the photographic machine is just what they need. It steers the eye from a singular point into the

19   See Claire Zimmerman, *Photographic Architecture in the Twentieth Century* (Minneapolis: University of Minnesota Press, 2014).
20   See Alexander Henning Smolian, "Serie oder Persönlichkeit—zum Technikverständnis von Rudolf Schwarz," *Wolkenkuckucksheim/Cloud-Cuckoo-Land* 19 no. 33 (2014), 193–209, cloud-cuckoo.net/fileadmin/issues_en/issue_33/article_smolian.pdf, accessed December 16, 2021.
21   Conrads et al., *Die Bauhaus-Debatte 1953*, 48.

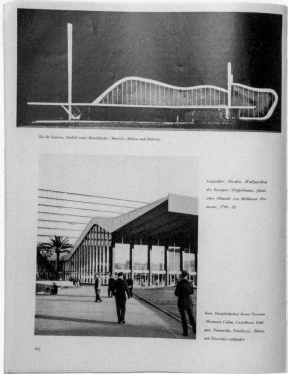

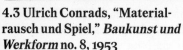

4.3 Ulrich Conrads, "Material-rausch und Spiel," *Baukunst und Werkform* **no. 8, 1953**

architectural stratosphere, whereas the true architect elevates a community of people into a common, completely clarified form."[22] The significance of the photographic image in architecture, both as a means of working and as a means to coalesce an interwar avant-garde throughout Europe, is well documented.[23] The Bauhaus had participated in and benefited from these parallel developments in photography and publicity. A very different visual culture and photography preoccupied *Baukunst und Werkform* in the early 1950s. **[4.3]** A photographic essay in the August 1953 issue by Ulrich Conrads entitled "Material Intoxication and Play: Notes on the Situation of the *Neues Bauen*" argues against the assertion that "play and intoxication have nothing to do with modern architecture; they are remnants of a time when court and church architects were always compelled to achieve the most precious, splendid, celebratory and largest. [...] But today [...] we know the arguments too well: Socialism, need, hard times, sobriety, functionality."[24] A reverse print of a 1905 cable and truss drawbridge, its filament-like members white, seen from below against the largely black background, faces an interior image of a Gothic cathedral, its massive stone tracery foregrounded in strong two-point perspective. Another spread compares a cast concrete storage building by Pier Luigi Nervi to an oblique exterior photograph of a sixteenth-century guild house in Strasbourg; the two photographs' perspective lines meet almost symmetrically in the magazine's binding. Perhaps the strangest pairing is a photograph of the UN Secretariat Building, still surrounded by the construction site that would produce the rest of the complex, with a seventeenth-century Wurzburg facade. Conrads's photographs of historic and current buildings argue for the intoxication of materials (*Materialrausch*) against the truth of materials (*Material-gerechtigkeit*). He proposes eroticism (*Erotik*) in favor of the "joyless harmony" purveyed by "serious" architects while never deserting the idiom of modernism. Conrads's final sentences leave no doubt about his affinity for Schwarz's position:

"This is not a call for "back to nature," as it might be misunderstood. Because when we speak about "fundamental experiences," we meant *our* experiences, the experience of the "here and now." [...] But those who—since we have spoken about material—define this approach as truncated materialism should be told, in lieu of any number of other retorts: "Physicality is the endpoint of God's path." It seems to us that there is enough in this statement to meditate upon for a good while longer."[25]

22   Conrads et al., *Die Bauhaus-Debatte 1953*, 38.
23   See Zimmerman, *Photographic Architecture* or Beatriz Colomina, *Privacy and Publicity: Modern Architecture as Mass Media* (Cambridge, MA: MIT Press, 1994).
24   Ulrich Conrads, "Materialrausch und Spiel: Notizen zur Situation des neuen Bauens," *Baukunst und Werkform* no. 2/3, no. 8 (1953), 392–407.
25   Conrads, "Materialrausch und Spiel," 407.

Throughout the Bauhaus debate, *Baukunst und Werkform*'s editors demonstrated their finesse, using photography in a strategic and nuanced manner. In both issues dedicated to the debate, their juxtapositions of comparable images with divergent texts take aim at the International Style practice of eliding the work of radically different architects to assert a unified style. *Baukunst und Werkform*'s illustrations, by contrast, revealed stylistic commonalities between the two architects whose philosophical disagreement was at stake. For example, next to a text written by Franz Meunier, Leitl's close associate, and the text editor for *Baukunst und Werkform*, is a Bauhaus-era image by Herbert Bayer. Dating to 1931, it shows a still life of a cone, sphere, drafting triangle, and pen, which cast a sharp shadow onto a folded newsletter with the heading "Bauhaus." The overleaf page depicts a 1928 Schwarz project for a church composed of three tall cylinders, reprinted from *Die Schildgenossen*. Cone, sphere, and cylinder: the classical Platonic solids imply a formal affinity between Bauhaus and Schwarz. Neither image is referenced in the texts. They constitute their own, visual rhetoric.

Several pages later, above a text by former Bauhaus student Paul Klopfer are two photographs of prismatic, white stucco and glass villas, both viewed past a fringe of overhanging foliage. On the left is Schwarz's Volk House (Offenbach, 1933–1934) and on the right, Gropius's 1935 house for British Politician Benn Levy near London. The two photographs' composition and prominent foliage foreground their similarities: both display garden-side views, pipe railings, flat roofs, and expansive glazing despite differences in the windows' configurations, which comprise tall French doors in Schwarz's building and horizontal band windows in Gropius's. **[4.4]**

As a graphic argument, the published images underline affinities, an approach that might have been intended to assuage offended readers by pointing to similarities between the two architects, both on the side of modern architecture. This approach, however, might also be read differently, as a way of underscoring the distinction Schwarz had made: that a genuine critique of the Bauhaus was *not* concerned with appearance, nor could it be reduced to formal or stylistic preference. The similarities depicted in the photographs prompted readers to think more deeply about the distinction between the two factions at war in the text. In his suspicion of purely visual argumentation, Schwarz set himself apart from the publicist methods of the Gropius Bauhaus and its continuation in the United States.

4.4 Villas by Rudolf Schwarz (left) and Walter Gropius (right), *Baukunst und Werkform* **no. 2/3, 1953**

Baukunst und Werkform tended to publish little of the architecture emerging from the United States, although this scant coverage might well have been out of step with its readership. An advertisement on the back cover of the July 1951 issue offered no fewer than thirty American books on architecture, planning, décor, and lifestyle. Their titles reveal an American market at odds with the serious, text-heavy content of the magazine in which the advertisement was placed: *Window Displays, The Specialty Shop, Furnishing with Color, America's Best Small Houses.* These were books directed at the homeowner and the industry charged with attracting his (or her?) disposable income. In its editorial content, by contrast, *Baukunst und Werkform* featured primarily European projects and industrial arts. As an example, in the eight 1953 issues not dedicated at least in part to the Bauhaus debate, the featured articles and illustrations showed recent work in Scandinavia, Northern Italy, and France. Only two American authors were included, neither of whom were canonical or commonly known: Saul Steinberg, whose ironic architectural drawings and caricatures sent up big cities, highway-hugging suburbs, and stick-built "machines for living;" and Bruce Goff, an autodidact to whose inimitable art and architecture the entire July issue was dedicated, without comment by the magazine's editors.

One notable exception to the dearth of American architecture are the pages dedicated to Mies van der Rohe on the occasion of his sixty-fifth birthday in 1951. The special affinity among this cadre of German architects for him and his work set Mies apart from the other expatriate Germans in the United States. Leitl's hyperbolic text, accompanied by a series of construction details and photographs otherwise rare in this magazine, ends with a quotation from a conversation held during Mies van der Rohe's most recent visit to Germany. In the context of the Bauhaus debate and its recasting of German cultural history, the last sentences are particularly striking:

"Surely, Mies's trailblazing work has already become part of the history of modern architecture, but the creative, pedagogic power that emanates from him is the strongest reality. Mies van der Rohe is a classic of modern architecture. His work, his path— followed with unshakable calm and magnanimity—is disturbed neither by conflict nor by fluctuations in the opinions of the day. Every building and every detail that comes from his hand has the absolute balance and clarity that only few architects have achieved in the haste of everyday building. [...] When we last met Mies van der Rohe in Berlin, the newspapers were full of complimentary reports on the record-breaking accomplishments for Speer's *Reichskanzlei,* which had risen from the ground in only a year. Mies said only one sentence on the subject: "Now they are proud that they accomplished this in one year but they don't know how difficult it is to make even only a baseboard correctly." It is this knowledge that we can all always learn from Mies again."[26]

Leitl juxtaposed Mies van der Rohe's deliberateness and slowness— an unlikely characterization given his prolific postwar American production—with Speer's vulgar speed. The photographs of towering steel frames and foundation footings many times the size of construction workers were described not as examples of cutting-edge technology, as another rhetorical strand would have had them, but instead, as classics beyond "the opinions of the day." Even if it seems hard to believe that a baseboard detail is the essential difference, for Leitl and his circle, the act of construction at the scale of such details seems to have been an article of faith.

Schwarz, for his part, allowed this appreciation for the integrity of construction details to include the Bauhaus, despite his critiques. Even the detail that failed was evidence of commitment to untried forms of building. But hidden within his defense of the Bauhaus's material experimentation was another critique: that material or technological logic did not validate an architectural work. The criteria should not derive from the ability to keep out rain or cold, he argued:

26   Alfons Leitl, "Anmerkungen," *Baukunst und Werkform* 5 (May 1951), 11.

"It is a riveting moment when an architect finally, finally, is permitted to build his glass cube, even if the excuse for it is a factory building, and it is reassuring and almost metaphysically necessary that its roof leak and that as a whole, it perform as if it were a greenhouse. There is nothing aggravating and nothing wrong about that; but the architect should not merely insist that this glass cube is the result of functionalist calculus."[27]

A glass cube as factory building: Schwarz's words are a thinly veiled reference to Gropius's Bauhaus building, with its concrete structure and industrial glazed facade. The construction of a factory with architectural aspirations could be "riveting," according to Schwarz, but only if its intellectual underpinning transcended functionality. Schwarz took functionalism to task not for claiming construction integrity, from the lack of which many early modern buildings suffered, but instead for its aspiration to bridge the gap between intellectual ambitions and their physical expression. By separating polemic from the physical object it deployed, Schwarz also positioned himself to stage a more sweeping critique. The imperative that modern architecture express function, construction, and material integrally was a foundation of prevailing rhetoric. Schwarz dismissed this imperative. Architectural ambitions, he explained, are myriad. Recourse to a crude "materialist" mandate was no way to justify a form by virtue of the way it housed activities and the manner in which it was put together.

The visual training adopted from the Bauhaus model and further developed at Harvard's Graduate School of Design under Gropius returned each year to first principles of composition as a way to codify artistic method through its fundamentals: space and color. To place empirical visual principles alone at the center of an architect's training ran counter to Schwarz's call for humanist pedagogy. Schwarz explained this view explicitly in the second article he wrote for Leitl to conclude the Bauhaus debate: "Certainly architecture cannot float freely in space as if it were objectless painting; precisely this was the greatest danger of the "Bauhaus Style." "[28] Architecture that floated "freely in space" on the basis of a conviction that space itself had somehow changed its essence was untethered from the historic dictates of physical gravity and spiritual transcendence, which were so important to Schwarz.

From the start of the Bauhaus debate, Schwarz had advocated for a re-evaluation of historical style, the perennial nemesis of avant-garde modern architecture. He dismissed the idea that style could be a proxy for quality. He defended the architects of the past against the dogma of anti-eclecticism when he wrote, "I consider it to be a sign of an ignoble and narrow mind to despise a genius only because it makes use of an appropriated language. A genius goes its own infallible way and changes its garb."[29] He urged reconsideration of the nineteenth century, much maligned in the literature of modern architecture, and recast the history of German architecture along spiritual lines that were expressed in style: the Gothic and the Antique. These two tendencies, he claimed, had always suffused German culture, from Goethe and Karl Friedrich Schinkel to Novalis and Franz Brentano:

"For the untalented, style is a recipe for making art without actually being able to; for the talented, it is a vocabulary. [...] Perhaps the great historical achievement of the Germans is less in the invention of new forms, but rather in the illumination, amalgamation, and unification of existing forms. Gothic and Antique were actually never historical subjects for the Germans but rather, intimate potentials. [...] For the young Goethe, the Strasbourg Cathedral was not the past but rather, a living sign of German and Christian spirit. It was not a matter of remaking everything that had ever been German. [...] Perhaps the two forms of the world have until today remained the German fate, and it is our destiny to be located between both possibilities of existence. [...] Is it so difficult to discover the living Gothic in Bartning's Star Church or the living Antique in the great works of Mies? What matters to us is that there is a great, living

27   Rudolf Schwarz in Conrads et al., *Die Bauhaus-Debatte 1953*, 44.
28   Rudolf Schwarz, "Was dennoch besprochen werden muss," *Baukunst und Werkform* 7, no. 4 (1953), 193–95, here 194.
29   Rudolf Schwarz in Conrads et al., *Die Bauhaus-Debatte 1953*, 41.

heritage in our art that is sufficient up to the present day and is carried by great architects whose interest was not in making buildings but in offering humanity its great space, and who all speak with one another across time."[30]

By questioning the importance of originality and siding with history, Schwarz implicitly challenged the modernist conviction that each era had its own, unique expression, an expression that acknowledged technological advancement as much as *Zeitgeist*. Schwarz countered that architecture was not *of* a time but "across time." It was no less striking to claim that the "German talent" consisted in recombination, not invention. The concept that the Antique and the Gothic were "intimate potentials" giving rise to vocabularies in which the "talented" can work, not as raiment or superficial style, contradicted familiar characterizations of historicizing architecture as inherently retrograde.[31] And if indeed the German talent was a matter of adaptation rather than invention, then the ambitions of the Bauhaus were misguided from the start. Bartning as Gothic, Mies as Antique: what better concrete examples of how these two "intimate potentials" might come to fruition in the present. This differed utterly from the ideal of a single, unifying modern architecture. This was a very different path to contemporary architecture than the one that ran, by way of originality, from the Bauhaus to Gropius's Harvard.

Schwarz otherwise offered few specific references to either architects or buildings. One exception is his tangential praise of Jugendstil, a movement relatively marginal to the postwar historiography of the modernist canon but championed at the 1951 Darmstädter Gespräch, at which Schwarz had spoken so forcefully. This rhetorical distinction between architectural artifact and architectural culture is fundamental to understanding Schwarz. He was concerned with the intellectual and philosophical weakness of contemporary architectural thinking; he was unconcerned with stylistic preference.

Schwarz's aspiration to recast German modern architecture within a context of historical continuity was not an idle academic undertaking. It was part of his larger desire to reassert modern architecture's historicity de facto. The Bauhaus stood in the way. Rejection of history, according to Schwarz, permeated its curriculum well beyond its insistence on empirical visual exercises. By expunging the humanities from the education of future architects and designers, the Bauhaus had silenced an architectural discourse that stretched across history and human experience. To Schwarz, this loss of historical continuity was as much to blame for the lack of critical interest in Leitl as an architect as was the division of labor among architects and the loss of humanist training:

"As our conversation intensified, I expressed the opinion that the origin of the strange muting of the conversation among architects might be deeper, and perhaps could be sought in a greater break with Western tradition that we had experienced. The master dictated to me that I was to write all this down, and I promised, although with concern. He was still convinced that the break with tradition was the fault of the Nazis; I nurtured in my heart the more terrible conviction that this had occurred when materialism had entered Western thinking. He was genuinely distressed that I seemed to consider the entire Nazi mess entirely inconsequential; the Reichskanzlei has been taken apart and next year, the Federal Building Department will build an entirely functioning replacement in Bonn. [...] Anyone who allows himself to be seduced by Nuremberg culture is as much beyond help as anyone who is electrified by a parade march; such things will always be, it belongs to the stupidity of nature that such things recur. [...] I said I believed, however, everything that occurred before then was much worse because it was more traitorous and more seductive. The master was truly unhappy when I revealed to him that I had never thought much of the Bauhaus and the activities around it, and had said as much even as a tender youth."[32]

30   Conrads et al., *Die Bauhaus-Debatte 1953*, 41–43.
31   See Werner Oechslin, *Otto Wagner, Adolf Loos, and the Road to Modern Architecture*, trans. Lynnette Widder (Cambridge: Cambridge University Press, 2002).
32   Rudolf Schwarz in Conrads et al., *Die Bauhaus-Debatte 1953*, 39.

The irony in this passage is as obvious as its heavily polemical tone. Schwarz was only two paragraphs into his essay but had already abandoned the conceit of a reported conversation with Leitl. His comments on the National Socialist regime are at best irresponsible, not only because of Leitl's worries about his wartime efforts for Hermann Rimpl. Schwarz himself, although never a member of the National Socialist Party, had spent the latter part of the war planning towns for "a new agricultural population"[33] in the Lorraine region of occupied France. His offhand depiction of Leitl as "truly unhappy" seems simply unfair, especially considering Leitl's efforts at *Baukunst und Werkform* to open discussion of wartime collaboration.[34] Why, then, would Schwarz ridicule Leitl publicly? And how could he equate the Bauhaus's role in destroying the "great Western conversation" of the interwar period to that of National Socialism? What was at stake when he descried the "anti-spiritual terrorism of dictatorial groups, namely the Bauhaus literates and later, of course, the masters of the Thousand Year Reich?"[35]

The impulse to repudiate history was endemic to much modernist rhetoric, a fact Schwarz repeatedly referenced. He harped on the historical rupture caused by those he criticizes, calling them almost interchangeably Bauhaus, materialist, and functionalist, "with their appearance dated as the Year One and before which, everything was barren and empty."[36] Only by breaching that "Year One" rhetoric, he argued, could one "freely view a young Europe, unfurling in a thousand hopes, as it had been in the decades before the war."[37]

With the end of the war had come another kind of year zero in Germany. It promised a clean slate in contrast to the punitive treatment to which the country had been subject in the interwar period. But it also created a void within national and cultural identity. The total rejection of history after the war was an immediate reaction to the abuse of history by the Third Reich. In 1953, so Schwarz, the "charlatans" of that earlier era still prevailed, their rhetoric suspending culture equally between false history—a legacy of Third Reich—and false ahistoricity. As he described it, "the masters of the Thousand Year Reich have become the keepers of tradition [...] We want to make their squinches and architraves difficult for them [...] [and for] the bastion of the avant-gardists who today still believe in their Year One."[38] In other words the Bauhaus, no less than National Socialism, albeit in very different ways, had condemned Germany to a cultural vacuum. The Bauhaus's eternal return to first principles, its insistence on always starting anew, took on even greater dimensions amidst the postwar political reality of a "zero hour." This slippage between Bauhaus modernism, National Socialist pseudo-history, and the cultural crisis of postwar West Germany was the most controversial part of his article. The equivalency was sensationalistic. But in truth, the synergy between the rise of international modernism in West Germany and remaining tendrils of National Socialist bureaucracy was part of practice in the 1950s.

There was another problem ancillary to reducing the history of architecture to a history of styles. By appropriating an architectural idiom and proclaiming its ideology loudly, so Schwarz, the Bauhaus had undermined those who foresaw developing other strands of modern architecture. It must have deeply irritated Schwarz that precisely this same ideology had propagated itself in the United States, and was now ready for re-importation to the homeland it had forsaken.

"One might accuse me of stirring up old dirt unnecessarily. But no, there is bitter necessity for this, so that fronts can finally be dissolved that are not fronts at all. The Bauhaus has achieved a great success, a success of publicists. As reprehensible as its ideologies were, the literarily-inclined lapped them up like milk and honey, and in an instant it was the defined dogma of all writers that vital architecture was indeed that of the Bauhaus and that the truly contemporary architect was only he who had broken with Western tradition. All others of us, however, were marked for decades. We were placed in the same tub and thrown out with the rest of the

33   Wolfgang Pehnt and Hilde Strohl, *Rudolf Schwarz, 1897–1961: Architekt einer anderen Moderne, Bewohnte Bilder* (Ostfildern-Ruit: Hatje Cantz, 1997), 100, describes Schwarz's work during the National Socialist period.
34   In 1949, Leitl had written, "We all, or most of us, were no heroes, or only very partially. Otherwise, we would no longer be here. We were all somewhere, and we also did work. [...] Our contracts all bore the signatures of military financial ministers, Gau leaders or SS leaders (even my own)." See Durth, *Deutsche Architekten*, 423–24, fn. 145.
35   Rudolf Schwarz in Conrads et al., *Die Bauhaus-Debatte 1953*, 43.
36   Conrads et al., *Die Bauhaus-Debatte 1953*, 40.
37   Conrads et al., *Die Bauhaus-Debatte 1953*, 39; Schwarz explains that he intends "to backdate Year One" to circa 1900, a familiar art historical shorthand for Jugendstil.
38   Conrads et al., *Die Bauhaus-Debatte 1953*, 46.

bathwater into the gutter. We were forced to make difficult inroads in industrial building, urbanism, church building, and literature to show that we were of a completely different nature. Our opponents have learned the entire phraseology by heart and have not forgotten it even today. One need not expect of one's enemy that he be any more gifted than average. Anyone who thinks that all this is past should read the diatribe that Mr. Tamms from Düsseldorf has sent, as I write, to the *Neue Zeitung*: the masters of the thousand-year Reich have become the defenders of tradition. [...] We do not want to make their squinches and architraves easy for them: tradition is ours. Or he might visit the bastions of the Avant-Gardists who even today believe in the 'Year One.' He would be immersed in a deadly lack of ideas and boredom in their publications which have slowly become fashion magazines (everyone is wearing corrugated metal and human organs).

      Dear Mr. Leitl, I sincerely believe that my text will not cause you any joy, but I believe that it has to be. We really must return to the space of truly great tradition and divest everything that is counter to its spirit; we must return to true discussion."[39]

Schwarz was right: his article caused Leitl no joy at all. The magazine's next issue, a double February / March combination, gave voice to the avalanche of responses in defense of the Bauhaus and its masters. Gropius condescendingly chose not "to answer Schwarz directly"[40] on this occasion—in fact, there is absolutely no correspondence between Gropius and Schwarz in the former's absolutely meticulous archive— but he was glad to encourage his advocates to launch attacks on his behalf. His response seems strangely choleric, given *Baukunst und Werkform*'s small, largely domestic circulation. It was not a publication that Gropius regularly read, and it is not included among the clippings in Gropius's voluminous scrapbooks. Gropius wrote to the magazine directly in order to request that Leitl send him the two 1953 issues by special order; this letter is the only documented correspondence between Gropius and Leitl.[41] The stakes seem to have been inordinately high. What was it about this article that so provoked Gropius? And what does the heated exchange in the pages of the magazine communicate about the complex allegiances among German architects, all advocates of modern architecture, on both sides of the Atlantic?

    In the short weeks between the initial publication of Schwarz's essay and the press date of the next issue, there was a flurry of correspondence between Gropius and the magazine's West German readers, who had been outraged by Schwarz's claims. Gropius apparently had little to fear from posterity but immediately developed his strategy for responding in a terse note refuting Schwarz's "reverse polemic,"[42] which he sent to his faithful minion Richard Döcker. This note was published in both Leitl's modest journal and *Die Neue Zeitung*, the American-published newspaper in West Germany.

    In a separate letter sent privately to Döcker as well as in the version intended for publication, Gropius parried Schwarz's "Bilde Künstler, rede nicht" with his own quotation from Goethe: "Lass dich nur zu keiner Zeit / Zum Widerspruch verleiten. / Weise fallen in Unwissenheit, / wenn sie sich mit Unwissenden streiten"[43] (as a prose translation, "never allow yourself to be misled into contradiction; the wise fall into ignorance when they fight with those who are ignorant"). The scale of Gropius's agitation behind the scenes, evident in his correspondence, belies his aloof recourse to Goethe.

39   Schwarz in Conrads et al., *Die Bauhaus-Debatte 1953*, 46–47.
40   Conrads et al., *Die Bauhaus-Debatte 1953*, 60.
41   Walter Gropius Papers, 1925–1969 (MS Ger 208). Houghton Library, Harvard University.
42   Conrads et al., *Die Bauhaus-Debatte 1953*, 122.
43   Quoted from Conrads et al., *Die Bauhaus-Debatte 1953*, 59.
44   Paul Betts, "The Bauhaus as Cold-War Legend: West German Modernism Revisited," *German Politics and Society* 14 no. 2 (39) (Summer 1996), 75–100.

For much of the disgruntled readership of *Baukunst und Werkform*, however, the Bauhaus was inherently worth defending. It was a connection to, not a disruption from, a meaningful history.[44] By virtue of the school's closure in 1933 under political duress, it had come to represent a culture of opposition to National Socialism. Like such expatriate figures as Thomas Mann or Theodor Adorno in their reassertion of German culture, the Bauhaus served as a reference point for an untainted tradition. Such reference points were particularly important at a moment that fell uncomfortably between the "zero hour" and whatever might come after. The widespread reception of the Bauhaus in West Germany after 1945 indicates its importance to cultural memory, well beyond architecture.[45]

Hermann Mäckler's letter of response in the February / March double issue exemplifies this tendency in asserting the ongoing significance of the Bauhaus in Germany as well as internationally. His article carried ironically the pompous title "Praeceptor Germanie et Europae" (Master of Germany and Europe), which, in Mäckler's view, Schwarz had claimed for himself "as others [had] before."[46] There was no mistaking Mäckler's insinuation that Schwarz was as dictatorial as the Third Reich had been. By contrast, Mäckler describes Gropius as "worthy of affection."[47] It is not Schwarz, the self-proclaimed tastemaker, who can rightfully claim mastery over Germany and Europe, Mäckler argues, but rather the Bauhaus:

> "What is the state of *your* historical desires? [...] Why, in fact, are you so deeply concerned with the Bauhaus in its historical form? Was it not liquidated almost 20 years ago? Shouldn't this only really be of interest to historians? Is it not true that a bit has happened in the world of building since the departure of the Bauhaus? [...] Are there not "things that are being decided" and thus offer matter for legitimate discussion? Important and valid things that, nota bene, are fundamentally connected with the past existence of the Bauhaus?"[48]

To prove the extent to which "important and valid things [...] are fundamentally connected with the past existence of the Bauhaus," Mäckler listed the current positions and locations of the original Bauhaus masters. At the top of his list is Gropius, "Architect, founder and director of the Bauhaus, most recently Chairman of the Department of Architecture, Harvard University, USA."[49] The next four names—Josef Albers, Herbert Bayer, Marcel Breuer, and Lyonel Feininger—were also in the United States; Albers and Breuer likewise enjoyed the title of professor at an Ivy League university. Laszlo Moholy-Nagy's name appears towards the end of the list, "photographer, set designer, writer, Director of the Institute of Design, Chicago, deceased 1940 in Chicago."[50] Of the thirteen men on Mäckler's list, six had emigrated to the United States and four of those held leading academic positions. As if aiming to add weight to his claim that the Bauhaus remained associated with "important and valid things," Mäckler concluded by asking about other Bauhaus masters: "How do things stand, for example, with Johannes Itten, with Gerhard Marcks, or with Paul Klee, whose most beautiful pictures I saw in Chicago in the home of Mies van der Rohe?"[51] Presence in America, it seems, has become a touchstone for validity, even for those who, like Klee, had perished without ever leaving Europe. Mäckler's Bauhaus remains important because it is in the United States, where "important and valid things" are located.

Leitl himself understood that the Bauhaus was central to the exchange between Germany and the United States, although the balance of power had dramatically shifted since the Weimar and Dessau eras. The photographs he published in *Baukunst und Werkform* depict the very different trajectories taken by Schwarz and Gropius in their architecture from the 1910s to the present. The four examples of Schwarz's work bespeak a consistent interest in the simple box: the cylindrical church and house in Offenbach already discussed, the Fronleichnam Church as published in 1930, and the Anglican garrison church. The same 1953 issue included four different images of the Bauhaus building and two of the masters' houses, including plans of both buildings, as well a view of Gropius's housing in Berlin-Siemensstadt from 1929. It concluded with two Breuer houses in Massachusetts. These images differ markedly from the preceding spread showing the Schwarz and Gropius villas, whose white stuccoed surfaces appear in naturalistically gradated shadows in classically composed frames. Foreground tree boughs balance the

45   Betts, "The Bauhaus as Cold-War Legend," 78; Betts notes that although the Bauhaus debate was reported in the popular press, other architecture periodicals made no report of it. He interprets this reaction as indicative of a relative disciplinary indifference to the Bauhaus legacy at that time.

46   Conrads et al., *Die Bauhaus-Debatte 1953*, 71.

47   Hermann Mäckler to Walter Gropius, July 21, 1950 (carbon copy), Series III, file 1153, Walter Gropius Papers, 1925–1969 (MS Ger 208), Houghton Library, Harvard University, 65.

48   Mäckler to Gropius, July 21, 1950.

49   Mäckler to Gropius, July 21, 1950.

50   Mäckler to Gropius, July 21, 1950.

51   Mäckler to Gropius, July 21, 1950.

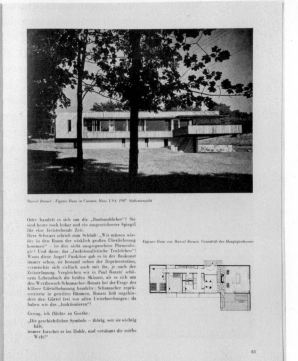

4.5 Marcel Breuer, two houses in the United States, *Baukunst und Werkform* no. 2/3, 1953

diagonals of a stair, in the case of the Schwarz villa, or the curved wall and slight perspectival recession of a balcony overhang in the Gropius villa, to produce classically composed views. [4.5]

The choice of two Breuer houses in lieu of Gropius's own house in Lincoln, Massachusetts, or even one of the several house projects on which Breuer and Gropius had collaborated, is curious. Gropius's Lincoln house of 1938 could have related to those earlier houses in the same issue; Gropius's larger American projects could have complimented the Siemensstadt images. Either would have yielded images expected of a Bauhaus idiom, as Breuer's projects did not. Perhaps this was the point: crossing the Atlantic had changed what could be attributed to the Bauhaus heritage. As Mäckler pointed out, "Who still builds to the letter of the formal laws of that Bauhaus?"[52] Under these conditions, however, who could be certain about what constituted the Bauhaus? It seemed even more difficult to assert its relevance to an emergent, uniquely West German cultural moment.

Gropius's relationship to his German past had been tempered by the effect of emigration on his self-image. Lent particular urgency by the fact that his country of origin was the enemy, the American tradition of assimilation played out for him in conflicting ways. His many scrapbooks attest to his compulsion to remain in Germany's public eye but the letters he sent to his German colleagues communicate his ambivalence. One example is in a 1946 exchange with Fritz Hesse, the mayor of Dessau during the Bauhaus years, who had been reelected after the war. A desperate Hesse, whose city lay in ruins, wrote to propose an international exhibition of Bauhaus work for the fall of 1946. As described in a clipping from the Dessau *Tägliche Rundschau* newspaper that Hesse enclosed in his letter, the exhibition would prove that "the Bauhaus building has once again become a central location of important work." Hesse wrote, "I would like to add that we place inordinate value on the Bauhaus exhibition's including submissions from emigrated *Bauhäusler*, so that the world can see the value of the Bauhaus idea, and the work of the Bauhaus in Germany, documented as clearly as possible."[53] Gropius responded with several suggestions for the exhibition, then added an observation that might have surprised the letter's recipient:

"I have learned much here about democracy. I believe that the United States is closest to what we once anticipated in a true democracy. That, although we do seem reactionary in this instance as a victor nation. You would observe many aspects of life here with particular interest."[54]

52   Mäckler to Gropius, July 21, 1950.
53   Fritz Hesse to Walter Gropius, February 14, 1946, Series III, file 876, Walter Gropius Papers, 1925–1969 (MS Ger 208), Houghton Library, Harvard University.
54   Walter Gropius to Fritz Hesse, May 30, 1946, Series III, file 876, Walter Gropius Papers, 1925–1969 (MS Ger 208), Houghton Library, Harvard University.

Whatever Gropius meant by "we" was transformed over the course of these few sentences. The first was a German "we," one that included both Gropius and Hesse and had anticipated a "true democracy." The second "we" included only Gropius, part of the "victor nation" to which he now belonged. With his inclusions and exclusions Gropius signaled his changed identity, a change that extended to many of the Bauhaus masters and even more so to its academic ideas. This Americanization was thorough; Gropius must have embodied it even in daily contact with students. In 1998, reflecting on her years at Harvard's Graduate School of Design, former Gropius student Edith Aujaume was surprised when asked about her experience studying with a German at the height of World War II. "What do you mean?" she asked when pressed. "Gropius was not German!"[55] And so he would have had it. In a 1951 letter to Theodor Heuss, during the period in which Gropius unsuccessfully attempted to secure civil servant pensions for the families of former Bauhaus masters, Gropius referred to himself directly as a "former German," troubled by the way his country of origin treated the bearers of its cultural heritage, embodied by the Bauhaus.[56] By 1953, the Bauhaus was arguably no longer German any more than Gropius. It was part of the story of modernism, a story whose prologue may have been European but whose primary action was American.

Gropius was far from the only important expatriate to engage American postwar culture and to advocate for the "discourse of the creative mind that posited knowledge as a key economic and political resource."[57] As European artists left sites of conflict for the security of the United States, they took publicly to rejecting their home countries in sweeping terms. An editorial statement in the liberal-leaning cultural magazine *Partisan Review* in its 1952 symposium-in-print "Our Country and Our Culture" exemplifies ideas about the decline of Europe as a corollary of American power:

> "The purpose of this symposium is to examine the apparent fact that American intellectuals now regard America and its institutions in a new way. [...] The American artist and intellectual no longer feels 'disinherited' as Henry James did, or 'astray,' (and curly) as Ezra Pound did in 1912. [...] We have obviously come a long way from the earlier rejection of America as spiritually barren [...] and the Marxist picture of America in the thirties as a land of capitalist reaction.
>
> Essential in the shift of attitudes is the relationship of America to Europe. For more than a hundred years, America was culturally dependent on Europe; now Europe is economically dependent on America. And America is no longer the raw and unformed land of promise from which men of superior gifts like James, Santayana, and Eliot departed, seeking in Europe what they found lacking in America. Europe is no longer regarded as a sanctuary; it no longer assures that rich experience of culture which inspired and justified a criticism of American life. The wheel has come full circle and now America has become the protector of Western civilization, at least in a military and economic sense."[58]

This sense of superiority was, however, not without nagging doubts, like those Gropius voiced when he admitted that "we do seem reactionary in this instance as a victor nation." One way to assuage these doubts was through the words of naturalized Europeans. An article published in *Partisan Review* in the year of the Bauhaus debate by expatriate philosopher and critic Ludwig Marcuse offers a stark example. Marcuse was part of the large German expatriate community in southern California. Writing in German that was then translated for publication, he characterized European intellectuals as "a species, which cannot live without a protective ideology, for they are professionally accustomed to it. They need a scapegoat who is to blame for everything. [...] In the lives of many European intellectuals, America plays a leading role as scapegoat."[59] This "blame" recalls Gropius's words to Hesse. Marcuse went further:

> "It has always been Europe's revenge to degrade America to the rank of a country of barbarians, but never before has there been so much

55   Edith Aujaume in conversation at Columbia University Graduate School of Architecture, spring 1999.
56   Walter Gropius to Fritz Hesse, June 21, 1951, Series III, file 877, Walter Gropius Papers, 1925–1969 (MS Ger 208), Houghton Library, Harvard University.
57   Anna Vallye, "Design and the Politics of Knowledge in America, 1937–67: Walter Gropius, Gyorgy Kepes" (PhD diss. Columbia University, 2011), 2.
58   *Partisan Review*, May–June 1952, 283–4.
59   Ludwig Marcuse, "European Anti-Americanism," *Partisan Review* May/June 1953, 314–20, here 317.

reason to crave revenge. Europe's megalomania needs America as a contrasting background for its own greatness—which no longer exists. [...] Europe's Anti-Americanism is simultaneously European self-hatred, a split personality which tries to insist the judge and the accused are two different people. But judge and accused are one— even though day after day sees the publication of the same old books about America, in which the authors shed crocodile tears over American technology, notwithstanding the fact that it impresses them so profoundly that they would love to crawl into every big machine, provided they got the chance."[60]

There was little space between personal and professional sentiment. Here, too, Marcuse's own biography shows the depth of this personal conflict between his German and American identities. As part of the German diaspora in southern California in the 1930s, he ridiculed "HeinrichMann, Alfred Döblin, Leonard Frank [and] Walter Mehring, unable to speak English, knowing nothing of filmmaking, full of contempt for the industry" but still trying to work in so-called "film factories."[61] Yet fewer than five years after writing his article, Marcuse had completed his own return emigration, moving back to Germany where he lived the rest of his life.

Gropius's return under US government auspices to West Germany could not avoid similar ambivalence, sometimes tinged with acrimony, about national identity. In official correspondence and publicly reported conversations, Gropius demonstrated good will towards his former homeland in his role as US Army advisor; but his condescension towards Richard Döcker is revealing. Döcker, whose resistance to National Socialism led him to leave architecture and instead to study biology, maintained regular contact from the time Gropius left for London, and even wrote a note of congratulations in 1937 upon Gropius's invitation to Harvard.[62] Döcker's letters are melancholic and resigned except for a brief period after the war when he tried to convince Gropius to reinstate the Ring. According to Döcker's plan, Walter Gropius, Ludwig Mies van der Rohe, Ludwig Hilberseimer, Martin Wagner, Erich Mendelsohn, and Ernst May all of whom had emigrated, would nonetheless rejoin the Ring in order to form a German delegation to the Congrès internationaux d'architecture moderne (CIAM).[63] Gropius did nothing to assist. The plans became yet another of the major disappointments in Döcker's life. No German delegation was ever established. Lowering his sights, Döcker hinted in later letters how much he would enjoy attending CIAM conferences anyway, proposing that Gropius extend invitations to the London and Bergamo meetings. Gropius ignored every request. Still, during the Bauhaus debate, Gropius chose Döcker as his proxy against Schwarz.[64] Gropius's concerns for Germany seem ultimately self-serving.

Nonetheless, the US occupying forces brought in Gropius to advise on rebuilding. He was seen as representing both cultural and practical positions, able to sway beliefs and provide concrete advice. While for the Americans he was a source of inside knowledge on Germany, West Germans were of two minds. Perhaps he could be their advocate, but often he seemed out of touch, unable to comprehend the challenges they were facing. Gropius tended to intercede on issues important to himself but with little impact on the daily practice of architecture. In 1947, he recommended to General Clay that financial support be provided for the Werkbund.[65] In 1948, he tried—albeit unsuccessfully—to throw his influence behind a new, de-Nazified set of building norms, replacing those established by party member Ernst Neufert, who had been a professor at the "other" Bauhaus after Gropius's school departed Weimar and, perhaps more saliently, had worked actively for Speer during the war.[66] Gropius referred to him only obliquely when he spoke of "Nazi ministers."[67]

Reception of his tours was mixed. A letter from Otto Bartning, then head of the architects' union, asks for his help following a 1947 visit: "All of us who are wrestling with the new rebuilding, hope for great assistance from the weight of your visit and thank you for it."[68]

60   Marcuse, "European Anti-Americanism," 317–320.
61   Ludwig Marcuse quoted in Alexander Stephan, "Communazis": FBI Surveillance of German Émigré Writers (New Haven: Yale University Press, 2000), 48.
62   Richard Döcker to Walter Gropius, January 26, 1937, Series III, file 646, Walter Gropius Papers, 1925–1969 (MS Ger 208), Houghton Library, Harvard University.
63   Richard Döcker to Walter Gropius, January 9, 1948, Series III, file 646, Walter Gropius Papers, 1925–1969 (MS Ger 208), Houghton Library, Harvard University.
64   Letters between Walter Gropius and Richard Döcker, 1934–53, Series III, file 646, Walter Gropius Papers, 1925–1969 (MS Ger 208), Houghton Library, Harvard University; and Durth, Deutsche Architekten, 341–51.
65   "Bericht für General Lucius D. Clay, den Militärgouverneur für Deutschland (U.S.Zone)," Baurundschau 9 / 10 (1948), 76–78.
66   Letters between Walter Gropius and Richard Döcker, November 2 and 7, 1948, Series III, file 646, Walter Gropius Papers, 1925–1969 (MS Ger 208), Houghton Library, Harvard University.
67   In Walter Gropius to Richard Döcker, November 7, 1948, Gropius is specific: it is Neufert's "arbitrary" norms he is criticizing.
68   Otto Bartning to Walter Gropius, August 9, 1947, Series III, file 416, Walter Gropius Papers, 1925–1969 (MS Ger 208), Houghton Library, Harvard University.

A November 1947 letter from Döcker speaks, gently, to the sense that Gropius had missed the point:

> "Your visit in Germany was doubtlessly very multifaceted but perhaps inadequate to give you a full image of the actual situation, particularly in regard to our professional work and chances. [...] But I do assume that you have gotten an overview of the desperate state and horrible conditions in our cities and their people. It is not easy to find recipes for help, particularly not when all means, even the most primitive, are so limited as they are among us at the moment."[69]

The lectures Gropius held were not only positively received. In 1947 he spoke in Berlin, Frankfurt, and Munich, and focused on American town planning, prefabrication, and standardized house building, and the relationship between technology and the human being.[70] Published as an open letter to General Lucius Clay, his conclusions and recommendations amounted to a combination of advocacy for organizations and people to whom he had personal affinities, such as the Werkbund, CIAM, and the "Bauhaus movement." It is interesting to speculate on what he meant by the latter. Perhaps it was the Geschwister Scholl Foundation, founded in 1946. Perhaps it was a response to the emergent Cold War reality that juxtaposed East German rejection of modern architecture and the Bauhaus to its embrace by the West.[71] Either way, Gropius wanted badly to ensure the legacy of the Bauhaus.

Gropius advocated for policies that would have resulted in large-scale de-urbanization. This proclivity perhaps in part reflected prevailing CIAM ideas and perhaps expressed his American experience. He supported an eminent-domain-like exercise of power at city scale, which would likely have prevented the reconstruction of large swaths of bombed urban fabric by fiat. He proposed resettlement through small planning units comprising five to eight thousand people, less than the population of four or five Berlin city blocks prior to the war. To advocate for less dense building may also have seemed pragmatic: Gropius appears to have been dubious that rebuilding could proceed apace under the conditions he encountered. Over and over in his speeches, he insisted that the material and technological wealth of the United States was a prerequisite to any true contemporary city building; and he never failed to point out that both were absent in West Germany, an observation hardly endearing to his audience.[72] He emphasized a need for patents to stimulate market forces in innovation and critiqued the use of salvaged building materials as a true alternative to fast, high-quality building. At a moment when salvaged rubble was the most common building material, Gropius's discussion of state-of-the-art technology and materials was tone deaf and self-aggrandizing. It allowed him to promote his own prefabricated building product, the General Panel System, which he used to illustrate the open letter he provided for publication in West Germany. By insisting that architectural libraries, exhibitions, and guest lectures be imported from "cultural areas in other countries,"[73] he conveyed his disdain for his German colleagues and his conviction that progress could only come from outside.

Praise came from unexpected quarters, however.[74] The author of the glowing report was Rudolf Hillebrecht, a high-ranking de-Nazified architect "between the two fronts,"[75] who had successfully transitioned from prominence within Albert Speer's Ministry to equal prominence within West Germany. As of 1941, Hillebrecht had been second in command for the Amt für kriegswichtigen Einsatz (task force for wartime necessities), the city planning and reconstruction agency led by Konstanty Gutschow under Speer's auspices. After internment as a prisoner of war in the British sector from 1944 to 1945, Hillebrecht was released to work with other useful experts establishing strategies for the reconstruction of war-damaged cities in the British sector. In 1948, he was elected Hanover's head of urban planning.[76] Hillebrecht, who had collaborated on a 1934 competition with Gropius, ended on a personal note:

> "Gropius himself, always at pains to keep his intellectual horizon as broad as possible; who on the one hand radiates his influence in all

69   Richard Döcker to Walter Gropius, November 19, 1947, Series III, file 646, Walter Gropius Papers, 1925–1969 (MS Ger 208), Houghton Library, Harvard University.
70   "Professor Gropius gibt gute Ratschläge," *Baumeister* (November / December 1947), 389–91.
71   Wolfgang Thöner, "Bauhaus in der DDR: Im Schatten der Parteiideologie," *Der Spiegel*, https://www.tagesspiegel.de/kultur/bauhaus-in-der-ddr-im-schatten-der-parteiideologie/24157522.html, accessed November 13, 2021.
72   "Professor Gropius gibt gute Ratschläge," 389.
73   "Professor Gropius gibt gute Ratschläge," 390.
74   See, for example, Karl Bonatz, "Anmerkungen zu den Presseinterviews mit Professor Gropius und zu seinem Vortrag im Titania-Palast am 22. August 1947," *Neue Bauwelt* (1947), 550.
75   Durth, *Deutsche Architekten*, 312–22.
76   Hillebrecht's professional success and its meaning for his reputation were clear by 1959, when he would grace the cover of *Der Spiegel*, which celebrated the "miracle of Hanover." See "Das Wunder von Hannover," *Der Spiegel* (June 3, 1959), 56–69.

civilized countries of the world; whose thoughts stand at the center of a broad international circle—he is and remains stamped by Germanness. And I was happy to have this impression verified by him."[77] Hillebrecht's impression seems strangely at odds with Gropius's open letter to General Clay, which appeared on the pages that followed Hillebrecht's notes: Gropius's "we" was explicitly American. Only in the beholder's eye was he still "stamped by Germanness."

As he hinted in his letter to Fritz Hesse,[78] Gropius's American identity was closely bound to his beliefs about democracy. So too was his part in an emergent relationship between architecture and politics in America, one that imagined the confluence of two Cold War imaginaries: "visual culture"[79] and supranational democracy. This vision of democracy could be propagated by the twinned tools of international development and postwar reconstruction.[80] Both its analytical methods, applied to all sectors through the newly minted field of "management," and the cultural production in which it clothed itself were, for Gropius, inherently and indelibly linked to the visual training he had pioneered. This link was not some figment of his imagination. He had ample confirmation. Had he wished, he could have pointed to evidence provided by figures whose paths had crossed, or re-crossed, his own after he emigrated to Cambridge in 1937. Among them was Albert Wohlstetter, economist, political strategist, RAND corporation analyst, and early in his career, president of Gropius's own General Panel Corporation. He could have spoken with members of the important International Unity of Science movement, including Otto Neurath and Rudolf Carnap; and with Gyorgy Kepes, who arrived in Cambridge a full decade after Gropius to take up with redoubled conviction the cause of visual education.

Of these four, Wohlstetter was the one who most directly connected Gropius to the areas of enterprise and government responsible for spreading American "democracy" abroad. Wohlstetter's active interest in visual culture dated to his graduate studies, first in law, then in advanced mathematics and logic at Columbia University in the mid-1930s. After attending several art history lecture courses given by Meyer Schapiro, whom he described as "the most brilliant lecturer I ever heard,"[81] Wohlstetter proposed to Schapiro a project that would have applied linguistics-based structural analysis to the use of myth in art history. Although never completed, the project reveals Wohlstetter's commitment to the power of abstract structural analysis. It also underlines a conviction that would remain throughout his life: that art functioned as a legible register of societal meaning. One recently published and incisive analysis of Wohlstetter's work points to his importance within the larger postwar project of connecting visual communication to broadly interdisciplinary structural methods.[82] Such methods formed the basis for the problem-solving of that era, from war games to economic interventions to corporate management.

Gropius and Wohlstetter had met in a different context. Wohlstetter began his postwar professional life as manager and quality control officer in a California aircraft factory run by his brother. The company, Atlas, engaged an émigré architect to design their hangars: Konrad Wachsmann, Gropius's partner in the General Panel Corporation.[83] In 1945, Wohlstetter became the director of research, then vice president and ultimately president of Wachsmann and Gropius's undertaking. He remained with the General Panel Corporation until 1951, when the company disbanded. From there, he moved to a position of much greater visibility at the new RAND corporation, where under his direction visual culture came to be treated as a litmus test, a sign to be decoded by the social and political sciences in the interest of anticipating geopolitical actions. His work at RAND took him into even more powerful positions, including that of security advisor to the White House from 1961 until the end of his career. Although the discussions between Gropius and Wohlstetter seem to have largely been dominated by their efforts to rescue the General Panel Corporation,[84] Wohlstetter's work at RAND ratified the conviction that the visual imaginary was inextricable

77   "Professor Gropius gibt gute Ratschläge," 389–91.

78   Walter Gropius to Fritz Hesse, May 30, 1946, Series III, file 876, Walter Gropius Papers, 1925–1969 (MS Ger 208), Houghton Library, Harvard University.

79   Pamela M. Lee, *Think Tank Aesthetics: Midcentury Modernism, the Cold War, and the Neoliberal Present* (Cambridge, MA: MIT Press, 2020), 41–42.

80   As per papers presented by Sandrine Kott and Michele Alacevich at The Heyman Center for the Humanities "Disciplines" Series: "The Idea of Development—Development and Underdevelopment in Postwar Europe," October 10, 2014, Columbia University. The complexity of resource flows and monetary policy at the end of World War II is also described in Timothy Mitchell, *Carbon Democracy: Political Power in the Age of Oil* (London: Verso Books, 2011).

81   Albert Wohlstetter to his wife Roberta, cited in Lee, *Think Tank Aesthetics*, 60.

82   See Lee, *Think Tank Aesthetics*, 1–119.

83   Gilbert Herbert, *The Dream of the Factory Built House: Walter Gropius and Konrad Wachsmann* (Cambridge, MA: MIT Press, 1984), 284–85.

84   Wohlstetter's role in trying to negotiate better loan terms and to economize the house design is detailed in Herbert, *The Dream.*

from the struggle to defend and propagate "the democracy." This same conviction resonated strongly in Gropius's thoughts.

In 1938, a conference held at Harvard would have put Gropius in proximity to another group of scholars, several of whom had lectured at the Dessau Bauhaus in 1929, less than a year after Gropius's departure as director in April 1928. The Unity of Science movement, like Gropius, had emigrated to the United States during the war and like most of the Bauhaus cohort, had found new academic homes in Chicago and Cambridge. The group's efforts to distill, within empirical, structural analysis, all the knowledge required to understand and govern modern life were, from the first, associated with the reduction to first principles that guided modernist art and architecture. As Rudolf Carnap wrote in 1928:

> "We sense an inner kinship between the attitude on which our philosophical work is founded and the intellectual attitude which presently operates in entirely different areas of life; we feel this attitude in artistic currents, especially in architecture, and in movements which strive for a meaningful form of human life: of personal and collective life, of education, and of external organization in general."[85]

Recent scholarship has considered at greater length the Unity of Science movement's investment in the visual components of analytical method, architecture, and planning;[86] its emphasis on the visual communication of information in the interest of propagating its universalist ambitions had clear methodological and philosophical affinities with the visual education that was Gropius's life's work. Perhaps zeitgeist, perhaps more: the alignment between the Bauhaus masters and the Unity of Science group, many of whom Americanized at roughly the same moment, speaks to the hopes and ambitions pinned on visual culture.

There is no doubt that Gropius saw Gyorgy Kepes's work at the Massachusetts Institute of Technology as aligned with his own ideals for visual culture as a corollary to a new liberatory, universalist spirit. "I wonder whether you have come across Kepes's new book *The Language of Vision*? At last, after all our endeavors [...] someone has taken up again this problem of formulating in definite terms a language of design, making objective fact statements," Gropius wrote in 1945.[87] Kepes's ambitions went far beyond an attempt to make "objective fact" out of aesthetic judgment. As he wrote in *The Language of Vision*, "The visual language is capable of disseminating knowledge more effectively than almost any other vehicle of communication. [...] Visual communication is universal and international."[88] Kepes makes clear reference here to the principles defined by the Unity of Science movement; but his hopes for visual culture went still further. "To perceive a visual image implies the beholder's participation in a process of organization. The experience of an image is thus a creative act of integration," he averred. For Gropius, too, one of the essential roles of visual culture was to agitate against increasing specialization:

> "Our scientific age has dulled our perception for the entirety of our complicated existence by carrying specialization to the extreme. The professional expert [...] tries to free himself from the pressure of general responsibility. [...] This has brought about a general dissolution of cultural relationships, resulting in the dismemberment and impoverishment of life. Civilized man has lost his totality. [...] *I maintain that our disoriented society desperately needs the creative participation in the arts as an essential counterbalance to the advances of science and industry.*"[89]

Wherever he looked, Gropius could see confirmation of his convictions about visual culture. No wonder Schwarz's accusations cut so close.

Gropius himself described this parity between visual culture and the project of universal democracy in the speech he gave in Hamburg upon receiving the Hansische Goethe-Preis in 1956, only a few years after the bitter Bauhaus debate. He expanded these remarks for American publication in 1968 in a collection entitled *Apollo in the Democracy*. His fervor helps to explain his overreaction during the Bauhaus debate.

85　Rudolf Carnap, *Der logische Aufbau der Welt* (Hamburg: F. Meiner, 1998), cited in Ivan F. da Cunha, "Utopias and Forms of Life: Carnap's Bauhaus Conferences," *Princípios revista de filosofia* 24, no. 45 (Winter 2017), 121–48, here 126.
86　See Nader Vossoughian, *Otto Neurath: The Language of the Global Polis* (Rotterdam: NAi Publishers, 2008); Lee, *Think Tank Aesthetics*.
87　Walter Gropius to Alexander Dorner, quoted in Vallye, "Design and the Politics of Knowledge," 196.
88　Gyorgy Kepes quoted in Vallye, "Design and the Politics of Knowledge," 230.
89　Walter Gropius, *Apollo in the Democracy: The Cultural Obligation of the Architect* (New York: McGraw-Hill, 1968), 5–7.

Gropius's speech does not mention the prize he has been awarded or its meaning. Instead, he spoke about the value of American democracy, defined as much more than a political system. This democracy is an all-encompassing ideal, suffusing history, politics, and aesthetics:

> "By the word 'democracy' I mean neither the antique Greek form of government [...] nor do I mean the politically stressed European, American, or Russian special forms of present democracy. I speak of the form of life which, without political identification, is slowly spreading over the whole world, establishing itself upon the foundation of increasing industrialization, growing communication, and information services and the broad admission of the masses to higher education and the right to vote. What is the relationship of this form of life to art and architecture today?
>
> In a long life I have become increasingly aware of the fact that the creation and love of beauty not only enrich man with a great measure of happiness but also bring forth ethical powers."[90]

A key part of this love of beauty, according to Gropius, depended upon visual training to support what he called the ability to "reconstruct [...] the relationships between the individual phenomena of our world."[91] The Gropius Basic Design course at the Harvard Graduate School of Design represented exactly such a systematic visual education. To accept Gropius's abstract definition of "visual training" was to imagine that the Bauhaus heritage had transcended discipline specificity to function as a constitutive element of pure democracy. As an imaginary, "visual culture" became shorthand for a specific kind of intelligence, one that was agile, intuitive, and incisive. It found widespread favor in the postwar United States, as is evident in the adoption of visual training to fields as diverse as early childhood education teaching and efforts to quantify intelligence. These tendencies reached a fever pitch in the efforts referenced above: the work of the RAND corporation with anthropologists Ruth Benedict and Margaret Mead to expand the scale of the Rorschach test to decode whole societies;[92] the work of Neurath on his ISOTYPE system of universally understandable graphic icons;[93] the efforts of Kepes's Center for Advanced Visual Studies at the Massachusetts Institute of Technology.[94] These theoretical tendencies were present in the documents that argued for the founding of the Hochschule für Gestaltung in Ulm, later called the New Bauhaus, and in the words chosen by John J. McCloy, Director of the United States High Commissioner on Germany, to argue for official American support of it.[95]

To see the Bauhaus legacy as part of a new world order must have been incredibly compelling for Gropius: in its magnitude, this continuity enhanced his own personal success and reputation. The apotheosis of visual culture was tantamount to Gropius's contribution to the conquest of progress over history. In this light, Schwarz's attack on the intellectual integrity of the Bauhaus must have seemed intolerable. It threatened the conviction that Gropius's art school curriculum had been transubstantiated into a constituent of true democracy.

Although they shared little else, Schwarz and Gropius were equally adamant about the value of the Bauhaus as a touchstone for a new architecture that would adequately represent spiritual and political reawakening after the devastating war. For Schwarz, the Bauhaus belonged to the intellectual collapse that had precipitated Germany's descent into Fascism. It had to be rejected entirely. For Gropius, the Bauhaus was the cradle of a new visual sensibility that was inherent to a global democratic spirit. It had to be celebrated, along with its author Walter Gropius, as the *pax Americana* spread around the globe. But even those architects who occupied a position between the two extremes expressed their misgivings about Gropius's vision for the postwar architectural world order. While Gropius seemed ready to accept a depopulated Germany, to be rebuilt only if the materials, values, and technology of his new American homeland were somehow to appear, his more cautious defenders on the pages of *Baukunst und Werkform* believed

90   Gropius, "Apollo in the Democracy," 3–4.
91   Gropius, "Apollo in the Democracy," 6.
92   Lee, *Think Tank Aesthetics*, chapter 2.
93   Mikel Breitenstein, "Global Unity: Otto Neurath and the International Encyclopedia of Unified Science," https://www.ergon-verlag.de/isko_ko/downloads/aikovol10200613.pdf, accessed November 28, 2020.
94   Vallye, "Design and the Politics of Knowledge."
95   Paul Betts, *The Authority of Everyday Objects: A Cultural History of West German Industrial Design, Weimar and Now* (Berkeley: University of California Press, 2004), 142–45.

that German culture should be allowed to determine for itself how to deal with impulses coming from the United States.

Well before the Bauhaus debate erupted, Hermann Mäckler, who would submit to Leitl's magazine, *Baukunst und Werkform*, an eloquent defense of Gropius and the Bauhaus legacy, expressed a growing discomfort at the disequilibrium in the architectural exchange between Germany and the United States. In the early summer of 1950, Mäckler had traveled from Frankfurt to the United States and undertaken a cross country trip to destinations as wide-ranging as New York, Washington, Chapel Hill, Knoxville, the Grand Canyon, Los Angeles, San Francisco, Chicago, and Boston, where he visited Gropius. He sought out John Entenza, the Eameses, and their Los Angeles circle. In California, he also met with an earlier émigré to a very different America, Richard Neutra. In Chicago, he met Serge Chermayeff, then director of the Institute of Design prior to its merger with the Illinois Institute of Technology. Chermayeff owed his position in Chicago to Gropius's recommendation.

Cities and towns, émigrés and Americans, new architecture and broad landscapes: Mäckler's travels gave him a sense of what was afoot in postwar America. He described what he saw in a report that he sent with a letter to Gropius dated July 7, 1950. He used the letter to convey the consensus among his West German peers about how to best engage culturally with the United States. Although Mäckler confined himself to discussing schools of architecture and their curricula, the reservations he expressed could be understood as a harbinger of the Bauhaus debate:

> "In conversation with Bartning, Eiermann, Leistikow, Schwippert, Schwarz, and others, however, it was always asserted that a connection with America could only have a serious meaning and enjoy a thorough success if we in Germany had an independent school as a sort of locus to receive ideas. Only then, free of harassments of a *Weltanschauung* sort, would it be possible to do something for architecture within a new generation. [...] Likewise, the question of German participation in CIAM is also weighed down by such considerations."[96]

Without parity, Mäckler implied, Germans remained susceptible in their cultural development to the "harassments" of an American way of life, or *Weltanschauung*. Mäckler's careful wording bespeaks distress. He acknowledged the role in this imbalance of Gropius and his pedagogy. On the one hand, the Bauhaus heritage offered German architects the opportunity to feel that they were part of an increasingly powerful international architectural culture. On the other hand, the Bauhaus, subsumed by this American *Weltanschauung*, was a feint, effectively overpowering the nascent architectural culture that Mäckler and others like him were trying to foster in West Germany.

In 1951, Gropius had returned to Hanover to visit the *Constructa* building exposition. While he was there, he attended a private meeting, planned by his old collaborator Rudolf Hillebrecht, whom he had visited on a 1948 trip to Stuttgart. Hillebrecht's agenda for the meeting was to reconcile the conflicts that plagued his own biography. The event, he hoped, would bring together the "two sides"—the modernists and the architects of the Third Reich—in a detente overseen by Gropius. He likely also thought that this meeting would reinforce the importance of his *Constructa* as a symbol of Germany's fresh start.[97] Hans Scharoun, Otto Bartning, Hans Schwippert, and Rudolf Schwarz were among those prominent figures who declined his invitation. Leitl, interestingly, chose to attend. Gropius accepted and the meeting took place as envisioned. As Rudolf Wolters, another Speer protégé, reported,

> "We met [...] in a private home and grouped ourselves unforcedly around Gropius. [...] Shortly before the meeting began, Bonatz entered the room. [...] He introduced himself to Gropius: Bonatz. To general surprise, it became apparent that the seventy-three year old Bonatz and the sixty-nine year old Gropius, both institutions for German contemporary architecture, were meeting here for the first time in their lives. It was touching to observe how awkwardly

96   Hermann Mäckler to Walter Gropius, July 21, 1950, Walter Gropius Papers, 1925–1969 (MS Ger 208), Houghton Library, Harvard University.
97   Durth, *Deutsche Architekten*, 322.

98 Durth, *Deutsche Architekten*, 322–3.
99 Gropius, "Apollo in the Democracy," 3–4.

and modestly the two men, reserved and yet friendly, greeted each other and sat down smiling, their claws retracted."[98]

The symbolic value of this meeting, even though it was held at a private venue, should not be underestimated. No more than niceties were exchanged, but by reporting the mere fact of its occurrence, it was clear that the conflict between "then and now," as Leitl had written a few years earlier, was no longer particularly relevant. Paul Bonatz, politically exonerated by his timely emigration to Turkey, was still designing the weighty, prismatic architecture with which former Speer acolytes could comfortably associate themselves. Gropius represented an ascendant formulaic modernism with which many of the architects in attendance would make their postwar careers. By bringing the two men together, facile political attributions to architectural styles could be considered moot. There was no need for "engaging directly" in the debate that Schwarz would precipitate. At the meeting in Hanover, a modernist tradition as represented by Gropius made peace with its former enemies.

But seen in the light of the meeting in Hanover, the assertions that Schwarz made two years later about Gropius and his claim to Bauhaus posterity were not so far from the mark. Because they cut close, they earned Gropius's extreme reprisal. To correct Schwarz's rendition of the true intellectual atmosphere at the historical Bauhaus was not the point. To debunk Schwarz's alternate history of modernism was no more important. Gropius's need for the mythical Bauhaus coincided with his vision of a modern architecture synonymous with "a form of life which, without political identification, is slowly spreading over the whole world," one within which "the creation and love of beauty not only enrich man with a great measure of happiness but also bring forth ethical powers.[99]" The *pax Americana* meant that even wars fought by proxy on the cheaply printed pages of obscure magazines were worth winning by any means necessary.

Were he still alive, Ulrich Conrads might be surprised to learn that an offhand comment, one he probably would not recall, set in motion the years-long process that resulted in this book. More broadly, though, his impact on me is connected in no small part with the ubiquitous volume he edited of first-hand architecture theory documents.[1] That book sustained a rebellious utopianism that made me particularly receptive to that offhand comment when it came in an utterly different context.

I arrived at architecture school in 1986 via the New York postpunk club scene; my two best friends via San Francisco hardcore and Chicago art squats. We were united by our impatience with most of what we found that first semester. It felt trite, predictable, depleted. A house for a poet? A landscape made of lines, a path made of planes? Is Kandinsky running the studio? Gaston Bachelard?

We were drawn instead to the words that had produced modern architecture early in the century. They felt declarative, resistant, radically Peter Pan. They were essentializing and absolute, the opposite of a modernism that had become middle-aged. They met us at the places we'd come from. "Ideas die when they become compromises."[2] We found them in Conrads's book.

The book proclaimed the opposite of what we were taught in school. Modern architecture, we were asked to believe, had failed, maybe because it ignored the past or maybe because it was beholden to it; because it was politically naïve or because it duplicitously chose the wrong political side; because its truth in materials never panned out or because it lied by hiding materials beneath a layer of white stucco.

No doubt we were receiving the legacy of modern architecture at an awkward moment. The years of our education corresponded to the repudiation of postmodernist architecture, itself a repudiation of bland mainstream modernism favored by ruthless developers. Postmodernism's

---

1 Ulrich Conrads, ed. *Programs and Manifestoes on 20th-Century Architecture* (Cambridge, MA: MIT Press, 1971).
2 Walter Gropius, Bruno Taut, and Adolph Behne, "New Ideas on Architecture," in Ulrich Conrads, ed., *Programs and Manifestoes on 20th-Century Architecture* (Cambridge, MA: MIT Press, 1971), 46–48, here 46.

151

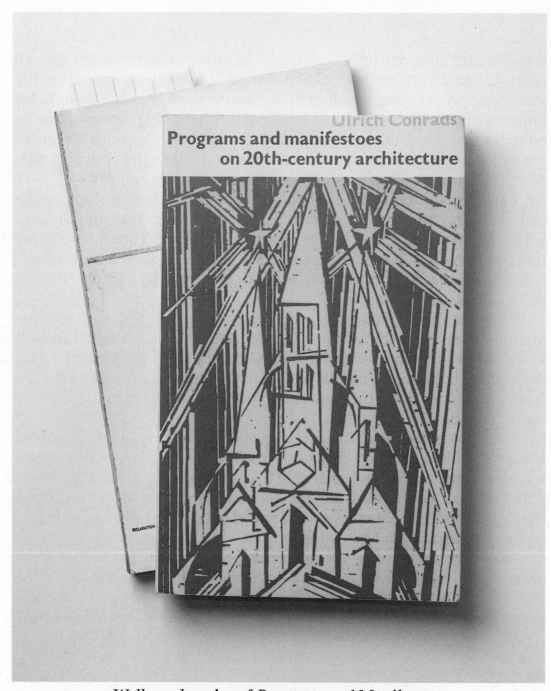

Well-used copies of *Programs and Manifestoes,*
edited by Ulrich Conrads, from the 1980s

sophistic hunt-and-peck use of motifs treated history as an inside joke, one whose ultimate punch line was the 2018 landmarking of the Chippendale AT&T building on Madison Avenue, itself a send-up of history: corporate headquarters dressed as highboy. Not that the architectural ideas offered us as an alternative were any funnier. Many relied literally on turgid critical theory, mostly French and Marxist in origin but without any Sixties-style socialist activism that might have redeemed it. We might be asked in our fall course to draw a school that took Foucault's *Discipline and Punish* into account, then in the spring, to design housing that foreclosed Freud's *Unheimliche*. Whatever. We figured out how to make sense of things by ourselves.

The language of manifesto spoke, across time, directly to our anti-establishment souls. Those manifestoes came to us in the small paperback anthology *Programs and Manifestoes on 20th-Century Architecture*, a brilliant Trojan Horse of modernist credo first published in English in 1971. It had been engineered by Conrads, identified laconically in the book as though he were its author, not its editor. On its cover, Lyonel Feininger's Bauhaus-as-Cathedral woodcut is reproduced in orange and pink, more candy wrapper than master icon.

At a moment of conflicting historiography, the anthology was pixie dust. Its authors, whether writing in 1906 or 1960, invoked a future radically better than our present: politically utopian, materially true, socially just. There was no compromise, no hedging, and definitely no reliance on footnotes for credibility. Only because these documents tell it in its own words, the story of modern architecture, a predictable canon in other narratives, reads instead like a whodunnit: an early rejection of nineteenth-century eclecticism, the embrace of flowing space and new materials, then finally the succession of charismatic masters from idiosyncratic Frank Lloyd Wright to sibylline Ludwig Mies van der Rohe, the organicists, and the rationalists. While affirming the apotheosis of all this in the International Style that emerged from a triumphant postwar United States, the book also nodded to a few pricklier outliers, eccentric Viennese and anarchic Parisians. But its greatest success was that the book put no filter between us and the original urgency with which each text speaks. We might have rolled our eyes when some instrumentalized version of Foucault or Freud appeared in our design studios; but those twentieth-century manifestoes?

Pure Johnny Lydon. "We are the poison in your human machine."[3] It was all there.

I read those manifestoes the way I listened to Public Image on cassette at my desk, a last holdover from club days: to maintain a tenuous claim to rebellion as I edged closer to conventionality. The little paperback anthology was one of the few things I bought off the required bibliography. It gave me a lifelong preference for primary sources. Received truths are rarely complete, or entirely true. The primary document outs it all.

Programs and Manifestoes does without running editorial intervention. One of only two books Conrads published in English, it remains in print even now. The extensive list of his German language publications reflects the range and complexity of his interests, from the French Romanesque and Gothic churches of his dissertation to his long fascination with cities. *Manifestoes* is by far his best seller in any language. The success was deserved. Without his book, many of the texts collected there might have disappeared. Young Turk in his early career, Conrads became an expert at preserving documents of dissent in his later years.

Conrads's tenacity was both personal and professional. Following the War—he had faced the the Soviet army at the Eastern Front, a colleague once told me with a meaningful look that kept me from ever asking for clarification—he completed his art history studies in 1951, after which he began work as an architecture journalist. In 1952, he joined the editorial staff of *Baukunst und Werkform*, a weekly periodical affiliated with the Werkbund, West Germany's assembly of artists, designers, and architects with aspirations to reestablishing Weimar-era productivity.

The periodical was remarkably curated, idiosyncratic in its editorial choices, committed to establishing a version of modernism distinct from Bauhaus traditions already subsumed in the International Style. In the densely illustrated essays Conrads published there, a visual culture prevailed that Conrads had begun to explore in his strangely associative 1950 doctoral thesis.[4] It was eclectic, pattern-conscious, and thoroughly formalist, superficially similar to Rudolf Arnheim's *Gestalt* analyses

---

3 Sex Pistols, "God Save the Queen," Virgin Records (1977).
4 A copy of Conrads's doctoral thesis is among the papers in his bequest at the Brandenburgische Technische Universität Cottbus-Senftenberg, Box 31.

but closer in spirit to the idiosyncratic, theologically-tinged concepts introduced in the late 1920s by the architect Rudolf Schwarz and the photographer Albert Renger-Patzsch. It favored stark, classically aesthetic black-and-white photographs that verged on pure geometry but always stopped short of the alienation for which the avant-garde advocated. *Baukunst und Werkform* was onto something very much its own, if hard to pin down, and Conrads was at its center. This, at a historic moment when the Bauhaus legacy was remaking visual culture elsewhere: expatriated and expropriated Bauhaus design dominated in the United States, from Madison Avenue where Herbert Bayer's graphics sold hair dye, to the surreptitiously propagandistic exhibitions on American lifestyle re-exported from Washington, D.C. to occupied Germany.[5] Perhaps resistance was futile, but at least initially Conrads and the thinkers whose work he helped to preserve were bound to try. Their attempts prevail, up to a point, in built form and in printed words.

And yet Conrads's interests from the early 1950s as expressed in *Baukunst und Werkform* were absent from his *Manifestoes*, not even included among those few outliers he allowed. The texts he selected mostly confirmed what had become established canon when the book first appeared in German in 1964, a canon even more entrenched several years later when it was issued in English translation. New to us, his late 1980s audience, those texts were snide and vibrant. To him, who had known them as the work of a generation barely older than he, they were the foundation of the architecture he had spent his career advocating. Perhaps he really did mean the anthology as a Trojan horse: the ideology of canonical modern architecture wrapped in the aura of antiestablishment declamation. If so, then perhaps this was instead the moment of his capitulation to a more conventional narrative. Or perhaps it was practicality. Conrads had a story he wanted told. And a book to sell.

I wish I had asked him what version of these speculations best described his attitude. When I met Conrads in 1992, he was the *ex officio* head of the editorial board behind the bilingual quarterly *Daidalos*, a lavishly produced thematic architectural journal he had founded in 1981.

---

5   See, for example, Jan Logemann, *Designed to Sell: European Emigrees and the Making of Consumer Capitalism* (Chicago: University of Chicago Press, 2020).

One day, six weeks or so after I began work there, he stood unannounced outside the balconied corner office I shared. He was on his way out, his overcoat draped across his shoulders and, I am fairly certain, a ream of A4 printer paper clamped under his arm. All of us addressed him as Herr Conrads, but in his absence we called him UC, the byline he had used for decades. The magazine's editorial board, all respected middle-aged men, courted his approval. I guessed that at least some of their deference was good manners. But I had also heard enough stories to know: the time was not long past when he had been an absolutist, as editor of both our quarterly and the weekly *Bauwelt* with which we shared offices. The UC I met had recently mellowed.

Towards the end of my tenure at *Daidalos*, my colleague Joseph Imorde and I were offered the opportunity to guest edit an entire issue on our own. We chose as our topic "space," with a set of qualifiers we thought were smart: "constructing space," "mental space," "the innervation of space," and the perennial architectural favorite of the late 1990s, "event space." We involved our friends, and soon the issue felt like a party for ambitious young intellectuals. The article I chose to write was an alibi to use one of my favorite quotations, attributed by a New York friend to his mentor, John Hejduk, dean at the Cooper Union in its 1980s heyday. "That is space," Hejduk was supposed to have said; "It warps the ether."

Ether notwithstanding, I would have done well to pay better attention to UC's recommendation during the meeting in which we announced our topic: "Everything to be said about space was said in 1951 in Darmstadt." He looked at me as he spoke, the only American in the room and the person least likely to understand his reference. Darmstadt: I knew the city only because of its unfortunate name, "intestine city." I had no idea what it meant for the history of architecture. It was also absent from UC's anthology. And yet he had cited this, a moment from the earliest days of his career, as though it were decisive. UC's reference to the 1951 Darmstädter Gespräch, the second in a series of conferences intended to rebuild cultural life after the Year Zero of the Third Reich, was for me a Trojan horse of another kind. Its topic, *Mensch und Raum*, stuck in the back of my mind. A few years later, back in New York, I sought out more. Columbia University's library had the published conference transcription. It must have been lively. Typeset in the book's wide margins are indications of

156

Ulrich Conrads at home in Berlin, 2005

the audience's spontaneous responses, applause, laughter, and shouted commentary. As I read, I was completely taken with what I found. There had been formal, prepared lectures, some practical and others speculative. Even more impressive were the unscripted discussions among the practicing architects in attendance. The surviving audio recordings of these lectures make clear that the speakers made few concessions to ensuring that intellectually demanding talks were understood. The lecture hall, UC later recalled to me, was overfilled and swelteringly hot. It is hard to imagine how the audience would have had the capacity to reflect upon and discuss what they had heard over the prior two days of lectures. Remarkably, the extemporaneous discussion is no less considered and perhaps even more interesting than those speeches. The participants somehow managed what we strove for as students but could not achieve as we navigated the rapids of mid-1980s architectural education: a serious, intellectually rigorous, unconventional effort to rethink the hermeneutics of modern architecture. It was valiant, heroic. I loved it. I still do, some twenty years later.

Well after I departed *Daidalos*, UC reappeared throughout my twenty years of intermittent research: as a young assistant at *Baukunst und Werkform*, as an arbiter of opinion at *Bauwelt*, and as founding editor of the *Bauwelt Fundamente* series of pocket-size paperback reissues of important architectural texts he selected. Among the reissued texts he chose to comment upon himself are *Mensch und Raum* as well as several volumes of otherwise lost writing by his postwar compatriots Schwippert, Schwarz, and Leitl, among others.

In 1997, *Daidalos* disbanded. During the years that followed, UC lost his sight to macular degeneration. For a man who had spent a lifetime transposing visual phenomena to printed words, this was an unimaginable loss. I saw him twice in Berlin, with students, before his death. He invited us to visit him at home, where I was surprised and thrilled to see him walk unassisted through his split-level living space. I asked him whether he had regained his sight. No, he responded, *"das kommt nie wieder"*—that will never return. He had learned to navigate synesthetically.

Over cookies we talked about *Mensch und Raum*, its protagonists, its debates, its architectures. I translated for the students. One wanted to know where he saw the impacts of Darmstadt in the present. *"Es blieb ohne*

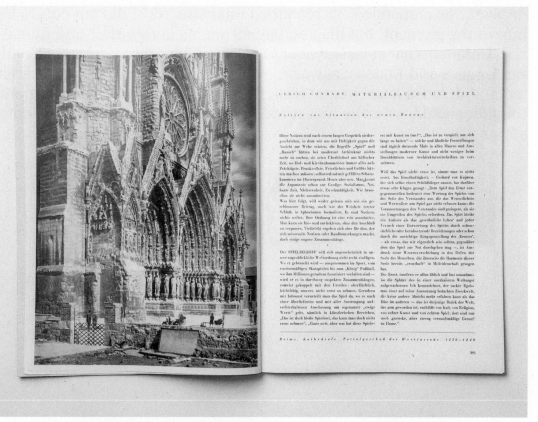

Ulrich Conrads, "Material Euphoria and Play," 1953

159

Antwort," he responded, "it remained unanswered." I did not contradict him in the moment, but his assessment seems both unfair and immaterial. Unfair, in that at least two of the Darmstadt presentations—Martin Heidegger's and Rudolf Schwarz's—found their audiences among architects, if decades later. Immaterial, in that the power of unconventional thought should never be measured by the degree to which it becomes status quo.

Modesty and Internationalism, 1953–1958

The chapter title quotes Hans Schwippert, *Notizen zur deutschen Beteiligung an der Welt-ausstellung Brüssel 1958*, (BA Koblenz: 1955), 1.

"The World of the Little Man"

The West German Pavilion at the Brussels World's Fair

West German architects were inclined to use sweeping, dramatic language to describe the impasse of their discipline in the early 1950s. It was no exaggeration. Any attempt to imagine a future architecture that could arise from the fundamentals of the "human being and space" had inevitably to defer to the immediate need for rebuilding. Continuity with any historic tradition, even that of interwar modernism, was at best tenuous, at worst damning. Given the mainstream narratives that governed the conception of international modernism, it was near-impossible to disentangle a heritage that could be acknowledged as specifically German. Even the Bauhaus had been expropriated: its intellectual legacy now lay on the far side of the Atlantic, its legacy buildings on the far side of the German-German border. The attempt to satisfy a desire for a "return to the valid and simple"[01] seemed bound to founder. Something quite different happened.

By the mid-1950s, the new West German republic's aspirational identity had found a way to express itself in architecture and design that was "a model of efficiency and simplicity,"[02] a consumer-friendly variant of the "valid and simple" which had been laid out in 1949. The new *Bundesrepublik* was a society in which the highest praise reserved for form was that it was "good"[03] or, for civil courage, that it accrued to the "little man." These tendencies converged in the first-ever West German World's Fair pavilion, built for the 1958 fair in Brussels. Staged in an impeccably constructed temporary structure designed by Sep Ruf and Egon Eiermann, curated and landscaped by members of the Werkbund, West Germany's inaugural entry followed a script written largely by Hans Schwippert. As the international press was quick to note at the time, it struck the perfect tone.

The legacy of Germany's presence at World's Fairs gave cause for apprehension in Bonn. The year 1937 had seen Albert Speer's portentous granite-clad steel tower in Paris.[04] Ludwig Mies van der Rohe's elegant pavilion in Barcelona in 1929, representing Weimar Germany, had been counted seminal even before it was dismantled at the fair's end. Simply by comparison to its antecedents, the 1958 pavilion would be closely observed for the way it represented Germany's salient values on the world stage. The expectations were clear and comparison inevitable, as Schwippert observed:

> "The German participation in the movement towards a new openness and lightness (German Pavilion Barcelona, Mies van der Rohe) has already made history *and achieved world recognition. How do things now stand [...] with us? [...]*
>
> The German contribution [in Brussels is] rich in expression but quiet and noble in its strength. You ask for a power that is strong enough to resist, in the future, a repeat of the debacle following 1933. I am an architect, not a prophet. My answer: At this time and place, the power was enough to compete with the shameful representation of that debacle in Paris in 1937, if not to erase it. Nothing less was required!"[05]

Schwippert's words make clear the degree to which Mies van der Rohe's modernism remained his reference point for an architecture of "openness and lightness," the same words Schwippert had used to describe the aspirations of his own Bundeshaus. And Schwippert was clearly convinced of architecture's political potentials. In that regard, he saw the 1958 pavilion as a way of writing, if not rewriting, German political history. Not satisfied merely to "compete with" Speer's pavilion and, by extension, the regime it embodied, Schwippert intended to erase it by means of architecture. Schwippert and the committee he helped put together was charged with delivering no less than a perfect embodiment, in architectural form, of a country about which little was known but whose simple existence was, in light of recent history, bound to elicit skepticism. West Germany would be, in Schwippert's words, "the object of particular attention. If it misinterprets the subject, ignores the spiritual

01   A statement by the editors in the first issue of *Baukunst und Werkform* reads, "The collapse destroyed the visible world of our lives and work. [...] We are left to return to the foundation of things [...] only. The valid-simple is useful." Reproduced in Johannes Busmann, *Die revidierte Moderne: Der Architekt Alfons Leitl 1909–1975* (Wuppertal: Müller und Busmann, 1995), 59.
02   Murrey Marder, "Brussels Exhibition [...] Spirit of a People is Reflected in its Architecture," *The Washington Post and Times Herald* (May 26, 1958).
03   Max Bill coined the term "The Good Form" in 1949 to describe what would become branded as German Design. See Paul Betts, *The Authority of Everyday Objects: A Cultural History of West German Industrial Design, Weimar and Now* (Berkeley: University of California Press, 2004).
04   On the materialization of Speer's pavilion, see Christopher Laws, "Art and Architecture Towards Political Crises: The 1937 Paris International Exposition in Context," https://culturedarm.com/1937-Paris-International-Exposition/, accessed December 16, 2021): "A surface of Bavarian granite masked a structure comprising three-thousand tons of steel; the granite rose in pillars with mosaics; and inside the pavilion, the floor was coated in red rubber."
05   Hans Schwippert, manuscript for "Notizen zur deutschen Beteiligung an der Weltausstellung Brüssel 1958," undated, GNM, DKA, NL, Schwippert, 5 and 8.

and political meaning of its demonstration [...] then the damage would be severe."[06]

World's Fair pavilions were, more often than not, conceived to advertise from a distance the image with which a country wished to be identified. As much large-scale sculpture as exhibition spaces, they competed with one another along the thoroughfares constructed for public promenade. In this regard, Ruf and Eiermann's design[07] departed radically from standard practice. Their "pavilion" was actually a ring-like complex of steel-framed buildings: four small, three medium, and one large. [5.1] The ensemble was set back from the main axis along which the other countries' pavilions aligned. The eight cubic volumes, laid out on a due north-south orientation, were accessed across a thinly dimensioned bridge, suspended from a single pylon. Even under construction, its spatial structure was legible: each pavilion was a vitrine for its contents, carefully selected by a committee of artists, architects, politicians, and curators to represent the workmanly quietude of West German life.

From the bridge, visitors entered the first of the two larger pavilions along a steel-framed walkway that connected all of the volumes in a rectangular ring. From there, movement was guided by the view from one glass building to the next. Walter Rossow's decoratively landscaped terrain slipped beneath the walkways and offered a park-like respite that would become much-loved by visitors pausing from the intensity of the fairgrounds. Attractions included a restaurant, a shaded seating area, and a small lagoon, all of which feature prominently in both official photos and souvenir snapshots. Each component building had been located to avoid disturbing the stands of existing trees that predated, and outlived, the fair; the buildings, because of the mature growth among which they stood, seemed always to have been there, or at least, it seemed that precautions had been taken to avoid any disruption.

The buildings above the brightly patterned landscape were, in appearance, the perfect inversion of the pavilion that had represented the Third Reich: in lieu of a towering block of Bavarian granite, cannulated with multistory columns and crowned by an outscaled, hook-taloned eagle, here were precisely dimensioned glass boxes, punctuated vertically by a delicate steel structure from which the facades were suspended. The actual, much heavier bearing structure was set back within the buildings, a structural concept with which both Ruf and Eiermann had experimented elsewhere. The glass buildings' contents were visible even from afar: brightly colored, graphically scaled images overlaid with the silhouettes of foreground objects and the moving forms of visitors. The buildings were at once billboards and exhibition halls. The people inside, all potential consumers of the West German lifestyle and products they were there to admire, became part of the architecture.

Although the pavilion by Ruf and Eiermann demanded no less precision or detailed execution than those designed by Speer or Mies van der Rohe, it kept its extravagances secret. Schwippert, in an undated draft typescript, discreetly described the project as built on "limited Federal means."[08] Its components were entirely prefabricated for installation in only a few months, between February and April 1957, after which they were transported to Brussels for mounting, a full year prior to the fair's opening.[09] The pavilion stood on site for less than half the amount of time required to produce and install it. As Imko Boyken, author of the only monograph on the building, acknowledged laconically on the verso of his book's final page, the building was "dismantled and scrapped" after its six-month occupancy during the World's Fair.[10] Little notice was taken in contemporary accounts of the pavilion's physical production, or of the frivolity of its destruction after only six months in place. Historical literature has done little to address this oversight.

Despite multiple comparisons that included the buildings within an idiom already known as "Miesian," unlike its famous antecedents, the Brussels pavilion was anything but an abstract expression of national identity. In every historical photograph, whether a professional image in stark black-and-white contrast or a fuzzy amateur snapshot made

06   Hans Schwippert, "Notizen zur deutschen Beteiligung an der Weltausstellung Brüssel 1958," October 14, 1955, B102/37723, BA Koblenz.
07   According to meeting minutes signed by Schwippert, Eiermann and Ruf were officially granted the commission on July 4, 1956, following the General Commissioner's acceptance of the exhibition concept Schwippert authored. AM TUM, schwi-135-201.
08   Schwippert, manuscript for "Notizen zur deutschen Beteiligung," 4.
09   Werner Durth and Paul Sigel, *Baukultur: Spiegel gesellschaftlichen Wandels*, 2nd rev. and enl. ed. (Berlin: Jovis, 2010), 531.
10   Immo Boyken et al., *Egon Eiermann/Sep Ruf: Deutsche Pavillons, Brüssel 1958*, Opus (Stuttgart: Edition Axel Menges, 2007), 55 verso.

5.1 West German World's Fair Pavilion under construction, Brussels, 1957

11　Fischer, Wend, and Generalkommisar der Bundesrepublik Deutschland bei der Weltausstellung Brüssel 1958, eds., *Deutschlands Beitrag zur Weltausstellung Brüssel 1958. Ein Bericht.* (Düsseldorf: A. Bagel, 1958). Fischer had been at the journals *Welt* and *Werk und Zeit*; his collaboration on the pavilion was noted as early as August 28, 1956. Aktennotiz, AM TUM, schwi-135-201.
12　Johannes Paulmann, "Representation without Emulation: German Cultural Diplomacy in Search of Integration and Self-Assurance during the Adenauer Era," *German Politics and Society* 25, no. 2 (83) (2007), 168–200.
13　Paulmann, "Representation," 168–200.
14　Paulmann describes the juxtaposition of the canoe to the USSR's neo-liturgical presentation of Sputnik as a stroke of genius in demonstrating how the oft-invoked *"Haltung der Zurückhaltung"* was an appropriate and powerful position for West Germany to assume in relation both to its immediate past and to its current position in the Cold War. Paulmann, "Representation," 168–200.

by a visitor, the spaces are full of people and heterogeneous objects. This holds true, as well, for the photographs published in the official guidebook produced by the West German General Commissioner with publicist Wend Fischer for the fair.[11] There can be no mistaking that the architecture was designed to ensure the visibility of everything it contained: deep, overhanging walkways used for installation and window-cleaning shaded the glazed facades to guarantee that the glass would always be transparent, never reflective in the glaring sun. The interior spaces and their various contents were always on display.

The presence of artifacts in this architectural setting was integral to the whole, which conceptually and physically was nothing other than a vitrine for the exhibition of West German–made objects. The relationship between architecture and its contents was reciprocal. Each object exhibited, even the least rarified, was constitutive of the whole as well as a worthy design exemplar in its own right. A case in point is the collapsible canoe, furnished by the Bavarian manufacturer Klepper in Rosenheim.[12] Even in the early 1956 architectural study and presentation model, the canoe was represented in miniature on the central pond.[13] As with every other product selected for the pavilion, its connotation went beyond its aesthetics. It signaled access to leisure activities and was equipped with nifty accouterments for the recreational sportsman or sportswoman. Furthermore, it was associated with adventure: two years earlier, a German physician had crossed the Atlantic Ocean in a canoe of similar model, a feat that garnered him coverage in *Life* magazine. This was a distinction that he and West German Chancellor Adenauer shared as the only two Germans to be featured since the war.[14] Produced by a firm that employed an impressive 1,500 workers, the canoe represented the readiness of Germany's domestic consumer product industry to restore the country to international presence by means of civil society. The boat's presence to scale in the architectural model indicates that Eiermann and Ruf, as well, recognized a need to showcase widely accessible design as part of everyday life.

The construction site that would ultimately become the 1958 Brussels World's Fair, as captured in photographs, is dominated by the

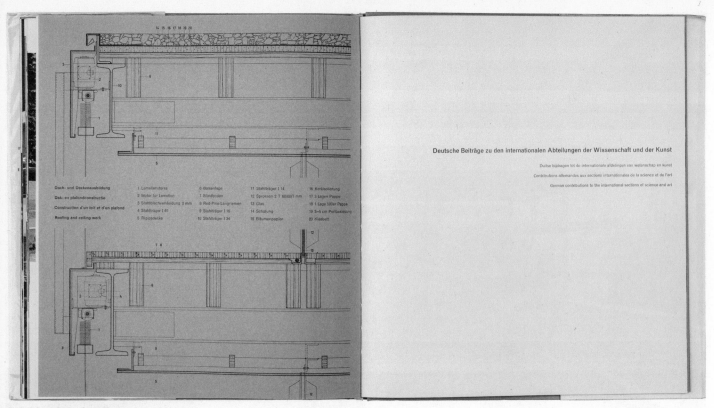

5.2 Simplified wall section showing roof and floor slab details, *Deutschlands Beitrag zur Weltausstellung Brüssel 1958. Ein Bericht.*

5.3 Interior stair and adjacent exhibit, *Deutschlands Beitrag zur Weltausstellung Brüssel 1958. Ein Bericht.*

enormous steel trusses of cranes, caught in the act of lifting prefabricated steel elements into place. With the notable exception of Le Corbusier and Iannis Xenakis's Philips Pavilion and the less-notable British pavilion, the fair's buildings were primarily long-span structures supported by steel columns and enclosed in steel and glass facades representing the "dazzling Modernity of [...] the nuclear age."[15]

Eiermann and Ruf's on-site handling of steel elements can be only superficially reconstructed from the few construction documents ever published: the two details and the building section included in the official catalogue from 1958 are all that was released, and they have been republished countless times until the present.[16] [5.2] The steel I-beams that carry the roof and floor plates are embedded and invisible. I-40 at the floors and I-34 in the roof, the steel is encased within a shell of sheet steel on the exterior surfaces and gypsum board or wood interior cladding, all affixed to more easily scribed and fastened wood members, which in turn remain invisible in the finished construction. The actual compressive members, large box columns measuring some fifty centimeters square, were offset from the building's perimeter by two and a half meters. At the buildings' edge, significantly slimmer elements stiffened with flanges running perpendicular to the glazing and tapered at ceiling and floor were used to stiffen the building against uplift and give the impression that the building was suspended from above. The published detail drawings do not represent the heavier columns but instead depict the lighter, finned mullions that hold the glass enclosure. By concealing the actual bearing structure beneath wood-clad ceilings and boxed columns, Ruf and Eiermann downplayed the tectonics, lionized in other countries' pavilions, of the long-span shed structure. A glance at the construction photos reveals just how massive the actual bearing structure was. The point, it seems, was not to be *overtly* heroic.

The pavilion's buildings seemed to levitate above the ground, a quality central to the architectural experience. This effect was created by periphery cantilevers that began above the brick-veneered bases on which each building stood, continued across the buildings' heights and terminated at the roof, which protruded beyond the plane of enclosure. Thinner white-painted steel elements at the edge of floor and roof plates, attached at the uppermost and lowermost floor plates by rectilinear stand-offs, reinforced this connotation. These, too, are not noted in the published detail, although they appear in sharp contrast in the black-and-white photographs that most often depict the building in publications. Covered walkways between the eight cubic component buildings, also carried on staple-shaped steel arches, used a similar stand-off, a detail that Ruf had developed in his 1950–54 Nuremberg Akademie der Bildenden Künste and that he would repeat in later projects. Tongue-and-groove red pine floorboards, into which the glazed facade disappeared, extended throughout the interior and continued onto the exterior walkways. Even the edge of the walkway was clad in red pine: a small piece of floorboard was connected to the edge grain of the last horizontal floorboard using mortise and tenon carpentry. The use of this less expensive soft wood, more prone to expansion and contraction over time than the more traditional oak or maple hardwood floorboards in common use, is the only concession apparent in the construction details to the pavilion's short life.

On the interior, stairs were free-floating, milled solid wood beams. [5.3] These heavy elements were realized in a material to match the red pine floor planes rather than in steel. The architecture juxtaposed heavy bearing members, expressed in the black-clad floor slabs and interior columns, with the impossibly light periphery members, including the barely offset, clad edges of the planes that made up floor and ceiling. The effect was simultaneously one of gravitas and levity, of repressed tectonic structure and highly articulated enclosure. It was philosophically aligned to, but visually unlike, its presumptive Miesian precedent.

With regard to site planning, Ruf's Nuremberg Academy and the Brussels pavilion evince a similar attitude toward a campus ensemble

15 Narration of a British newsreel, "Brussels: The World on Show," in *The World on Show* (British Pathé, 1958), https://www.britishpathe.com/video/the-world-on-show/query/Belgium, accessed January 25, 2016.
16 Compare the drawings in Fischer, *Deutschlands Beitrag*; Boyken et al., *Egon Eiermann/Sep Ruf.*

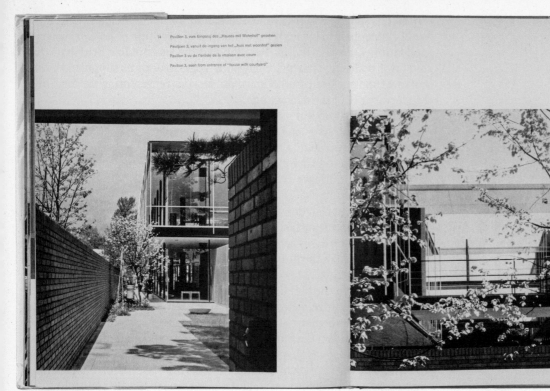

74　Pavillon 3, vom Eingang des „Hauses mit Wohnhof" gesehen

Paviljoen 3, vanuit de ingang van het „huis met woonhof" gezien

Pavillon 3 vu de l'entrée de la maison avec cours

Pavilion 3, seen from entrance of "House with courtyard"

5.4 Wall between pavilions 3 and 4, *Deutschlands Beitrag zur Weltausstellung Brüssel 1958. Ein Bericht.*

expressed in a larger parti: both were based on a series of loosely connected pavilions whose relationship to one another defined both identifiable interior courtyards and a larger landscape figure. This similarity in parti has often been cited as the grounds for the otherwise unsubstantiated but routine architecture-historical practice of crediting Ruf with the pavilion's site design while attributing to Eiermann its building design and construction concepts.[17] However, this simplistic separation of the two collaborators' roles is not supported by Ruf's handling, in other contemporaneous projects, of a material and construction palette closely related to that of the Brussels pavilion, albeit to different spatial ends. One such project is his Hochschule für Verwaltungswissenschaften (HfV) in Speyer. Because a whole new class of West German civil servants was to be trained at the HfV, the task of representing the new culture of West Germany was no less significant there than in Brussels.

Only a few images of the Brussels pavilion depict it as anything but fully transparent, a tendency that underscores the obvious interpretation of the architecture as a large-scale vitrine for the objects it housed. In contrast to the many images of the photogenic glass volumes, there is little documentation of the dark brick socle on which each sat. The buildings' juncture with the ground plane was largely ignored although much attention has been paid to the open landscape that stretched between buildings. Of the 208 pages in the book officially documenting the pavilion, only two spreads, reproduced here, show the clinker walls from which the glass "vitrines" cantilevered. **[5.4] [5.5]** The architecture that these walls defined is no less interesting than its better-documented corollary, and contributes importantly to the way in which the project addressed the private sphere.

The bottom edge of the glass vitrines marked a consistent datum, so that the site's changing slope had to be accounted for by varying the height of the bases on which the eight glass buildings sat. At the upper portion of the site, where the topographic differential was small, the brick-clad concrete base was merely a low retaining wall from which the glass and steel superstructure rose. Along the site's southwest corner, however, the brick-clad foundation walls were tall enough to enclose an additional lower story, which presented an opportunity to develop a spatial order that differed from the transparent vitrines above. These brick walls offered private spaces, which were sheltered from, although in direct proximity to, public activity. One example is right outside the

17　Boyken et al., *Egon Eiermann/Sep Ruf.* Greg Castillo cites Peter Blundell Jones as having provided a similar opinion, which Castillo also seems to accept. Greg Castillo, "Making a Spectacle of Restraint: The Deutschland Pavilion at the 1958 Brussels Exposition," *Journal of Contemporary History* 47, no. 1 (2011), 97–112, here 102.

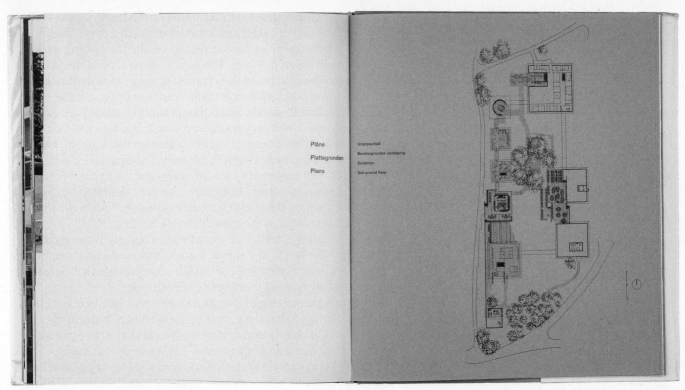

Pläne
Plattegronden
Plans

Untergeschoß
Benedengrondse verdieping
Souterrain
Sub-ground floor

5.5 Site plan, West German World's Fair pavilion, *Deutschlands Beitrag zur Weltausstellung Brüssel 1958. Ein Bericht.*

book-lined library, which, in the official publication, is populated exclusively by studious women. [5.6] [5.7] Outdoors, visitors relax, among them two women stretched out flat, basking in the sun on the round seating elements, their postures decidedly immodest for the standards of 1958. [5.8] The women depicted in these two photographs provide a subtext: the walled library is a space of decorum, the open porch, one of abandon.

Along the site's low point, a long, bracket-shaped brick wall formed the backdrop to Rossow's landscape. The wall configured an outdoor room at the lowermost small volume, then skirted the southernmost volume to form a narrow stair and seating area. At its terminus, the wall involuted, forming a small, brick-clad structure shaded by a thick stand of trees. This structure was a model house, facing onto a *Wohnhof*, or domestic courtyard, surrounded by the same brick wall that defined the house. [5.9] If the glazing and exposed steel construction begged comparison to Mies van der Rohe's Barcelona pavilion, so did these walls, for the way they extended past the boundary between interior and exterior or turned in on themselves to form separate courtyards. However, while Mies van der Rohe's rarified pavilion was empty, Ruf and Eiermann's was as full as a trade fair stall; while Mies van der Rohe's architecture was unerringly precise in placement and dimension, Ruf and Eiermann's was much more pragmatic and opportunistic. Sometimes the walls bypassed structural columns; sometimes they replaced them. Sometimes they obeyed purely functional or structural considerations. But they also signaled an architecture, intimate and enclosed, that was different in kind from the fully glazed boxes and their palimpsest of views above. While the glass boxes displayed the objects of everyday life to their best advantage, the brick-clad walls demonstrated the kinds of spaces in which everyday life would be at home.

The compact interior space of the model house was an abbreviated demonstration of how the typical West German lived, or aspired to live. [5.10] The disposition of elements—bathroom and kitchen core freestanding at its center, bedroom and living room defined by the encircling wall on two sides and enclosed by a continuous pane of glass toward which the two rooms were oriented—shared much with the small houses Ruf had realized for the Berlin Interbau exhibition of 1957–58. The glazed south-facing wall opened onto a garden, where a seating group and steel chimney occupied the place taken by a statue and reflecting pool in Mies van der Rohe's Barcelona pavilion. This tongue-in-cheek reference to the Miesian precedent affirmed the pavilion's larger message: that good

18 Schwippert, "Notizen."

19 "La Dernière Heure" (Brussels) dated May 2, 1958. Cited in Christopher Oestereich, "Umstrittene Selbstdarstellung: Der Deutsche Beitrag zur Weltausstellung in Brüssel 1958," *Vierteljahrshefte für Zeitgeschichte* 48, no. 1 (2000), 127–53, page 127. Also cited in Fischer, *Deutschlands Beitrag zur Weltausstellung Brüssel 1958. Ein Bericht..*

20 Expressions of concern for the way the physical world registered "spiritual" needs were frequent in the wake of World War II. I will note here only the 1947 CIAM VI statement: "We must combine social idealism, scientific planning and the fullest use of available building techniques. In doing so we must enlarge and enrich the aesthetic language of architecture in order to provide a contemporary means whereby people's emotional needs can find expression in the design of their environment." In John R. Gold, *The Experience of Modernism: Modern Architects and the Future City 1928–53* (London: E & FN Spon, 1997), 203.

design had been democratized. The detailing of the house's glass wall—mullioned in black-painted steel and set back beneath a deep, thickly dimensioned overhang—was robust, totally unlike the glazing details elsewhere in the Brussels pavilion. The heavy frame around the glass wall merged into the courtyard doorframe, equally thick in dimension. Above the glazing and set without a frame into the roof overhang, the ceiling plane continued outside without interruption, to form an exterior eave. The juxtaposition of heavy frame and absent header—the former clearly demarcating the difference between exterior and interior, and the latter implying continuity between these same two spaces—carefully balanced the desire to demarcate a private realm and the impulse to embody a new lightness in architecture. Both aspects were celebrated by the texts that accompanied the West German exhibition.[18] As in the library, the inside was decorous and the outside, free-wheeling.

The 1958 Brussels World's Fair was a first not only for West Germany but also for the New World Order that the war had wrought. Its ambitions were markedly different from those of the fairs that preceded it. The invitation to participating nations was worded accordingly:

"We want an accounting of human achievement in all areas of the Modern World: so that the people of the world are brought to the realization clearly and dynamically that they are responsible to return the humane to this world. [...] We wish that every nation is able to explain to the others its way of life, its philosophical and religious conceptions as well as its economic and social programs. If governance means the attempt to increase the happiness of a people, then all are invited to convey to the others what ideal it has of this happiness, and in what way it believes that it can ensure the material and moral prerequisites for it."[19]

Earlier World's Fairs had aimed to showcase progress and technology. At Brussels, however, the desire expressed in the invitation to convey the basis for "happiness" within the context of a "way of life" resonates with the language used in much of the postwar European cultural response to the war experience.[20] This expression of belief in the aspiration to everyday happiness must have spoken straight to Schwippert's heart. It was the apotheosis of his *Wohnwollen*, the neologism he had used to describe the profound urge to domesticity that, he thought, would guide architectural practice from Year Zero onwards. In practical terms, the invitation's phrasing offered an opportunity just as close to the heart of Schwippert as postwar German Werkbund president: to represent

5.6 Pavilion 8 library, unpeopled and staged with young women, *Deutschlands Beitrag zur Weltausstellung Brüssel 1958. Ein Bericht.*

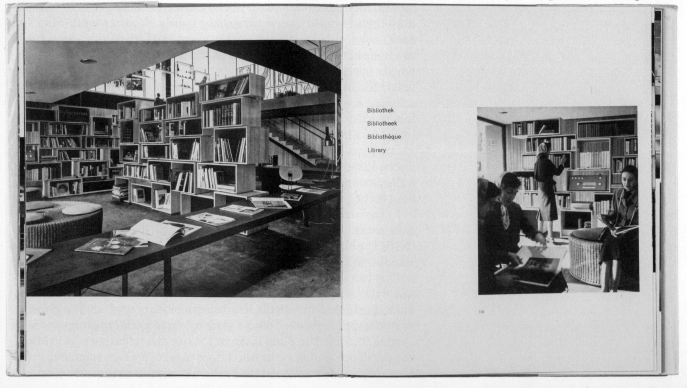

Bibliothek
Bibliotheek
Bibliothèque
Library

5.7 Pavilion 8 library, exterior view,
Deutschlands Beitrag zur
Weltausstellung Brüssel 1958. Ein
Bericht.

the swords-to-ploughshares transformation of demilitarized Germany as a producer of consumer goods. Schwippert, whose political connections were always lively, was among the first to be asked to respond when the invitation arrived in Bonn in late 1955. West German Minister of Economic Affairs Ludwig Erhard, his own house designed by Ruf, appointed Hermann Wenhold general commissioner to oversee the pavilion's development. Wenhold in turn articulated the core political intention that would guide all decisions: "the Federal Republic will avoid everything in its exhibition that might be perceived as arrogant."[21] Perhaps this intention explains the surprising official decision to pursue Schwippert's unorthodox proposal: to represent the country's progress in terms of the everyday. And although the design and curatorial team was chosen by March 1956, it was not until the February 1, 1957, meeting of the *Bundestag* that the government's decision to participate was officially announced.[22]

Initially, two concepts were presented to Wenhold: Schwippert's and that of Herbert Engst, director of the Northwest German Exhibition Association. Engst proposed a more conventional agenda of "products, progress, nationalism," focusing entirely on a broad history of technical progress and the German contribution to it, from Gutenberg to the present. This was in stark contrast to Schwippert's proposal, which emphasized the daily life of West Germany's new petty bourgeoisie and promoted the design of its environment and quotidian objects to describe the country's postwar identity. There was relatively little jockeying regarding the pavilion's content, a testament to Schwippert's well-chosen approach and to his political acumen. The decision was made within a few weeks. With Minister Erhard's support, Schwippert was selected as curator over Engst.[23]

Schwippert, in contrast to Engst, was explicit that progress and technology had fallen under a "dark shadow."[24] This was doubly true in Germany, which had subordinated the continent to the products of military technology. "This World's Fair, for the first time, I believe," he wrote, "is subordinated to an idea and is not to be a public arena for

21   Durth and Sigel, *Baukultur,* 530.
22   Printed report from *2ter Deutscher Bundestag, 189 Meeting in Bonn,* GNM, DKA, NL, Schwippert, Werkbund Binder (Friday, February 1, 1957).
23   *2ter Deutscher Bundestag,* 530. On March 17, 1956, the decision was made to pursue Schwippert's proposal.
24   Schwippert, manuscript for "Notizen zur deutschen Beteiligung," 2.

business and mercantile prowess, no longer a market for progress in the old style."[25] Schwippert short-handed this idea as the "habitual world of the little man" and the "life of [West Germany's] so-called masses."[26] His loose use of "the masses" is curious in Germany's Cold War context, but the modifier "so-called" insinuates a distinction: the lives led by his "little men" are private, not based on class consciousness. They are united by the benefits of modern design, evident in the qualities of work and domestic spaces that guaranteed their happiness. Good design, in Schwippert's account, configured the communal experience of the new, diligent, modest, and decidedly not belligerent West German citizen.

Schwippert's October 14, 1955, proposal was offered on behalf of the Werkbund, of which he had been president since 1950, and the Rat für Formgebung,[27] a consulting committee on design within the Ministry of Economics. Neither "ignorance nor frivolity nor arrogance"[28] would be permitted. Thanks to Schwippert's influence, Ruf and fellow *Werkbundler* Egon Eiermann were commissioned with the pavilion's architecture in 1956.[29] As planned, the exhibition included three primary areas of focus, each a potential platform to convey the new West German *esprit* by means of consumer goods and the environments in which they were used. Keeping political and economic interests in mind, Schwippert suggested that these themes "follow the broad lines of international interest and at the same time permit the appropriate consideration of German economic interests."[30] Each area would showcase a solidly middle-class world in which the objects of home and workplace "are becoming beautiful. The sad juxtaposition: here, filthy, lowly world of work, there; trusted home,here drudgery, there freedom; here factory, there idyll—begins to disappear. The apparatuses of the working world and the world of the home increasingly resemble one another."[31] The successful partnership of industrial production and good design was set against the backdrop of implicitly equitable distribution of wealth, which allowed all citizens access to an aesthetically inspired environment, even in a factory. The image of a society in which industrial labor was no longer "drudgery" undergirded West Germany's reformed international identity[32] as the joyful, new world of the "little man."

The initial proposal document already includes "sketched examples"[33] of these concepts, which appear in all of Schwippert's texts on the pavilion. As previously with *Wohnwollen*, he coined a new term to contain his vision: *Wohnwelt*, the world of inhabitation, in a narrow translation, or lifeworld more broadly, by which he meant the entire environment of everyday life. It was nothing less than a microcosm of a larger worldview. In practical terms, this focus allowed him to lionize the efforts of the postwar German Werkbund and to prove the benefits that design collaboration offered to industry. As he wrote,

> "Thanks to the consciousness of the exemplarily progressive sectors
> of German industry and the efforts of the German Werkbund
> and its affiliated organizations, few countries have at present such
> excellent objects to fulfill the needs of life and living as does Germany.
> [...] herein lies a German achievement which, only now attained,
> can make an extraordinary impression when represented clearly
> and unambiguously."[34]

While praising the role of industry, he was swift to explain that a "presentation as imagined by industry lobbies and market specialists, such as labor saving through rationalization or other problems, is still not enough"[35] to form the basis for the fair's exhibit. It was imperative that the "humanitarian-cultural and formal values as well as the capacity for comprehensive optical and spatial representation"[36] set the tone. Schwippert's contention, that ethics were implicit to the "optical and spatial representations" created by architecture and design, aligned with interwar modernist rhetoric. This was a very different context, however: an economy increasingly driven by consumer goods and a society in which the private sphere had come to be understood as the antidote to the horrific excesses of Fascist public appearance. Domestic design was meant to propagate good values one individual at a time. Consumer culture

25   Schwippert, "Notizen," 1.
26   Schwippert used both phrases ("die Wohnwelt des sogenannten kleinen Mannes in Deutschland" and "das Leben der sogenannten Masse") in October 1955, prior to the first meeting of the *Inhaltskommission* in December that year. See Schwippert, "Notizen."
27   Schwippert, "Notizen," 528–29.
28   Schwippert, "Notizen," 528–29.
29   In a protocol of the November 1956 meeting of the Werkbund, Schwippert reported that "a competition foreseen by the Director of Federal Building could be hindered, because and as long as the intellectual concept for the exhibition was still not decided. After a resolution by the cabinet, the Director of Federal Building asked Rossig, Eiermann, and Ruf to develop preliminary projects. The two projects showed adequate similarities so that a collaboration between the two architects was resolved, so as to secure the right form for the buildings." Rossig's name subsequently does not appear as an author of the project. "Typescript of the Protocol of the Deutscher Werkbund AG Meeting on November 17, 1956," GNM, DKA, NL, Schwippert. A separate document (AM TUM, schwi-135-201) indicates July 4, 1956, as the date on which Eiermann and Ruf were commissioned. Schwippert, Eiermann, Ruf and Minister Johannes Rossig had begun conceptual plans in May, 1956.
30   Schwippert, "Notizen."
31   Schwippert, "Notizen," 2.
32   Schwippert said, "We are trying consciously to avoid all sensational fireworks as they are common at conventions or fairs. What should, and will, make an impression is what we have to show in a sober and upstanding way: our efforts and achievements that aim to make the life and work of everyone in Germany more meaningful and more beautiful." Hans Schwippert, "Typescript of a Meeting on July 17, 1957 on the Topic of Whether the German Pavilion at the Brussels World's Fair Would Be Spectacular Enough," GNM, DKA, NL, Schwippert.
33   Schwippert, "Notizen," 1.
34   Schwippert, "Notizen."
35   Schwippert, "Notizen," 1–2.
36   Schwippert, "Notizen."

5.8 Pavilion 8, exterior with outdoor
lounge area, *Deutschlands Beitrag
zur Weltausstellung Brüssel 1958.
Ein Bericht.*

was a clever covert means by which to introduce moral education while
simultaneously buoying the economic stability on which a democratic
West Germany could build. Schwippert believed in this project deeply.
It was more complex than the typical "soft sell," which his historical
context—the use of domestic consumer goods as proxies for ideological
positions in the postwar period—might otherwise imply.[37]

No less evocative of earlier modernist rhetoric was Schwippert's
correlation between "glass and happiness," a trope closely associated with
Paul Scheerbart and Bruno Taut in the 1910s.[38] For Schwippert, however,
glass architecture was not part of a utopian future; it was evidence that
everyday life had achieved a new, joyous quality. Glass was equated
to openness, a position Schwippert had also taken in his comments at the
1951 Darmstädter Gespräch. The architecture of openness, he had stated
there, transcended the threats posed by the world around it: "it seems
to me that there is something quite peculiar here. In a time characterized
by unrest, fear and threat [...] we sense around the world a directive
of building that is anything but a bastion of refuge. [...] [it is] the brightness and lightness of our spatial desire."[39] Envisioning the World's Fair
pavilion, Schwippert expanded his parable, claiming that this phenomenon of parallel spiritual and architectural openness was now global.
This phenomenon had a definitive origin: "Mies van der Rohe, Barcelona
Pavilion!"[40] West Germany and its design culture was no less committed
to the "joy of life".[41]

"There is in the world a movement against the deadly serious,
the political situation, the dehumanization of the mechanized,
the threats of the new, ghostly threats of destruction and of 'progress,'
against the constant danger of human catastrophe, regardless of the
situation, which, in the most wonderful way, desires and asserts a new
levity, a new tenderness, a new grace.

The glass walls of the new architecture, the new lightness of the
office, workshop, factory, the delicacy of the new furnishings,
the friendliness of living amid greenery, the transformation of clothing,

37   Greg Castillo has described the use
of domestic goods as proxies by both Germany
and the Superpowers. Greg Castillo,
"Domesticating the Cold War: Household
Consumption as Propaganda in Marshall Plan
Germany," *Journal of Contemporary History* 40,
no. 2 (2005); Castillo, "Making a Spectacle."
See also David Crowley, "From Homelessness
to Homelessness," in Robin Schuldenfrei, ed.,
*Atomic Dwelling: Anxiety, Domesticity, and Postwar
Architecture* (Abingdon: Routledge, 2012).
38   Scheerbart is referenced in Schwippert,
"Notizen," 2.
39   Ulrich Conrads and Peter Neitzke, eds.,
Mensch und Raum: Das Darmstädter Gespräch 1951
(Braunschweig: Vieweg, 1991).
40   Schwippert, "Notizen," 2.
41   Schwippert, "Notizen," 2–3.

42   Schwippert, "Notizen," 2–3.

43   Schwippert, "Notizen," 2–3.

44   Statista, "Verteilung der Exporte ausgewählter Länder und Regionen weltweit nach Warengruppen im Jahr 1955." http://de.statista.com/statistik/daten/studie/249754/umfrage/sektarale-anteile-am-export-von-ausgewaehlten-laender-1955/, accessed December 16, 2021.

45   Wendy Carlin, "West German Growth and Institutions, 1945–1900," Centre for Economic Policy Research, University College London 1994, 29. https://www.ucl.ac.uk/~uctpa36/west%20germany%20in%20crafts%20toniolo.pdf, accessed December 19, 2021.

46   Schwippert as cited in Oestereich, "Umstrittene Selbstdarstellung," 2–3.

the decorative arts—these are all within a great effort of human resistance to threat, darkness and imminent chaos."[42] Schwippert understood architecture and design as resistant to larger, top-down forces, among them the political and economic interests that, in the past, had conspired to create an atmosphere of "darkness and imminent chaos." Instead, design was a means to allow a loosely organized community of individuals to find joy at the scale of their own daily lives. Strengthened in their moral fiber by their immediate environments, he contended, these individuals could, in aggregate, form the "great effort of human resistance." The irony of a national pavilion dedicated to demonstrating aggregated bottom-up resistance to politics may seem obvious. No less ironic was the characterization of consumer goods and architecture, produced only through application of large capital and industrial inputs, as the tools of individuals. Despite Schwippert's best hopes, consumer markets were politically agnostic. But Schwippert's idealism also gave less idealistic interests places to flourish. The liberative connotations with which he wished to imbue these interests did their case no harm.

His faith in the ability of architecture and design to generate joy in daily life extended to a final theme in Schwippert's manuscript: the beautification of the workplace. His attention to the workplace included not only its architecture but also "appliances, tools, machines, even vehicles!"[43] These had long been subject to design in Germany; but in 1955, these particular categories of goods accounted for 40 percent of West Germany's total exports by monetary unit.[44] Throughout the 1950s, West Germany maintained its economic growth by exporting what its industry produced,[45] a clear shift away from the exportation of raw materials, which had dominated the early postwar economy. The need to assure a place at Brussels for the West German consumer goods industry was a political and economic imperative.

Schwippert's hope that "the equipment of the working and domestic worlds is becoming the same"[46] was much more than mercantile. The elision of places of work and domesticity, according to Schwippert, was also evidence of the larger social movement towards joy:

"The sad juxtaposition [...] is beginning to disappear. [...] There are the same norms, the same materials, the associated color schemes; it is the same formal spirit of an honest life [made] from the possibilities of its time, which transform and unify both. [...] To show that this positive unification has captured the whole of daily life,

5.9 Courtyard house, exterior and views, *Deutschlands Beitrag zur Weltausstellung Brüssel 1958. Ein Bericht.*

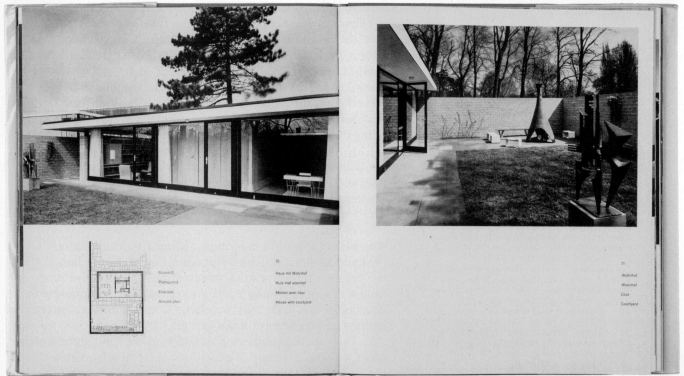

> and not only the hours outside of work, the vacation, would be yet another demonstration of the aspect of progress that seeks to humanize."[47]

The ubiquity of good design, for Schwippert, proved the ubiquity of an honest, humanizing life. This was true even in contexts where individual aesthetic preference had little role to play, in contexts where the "little man" had historically been oppressed. Schwippert credited the humanization of the entire West German *Wohnwelt* to a German industry newly enlightened by the Werkbund and its affiliates. One particular episode involving the appliance manufacturer Braun AG offers an example.

Schwippert was by no means naïve about the ways in which the intertwining of design and industry served West German economic strategy. The Rat für Formgebung, of which he was a member, had been founded with government support in 1950, specifically with the mission of being an "informal liaison between industry and consumer."[48] It was backed by Theodor Heuss, first president of West Germany, and Ludwig Erhard, both of whom foresaw significant West German economic growth by means of consumer goods. Erhard was even more concerned with safeguarding consumer satisfaction as a pillar of economic and political stability, a lesson learned from the household stability delivered early in the National Socialist regime.[49] By the late 1950s, West Germany's participation in international design fairs was seen as a political tool to stimulate export markets and to establish the country's profile. In Schwippert's pragmatic words, "the work on these kinds of [international design] exhibitions has the character of applied sales advice."[50]

The correspondence in 1956 between Schwippert and Max Braun, founder of Braun AG, indicates the degree to which this economic savvy was second nature to Schwippert and integral to the Werkbund's day-to-day. In this series of letters, Braun requested and received Schwippert's advice on how to deal with a conflict that had arisen at a joint meeting of the Swiss and Baden-Württemberg chapters of the Werkbund, which had been held at the Ulm Hochschule für Gestaltung (HfG) on October 20 and 21, 1956.[51] Werner Aebli, a Swiss architect, had used the occasion to excoriate the design of a Braun radio first marketed in August 1955. Developed in an early partnership with the Ulm HfG, the design had been well received and was considered a harbinger of the new type of West German consumer product to which both Werkbund and Rat für Formgebung aspired. Braun sent two letters to Schwippert for his revision and comment, one addressing Aebli's attack on the radio's technical quality and the other answering Werkbund members who had criticized the radio's form. With Schwippert's help, both letters became marketing opportunities rather than vitriol. As Braun wrote, "Please accept my heartfelt thanks for the enormous effort you invested in our letters to the Werkbund members. Your advice was particularly valuable because it showed us that we had not yet found the right tone."[52]

The first of the two, an open letter intended for publication, cleverly redirected Aebli's attack by feigning an assumption that Aebli "was motivated to these harsh words by personal experience" and had at some point "had complaints about one of our products, since we—like all manufacturers—have an unavoidable, small percentage of complaints."[53] The letter ended by offering that Braun's customer service could address any problems Aebli, as a consumer, might have, and by challenging him to find another middle European manufacturer whose comparable product was superior—in exchange for a DM 10,000 reward. By transforming the design critic into a disgruntled consumer who could be placated by company largesse, Braun's response became an opportunity to emphasize the company's commitment to its users.

The letter to Werkbund members addressed each point in the critique of the radio's design. As Braun wrote, it was "new for us that friends of the 'Good Form' would also appropriate arguments that otherwise only come from the opposing camp."[54] As a counter-argument, Braun proposed, "in the circle of people who deal immediately with questions of design, we would prefer to show directly what things are new with us.

47   Oestereich, "Umstrittene Selbstdarstellung," 3.
48   Betts, *Authority of Everyday Objects*, 181.
49   Betts, *Authority of Everyday Objects*, 182–83.
50   "Typescript of the Protocol from a December 15, 1956 Meeting of the Rat für Formgebung in Bonn," GNM, DKA, NL, Schwippert.
51   Gerda Breuer, "HfG Ulm und Werkbund," in *Das gute Leben: Der Deutsche Werkbund nach 1945* (Tübingen: Wasmuth, 2006), 7.
52   Max Braun to Hans Schwippert, December 18, 1956, GNM, DKA, NL, Schwippert.
53   Max Braun to Hans Schwippert, December 17, 1956 GNM, DKA, NL, Schwippert.
54   Open letter from Max Braun to Werner Aebli and the members of Werkbund, December 18, 1956, GNM, DKA, NL, Schwippert.

Therefore, today we are sending you our new radio catalogue. Our newest model, the SK4, is published in it for the first time."[55] The SK4, a combination radio and record player, was one of the first designs by the team of Hans Gugelot and Dieter Rams to go into production, and represented Braun's new design approach.[56] In supplying a catalogue, Braun's strategy was twofold: first, he conveyed his commitment to working with independent, academically well-regarded designers; and second, it transformed his critics into potential consumers. Braun AG and its products were particularly compelling evidence that West German design was gaining credence, on the domestic market and also on the international. By 1958, several Braun products, including the SK4, had been acquired by the Museum of Modern Art in New York.[57]

The HfG in Ulm, co-funded by the United States High Commissioner on Germany and the German Federal Republic, in its founding principles represented exactly the confluence between design forms and a reconceived German political life that Schwippert intended to represent in Brussels.[58] Debates about the distinction between the "Good Form" and the West German passion for freeform "kitsch" that would result in a broader rejection of industry collaboration at the HfG were still years away.[59] During the run-up to the Brussels World's Fair, the alliance that Schwippert cultivated among government interests, economics, diplomacy, architecture, and design held fast even at the "New Bauhaus" in Ulm. In a letter dated October 19, 1956, to HfG professor and Werkbund official Otto Haupt, Schwippert enlisted Haupt's support in communicating to his academic colleagues the "importance of the 'practical' case of Brussels."[60] A week later, on October 27, Schwippert wrote again to let Haupt know that

> "after a struggle of more than a year, my 'story' was made the 'script' for Brussels. This means: contents were determined by themes, groups, scale and sequence, were synchronized with the building (which was the first victorious battle of the summer), were organized, decided, and now decreed as no longer changeable."[61]

Throughout the history of its reception from its earliest design iterations to the most recent architecture-historical descriptions, the idiom of the 1958 West German pavilion has been compared to Mies van der Rohe's.[62] In all the many versions of text Schwippert wrote about the pavilion, he referenced only one architect: Mies van der Rohe, to whom he attributed the role of leading the "German contribution to this movement toward a new openness and lightness,"[63] a movement to which the West German pavilion aspired to contribute. Likewise, Alfons Leitl, now a practicing architect after his time as Editor-in-Chief of *Baukunst und Werkform*, referenced Mies in his text for the catalogue that was published by the West German state and offered for sale at the World's Fair. Mies van der Rohe, not the Bauhaus—despite the promise of the HfG—was the delicate strand of prewar tradition with which to establish continuity.

Of all those involved in the pavilion's development, Eiermann had the clearest and most current personal affiliations with Mies. In 1950, a few years after his appointment as Professor at the Technische Hochschule in Karlsruhe, he had persuaded the university to confer an honorary doctorate upon Mies van der Rohe, which was presented to him by Konrad Wachsmann during a visit to Chicago.[64] In the summer of 1953, as the Bauhaus Debate still reverberated, Mies visited Eiermann in Karlsruhe, where he toured the university and Eiermann's professional office. These events proved to be one-offs, however: there is no correspondence between the two men that attests to an exchange of architectural ideas.[65] Ruf had no documented contact with Mies until the early 1960s, during a trip to the United States. Despite Schwippert's and Leitl's comparisons, there is no evidence that the architecture of the 1958 pavilion reflects Mies van der Rohe's personal mentorship or that he exchanged ideas with its architects.

The work for which Mies van der Rohe was known by 1956, when design began, far exceeded the means available to Schwippert's "little man." In literal and metaphorical terms, it was important that West

55　　　Open letter from Max Braun to Werner Aebli, GNM, DKA, NL, Schwippert.

56　　　For an interview with Rams on the product and its development, see https://www.youtube.com/watch?v=2dXJFV-2JhM, accessed January 24, 2016.

57　　　See the model at the MoMA website, http://www.moma.org/collection/works/2649?locale=en, accessed December 17, 2021.

58　　　Betts, *Authority of Everyday Objects*, chp. 4.

59　　　Betts, *Authority of Everyday Objects*, 151, on Inge Scholl's 1962 article.

60　　　Hans Schwippert to Otto Haupt (carbon copy), October 19, 1956, GNM, DKA, NL, Schwippert.

61　　　Hans Schwippert to Otto Haupt (carbon copy), October 27, 1956, GNM, DKA, NL, Schwippert.

62　　　The comparison between the 1958 pavilion and Mies van der Rohe is typical, appearing in Castillo, "Making a Spectacle," 116; in Alexander Reichel and Henning Baumann, *Tragen und Materialisieren. Stützen, Wände, Decken*, Scale (Basel: Birkhäuser, 2013), elektronische Daten, 51; and in Alexandra Staub, *Conflicted Identities: Housing and the Politics of Cultural Representation*, Routledge Research in Architecture (New York: Routledge, Taylor & Francis Group, 2016), 113 caption 4.4.

63　　　Schwippert, "Notizen," 5.

64　　　Immo Boyken, "Ludwig Mies van der Rohe and Egon Eiermann: The Dictate of Order," *Journal of the Society of Architectural Historian* 49, no. 2 (June 1990).

65　　　Boyken, "Ludwig Mies van der Rohe."

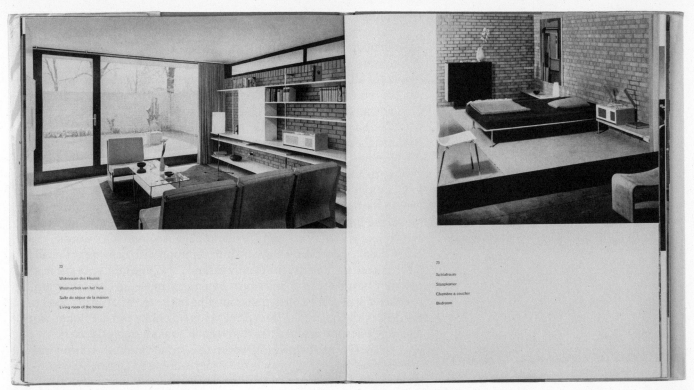

72
Wohnraum des Hauses
Woonverbrek van het huis
Salle de séjour de la maison
Living room of the house

73
Schlafraum
Slaapkamer
Chambre a coucher
Bedroom

5.10 Courtyard house, *Deutschlands Beitrag zur Weltausstellung Brüssel 1958. Ein Bericht.*

Germany avoid imagery that was "boastful," or *protzig*.[66] To calibrate the Mies of Barcelona by way of Chicago to that much more modest *Wohnwelt*, Eiermann, Ruf, Schwippert, and their collaborators would have looked hard at what, by then, had been extrapolated: the Miesian idiom, rather than Mies van der Rohe. Their result, described lay journalists during the World's Fair as at best "airy"[67] and at worst "a bit heavy handed and dull,"[68] was identifiable, it seems, in the way architectural form was derived from construction.[69] Doubly strange, then, that the reality of the pavilion's construction received little attention while its appearance was so touted, although this also might be argued in relation to the Miesian idiom as a whole. Schwippert's texts, peppered with ideas about construction already suggested in his presentation at the Darmstädter Gespräch of 1951, betray the motivation behind Eiermann and Ruf's detailing sleight-of-hand. By 1958, the challenge to West German modernist architects was no longer, as it had been in the early 1950s, a dearth of construction materials appropriate to transcendent "lightness." The challenge had instead become how to calibrate the evident material wealth and quality of German industrial production with a political and societal demand for an appropriately modest expression, which was something of a Trojan horse for quality and elegance. The term "Miesian" was shorthand for the solution, because of the way in which Mies van der Rohe's work was perceived both in the United States and, by extension, within the West German architectural demimonde.

By the time the pavilion's program and design were being developed, Mies van der Rohe's international standing was codified. He was, according to Henry-Russell Hitchcock, the de facto arbiter of the International Style, no longer merely one among "Le Corbusier, Gropius [...] Oud and the rest;"[70] he had become one of the three "generally accepted masters [...] among those interested in modern architecture."[71] Hitchcock also claimed that Mies's early work had been more strongly influenced by the classical proportioning systems of Schinkel than by industrial architecture, which, according to the canonical narrative, had so strongly influenced all early modern architecture. The assertion that Mies represented an apotheosis of discipline and clarity dominated his American reception in the first half of the 1950s. His other major American proponent, Philip Johnson, accordingly described the Lake Shore Drive apartments in a press release that accompanied a huge model of the Chicago project that was exhibited at the Museum of Modern Art in New York from March to May of 1950:

66　　The "boastful facade" refers to an article in the German magazine *Der Spiegel* from March 14, 1951, which described a discussion by Marshall Plan officers about blocking credit to Germany "as long as it lived above its means." The magazine offered statistics on "non-essential imports," including $210,000 for rum, $155,000 for cognac, $511,000 for cosmetics, and $136,000 for lobster. Citing problems with the liberalization of the German economy, for which Ludwig Erhard was in part responsible, the magazine claimed, "the current reconfiguration of German liberalization will tear down some façades that are too boastful for Germany." See "Zu protzige Fassade," *Der Spiegel*, March 14, 1951.
67　　Marder, "Brussels Exhibition."
68　　Howard Taubman, "Windows to the Souls of Nations; the Cultural Offerings at Brussels, a Critic Finds, Reveal More Than the Sponsors Intended," *New York Times* (September 7, 1958).
69　　Boyken, "Ludwig Mies Van Der Rohe."
70　　Henry-Russell Hitchcock and Philip Johnson, *The International Style: Architecture Since 1922*, lst ed. (New York: W. W. Norton, 1932), 43.
71　　Henry-Russell Hitchcock, "The Evolution of Wright, Mies & Le Corbusier," *Perspecta* 1 (1952), 8–15, here 9.

"Unlike the jagged and curved plan shapes of [Mies's] earlier projects, the new apartment towers are perfectly rectangular in plan, an undisguised expression of their regular steel frame. [...] These glass towers are monuments to order. Their simplicity is deceptive for, as in all great works of art, it is the result of a painstaking process of reduction until all that is left is the essential statement: a pure and unadorned crystal. When Mies came to the United States, he said: 'The long path [...] to creative work has only a single goal: to create order.' When that goal is attained, as it is being attained here, modern architecture will have reached another milestone along its 'long path' toward perfection."[72]

Johnson's characterization[73] makes no concessions to the fact that people lived in the building, although the press release's title, "Museum to Show Model of First All Glass and Steel Apartment House," cleverly noted that the project was a "first" in its residential genre. Johnson's words— "order" and "perfection"—have little in common with Schwippert's call for an architecture "against the deadly serious."[74] While Johnson's publicity text may best be read as the words of a major museum curator straining to couch a speculative apartment building in the terms of an art object, the description proved to be typical of the way Mies van der Rohe's work, and the "Miesian" idiom extracted from it, was characterized.

In the German-speaking world, this same characterization was proselytized by such figures as the American-based German-Swiss Werner Blaser and Sigfried Giedion, both of whom contributed essays to a 1956 issue of *Bauen + Wohnen* commemorating Mies van der Rohe's seventieth birthday.[75] Here, too, they described his architecture as expressive of "fundamental principles" intended to "make order in the desperate chaos of our era."[76] The accompanying images of projects, among which Lake Shore Drive was the first to appear, juxtapose a chaotic and heterogeneous outside world against Miesian order inside the building. **[5.11]** Photos of the Lake Shore Drive facade are regularly curtained, so as to underplay the tenants' inevitably diverse interior decoration. A photograph of the lobby, in which reflections of a traditional Chicago street and skyline are ghosted in a foreground reflection, contrasts the interior space to the hodge-podge of traffic lights, curbs, and cars on Lake Shore Drive, seen beyond the building's entry portico. The lobby is dominated by a carefully staged tableau: rarified Mies-designed seating, a glass coffee table, the steel bearing structure, and the steel facade mullions. As Blaser had written only a few pages earlier, "the creation of space, beginning with the structure, is architecture's true charge;"[77] but not, it seemed, the interplay with objects of everyday life to which the German pavilion would aspire.[78] From the book-matched Roman travertine pavers to the specially formulated black paint produced for the building's steel by Detroit Graphite,[79] this photograph also made obvious that the bespoke production of this luxurious, "Miesian" space came at a high material and construction cost.

For contemporaneous authors and thinkers who chose to apply the adjective "Miesian" to the Brussels pavilion, this term both included and transcended the specifics of any one of Mies van der Rohe's projects. It had become synonymous with a specific kind of modern architecture, ordered and "perfect" but also broadly applicable to different programs and locations. For German architectural circles, association with this idiom offered two advantages: its German origins, which implied continuity and tradition, and its undisputed international status. This latter association has been emphasized in more recent literature, both as a verification of the project's high quality and as a basis to critique its tropes.[80]

The pavilion came to be identified with a clever formulation that first appeared in an early review: *"die Haltung der Zurückhaltung,"*[81] the posture of restraint. It was as Schwippert had foreseen:

"How much *élan* do you think is needed today to achieve the ordinary? Today especially! Here *was* élan, but, you understand, of the kind that puts value on the way that the traces of labor and sweat are, as is common among civilized peoples for the past few centuries,

72 The Museum of Modern Art, "Museum to Show Model of First All Glass and Steel Apartment House," news release, 1950. https://www.moma.org/momaorg/shared/pdfs/docs/press_archives/1406/releases/MOMA_1950_0015_1950-02-23_500223-13.pdf.

73 There is no little irony in the fact that this "perfection" would ultimately frustrate Johnson. See Dietrich Neumann and Juergen Schulz, "Johnson's Grid," *AA Files: Annals of the Architectural Association School of Architecture* 70 (Spring 2015).

74 Schwippert, manuscript for "Notizen zur deutschen Beteiligung," 3.

75 See Werner Blaser, "Mies van der Rohe, Chicago School, 1938–56," *Bauen + Wohnen: Internationale Zeitschrift* 10, no. 7 (1956), 217–27 and Sigfried Giedion, "Der moralischer Einfluss der Architektur Mies van der Rohe," *Bauen + Wohnen: Internationale Zeitschrift* 10, no. 7 (1956), 227–29.

76 Blaser, "Mies van der Rohe," 217–18.

77 Blaser, "Mies van der Rohe," 217.

78 Durth and Sigel, *Baukultur*, 530.

79 Rico Cedro, "Restoring Mies van der Rohe's 860–880 Lake Shore Drive: When Less Is Not Enough," *CTBUH Journal*, no. 1 (2009).

80 The texts by Boyken and Castillo represent two versions of this later reception of the Brussels pavilion as "Miesian": Boyken et al., *Egon Eiermann / Sep Ruf*; Castillo, "Making a Spectacle."

81 The term, first used by Ernst Johan in his review of the pavilion, "Haltung der Zurückhaltung," *Werk und Zeit* (June 1958), is cited throughout literature that describes West German ambitions for a redefined national identity in the Adenauer period. See Paulmann, "Representation" and Castillo, "Making a Spectacle."

82   Schwippert, manuscript for "Notizen zur deutschen Beteiligung," emphases underlined in original.

removed in time. Thus it was, on the whole, a report on possibilities and powers that are available but—unfortunately—are too seldom used.

And it was, as a demand on today, much more than one is by and large willing to fulfill and realize in our German everyday life. Nothing less than the reconfiguration of the future. *Vision*, however, in the sense of its demands on the highest, forward-looking humane engagement with art, it was *not*.

Vision of such a kind is, by the way, one man's concern. I am thinking of Mies van der Rohe: Pavilion 1929 in Barcelona. It is beside the point whether it was one man or not, whether there was the necessary trust in him to realize what was consistently daring; it is equally irrelevant whether this daring was legitimated and, thereafter, accepted by us at home.

We were compelled, as a logical and realistic consequence of the program and guiding idea, this time to choose a *group*, a *team*. And what teamwork was created here, this is at least new, is something rare among us Germans; even more so, it is today, it is more modern than other extravaganzas elsewhere, it is a proper and superior result of this moment and hour. The fact that it was achieved with such decisive unity and closure is a first.

Team and Vision—say it isn't so [...] Here was not one head, there were 50, 60, 70 heads, designers, businesspeople, organizers, salespeople, collaborators, from culture, training, administration, education. The unity of their collaboration was the astonishing fact of a common effort."[82]

In Schwippert's recollection, the spirit through which the pavilion came into being was clear in the project's expression: the élan of the ordinary in which "traces of labor and sweat are [...] removed," just as civilized cultures would wish it, the product of many hands and not a single leading head. Here, too, was the difference to the Miesian, a style named for a single man, no matter what parallels Schwippert sought elsewhere. Self-effacement not heroism, collaboration not singular authorship, were new German virtues evidenced in Brussels. This new restraint and modesty were not to be understood as effortless, but the effort was not an "extravaganza." The values of transparency and elegance carried forward from Mies van der Rohe, the only American expatriate German architect consistently admired by Schwippert and his circle as though he had never left their fold, were to be tempered by modesty. It was this

5.11 Ludwig Mies van der Rohe, Lakeshore Drive Apartments, 1951, *Bauen + Wohnen* 1956

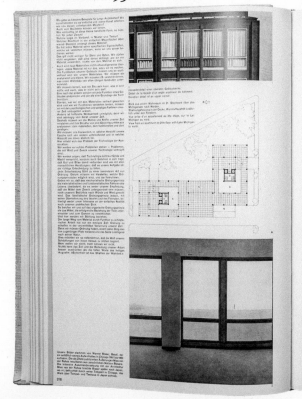
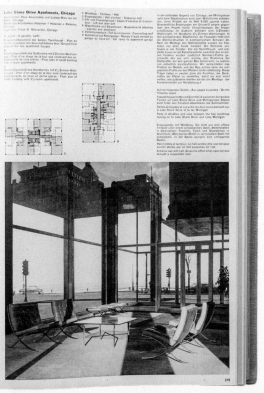

83   See "Flooded at the Farnsworth House" on the erasure of the welds in the Farnsworth House's socle. Mike Cadwell, *Strange Details, Writing Architecture* (Cambridge, MA: MIT Press, 2007).

84   Marder, "Brussels Exhibition."

85   Taubman, "Windows."

86   Taubman, "Windows."

modesty that set the West German pavilion apart from the costly procedures by which Mies's American projects concealed the effort of their production.[83]

Schwippert struggled to put into words the role to be played by architecture and consumer design objects in constructing and reinforcing the image of a workmanly, modest, universally accessible West German culture. A laboriously edited text, full of pasted-in typewritten scraps and handwritten notations, bears witness to his efforts to frame these ideas precisely, even after 1958. Nevertheless, his message was conveyed and embraced. The architectural and design idiom that Schwippert and his team established at Brussels was quickly accepted as the embodiment of a new, positive West German culture. Even before the pavilion had been completed, Ruf was becoming one of its foremost practitioners. In parallel to consumer goods manufacturing, the rapidly developing West German construction industry bespoke the dramatic pace at which the country had regained state-of-the-art quality. These achievements, too, were shown to advantage in Brussels, as described in the *Washington Post and Times Herald*:

> "Western Germany, risen from the thrashing in World War II to a dominant position in European production and financial well-being, has produced probably the most successful all-around exhibit in the fair. The German display is a model of efficiency and simplicity, with eight airy, attractive box-like structures of wood and glass, prefabricated and erected in eighteen days."[84]

The pavilion's overwhelmingly positive reception in both the European and the American press ratified the successes of Schwippert, Ruf, Eiermann, and the committee in calibrating enormous national achievement and understated design, an accomplishment that the American press contrasted to its own country's poorly planned, "impetuous"[85] gold-domed US pavilion. One journalist juxtaposed West Germany's discretion to the way the US pavilion had revealed some "uncomfortable truths we need not have paraded in public."[86] The pavilion of the Soviet Union was similarly excoriated in the press. The two superpowers had failed to do what West Germany had done: to correlate perfectly the country's reemergence as a design force with its government's desired political profile.

The chapter title quotes Leland King as cited in Jane C. Loeffler, *The Architecture of Diplomacy: Building America's Embassies*, 1st ed. (New York: Princeton Architectural Press, 1998), 88.

"New, Clean, and Spectacular"

The Allure of American Architecture in West Germany and the Influence of Skidmore, Owings and Merrill

Well before the average West German household could afford and enjoy everyday design objects, the value of architecture and environment was clear to the US occupying forces. The ensuing agenda to represent the "victor nation" abroad,[01] as put into practice in embassies, chain hotels, and cultural outposts designed by the most prominent American architects, seems blithely idealistic at present, in the era of a former US president who wanted to "make federal buildings beautiful again."[02] No less than baseball as a means to teach healthy rebelliousness to German youth, lampooned so unforgettably in Billy Wilder's *A Foreign Affair* (1948, Paramount Pictures), exhibitions of the "new, clean, and spectacular" architecture that housed the American way of life were meant to inspire West Germans to reimagine their entire lifeworlds.

Traveling exhibitions on architecture and planning were frequent in West Germany during the late 1940s and into the 1950s.[03] The Museum of Modern Art was a primary purveyor of this content, both independently and through US government-sponsored institutions such as the America House network.[04] Such exhibitions and the accompanying catalogues provided lay audiences and, to a significant extent, professional ones, the first close look at American corporate architecture.

The America House network in West Germany was initially an amenity housed in existing spaces to provide access to books, lectures, films, and other events. It was quickly understood as an increasingly important means for reeducation that could shift civil society towards greater democracy as defined from an American perspective. This agenda inspired curiosity; it also provoked suspicion. But in the absence of other possibilities, the libraries, films, exhibitions, and lectures provided by the America House system were hard to pass up.

Although cultural reeducation of the German people had been stipulated both in the Potsdam Treaty and the directive that established the military occupying government, the America House network was initially used only as an incidental contributor to that goal.[05] Established in 1945 with the founding of two small libraries, one funded privately and the other by the US government, the first America House collections were no more than cast-offs of military reference books. The network was not officially mentioned in congressional reports until two years later. By 1947, the ominous-sounding Anglo-American Psychological Warfare Division, which had taken over responsibility for the two libraries, was dissolved, and the America House project was transferred to the education department of the occupying governing body, the Office of Military Government in Germany.[06] The two libraries were consolidated and moved from Marburg and Bad Homburg to Wiesbaden, where an American garrison is located even now.

Prior to the deterioration of relations with the Soviet Union and the start of the Korean War, the stated purpose of the America Houses was to publish and promote the German-language daily *Die Neue Zeitung*, a paper from which Walter Gropius, incidentally, often clipped articles for his scrapbook. The other purpose was to oversee the revitalization of non-political German public life and culture. As the network slowly expanded, each America House was also required to have a library holding books that were selected (or censored) according to clear policy guidelines. By the time responsibility for the building and maintenance of these "information centers" was passed to the Office of Military Government in Germany, library and exhibition spaces were mandated at each location.[07] There were already twenty America Houses in West Germany by 1947 and, at the height of the program, there were twenty-seven in major cities as well as a network of 136 libraries in smaller cities. The early America Houses were allocated space in retrofitted existing buildings, but, starting in 1951, funding was granted to build seven new, dedicated America House buildings, with others to follow.

01   Fritz Hesse to Walter Gropius, February 14, 1946, series III, file 876, Walter Gropius Papers, 1925–1969 (MS Ger 208), Houghton Library, Harvard University.

02   Elizabeth Blair quoting Donald Trump, "'Ugly,' 'Discordant': New Executive Order Takes Aim at Modern Architecture," All Things Considered, December 21, 2020, https://www.npr.org/2020/02/13/805256707/just-plain-ugly-proposed-executive-order-takes-aim-at-modern-architecture, accessed January 18, 2021.

03   Hermann Schäfter, "Kulturelle Wiederbelebung. Ausstellungen in Westdeutschland von Kriegsende 1945 bis in die 1960er Jahre," in Klaus Hildebrand, Udo Wengst, and Andreas Wirsching, eds., *Geschichtswissenschaft und Zeiterkenntnis von der Aufklärung bis zur Gegenwart: Festschrift zum 65. Geburtstag von Horst Möller* (Munich: Oldenbourg, 2008), 645.

04   Carola Hein, "The New York Museum of Modern Art: Engagement in Housing, Planning and Neighbourhood Design," in Robert Freestone and Marco Amati, eds., *Exhibitions and the Development of Modern Planning Culture* (Surrey: Ashgate, 2014), 254.

05   Karl-Ernst Bungenstab, "Entstehung, Bedeutungs- und Funktionswandel der Amerika-Häuser: Ein Beitrag zur Geschichte der amerikanischen Auslandsinformation nach dem 2. Weltkrieg," *Jahrbuch für Amerikastudien* no. 16 (1971), 189.

06   Bungenstab, "Entstehung, Bedeutungs- und Funktionswandel," 192.

07   Bungenstab, "Entstehung, Bedeutungs- und Funktionswandel," 195.

08   Bungenstab, "Entstehung, Bedeutungs-
und Funktionswandel," 198.

09   Schäfter, "Kulturelle Wiederbelebung," 645.

10   See Bruno Taut, *Die neue Wohnung: Die
Frau als Schöpferin*, 2nd ed. (Leipzig: Klinkhardt
& Biermann, 1924) or Walter Gropius, *Bauhaus-
bauten Dessau*, Bauhausbücher (Munich: Albert
Langen Verlag, 1930).

11   Reinhold Wagnleitner, "Propagating the
American Dream: Cultural Policies as Means of
Integration," *American Studies International* 24,
no. 1 (1986), 75.

12   Greg Castillo, "Domesticating the Cold
War: Household Consumption as Propaganda
in Marshall Plan Germany," *Journal of
Contemporary History* 40, no. 2 (2005).

13   Sonja Schöttler, *Funktionale Eloquenz:
Das Kölner Amerika-Haus und die Kulturinstitute
der Vereinigten Staaten von Amerika in Deutschland*
(Worms: Wernersche Verlagsgesellschaft, 2011), 9.

14   Imma von Guenther, "Wie lebt
Mr. Average in Amerika?" *Die Zeit*, April 9 1953,
http://www.zeit.de/1953/15/wie-lebt-mr
-average-in-amerika, accessed December 16, 2021.

An overview of the kinds of lectures and exhibitions offered through the America House network gives a sense of how democracy was presented, with the American lifestyle as its natural expression. Lectures with titles such as "The American Constitution," "Freedom and Slavery," "Organizations of World Peace," or "American Democracy"[08] complimented exhibitions that explored the lives of women farmers or the interiors of American homes, urban and rural.[09] It is clear that exhibitions such as these were intended to appeal to women, who were seen as forces for change by means of their influence on domestic environment. Such appeals had been widespread during the Weimar era among architects such as Bruno Taut and Walter Gropius.[10] After 1947, it was even more broadly used to export American cultural values not only into West Germany but also throughout Europe and Latin America.[11] As reconstruction accelerated and the economy stabilized, the appeal of lifestyle and lifestyle objects grew apace, and the strategy of appealing to both genders' consumer desire grew in importance, perhaps reaching its apogee in the infamous "Kitchen Debate" of 1959.[12] Architecture could be cast expediently as a harbinger of a better life.

For the purpose-built America Houses, architecture was not merely an exhibition or lecture topic. It was an immersive experience. This was particularly true in the case of Skidmore, Owings and Merrill (SOM). The photographs exhibited, the walls on which they hung, the spaces those walls defined: in short, the whole atmosphere of the slick, new America Houses had been developed by Gordon Bunshaft's SOM team.[13]

Architecture was not depicted as a lofty cultural achievement but rather as a defining factor in the everyday life of "Mr. Average."[14]

6.1a Dollhouse-scale skyscraper and set-back apartment buildings (6.1a); suburban and rural homes (6.1b), *So wohnt Amerika,* **1949**

Models, pictures, graphs and statistics tell the story of the "So Lives America" Exhibition now touring cities of the US Zone.

Model of apartment house getting finishing touches at Nuremberg studios last summer.

Tilt-up methods of construction and prefabricated houses evoked the keenest interest, for many who saw the Frankfurt Fair exhibit obviously felt that by exchanging techniques and borrowing ideas, Germany's numerous postwar housing problems well may benefit from American housing experience.

15 "So wohnt Amerika," *Information Bulletin* (December 1949), 63–67, http://images.library.wisc.edu/History/EFacs/GerRecon/omg1949Dec/reference/history.omg1949dec.ioo28.pdf, accessed December 16, 2021.
16 Hein, "New York Museum of Modern Art," 255.
17 "Architektur der USA seit 1947 exhibition catalogue," (Stuttgart: Dr. Cantz'sche Druckerei, 1950), 5.

The 1949 exhibition *So wohnt Amerika* (So Lives America) is an early example. It depicted the architecture of the American lifestyle from set-back urban towers to suburban Cape Cod houses, with prototypical spaces presented in the form of large, dollhouse-like models.[15] **[6.1]** The direct appeal of conveying cultural norms by picturing everyday spaces, albeit often in staged photographs empty of people, allowed visitors to project themselves into the situation depicted.

Another exhibition immediately relevant to a professional audience, the 1950 *Architektur der USA seit 1947*, followed a year after *So wohnt Amerika*. It drew from a familiar pool of American architects whose work would later be featured in the Henry-Russell Hitchcock and Arthur Drexler-curated Museum of Modern Art (MoMA) exhibition *Built in the USA—Since 1932*, which also traveled to Europe in 1952.[16] These architects included Philip Johnson, Richard Neutra, Serge Chermayeff, Marcel Breuer, Ludwig Mies van der Rohe, Erich Mendelsohn, Frank Lloyd Wright, and Eero Saarinen. The American Institute of Architects had selected these participants for the Seventh Pan-American Congress in Havana; a few more were added for the German show.[17] There were five projects by SOM, in quantity second only to Pietro Beluschi's six. Alongside the houses, schools, and museums of these more well-known figures were hospitals, commercial and office buildings, and urban planning projects by architects working in smaller cities: William Pereira, the firm of Stevens and Williamson, Ernest Kump, and I.M. Pei, who was then working for Webb and Knapp. A special category entitled "recreation" even included temporary structures by John Lautner, later famous for his houses featured in James Bond films. These were largely the corporate firms that

6.1b

A simple one-family residence outside Chicago, away from big city smoke, grime and noises.

Galena, Ill. home of General Ulysses S. Grant, Civil War (1861 — 1865) hero and 18th President.

Springfield, Ill. home of Abraham Lincoln (1809 — 1865) before he became 16th President.

Impressive modern apartment building, complete with luxurious penthouses, reaches 25 stories into the sky.

One-family homes are preferred. At right, typical post-World War II group of semi-detached houses.

LEVER HOUSE
Office Building for Lever Brothers Company
New York, N. Y. (now under construction)

This office building of blue heat resistant glass and stainless steel will front on Park Avenue between 53rd and 54th Streets, occupying one third of a city block. The street floor is an outdoor concourse with clear open space from 53rd through to 54th Streets, interrupted only by the columns which support the building, and a glass enclosed lobby. In the rendering below of the street floor the columns are indicated by the black dots while the dimensions of the lobby can be traced by means of the white lines forming an oblong on the right side of the rendering. A single office floor on the second floor provides 22,000 square feet of office space and forms the base for the 21 story tower which occupies 25% of the site area. Each floor of the tower provides 8700 square feet of space. The third floor, enclosed in glass from floor to ceiling, will hold the employees cafeteria looking out on the terrace gardens.

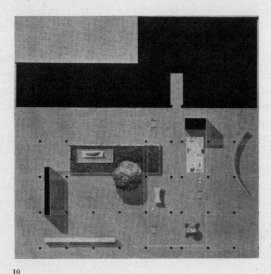

10

6.2 Skidmore, Owings and Merrill, Lever House Model, Museum of Modern Art, 1950

had emerged since the war. Wall text attributed projects not only to their architects but also to engineers and interior designers. As the introductory text explained, "This exhibition shows emphatically— as a viewer in another country may not tend to observe—the remarkable progress which Modern architecture has made in the US since the war, both as in the planning of exterior areas and on the interior—lighting, furniture etc."[18] Whereas the earlier exhibition had included all the stylistic heterogeneity that actually characterized the American landscape, these later shows told a different story: the apotheosis of modernist architecture in the United States.

In that story, modern architecture was largely inextricable from the rise of the corporation, both as its client and as its business model. Skidmore, Owings and Merrill occupied a special position here, since it was the first architecture firm large and structurally complex enough to qualify as corporate, and also produced work that expressed the commitment of corporate business structures to the leveling capacity inherent to management principles. "So it is that today in America, large buildings are not designed by individuals but instead by an entire staff of specialists,"[19] German émigré journalist Fritz Neugass wrote in his review of the Museum of Modern Art's 1950 exhibition dedicated to SOM. Neugass contrasted SOM's disinterest in the authorial with the precedents set by Le Corbusier, Mies van der Rohe, Robert Maillart, and Alvar Aalto, a list that could have been cribbed from Sigfried Giedion's 1941 *Space, Time and Architecture*. The MoMA show underscored SOM's utterly different proposition: that museum-worthy architecture could be achieved by designers who would remain nameless, and that the corporate model was in fact the

18   "Architektur der USA seit 1947," 6.
19   Fritz Neugass, "Die neue Architektur: Amerika besinnt sich auf einen eigenen, zeitgemässen Stil," *Sonntagsblatt Staats-Zeitung und Herold* (November 5, 1960), 5c.

only way to come to terms with the problems posed by the new scale of the postwar economy.

The MoMA exhibition included only projects either under construction or completed in 1950. Like the America House exhibitions, it featured large models, in this case produced specifically for the exhibit by Theodore Conrad, a model builder who in his own words had "built all of lower Manhattan below Houston Street."[20] An exhibition byline crediting equally the architecture firm, its model builder, and its graphic designer points to the radically anti-individualistic approach to authorship. The catalogue stated:

> "When the Museum invited Skidmore, Owings and Merrill to exhibit its recent buildings, it did so because this firm, composed of a group of single designers working exclusively in the modern idiom, produces imaginative, serviceable and sophisticated architecture deserving of special attention. The single designers who function within this organization have no fear of a loss of individuality. They are able to work within their corporate framework because they understand and employ the vocabulary and grammar which was developed from the esthetic conceptions of the twenties. They work together animated by two disciplines which they all share—the discipline of modern architecture and the discipline of American organizational methods."[21]

This was fairly standard rhetoric for SOM—Gordon Bunshaft, one of the few SOM design partners known by name, was famously resistant to any architectural historical claims about his work[22]—but it was quite unusual for a museum known to celebrate connoisseurship. The catalogue did its best to bridge the gap by comparing SOM's work to the architectural canon MoMA celebrated. It described the Northern Indiana Hospital for Crippled Children, a 53,000-square-foot building organized around a courtyard, as offering "privacy as well as a feeling of space by continuing the interior wall. This feature was introduced by Mies van der Rohe in the Barcelona Pavilion in 1929."[23] MoMA used the opportunity to produce an architecture-historical pedigree, which SOM had declined to volunteer.

A photograph of a model for the Lever House makes a stronger argument for comparison with the Barcelona Pavilion. [6.2] The photo depicts the building as a tonal rendering of its elements in shadows cast by column grid, walls, indoor-outdoor planter, and two butterflied elements. Barely visible white lines indicate the building's perimeter. The photograph describes beautifully the continuities of interior and exterior, the juxtaposition of built and unbuilt elements, and the balance of orthogonal and non-orthogonal geometries that characterized Isamu Noguchi and SOM's collaboration. It contrasts with other projects in the show, represented in drawings so dry that non-architects, even those willing to visit a MoMA show, would scarcely have been able to appreciate them: the gridded, repetitive facade drawings of the Heinz Vinegar Building or the Lake Meadows housing, both included in the catalogue, seem particularly inscrutable.

What was at stake here, however, was not simple aesthetics. Neugass put a point to it:

> "So it has happened that today in America, large buildings are not built by individuals but by a whole staff of experts. One of the most successful Modern architecture collaboratives today is the firm Skidmore, Owings & Merrill, which supports three offices in New York, Chicago and San Francisco. It comprises nine partners and keeps a staff of no fewer than 322 specialists and employees busy. As needed, this staff is swapped out among the various offices and construction sites. [...] Thanks to their extraordinary organization, they are in the position to build whole cities."[24]

Indeed, SOM had already built a whole city in Oak Ridge, Tennessee, one whose quantitative model was Louis Skidmore's small hometown;[25] those who lived in this new city were responsible for building America's atomic bomb.[26] Oak Ridge became a template for the kind of project at which SOM excelled: it allowed the firm to set numerical standards for

20   David Dunlap, "Theodor Conrad, 84, Modeler and Architecture Preservationist." *New York Times*, August 20, 1994, Section 1, Page 29. See http://www.nytimes.com/1994/08/20/obituaries/theodore-conrad-84-modeler-and-architecture-preservationist.html, accessed December 16, 2021.

21   "Skidmore, Owings & Merrill," *The Bulletin of the Museum of Modern Art* 18, no. 1 (1950).

22   Reinhold Martin, "The Bunshaft Tapes: A Preliminary Report," *Journal of Architectural Education* (1984–) 54, no. 2 (2000), 80–87.

23   "Skidmore, Owings & Merrill," 6.

24   "Skidmore, Owings & Merrill," 6.

25   The speed at which the master plan was prepared meant that precedents were drawn from the architects' experience; there was no time for academic research. Lawerenceberg, Indiana, was used to calibrate civic and retail amenities (shops, libraries, schools) against the anticipated number of inhabitants and families. The proportional rules of thumb developed in this way became standards, as Walter Metschke, who ran the team that produced the plan, recalled. Walter G. Metschke, "Memoirs of Walter G. Metschke / Compiled under the Auspices of the Chicago Architects Oral History Project, the Ernest R. Graham Study Center for Architectural Drawings, Department of Architecture, the Art Institute of Chicago," in *Chicago Architects Oral History Project* (Chicago: The Art Institute of Chicago, 1998), 40.

26   Hyun Tae Jung, "Organization and Abstraction: The Architecture of Skidmore, Owings & Merrill from 1936 to 1956," (PhD Diss., Columbia University, 2011) (3454018), 116–17.

civic amenities, to lay out roads, and to determine housing and landscape typologies that soon became the standard scaffold upon which new suburban towns were modeled across the postwar American landscape. Little imagination was needed to realize that this capacity would be welcome in rebuilding a country left largely in ruins by the war that had made it, if temporarily, a ward of the United States.

SOM's wartime work, both at Oak Ridge and through its research collaboration with the Pierce Foundation on the use of inexpensive, lightweight framing and sheet material for housing, positioned the company to have significant impact on construction as well. In addition to its better-known work with Cemesto, a concrete board product developed in the 1930s, SOM had used Oak Ridge to explore numerous materials whose development had been accelerated through the war effort and that, after the war, were remarketed for the construction industry. These included weather-resistant exterior plywood, latex glues, caulk, concrete board, and improved gypsum board, all components of the "dry" construction pioneered in the 1940s and still in practice today. Many of these products, originally developed for use in other industries—for example, caulk was originally used as a superior alternative to canning wax for preserving vegetables—found new applications during the war. The use of marine-grade plywood in aerospace and shipbuilding is familiar in the literature of material technology transfer, but advances in organic and synthetic polymers were perhaps even more transformative for construction.

Early sheet construction materials, including Masonite, the first commercially produced sheet construction material in the United States, and Cemesto, were typically wood or paper pulp–based.[27] The lignans in the pulp, subjected to intense pressure in the process of making panels or sheets, were strong enough for cladding purposes. Naturally derived adhesives such as silicate of soda, asphalt, or even flour paste were added to complement the lignans' bonding capacity; other additives such as rosin, wax, or clay were intended to lend fireproofing, waterproofing, and insect-resistant properties.[28] The constituent materials and production methods remained unchanged from 1928, when the first Masonite panels were produced, until around 1940.

The primary challenge to sheet construction materials as part of the building structure or envelope was the need for waterproof glue. Prior to World War II, casein glue, derived from milk whey, had the highest commercially viable degree of water resistance and was used for sheet materials, including in the production of plywood. This did not produce exterior grade sheet wood, however. Synthetic resin-based glues, chemically developed in 1934, were far superior in performance.[29] Military demand for exterior grade plywood spurred the commercial development of resin adhesives; SOM's Oak Ridge was one of the earliest large-scale applications of exterior plywood for building construction before it was widely availabe to civilians.

The development of sealants during the 1940s, mostly for high-performance machines, accelerated the genre of construction in which SOM excelled: the glass curtain wall. Putties made of organic oils, such as linseed, tung, castor, or even fish liver, mixed with calcium carbonate, had been commonly used to seal glass into window frames throughout the 1920s.[30] Because this putty had to be replaced at regular intervals, it was impractical for larger glass facades. The elastomeric sealants that emerged in the 1940s were different. Because they remained pliable, they could absorb much greater differential movement between components. Derived from rubber, the first synthetic building sealants became available in the United States in 1935 from Thiokol Corporation, a company whose name became synonymous with this type of sealant.

Rubber gaskets had been used since the mid-nineteenth century in engines, pipe fitting, and shipbuilding. In building construction, compressible textile fiber served instead to tighten components installed against the building frame, such as windows or doorframes. Often tar or oil-saturated rope or twisted cloth was positioned between the frame and the wall to fill gaps, block water and air infiltration, and ensure a snug fit.

27   The first commercially produced particle board was made in Germany in 1887, when an inventor named Hubbard made "artificial wood" using wood flour and egg white-based glue. Roger M. Rowell, *Handbook of Wood Chemistry and Wood Composites*, 2nd ed. (Boca Raton: CRC Press, 2013), 399.

28   Carol S. Gould et al., "Fiberboard," in Thomas C. Jester, ed., *Twentieth-Century Building Materials: History and Conservation* (New York: McGraw-Hill, 1995), 89–94.

29   Andrew McNall and David C. Fischetti, "Glued Laminated Timber," in Jester, *Twentieth-Century Building Materials*, 137–38.

30   Michael J. Scheffler, James D. Connolly, "Building Sealants," in Jester, *Twentieth-Century Building Materials*, 272–74.

As the demand for reliable, steady-state interior climate grew, however, the use of compressible linear gaskets gained traction. In this area, too, wartime developments in material science and aerospace created new opportunities for more airtight building envelope construction. Curtain wall construction would be unimaginable without gaskets to absorb tolerances and ensure weather-tightness; but even in SOM's early Cemestos houses, the prefabricated windows were gasketed, an early crossover of technology from military to civilian applications.

The ability to move technologies from high-performance to building construction spheres was empowering for architects. Invited to participate in a conference by the American Institute of Architects / Association of Collegiate Schools of Architecture (AIA / ACSA) on the impact of new materials on architecture in 1960, Frank Frybergh of Skidmore, Owings and Merrill's New York office described what SOM might uniquely have experienced for the first time at Oak Ridge:

> "Gone are the days when the architect was forced to use building materials without being able to exert his influence on their design or quality. Now the architect not only invents new uses for familiar products but also influences the design and quality of new materials.
>
> Just as an illustration I want to mention the influence the architect has exerted on the use of sealants. As late as ten years ago polysulfide base Thiokol sealants were used for sealing of jet fuel tanks only. Architects have seen the great potential of this material and have advocated and pioneered its use for building construction. Now it is difficult to imagine a metal and glass curtain wall without the use of this or some other synthetic sealing material."[31]

The Oak Ridge project was able to exploit the enormous potential of these new technologies for the problem of building construction. Because of SOM's role as designer, overseer, and researcher linked to the emergent building industry, the company had particularly good access to these developments. It was not only the company's corporate structure and capacity for knowledge transfer that positioned it to obtain and realize its postwar commissions but also its connections to an emergent, eager building products trade. This advantage would prove influential as SOM went on to realize a series of buildings for the United States High Commissioner on Germany.

The West German architectural press published surprisingly little of SOM's work before the second half of the 1950s, despite the firm's prominence in US-sponsored exhibitions. One of the earliest, if not the first, German-language SOM monographs was aimed at a different readership. *Bürobau mit Blick in die Zukunft* (office building with a view into the future) by Claus W. Hess, a seventy-page hardcover illustrated with Ezra Stoller photographs and architectural line drawings, told the story of its author's visit to the corporate campus of Connecticut General Life (1957). Billed on the title page as a business consultant, Hess wrote in an accessible style, peppering his German-language text with English phrases: "a good place to work"[32] or "work does not want to go upstairs."[33] He quoted verbatim his correspondence with the "six friendly women"[34] responsible for "curious international visitors."[35] He wondered aloud whether such a pleasant place could really be a place of work.

Hess seemed to address German companies planning new corporate headquarters. His book explains the advantages of building outside the city and gives directives on space planning, programming, the erection and use of test "mock-ups," as well as criteria for choosing an architect, general contractor, and interior designer. In the Connecticut General Life campus, its planning, and its execution, he recognized a new organizational paradigm. Despite his simple language, Hess described in great technical detail the lighting, heating, and acoustic systems integrated into walls and ceilings. The architects' report, reprinted in his book, includes a three-page list of all subcontractors and suppliers involved in the project. Completed by the trifecta of SOM, Turner Construction, and Knoll

31   Frank Frybergh, "Materials," *Journal of Architectural Education (1947–1974)* 16, no. 2 (1960), 33–34, here 33.
32   Claus William Hess, *Bürobau mit Blick in die Zukunft: Bericht über Connecticut Life Insurance Co., Bloomfield, Conn. USA* (Barmstedt: Schnelle, 1959), 18.
33   Hess, *Bürobau mit Blick*, 52.
34   Hess, *Bürobau mit Blick*, 9.
35   Hess, *Bürobau mit Blick*, 10.

36   Benno Kroll, "Aufstieg und Fall
der Gebrüder Schnelle," *Manager Magazin*,
1972, 67–69.
37   Carsten B. Horsley, "Some Second
Thoughts on Open-Plan Offices," *New York
Times*, March 18, 1979, R1; cited in Kroll,
"Aufstieg und Fall," 68.

Furniture, with Florence Knoll as interior designer, the Connecticut
General Life Building represented the state of the art in corporate
headquarters for a West German, or really any, audience in the
late 1950s. **[6.3]**

Hess also detailed the emerging science of human resources and
its spatial implications. Of the 2,000 employees on the campus, only 400
were men; of the remaining 1,600 women, only one-third were married,
a fact Hess pointedly noted. To ward off attrition and turnover, a concern
arising from the company's relocation outside the city of Hartford,
the campus included hair salons, shops, watch and shoe repairers, a movie
theater, bowling alley, shuffleboard, ping pong: it was a corporate
campus masquerading as a cruise ship for single women. This was an all-
encompassing environment beyond the glass partition walls that
SOM had specially designed to delimit each employee's cubicle.

Hess's report is more than an incident in SOM's influence on West
German spatial practices. The publishers, the two brothers Eberhard
and Wolfgang Schnelle, had founded their consulting company in 1959,[36]
the year of Hess's publication. Known later as the "Quickborn Team,"
the Schnelles quickly became international consultants on the *Bürolandschaft*,
that maze of oversized offices, cubicle furniture, equipment, and
accouterments which defined the 1960s corporate park. Their clients
included large West German corporations, among them Lufthansa,
Bertelsmann, and Krupp; but they also ran a New Jersey office to service
clients like IBM and Kodak. Even *The New York Times* reported that
the open office system was said "to make offices more efficient, more
economical, more flexible and more democratic."[37] By the time the
Schnelles sold their company in 1972, the Quickborn Team had effectively
repackaged the architecture of American corporate culture as pioneered
by SOM and re-exported it as a billable service.

Although SOM's German office was closed by then, architecture in West
Germany looked intently, if for other reasons, to the SOM model of the
mid-1950s. Critiques of postwar streetscapes and the idiom in which they
had been built were increasingly strident. The gridded infill facade,

**6.3 Skidmore, Owings and Merrill,
Connecticut General Life
Headquarters, 1957**

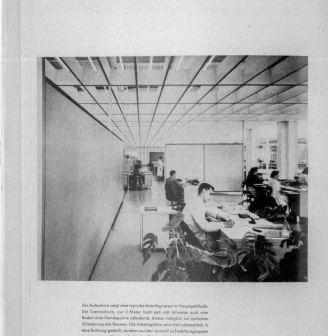

Die Aufnahme zeigt eine typische Arbeitsgruppe im Hauptgebäude.
Die Trennwände, nur 2 Meter hoch und sich teilweise auch vom
Boden eine Handspanne abhebend, dienen lediglich zur optischen
Gliederung des Raumes. Die Arbeitsplätze sind nicht schematisch in
eine Richtung gestellt, sondern wurden sinnvoll zu Funktionsgruppen
zusammengeschlossen. Auch der Gruppenführer im Vordergrund
sitzt im Gegensatz zu den anderen auf einem Teppich. Teppiche,
Stellwände und Pflanzenarrangements ersetzen also festgemauerte
Wände in äußerst sinnvoller, nämlich variabler Weise als Rang-
abzeichen der Bürohierarchie.

Das Foto zeigt das Fehlen des bei uns typischen Mittelganges zu-
gunsten einer lockeren Arbeitsplatzanordnung.
Registratur- und Karteischränke werden dorthin gestellt, wohin sie
funktional gehören.

a staple for the first wave of West German rebuilding, had, in part justifiably, come to epitomize architects' and planners' failure of imagination. The term used by architectural critics and journalists was *Rasteritis*,[38] grid as contagious disease. Walther Schmidt, editor of the periodical *Bauen und Wohnen*, had coined the term in 1947[39] to describe the impulse to base a building's facade exclusively on its underlying structural grid. For Schmidt, blind reliance on the grid, and adherence to the standardized building dimensions it reflected, stripped the architect of any discretion. It was a tendency that would

> "cast shadows on the future. It is a fact: consistent building norms, and the ordering of building dimensions, is a great event. It also seems to us to be one of the most important, consequential, and urgent tasks that the hour demands of us—the most important, because the rationalization of our building construction process that alone can help us depends upon it; the most consequential, because [norms] can no longer be changed once production facilities have been calibrated to them; and the most urgent, because they must and can be introduced now, before the reconstruction of our building material and building industries."[40]

Even more was at stake than the opportunity for architects to influence construction; it was a matter of philosophical and political importance. The streetscape manifested the values of society. If individual will, decision-making power and liberty were to thrive, then the environment would have to play its part. As Schmidt continued,

> "If its use grows out of control, then the grid can come to symbolize lack of freedom, condescension, and recurrent impediment. [...] In the open landscape, one can wander freely but in a system of perpendicular crossing streets, one can only march or perhaps sneak along. We have had our experience with how 'marching' tends to go and as well, with those who have chosen to sneak along. [...] Human freedom operates only in a narrow space between necessities. It is a human and an artistic duty not to limit or distort this narrow space with pseudo-necessity [...] but rather—literally—to *test its dimensions freely*."[41]

Schmidt's fears were seconded in the decade that followed. Architects and the gridded facades they designed, according to Bauhaus graduate Hubert Hoffmann,[42] "in their dull monotony so fittingly symbolized the anonymity of their society."[43] Other critics decried the tedium these facades brought to city streets.[44] Still others faulted an overly hectic attempt to rebuild, whether for social or economic benefit.[45] Consensus on an alternative was only beginning to emerge.

That alternative was given a name nearly ten years later, on March 12, 1956, by the Berlin weekly *Bauwelt*: the "good grid." Its cover image bore the title "Grid? Then please, as well-done as it is here."[46] The title was borrowed from a text in the issue that contrasted the "good grid" to Paul Schwebes and Hans Schoszberger's recent buildings at Berlin's Breitscheidplatz near the zoo:

> "Inasmuch as an architect knows how to use a grid [...] he has no need—as a new pair of architects intend for their buildings bordering the Berlin Zoo—to 'blur' function as it determines form. Wouldn't these two colleagues prefer first to head to the Acropolis equipped with diagonal struts and St. Andrew's crosses, or to Rome or Paestum, and cover up the interminable monotony of classical verticals in the columnar orders there?! Others may wish to use the grid but please, done well."[47]

The author, hiding behind the byline "Z," cast Schwebes and Schoszberger as philistines who misunderstood even the "good grid" of classical architecture. Z. offered a counterexample, which, he claimed, looked neither to the past nor to the present but met exactly the aesthetic demands of the present: the American consular buildings in Germany, all by Skidmore, Owings and Merrill.

Another publication to take up the Rasteritis challenge was the illustrated volume *Neue Deutsche Architektur* (1956). Edited by Hoffmann,

38   See Werner Durth, *Deutsche Architekten. Biographische Verflechtungen 1900–1970*, Schriften des Deutschen Architekturmuseums zur Architekturgeschichte und Architekturtheorie (Braunschweig: Vieweg, 1986), 357–8; Dirk Dorsemagen, "Büro und Geschäftshäuser der 50er Jahre. Konservatorische Probleme am Beispiel West-Berlin," vol. I (Diss., Berlin Technische Universität, 2004), 72–73.

39   Walther Schmidt, "Rasteritis," *Bauen und Wohnen: Zeitschrift für das gesamte Bauwesen* 2 (December 1947), 290–92.

40   Schmidt, "Rasteritis," 290.

41   Schmidt, "Rasteritis," 292.

42   Baunet, "Hubert Hoffmann." http://www.baunet-info.com/research-networking/artists-groups-topics/hubert-hoffmann/, accessed December 16, 2021.

43   Hubert Hoffmann, "Introduction" Gerd Hatje and Hubert Hoffmann, eds., *Neue Deutsche Architektur* (Stuttgart: Verlag Gerd Hatje, 1956), 5.

44   Ernst Alberts, "Leserbrief," *Bauwelt* 11 (1956).

45   Dorsemagen, "Büro und Geschäftshäuser," 72–73.

46   *Bauwelt* 11 (1956); its cover reads, "Rastern?—dann bitte gut wie hier."

47   *Bauwelt* 11 (1956), 245.

Karl Kaspar, and the typesetter-turned-art-publisher Gerd Hatje, it took seriously its intention to document West German architecture at the moment of its publication. The introduction poses the book's title as a question: "German architecture?" It began by explaining that the first response to the desperate need for new building in bomb-scarred cities did not constitute an architectural agenda.[48] Much had been built since the end of the war, but the editors warned their readers against being impressed "by the quantity of building [...] 400,000 new apartments each year are not necessarily a cultural achievement by any means! Architecture cannot be captured in materialist, additive thinking; its evaluation requires intellectual standards."[49]

These new standards are, by implication, captured by the buildings in the book, all of them "clear expression[s] of building for our time" and "characteristic of Neues Bauen."[50] The authors compare them to only one other moment in German architectural history, the period that started at the end of the First World War, when a balance was found between the attraction of industrial architecture and "all vital and spontaneous emotions" expressed in Jugendstil.[51] The moment had come to an end in 1933, when "the development breaks off, Neues Bauen was ostracized, its protagonists had to emigrate or were condemned to inactivity."[52] Since then, Germany had relinquished its role at the epicenter of modern architecture. As they observed,

> "Other European nations [...] used the opportunity to exploit the insights of Neues Bauen and developed it further. So it is today that the roles of giver and taker are reversed, and what was once the center is now most often the receiving party. [...]
>
> Without a doubt, German architects after 1945 picked up many of the ideas that other nations had evolved during the period of our spiritual isolation. Today, we still remain in a stage of absorbing and reworking. [...] The quality of intellectual production can also be measured by its success in developing further a borrowed idea and transforming it."[53]

The gridded facade was proof of how far German architecture had fallen: the *Rasterfassade* "because of its monotony has done much to put cheap arguments in the hands of the adversaries of modern architecture to claim its purported lack of expressive means."[54] In the hands of mediocre West German practitioners, the tenets of modern architecture had produced facades so bad that they undermined the modernist cause.

Nonetheless, the demonized gridded facade makes countless appearances in the projects that the editors selected for the pages that followed. If the measure of Rasteritis was an automatic correlation between structure and facade design, it seems logical to expect an emphasis on detail drawings or construction photographs that communicated artful calibration between the two. But instead, only a single construction drawing is included, for Egon Eiermann's 1954 Burda-Moden publishing house in Offenburg. **[6.4]** As if to frustrate any attempt to make sense of what distinguishes a "good grid" from a bad one based on construction, the drawing shows that Eiermann's facade is a thoroughgoing hybrid of materials rather than the clear expression of a single material and its constructional logic, as the *Neues Bauen* tradition might have demanded. Bent sheet metal facade columns prove to be no more than formwork for cast concrete infill, backed by a layer of insulation and finished on the interior with fiber cement board. Only every other facade support abuts an interior partition wall, but the interior spaces are not expressed at all on the exterior. The frames and stops that hold exterior infill panels are fiber cement, but they are milled and conjoined as if they were made of wood. Any claim to truth in construction is further occluded by the facade structure, which is suspended on tension members from the top of the building, obscuring the traditional compression columns that hold up the real bulk of the building.

After leaving the architects they feature with little to their credit besides "further developing a borrowed idea and transforming it,"[55]

48   See Otto Bartning, ed., *Mensch und Raum: Darmstädter Gespräch 1951* (Darmstadt: Neue Darmstädter Verlagsanstalt, 1951), 33. The preamble to the Darmstädter Gespräch had cast the problem of homelessness as fundamental to any architectural agenda post-1945.
49   Hoffmann, "Introduction," vii.
50   Hoffmann, "Introduction," vii.
51   Hoffmann, "Introduction," x.
52   Hoffmann, "Introduction," xii.
53   Hoffmann, "Introduction," viii, xii.
54   Hoffmann, "Introduction," viii–ix.
55   Hoffmann, "Introduction," xii.

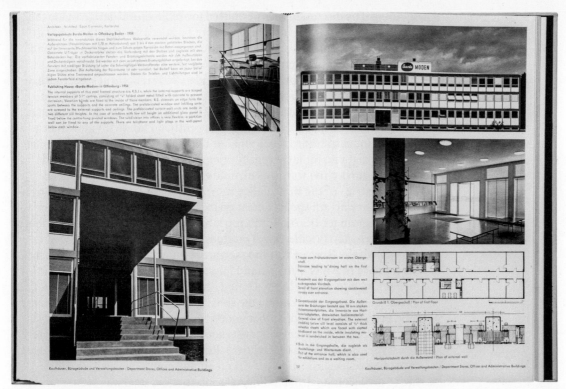

6.4 Egon Eiermann, Burda-Moden publishing house 1954, in *Neue Deutsche Architektur* 1956

Hatje, Hoffmann, and Kaspar offer one specific recommendation, and thus arrive at the same conclusion as *Bauwelt*'s Z.:

> "The observably high quality of the occupying force buildings, consulates and America Houses by the American architecture office Skidmore, Owings and Merrill has not remained without influence on the latest developments in Germany. By collaborating on these buildings, a large number of German architects have come in immediate contact with American planning methods. Inspiration from the controversial UN building, Lever House, and from department stores and office building has also been absorbed to greater or lesser degrees."[56]

Architects and corporate heads were not the only West German audiences responsive to SOM's new approach. The building industry was still dominated by the specialized, mostly regional producers of building components and the skills of those workers who would install their products, both organized by trade: a local steel company might produce structural trusses as well as facade systems in metal, to be handled on site by trained metalworkers, while the glass in the facade had to be provided by a different company and installed by glaziers. Slow, labor-intensive masonry dominated residential construction and was common in other building types as well. But as the industry retooled, especially to deliver products for the multistory and long-span commercial buildings that favored faster construction methods, the American paradigm represented by SOM and increasingly appreciated by architects offered business advantages that would lead to the emergence of large, market-determining manufacturers.

In the United States, which had seen dramatic increases in steel production during the war,[57] the use of steel as a structural material for new high rise and long-span construction offered an easy avenue for the industry's transition to a civilian economy. Of course, a "steel building" is always a composite between the steel bearing structure and other materials that form floors or enclosures. Claims to truth in construction should always be subject to scrutiny. When used to support a curtain wall, however, the steel bearing structure maintains its primacy as the most effective building material when used in tension: the steel verticals from which a curtain wall facade "hangs" can be proportionally thin and delicate without compromising performance. The mullions that subdivide the curtain wall into smaller units are dimensioned to account for manufacturing limitations to the size of planar infill materials. These mullions dominate the facade's expression to the extent desired by the architect's

56   Hoffmann, "Introduction," xii.
57   See, for example, Chang Woo Jung, "A Comparison of the Mining and Metallurgic Industry in Germany, Japan, Russia, the U.S, and Chile 1850–1950" (Term paper, Korean Minjok Leadership Academy, December 2010), section IV.4, http://www.zum.de/whkmla/sp /1112/jcw/jcw2.html#iv4, accessed December 16, 2021.

detailing. The discretion thus permitted to architectural design made the curtain wall, unlike the infill or shopfront facade, a boon to the "good grid."

The development of steel facade construction in a West German postwar context frequently evolved from the know-how that older companies had developed earlier as bridge and structural steel fabricators. American requisitions of export steel and coal during the Korean War meant that Ruhr steel was not initially available for domestic use. Early measures enacted under the Morgenthau Plan to divide larger German industries into much smaller units also initially limited production. But distaste for large legacy companies, all of which supported logistics during the war, was ultimately superseded by expedience.[58] The industries of the Ruhr valley were significant enough to Germany's recovery to warrant specific mention in President Truman's December 1947 "Program for US Aid for European Recovery."[59] A primary contributor to the *Wirtschaftswunder*, steel production rates in the five years from the start of the Korean War in 1950 through 1955 increased by 177 percent in response to American demand for steel, used presumably for armaments. Despite export to the United States, the rate of steel construction in Germany increased during the same period by 163 percent, outpacing food production and consumer goods.[60]

Availability of steel for construction did not translate immediately into a sophisticated facade industry. Rolled steel production did not resume at profitable levels until 1950.[61] Even among companies with historic ties to precision steel machining for construction, steel was often marketed for long-span structures such as bridges or industrial buildings. Aluminum alloys, available domestically for building product applications as early as 1948,[62] were the materials of choice for facades. Aluminum, softer and easier to extrude into profiled linear elements than steel, was seen as an ideal substitute for traditional wood windows as long as wood was a limited resource.[63] Used for windows or shop fronts, aluminum was self-supporting, although for larger facade spans, steel subconstruction was still needed. From a business perspective, this suited the several companies that offered both steel bearing structures and aluminum window elements.

One such company was Josef Gartner GmbH.[64] By 1954, only three years after producing its first commercial line of aluminum display vitrines, windows, and glazed partition walls, Gartner delivered a fully-patented operable facade system for the Kaufhof department store corporate headquarters in Cologne.[65] Only every third facade element was supported by the seven-story concrete structure, designed by Hermann Wunderlich and Reinhold Klüser.[66] Running above enameled glass at the spandrel and clear glass at each story, the aluminum mullions defined a tartan, equally dimensioned in vertical and horizontal. This innovative facade system earned the project a two-page spread in the "Construction" section of the August 1955 issue of *Bauen und Wohnen* and two pages in *Neue Deutsche Architektur*.

Bauen und Wohnen described in purely technical terms the new Kaufhof ensemble, which included an office tower, warehouse space, underground garage and delivery area, cafeteria, and showrooms. Its size alone was impressive: 22,000 square meters and a 25-meter free span at the entry to the service courtyard, a "modern" reinforced concrete structural system.[67] It was constructed in twelve months. More than a quarter of the text dedicated to the building's technical description focuses on the facade. The author's excitement was evident: "the facade was hung freely in front of the structure as an exterior skin and installed as components (*Montagebauweise*). The vertical and horizontal mullions in the facade are executed in aluminum, technically anodized. Spandrel and parapet are dark green wire glass and the integrated tilt-and-turn windows are mirror glazed."[68]

Technical advancement was swift, as building heights increased and new materials were introduced. Among these was Thiokol rubber, already used in the United States in the 1930s and widely used by SOM as of the late 1940s[69] but new to German construction. One documented

58   See Werner Bührer, *Ruhrstahl und Europa: Die Wirtschaftsvereiningung Eisen- und Stahlindustrie und die Anfänge der europäischen Integration, 1945–1952, Schriftenreihe der Vierteljahrshefte für Zeitgeschichte* (Munich: R. Oldenbourg, 1986), especially part III; and Durth, *Deutsche Architekten*, 258.

59   Harry Truman, "Program for US Aid for European Recovery, December 19, 1947," reprinted in "In der Vergangenheit nach Zukunftsperspektive Ausschau halten: Die Vereinigten Staaten von Amerika und Deutschland 1945–1950 und danach," *Zeitschrift für Kulturaustausch*, 1987, 362.

60   Tamás Vonyó, "The Wartime Origins of the Wirtschaftstwunder: The Growth of West German Industry, 1938–55," *Jahrbuch für Wirtschaftsgeschichte* 55, no. 2 (2014), table 2, https://eh.net/eha/wp-content/uploads/2013/11/Vonyo.pdf, accessed December 19, 2021.

61   Information from Josef Gartner GmbH, including project list, provided to the author by Monika Niklaser via email, July 12, 2010.

62   Niklaser, email, July 12, 2010.

63   *Donau Zeitung* special issue (November 10, 1951), unpaginated.

64   Gartner, purchased in 2001 by the Permasteelisa Group, became internationally recognized for its innovative high-performance curtain wall systems. Gartner, "History," https://josef-gartner.permasteelisagroup.com/history, accessed December 16, 2021.

65   Niklaser, email, July 12, 2010.

66   https://agrippaviertel.koeln/hauptverwaltung_kaufhof/, accessed January 21, 2022.

67   "Der Kaufhof-Hauptsitz," *Bauen und Wohnen: Zeitschrift für das gesamte Bauwesen* 1955, 252.

68   "Der Kaufhof-Hauptsitz," 252.

69   Frybergh, "Materials," 33–34.

70   Niklaser, email, July 12, 2010.
71   The Düsseldorf town planner who envisioned the tower required de-Nazification to practice. On Tamms's planning, see Friedrich Tamms, "Düsseldorf, eine neue Stadt," *Der Architekt BDA* IV (1955), 421–25.
72   Hellmuth Völkel, "Mantelwände bei Skelettbauten," in *Bauwelt* 16 (1958), 366–67.
73   Gartner reported that visitors called the exhibition the *Gartner-Schau* (Gartner show) rather than a *Gartenschau* (garden show).

use of rubber gaskets came two years after the Kaufhof buildings, in Gartner's first prominent steel and aluminum facade, fabricated for Paul Schneider-Esleben's Mannesmann tower in Düsseldorf (1957–1958).[70] The building's design was well-publicized[71] but its significance for facade construction was enormous, as is clear in a *Bauwelt* feature written on the occasion of its enclosure.[72] The magazine's April 21, 1958, cover was a close-up photo depicting the hoisting of a window element against the background of its gridded intermediary back-up structure.

Gartner was by no means the only company to transform its production from bespoke, singular elements to full facade systems; it was also not the only company to readjust its aesthetics over the course of the 1950s. The building industry initially seemed ambivalent about architecture's appearance in the early postwar period despite architects' concerns with style. Even as late as 1952, Gartner represented itself with both the heavy monumentality of the 1930s and the modern glazed facades of the 1950s. A 1952 promotional calendar attests to this stylistic ambivalence. **[6.5]** The calendar images promote Gartner's high technical capacity, whether in machining custom hinge hardware for Paul Schmitthenner's mammoth solid-wood garage doors, or in fabricating an ethereal greenhouse system for the 1950 German Federal Garden Show (*Bundesgartenschau*) in Düsseldorf.[73]

Contemporaneous advertisements in *Bauen + Wohnen* reflect changes in stylistic tendency and industry strategy among manufacturers of products ranging from brick or glass to water heaters, furniture, or home textiles. Not to be confused with the nearly epigonous *Bauen und Wohnen,* published in Ravensburg, Germany, this magazine was published in Switzerland and focused on communicating new construction techniques and details. As late as 1954, these ads reflected a more narrow and traditional market segmentation. By 1956, however, companies offered complete building systems and by 1957, these kinds of systems were proprietary.

One such example is Jucho, a window manufacturer, which supplied the steel frames for Ruf's Akademie der Bildenden Künste. Like Gartner, Jucho had begun as a steel bridge-building company in the late nineteenth

6.5 Josef Gartner GmbH, promotional calendar, 1952

Architekten: Hochbauamt der Stadt Stuttgart   Foto Weber

Gartenschau Stuttgart 1950. Große Ausstellungshalle, elektrisch geschweißt, Konstruktion und Ausführung GARTNER

1952   J U N I   30 Tage
Pfingstsonntag   Pfingstmontag
1   2   3   4   5   6   7
Sonntag   Montag   Dienstag Mittwoch Donnerstag Freitag Sonnabend

Architekt Prof. Dr.-Ing. Schmitthenner   Foto Fels

Straßenmeistereien der Autobahnen Karlsruhe, Seckenheim und Darmstadt
Verwindungs- und senkungssichere Holztore auf Stahlrahmen, mit handgeschmiedeten Bändern und GARTNER-Patentverschlüssen

1952   M A I   31 Tage
                                    Himmelfahrt
18   19   20   21   22   23   24
Sonntag   Montag   Dienstag Mittwoch Donnerstag Freitag Sonnabend

century[74] and in the 1930s and early 1940s had been a major manufacturer of steel and steel-copper windows for commercial, industrial, and residential buildings.[75] A January 1954 advertisement that ran in both *Bauen + Wohnen* and in *Der Architekt BDA* was dominated by an image of the Trinkaus Bank building in Düsseldorf, completed in 1951 after a design by Helmut Hentrich and Hans Heuer. **[6.6]** Never featured editorially in *Bauen + Wohnen*, the project elicited approval from its architects' former mentor Albert Speer, who saw it first in 1955 in a book he had been permitted to borrow from the Berlin *Amerika-Gedenkbibliothek:* "The Trinkaus Bank building, designed by Hentrich, who once belonged among my architects: with the rectangular double columns, infilled with glass planes, the building recalls the OKW [*Wehrmacht*] facade planned for Berlin."[76] Association with Speer was not necessarily good advertising. The building was likely selected for the ad because of its technically challenging infill *Rasterfassade*, but its affiliation with the kind of architecture Speer approved of may have been another reason for the transition to the curtain wall facade, which was both easier to produce and install and more amenable to modernist stylistic preferences.

The building was already three years old by the time Jucho's advertisement appeared but it was without doubt a model of window manufacturing precision. The Trinkaus is a *Rasterbau*,[77] its heavy, trabeated limestone facade grid infilled with tripartite black and bronze window elements. The bronze frames on the window units divide by three again: a high transom, a vertical transparent panel, and a lower black enameled panel into which a brass stud is set. The windows' large size, bimetallic composition, and precision juncture to the limestone-clad columns all required enormous skill, a selling point for Jucho despite the building's stylistic drawbacks.

Another advertisement of that same year for the metal fabricators' consortium Vereinigte Deutsche Metallwerke AG deflected problems of architectural style by using a line drawing instead of a photograph. **[6.7]** The drawing depicts a nine-story building with a shallow sloped roof, cropped at the top of the page. A network of lines renders a facade that might be in any style: traditional, with three over three windows and open parapets, a gridded infill facade, or a curtain wall. At least as importantly, the suggestive drawing cleverly sells not a tangible product but instead the know-how required to realize this or any facade in metal. The ad text offers a variety of architectural metalwork, from anodized sheet metal surfaces to rolled or extruded profiles for facades and furniture to roofing products, limited only by the architect's imagination. All this, "in contemporary construction-based design applications (*Formgebung*), make it possible to use the beautiful, useful material aluminum not only decoratively but also for construction purposes. [...] Request our technical advice with no obligation."[78] This wording implies that the facade industry was eager to offer architects the opportunity to collaborate on creating the facade, roofing, and cladding systems of their choice. It implies that each building was bespoke, unique, and craft-dependent rather than a collation of mass-produced industrial parts. These qualities substantially benefited SOM in realizing its buildings only with German-sourced materials despite the fact that their design innovations would have surpassed what the market otherwise offered.

By 1956, Jucho had moved on. An "office building in Baden-Oos" clad in a continuous gridded envelope described simply as a "metal facade"[79] represented the company's sales pitch. **[6.8]** The text lists Jucho's products as steel windows for residential and industrial applications, thermopane steel windows, aluminum windows, and aluminum interior acoustic partition walls but not facade systems, in seeming contradiction to the image above it. Perhaps, on closer inspection, an observant consumer would realize that the many open windows in the photo were Jucho products? More likely, Jucho's image choice was intended to associate the company with state-of-the-art curtain wall facade construction and to imply that Jucho was the right partner for achieving such facades. As in the case of the Deutsches Metallwerk AG advertisement,

74   "Zum fünfzigjährigen Bestehen der Firma C.H. Jucho in Dortmund," *Die Bautechnik* 5, no. 31 (July 15, 1927).

75   C. H. Jucho, "Jucho-Kupferstahl-Fenster für Büro-, Geschäfts- und Wohnhäuser und Siedlungsbauten," (Dortmund, 1931) (industry pamphlet).

76   Albert Speer cited in Durth, *Deutsche Architekten*, 308.

77   Roman Hillmann includes the Trinkaus Bank in his list of Rasterbauten of the 1950s, although he does note the building's "heavy tectonic form." Roland Hillmann, *Die Erste Nachkriegsmoderne: Ästhetik und Wahrnehmung der westdeutschen Architektur 1945–63* (Petersberg: Michael Imhof Verlag, 2011), 122.

78   *Bauen + Wohnen* 8, no. 2 (April 1954), n.p.

79   *Bauen + Wohnen* 10, no. 4 (April 1956), n.p.

80   Ernst Zietzschmann, " 'Team-work':
"Eine Architekturfirma mit 322 Mitarbeitern,"
Bauen +Wohnen: Internationale Zeitschrift 6,
no. 3 (June 1952), 139–45. A second article
appeared in October 1952 in the same periodical.
It included a three-page spread of a small
drive-up laundromat in California completed in
collaboration with Gardner Dailey. See Ernst
Zietzschmann, "Wäscherei in Kalifornien,"
Bauen + Wohnen: Internationale Zeitschrift 6, no. 5
(October 1952), 264–67. A two-year hiatus
followed before *Werk* published an article on
Lever House in 1954; see "Das Lever House
in New York," *Werk* 41, no. 2 (1954), 49–54.
81   *Bauen + Wohnen* 6, no. 3, cover.
82   Zietzschmann would become president
of the North Rhine-Westphalia chapter of the
German Werkbund from 1959–65 and later
a professor at Hanover's Werkkunstschule. See
Markus Jager, "Vom Bauhaus zur Werk:
Kunstschule das Fakultätsgebäude von Ernst
Zietzschmann," *Jahrbuch Hochweit* (2019), 6–9.
https://www.archland.uni-hannover.de
/fileadmin/archland/FAKULTAET
/MarkusJager_HOCHWEIT2019.pdf.
83   Zietzschmann, "Wäscherei," 139–40.
84   "Bonn," in *SOM News* (Skidmore,
Owings & Merrill, 1953).

the firm seemed open to collaboration and to adapting its products as desired.

By 1957, however, this collaborative spirit seems to have given way to proprietary systems designed, patented, produced, sold, and under warrantee by a manufacturer. A photo of Skidmore, Owings and Merrill's Manufacturers Hanover Trust building, completed in 1954 but not published in Germany until January 1956, dominates a quarter-page advertisement from the January 1957 issue of *Bauen + Wohnen*. **[6.9]** "New York's most modern building"—although the building was already three years old—was used to sell "the most modern lighting in the world," for which the advertiser was an exclusive German agent. Offered as a complete package that included a "very practical" ceiling suspension system, all under patent protection, the MARLUX light ceiling was detailed in a catalogue that readers were urged to order. The know-how was built into the proprietary system available for purchase. Facade manufacturers soon followed suit.

The 1951 opening of SOM's office in West Germany predated by a year the earliest mention of its work in the German architectural press.[80] The article appeared in the June 1952 *Bauen + Wohnen* issue on "large structures"[81] and was the only article in that issue to profile an architectural office rather than a single project. Its author, Ernst Zietzschmann,[82] borrowing heavily from the catalogue to the 1950 exhibition of SOM at the Museum of Modern Art, offered a familiar narrative: SOM could prevail as a new model of architectural practice because of its consensus on both modernist idiom and corporate business organization as a delivery method. "In that sense," he wrote, "a fact that we find quite remarkable is tested: the possibility of frictionless collaboration among very many individuals. [...] The individual designers who work within such an organization have no concerns about letting go of their personalities."[83] Otherwise, the German press was quiet around SOM for the next couple of years while the firm went about delivering its projects to the United States High Commissioner on Germany (HICOG).

A notice in the August 15, 1953, issue of *SOM News*, an internal publication for disseminating information among the firm's numerous offices in places as far-flung as Morocco, Turkey, and Japan, celebrated the opening of the Bonn office in winter 1951.[84] It featured a rendering of the American Consulate in Bremen, then nearing completion, and cited Gordon Bunshaft, located in New York, as partner-in-charge, and David Hughes, who had been stationed in Germany since the office opened, as on-site project manager.

"Bonn" was a geographic simplification: the office was located in Bad Godesberg, in the greater Bonn-Cologne region, where HICOG was

6.6 C.H. Jucho window company, advertisement 1954

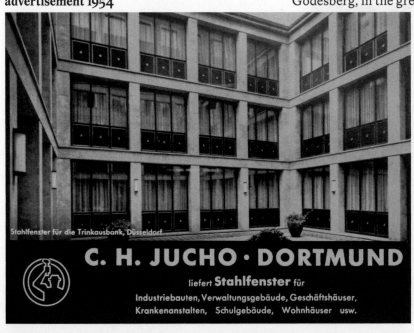

85   Zietzschmann, "Wäscherei," 139.
86   Natalie de Blois in conversation with the author, June 21, 2010.
87   King was responsible for giving the commissions for the US embassies in Rio and Havana to Harrison Abramovitz. He served in the Foreign Building Operations from 1938 to 1953. Tanya Schevitz, "Leland King: Backer of Modernist Embassies." *SFGate* (May 4, 2004). http://www.sfgate.com/bayarea/article/Leland-King-backer-of-modernist-embassies-2762155.php, accessed December 16, 2021.
88   Natalie de Blois in conversation with the author, June 21, 2010.

headquartered. Period photographs show a long, fluorescent-lit drafting room. Rows of simply built tilt-top drafting tables, three abreast, line the room in which some thirty to forty architects and draftsmen worked. Although dwarfed by SOM's US operations, the Bad Godesberg office, operated in collaboration with Ruf's one-time associate Otto Apel, was perhaps the largest architecture office in Germany at the time. Its organizational structure parroted the SOM corporate organization which, as the 1952 *Bauen und Wohnen* article put bluntly, was "the largest commercial business in the field of architecture."[85] The office hierarchy is obvious at a glance. "Germans who worked on drafting tables all wore white coats to keep clothing clean," as Natalie de Blois, Bunshaft's protégé and a design architect for the consulates, recalled in 2010.[86] White coats drafted; suit jackets—the Americans—supervised. **[6.10]**

According to de Blois, the projects were overseen from the United States through the New York office; Leland King, head of the U.S. Department of State Foreign Building Operations,[87] advocated for the firm in Washington, D.C., where Bunshaft often accompanied him for presentations. While Bunshaft traveled to Germany no more than two or three times per year, de Blois spent nearly a year there between 1952 and 1953 following her Fulbright grant in Paris. She recalled that the New York team was rarely involved in projects after the design phase. No one on the SOM team spoke German, she noted, but "we communicated well. [...] We did not discuss modern architecture or the International style [...] It was not extraordinary. One said 'good morning' every day."[88]

6.7 Vereinigte Deutsche Metallwerke, advertisement 1954

6.8 C.H. Jucho window company, advertisement 1956

6.9 Marlux brand lighting advertisement with SOM's Manufacturers Hanover Trust, 1957

89   De Blois, June 21, 2010.
90   Gordon Bunshaft Architectural
Drawings and Papers, 1909–1990 (bulk 1950–
1979), Columbia University Series VII:
Publications—*SOM News* and Photographs.
91   "Amerikanische Generalkonsulate in
Bremen, Düsseldorf, Frankfurt und Stuttgart"
Bauen +Wohnen: Internationale Zeitschrift 10, no. 4
(1956), 113–18.

She remembered the name of her German collaborator nearly fifty years later: Mr. Becker. And although she did not complete detail or construction documents, de Blois was certain that the SOM office in Bad Godesberg worked exclusively with German manufacturing and construction firms. This practice would have been consistent with the use of foreign credit vouchers, intended in the frame of the Marshall Plan to bolster the local economy, to pay for construction. Even in the early 1950s, she recalled, "Germany had a sophisticated building industry. No American products were used in the German projects."[89]

Beyond de Blois's anecdotal information, the relationship between the German employees of SOM in Bonn, the American architects sent to run the office, and Otto Apel, the German architect who was signatory on the consular projects, is difficult to reconstruct. Information has to be extracted from the construction documents, all of which bear both SOM's and Apel's title blocks. They are labeled in German and the names of the draftsmen who signed the drawings are German, confirming de Blois's recollections. No project correspondence or job book has yet been located, however, to describe the working relationship between New York and Bad Godesberg. Apel's office archives from that era also seem to have vanished.

Documents in the Gordon Bunshaft collection[90] indicate that authorship for the projects was attributed equitably. Photographs of the earliest German projects, housing for consular employees in Bremen, are labeled as projects by SOM "in association with Otto Apel." An April 1956 article in *Bauen + Wohnen* inverts this attribution, crediting Apel and his project architect Franz Mocken with all four consulates, although noting in smaller typeface, "in collaboration with Skidmore, Owings & Merrill, Architects and Engineers, New York."[91] By the magazine's publication date, with SOM long gone from Germany, Apel's authorship

6.10a Skidmore, Owings and Merrill/Otto Apel site office, Bad Godesberg 1952–1953

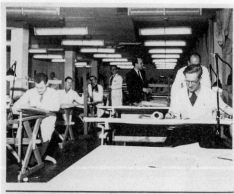

2 German Staff
and
Ed Petrazio US
in rear

Sherwood Smith US
2 German Staff

6.10b

for the buildings had become plausible, although when first built, they would have differed radically from everything around them.

During its five years of operation in West Germany, within the Consular and America House building program administered by the US Department of State and the HICOG, SOM completed four consulates: Bremen (1952–1953), where housing was included in the project, Düsseldorf (1953), Frankfurt (1954–1955), and Stuttgart (1954–1955). A fifth consulate project was planned in Munich, but the city's building administration, which judged SOM "arrogant,"[92] rejected the project and HICOG retracted the commission. The difficulties in Munich marked the end of SOM's German work. In summer 1954, its staff moved to a smaller space in Frankfurt am Main which, in turn, was closed in spring 1955 upon completion of the Stuttgart consulate.[93] By then, SOM's influence was solidly established through those who had worked in its offices, and indirectly, through publications.

SOM's German projects are typical in appearance and conception to the firm's work elsewhere at that time: facades in controlled relief, realized in offset planes of structure, infill wall, spandrel, window frame, glazing, and in some cases an additional exterior frame that emphatically redelineates the underlying grid. The materials used, including aluminum windows, gray spandrel glass, and shell limestone in Frankfurt [6.11] and Stuttgart or white-painted steel windows, Roman travertine, and exterior aluminum frames in Bremen, were luxurious by German standards, representative of American wealth and gravitas. So, too, were the sleek glazing details. The specificity of each facade component and the degree to which it was integral to the facade as system far exceeded facade construction then popular in Germany. While SOM's facade design comported well with

92   See Loeffler, *The Architecture of Diplomacy*, 96. According to Loeffler's research, SOM did not contact anyone in the city building administration prior to submitting a proposal. This, although the April 15, 1954, issue of *SOM News* reported that the Munich consulate had "reached the stage of working drawings."
93   The closing of SOM's German office was announced in the August 15, 1955, issue of SOM News under the heading "Here and There": "Edward G. Petrazio has been assigned to the Chicago office after two and one-half years in Germany. With the completion in June of the remaining consulates in Stuttgart and Frankfurt, the SOM office in Frankfurt has been closed." Many of the architects active in the German office became associates in the 1950s: Paul Pippin, Edward Petrazio, Sherwood Smith, Carl Bitter, David Hughes, and Natalie de Blois.

the US building industry in the early 1950s, it was utterly unlike the pieced steel angles that Ruf had used to assemble window frames and facade glazing for the Akademie der Bildenden Künste or the kinds of products offered in magazine ads.

The facade details for the Bremen consulate, drafted in Bad Godesberg in July 1952, just as Ruf's office was detailing the Akademie der Bildenden Künste, reflect assumptions about material and construction that are radically different from those made by Ruf's employees. SOM's details demand highly specific components. They depict bays of six windows above six identically dimensioned travertine spandrel panels, set forty milli-meters proud of the exterior frame, which comprises white-painted I-section columns into which aerated concrete was cast in place. The storefront glazing system is detailed as stick construction, pieced together on site to absorb only minimal tolerances in the structural frame. In the horizontal, slotted tabs welded to the steel facade fascia are bolted through an L-angle on the interior side, and on the exterior through an unequal leg C-channel to which a threaded nut has been welded. A highly specific steel angle, customized for the fixed frame, was bolted into place on the C-channel; the operable frame, another function-specific shape with a smaller U-shaped thin-gauge steel glass stop, was then installed. In the vertical, a welded L-section was used to anchor the frames to the concrete structure and, on its interior side, to receive the leading edge of an insulated panel, which abuts the acoustic dropped ceiling. A V-shaped exterior trim of thinner-gauge steel, affixed with a setscrew, was then clipped over the bolts, which connect the fixed frame to the interior back-up structure.

The Bremen documents assumed the capacity to produce sophisticated, function-specific facade elements in Germany. The drawings also specify large quantities of sheet aluminum, a rare commodity at that time. Moreover, the facade drawn for the Bremen consulate was conceived as a system. Each piece serves a legible function: back-up structure, anchor-age, fixed frame, operable frame, weather protection, and drip. Were the elements of this system reconfigured, however, they could have produce a similar, but different facade. An economy of scales is implicit in the Bremen facade as system, which, by extension, would shape the future of the construction industry.

The record set of construction drawings for the Düsseldorf consulate indicates that its design and planning overlapped with work in Bremen. [6.12] Jack Gensemer, the architect who directed HICOG's building initia-tives, approved all but the final plot plan on October 19, 1953, at which point everything from the structural system to the species of street trees was determined. The final drawings were approved in December 1953.[94] This is the briefest drawing set of all the consulates, with only nine draw-ings, two of them window details. Another sheet includes only suspended ceiling details with integrated fluorescent lighting, an indication that the ceiling systems already available in the United State were yet not available in Germany.[95] The microfilm files of the drawings are extremely poor quality, perhaps because the originals were drawn quickly in pencil on coarse paper. Many annotations are handwritten rather than lettered with a template, as was used in the drawing sets for the three other consulates. The corners cut on drawing quality would be consistent with faster production.

A tight delivery schedule might explain its many similarities with the Bremen consulate, including the steel I-sections used as columns and beams. In Düsseldorf, steel U-channels were used as beams to create an exterior horizontal steel surface flush with the flanges of the structural I-beam columns. All interior steel structure was subsequently embedded in concrete for fireproofing. The only architectural steel is in the finished buildings' facades. Nonetheless, there are significance differences in the two building's structural characteristics. Whereas the floors in the Bremen consulate were concrete cast as flat plates, the Stuttgart consulate had a waffle slab configuration, which allowed for longer spans with less material weight. Although not yet explored in the Düsseldorf design, the waffle slab in combination with prefabricated concrete planks would facilitate the spatial concept of the two subsequent consulates.

94   As per the dated signature on the microfilm-preserved drawings found in the collection of Skidmore, Owings and Merrill, New York City.
95   SOM's Manufacturers' Hanover Trust building on Fifth Avenue, already occupied in 1954, used a commercially available acoustic dropped ceiling system later marketed in Germany, to name one example.

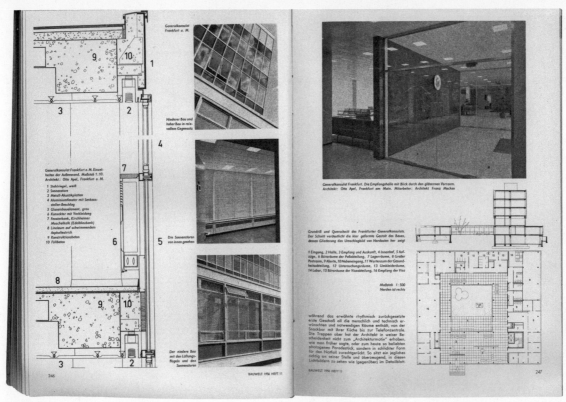

6.11 Wall section and photographs in *Bauwelt* 1956

The Düsseldorf consulate facade is also similar to that in Bremen, both of them detailed as slightly proud of the white-painted, exposed steel frame. There are subtle differences in the detailing of the two, however, perhaps as a result of on-site experience or the facade contractors' advice. Although exactly the same steel window angles are used—single pane glazing, no indication of weather stripping or gaskets—the depth of the V-shaped steel counter-flashing in Düsseldorf is reduced as compared with that in Bremen.

The published construction details distinguish the buildings from the notorious *Rasterfassade*, in which the facade grid is nothing more than the building's vertical and horizontal structural elements clad to withstand exterior exposure and to conceal deviations or tolerances. In the consulates, the flanges of the structural steel I-beam columns are exposed on the exterior, perfectly in plane with the U-channels into which the floor slabs sit. The structural grid, usually subject to the laxer tolerances of "rough" construction, is itself a precisely built surface finish. In the order of their construction, the consulate facades invert the way trades typically interacted in West German practice: rather than reserving high-precision trades for infill and finish materials, both buildings were first built using high-precision welded and bolted steel, then stabilized with lower-precision cast concrete. And unlike the usual *Rasterfassade*, the exterior facade elements are set in front of, rather than in plane with, the facade grid. This choice facilitated the prefabrication of the six window frames abreast, as in both the Bremen and Düsseldorf consulates. Adjustments during installation could be made using slotted connections to the welded angles that attached the window elements to the wall. The finesse evident in Jucho's Trinkaus Bank was obviated by SOM's approach to facade construction.

Although the approval dates next to Gensemer's signature are separated by only months, the differences between the earlier Bremen and Düsseldorf consulates and the two final consulates in Stuttgart and Frankfurt are enormous. The two earlier consulates differed in technique and appearance from their West German context, but their designs included many recognizable characteristics. SOM's final two consulates introduced another architectural strategy that further liberated the building envelope from its back-up structure.

The first two consulates had simple structural systems: three rows of parallel columns, stabilized against wracking by stairs, bathroom

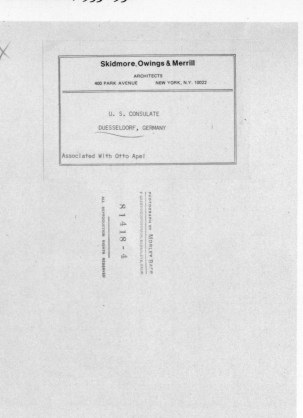

6.12 Skidmore, Owings and Merrill/Otto Apel, American Consulate General, Düsseldorf 1953

cores, and floor slab. On each floor, a double-loaded corridor ran to one side of the interior column row, defining deeper rooms on one side of the corridor than on the other. The columns in the corridor were offset from the longitudinal partition wall and detailed with great care, as the several sheets of drawings dedicated to difficult junctures of wall, columns, and corners attest. Both exterior rows of columns were in plane with the building envelope, so that the interior structure registered in the building's exterior steel framing members. By contrast, in the Stuttgart and Frankfurt consulates the columns stand free from the exterior wall, independent from although calibrated to the rhythm of the building envelope. This latter strategy permits much more complex floor plans in which larger spaces and smaller spaces are contiguous. Corridors are no longer the backbone of the building's planning but instead are used only where opportune and otherwise omitted. **[6.13]**

The setback of column from envelope opened up possibilities for the facade. Offset curtain walls benefit bearing structure performance: the weight of the facade positively stresses the back span of columns behind the edge cantilever. This means that both slab and column can be more thinly dimensioned. In addition, the gap between column and envelope could be hollowed out for heating and cooling systems, concealed behind the facade spandrel elements; very literally, the building envelope contributed actively in calibrating interior climate. SOM's New York office had only recently used this strategy in its headquarters for Manufacturers Hanover Trust (1954).

As noted in the April 15, 1954, issue of *SOM News*, the two last consulates were also the "first concrete frame office buildings to be built under the SOM program for the State Department."[96] Square columns, plastered over protective metal corner profiles to ensure sharp edges, stand 24.5 centimeters from the facade.[97] Drawing sets from both the Stuttgart **[6.14]** and Frankfurt consulates include sheets dedicated only to the juncture of interior partition walls, columns, and mullions at the buildings' perimeter, demonstrating the complexity required of an elegant solution that also could leave the columns freestanding.

The construction sets depict a hybrid bearing structure of cast-in-place columns, some with precast concrete elements as lost formwork,[98] steel I-beams, and precast lightweight concrete floor elements. The precast

96   *SOM News* (Skidmore, Owings & Merrill, April 15, 1954), unpaginated.
97   See drawing A007 in the Frankfurt Consulate set or A005 in the Stuttgart set, SOM Collection, New York City.
98   Annotations on working drawings for both consulates show that Ytong prefabricated aerated concrete elements were used for some vertical elements and for spanning floor elements.

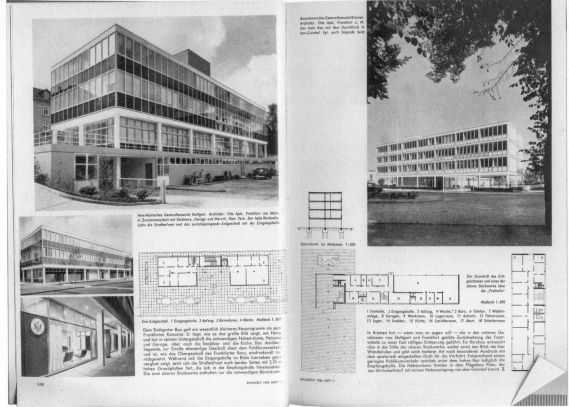

6.13 American Consulates General in Stuttgart and Bremen, *Bauwelt* 1956

floor elements, manufactured by West German subsidiaries of a Swedish company and sold under the brand name Ytong, were a staple of postwar West German reconstruction. Notably they were unavailable in the United States; their use indicates the latitude allowed to the Germans working in SOM's office.[99] In Germany, they were considered important to accelerating construction at a moment when new buildings were sorely needed. Ludwig Erhard, for whom Sep Ruf would later build a villa, advocated for the product manufacturer at the Bundestag in March 1952, praising its contribution to quick, energy-efficient housing construction.

The combination of concrete columns and steel beams was extremely unusual for such relatively short span structures. Advantages in construction speed gained by using steel and Ytong for the horizontal bearing structure would have been reduced by the time-intensive interplay of trades as steel and concrete workers tag-teamed. By contrast, for the concrete-filled steel skeletons in the first two consulates, the two trades would have worked sequentially. To some extent, the construction of the later two consulates reflects the distribution of responsibility in the Bad Godesberg office. The column placement, wall-to-column junctures, and curtain wall detailing reflected SOM's US practices; the expanded use of Ytong and concrete rather than steel were typical of West German construction.

The two buildings' facades are nearly identical: exactly the same sheet of curtain wall details is included in both sets, approved by Gensemer on exactly the same day, July 13, 1954.[100] **[6.15] [6.16]** The two upper stories comprise an operable steel window system above an opaque spandrel panel. The profiles are in much lower relief than in the facades of the first consulates, less than 25 millimeters between the leading edge of the mullion and the glass or spandrel panel, whereas the offset was 30 millimeters in the Bremen and Düsseldorf projects. The use of a concrete bearing structure required a different approach to facade anchorage as well. In lieu of connections welded to structural steel prior to concrete work, slots were cut in the concrete floor after casting. Steel fins were mortared into the concrete and the fixed frames of the window or spandrel elements bolted to them. A rectangular steel cap covered the bolt. The cap was not tapered to appear more slender, a detailing technique used in the earlier consulates, and the fasteners were left visible. The assembly's dimension of 55 millimeters, 70 at the base of the

99   The material had been used for non-bearing walls in SOM's Bremen consular housing as well but played only a minor role in the Bremen and Düsseldorf consulates. *SOM News* (Skidmore, Owings & Merrill, December 15, 1953).
100   Both drawings are signed by Gensemer and stamped "approved" with this date noted.

101   Item under "notes," *SOM News* (Skidmore, Owings & Merrill, August 15, 1955).

103   Item under "notes," *SOM News* (Skidmore, Owings & Merrill, August 15, 1955).

103   *SOM News* (Skidmore, Owings & Merrill, April 15, 1954).

104   "Der Stadtrat sagte NEIN zu dieser Fassade," *Abendzeitung* (Munich, March 4, 1954). Ruf was fast to react to the SOM debacle. His consulate job book includes this article as a clipping as well as a document dated March 13, 1954, describing a new massing and facade strategy for the same site. This later document suggests "greater emphasis" on the vertical rather than the horizontal and is likely Ruf's counterproposal. A letter dated October 1954 from a real estate lawyer reports that the site for which SOM's proposed building had been rejected was still foreseen, and that, as a basis for negotiations between HICOG and the city of Munich, "no other American architect" would be commissioned.

105   For a thorough account of the site planning issues, see Irene Meissner, *Sep Ruf 1908–1982*, Kunstwissenschaftliche Studien (Berlin: Deutscher Kunstverlag, 2013), 136.

106   Meissner, *Sep Ruf 1908–1982*, 128.

curtain wall, was 25 millimeters thicker than in the earlier projects. The effect was much more robust. With its flat relief and heavier dimensions, the curtain wall in the Frankfurt and Stuttgart consulates represented a very different aesthetic. Although the way the structural frame was constructed owed more to West German standard practice, the facade aesthetic was distinctly different from the more highly profiled, filigree appearance of contemporary German architecture, including that of Ruf and Schwippert.

In the fall of 1954, as SOM's German office was downscaled and relocated to Frankfurt, its two New York employees "on loan" to the German projects, Sherwood Smith and Carl Bitter, returned to the home office.[101] By summer 1955,[102] with the completion of the Frankfurt and Stuttgart consulates and with the embarrassing loss of the Munich project, SOM's German office closed. The managing architect, Edward Petrazio, returned to the Chicago office. Perhaps by 1956, SOM's interest in German work had been eclipsed by its other, larger possibilities elsewhere in the world.

The Munich debacle must have been shocking, given SOM's reputation for competence. A note in the April 15, 1954, issue of *SOM News* told employees that "two additional consulates (Munich and Stuttgart) have reached the stage of working drawings"[103] but on the ground, the facts were different. In February 1954, Munich's building commission ended SOM's bid to realize an American consulate on the edge of the English Garden.[104] During the design process, the Bad Godesberg office had neglected contact with local officials, which was especially important given the contentious site.[105] Ruf, who at that time was involved in several projects for HICOG in Bonn,[106] persuaded Gensemer that he could salvage the project. His good relations with both Munich bureaucracy and American administration resulted in a direct commission in October

6.14 Skidmore, Owings and Merrill/Otto Apel, American Consulate General in Frankfurt, wall-to-column junctures, 1954

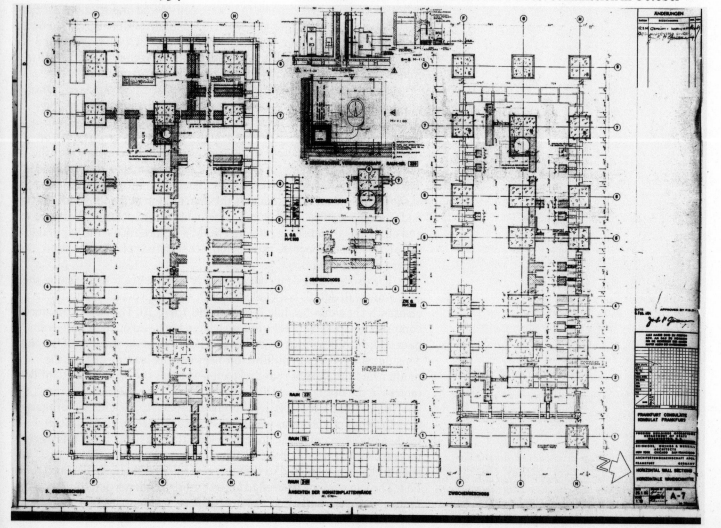

107 In a letter to Ruf dated October 21, 1954, from Ernst Werner, the agent retained by the United States to negotiate with the Munich Commission on Rebuilding (Wiederaufbau-referat), assurances are given that "no other American architect will be commissioned but instead, that exclusively Prof. Ruf working together with the state official Director Gensemer [...] will execute the architectural direction." On April 4, 1955, Gensemer wrote to Ruf: "I am very glad you were able to find an opportunity to visit the completed American consulate in Bremen. [...] I am sending you under separate cover a set of working drawings of the Frankfurt consulate in order that you may see the type of complete drawings and details which were made for our projects." Collection of Notburga and Elisabeth Ruf.

108 There is no record to indicate that Ruf subscribed to any American architecture periodicals, and he was not, until much later, in correspondence with German émigré architects in the United States. There are no US journals in the extensive office archive maintained by Ruf's daughters. Later correspondence with Gropius, Mies, and Neutra begins in the 1960s. Collection of Notburga and Elisabeth Ruf.

109 Collection of Notburga and Elisabeth Ruf.

of 1954. In April of 1955, HICOG's agent sent him a set of SOM's drawings for the Munich project and the construction set for the Frankfurt consulate; Ruf also visited the Bremen consulate.[107] Although Ruf's collaborations with Otto Apel predated the consulates, the Munich commission marks Ruf's first serious documented encounter with American construction and detailing methods.[108]

Ruf's initial project with at least three variations went to Jack Gensemer in March 1954, almost immediately after SOM's dismissal. SOM had designs for two sites: on Briennerstrasse, the formal boulevard laid out by Leo von Klenze, and on the edge of the large English Garden, a public park in the city center. Ruf developed schemes for both sites but advocated for the latter, in which the building was reoriented for greater transparency from the park, a strategic move to allay the city building commission's objections. The building was ultimately realized in this position. By November 1954, Ruf had engaged the services of a real estate lawyer to help track the project; in January, he received a lengthy letter from Gensemer, including sketches and amendments to the plans, as well as initial design approval.[109] Final confirmation from the Foreign Building Office arrived from Washington in August 1955, and Gensemer encouraged Ruf to begin working drawings. The city of Munich issued permits for Ruf's project in early October 1955 and construction commenced soon thereafter.

The Foreign Building Office and HICOG had a strong hand in the building's design: with such a quick turnaround from approval to construction, detailing would have had to be streamlined and recourse made to existing building techniques and products that had proven effective. The consulate is radically different in appearance from Ruf's other contemporaneous buildings. In contrast to the tapered, cantilevering roof planes and the transparent, filigree glazing typical of his work around 1954, the consulate is stolidly prismatic, its aluminum-gridded

6.15 Skidmore, Owings and Merrill/Otto Apel, American Consulate General in Bremen, horizontal facade section, 1953

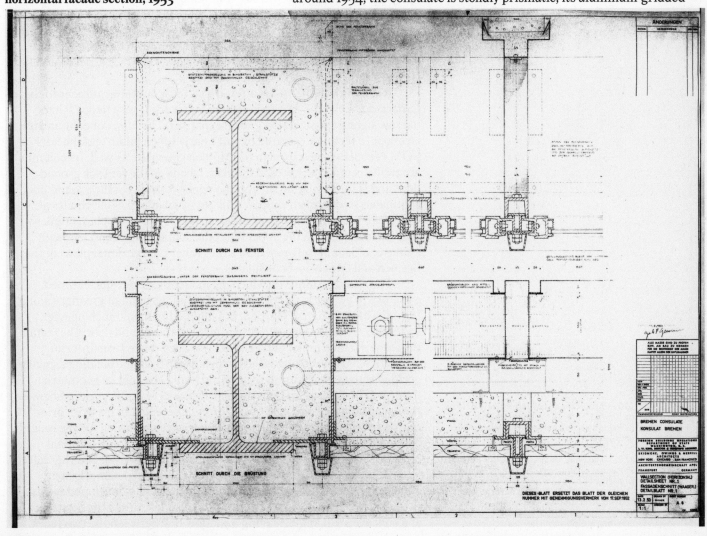

glazing set in very low relief against the stone-clad structural skeleton. The facade strategy is a hybrid between the exposed skeleton facades of the Bremen or Düsseldorf consulates and the continuous, multistory curtain wall construction used in Frankfurt and Stuttgart.

Through the drawing sets he received and the construction contacts HICOG likely supplied, Ruf was privy to a body of knowledge otherwise only accessible to those German architects who had worked directly with SOM. Ruf's highly developed sense for construction intricacies and his deep investment in the architectural expression of details would have been well served by this knowledge. It put him at the cutting edge of the growing shift toward curtain wall detailing: it allowed him to test a weightier modernist style and to realize it in a broad palette of rich materials. It also would have empowered him in dealing with fabricators and building product industry players eager to develop more highly specialized product systems after the American model. Ruf's work from this point onward departs from the idiom he had championed in the early 1950s to expand upon the style he adopted for the HICOG buildings, a style already established by SOM.

Despite its importance for Ruf's developing idiom, not much documentation survives of the construction process by which the Munich consulate was realized. Presumably because of US Department of State security requirements, his office archives retain only a single blueprinted set of drawings from November 1, 1955, but no construction drawings. The job book contains no more than preliminary correspondence with suppliers of building products and contractors. Extensive preserved correspondence dealing with project administration from its early moments does affirm the freedom Ruf exercised in design considerations, although these letters are not accompanied by sketches or images. Any HICOG drawings that may have survived were lost after German reunification,[110] by which time none of the consulate buildings except for the one in Munich was owned or occupied by the US government. Period photographs and the contemporary condition of the building, altered from the original design, are the only other sources of first-hand information. Despite the sparse evidence, it is clear that Ruf grasped quickly which aspects of SOM's German style he wished to adapt. **[6.17]**

Ruf's work of the 1950s offered a strong counter-argument to the *Rasterfassade*. He translated his passion for facade transparency[111] into narrow sight lines and large glazed expanses. The offset of column and envelope, a technique shared by Ruf's early 1950s idiom and the later SOM consulates, was used in the Munich consulate as well. Its columns are twelve centimeters behind the glass facade on the set-back ground floor and significantly farther on the upper stories. On the ground floor, continuous steel-framed window walls, to which the rows of cylindrical, white-painted columns run parallel, envelope the open-plan, publicly-accessible spaces. On the upper floor, the double-loaded corridor with banks of offices closely resembles the rather conventional plans of the Bremen and Düsseldorf consulates.

The round columns on which the main office tract sits, elevated one story to permit a clear view to a continuous band of greenery along the edge of the English Garden, are doubled to form much heavier, 45-centimeter-deep piers, elliptical in plan, on the ground floor. They retain the same surface finish and geometry as they move from interior to exterior and are distinguished by their depth from the building's smaller gridded square columns on the ground floor. The special geometric treatment of these piers is unique in Ruf's oeuvre of the period. Likewise, the use of columns as a grid has no direct precedent in his work prior to the consulate.[112] It does recur, however, in his planning for the roughly contemporaneous Theodor Heuss pavilion at the German National Museum in Nuremberg (1955–1958) and in projects developed thereafter.

On the ground floor, the two perpendicular glazed walls meet at negative corners, repeating the details SOM had developed for its two curtain wall consulates, in which the facades turned the corner at a concave steel angle, leaving a shadow line between the two faces.

110   According an email from Harald Nethe on June 30, 2010, all the State Department drawings were abandoned when the Bonn embassy was closed.
111   Bartning, *Mensch und Raum*, 107.
112   The Neue Maxburg (1954–57, Ruf and Pabst) has decoratively clad round columns in parts of its facades and public spaces, but these are clearly related to the repetitive bearing structure elsewhere in the building and are not expressed to the same degree as free-standing sculptural elements.

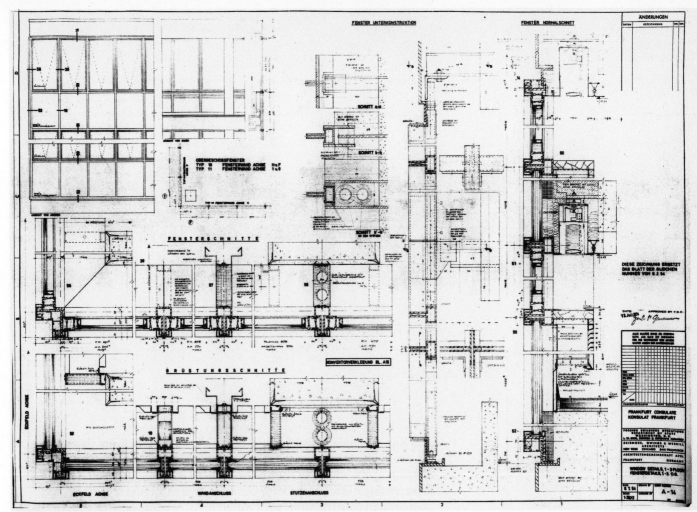

6.16 Skidmore, Owings and Merrill/Otto Apel, American Consulate General in Frankfurt, horizontal facade section, 1954

The facade is thin on this lower floor, with an overall thickness of eight centimeters. On the upper stories, Ruf developed a facade system that covers all three floors continuously, alternating between operable hopper windows and stone spandrel panels infilled with the local Kirchheimer Blaubank limestone typical in Munich.[113] The building's cornice, the lowest floor plate, and the location of its structural columns are marked in the facade by solid elements clad in a lighter limestone from the Jura mountains. The effect combines the infill facade strategy used by SOM in Düsseldorf and Bremen, albeit without those buildings' horizontal framing elements, with the continuous low-relief facades developed for the Frankfurt and Stuttgart consulates. Although the width of Ruf's facade elements is slightly greater, creating a different proportion than SOM's, the facade mullions and the window frame design most closely resemble SOM's two later consulates: flat cover channels without visible fasteners double as fixed frames around the operable windows, which tilt into the building to open. Ruf's choice of material for the spandrel panels, on the other hand, follows the precedents set in Bremen and Düsseldorf. The gold anodized finish on the facade metal indicates, however, that his window mullions were made in aluminum rather than steel, which cannot be anodized. This change would have made the facade system simpler to fabricate, since most contemporaneous German facade systems were aluminum. These material adjustments mark another instance of Ruf's capacity to assimilate selected elements of SOM's architecture into to a more standard German construction context.

Even without a full set of working drawings to study, it is obvious that the robustness of the Munich consulate's facade detailing is at odds with the idiom developed by Ruf in his earlier or other contemporaneous buildings. At the turning point between the style of his immediate postwar work and the projects that would elevate his practice to an international scale,[114] the consulate marks his transition to a different set of architectural interests, material choices, and stylistic preference. From the architecture

113   Building description by Ruf, Collection of Notburga and Elisabeth Ruf.
114   Meissner periodizes the work from 1954–58 as "international" in terms of both location and importance. She includes the German pavilion at the 1956 World's Fair. Meissner, *Sep Ruf 1908–1982*, 228–55.

6.17 Sep Ruf, American Consulate in Munich, perspective, plan set, November 1955

of minimal means and full transparency, Ruf turned from this moment toward an architecture perhaps more appropriate to the wealth of building materials and sophistication of building products that were now increasingly available in West Germany. His encounter with SOM and American construction types would register in his oeuvre and become at least one of many motivating factors for the kind of architecture he would produce from this point on.

Without so much as minimal abridgment, the contents of Sep Ruf's architectural office in Munich were transported upon his death in 1982 to the house he had designed exactly thirty years earlier for his family on Lake Tegern some fifty kilometers away. The volume of documents would certainly have made the move an enormous undertaking. All of it remains intact, in the custody of his daughter, Notburga, an architect who worked for her father, and her daughter, Elisabeth, whom Ruf adopted, making him a father figure to both.

I first found their names among the acknowledgments in one of the few Ruf monographs I could find in the early 2000s when I began my research on West German postwar architecture in earnest. After a Munich friend found their address for me, I wrote a formal letter in my best German. I had no idea what to expect of their collection. I hoped that it included Ruf's construction documents; my intuition, after visiting a few of his buildings, was that these would be important for understanding his work, but no such drawing had yet been published. The answer to my letter arrived via email, assuring me that such drawings had survived and offering to prepare them for me to study as soon as I could visit. This generosity, so unexpected, was also a reprieve. Had the Rufs declined my request, I would have given up my research entirely. The archive of Ruf's drawings at the Technische Universität München was closed and would remain closed for years.[1]

Sep Ruf, a committed practitioner of modern architecture in conservative Bavaria, was known later in his career for such major clients as IBM, the German National Museum, and the Bavarian State itself. Precise, astute, and agile, he also had unique access to the political forces that remade West German cities and public buildings. He was as charismatic and politically savvy as any of the postwar heroes that architectural history has lionized: Eero Saarinen, Oscar Niemeyer, I.M. Pei,

---

1 The outcome of that closure was the first comprehensive monograph on Ruf: Irene Meissner, *Sep Ruf 1908–1982*, Kunstwissenschaftliche Studien (Berlin: Deutscher Kunstverlag, 2013). As a work of scholarship, it was more than worth the wait I was asked to endure, despite the frustration it caused me.

Akademie der Bildenden Künste, plaster casts, 2019

Wallace K. Harrison, Lúcio Costa. That his work ever receded from the public imagination even in his native region seems nothing if not peculiar.

The Ruf family's stories intersect with postwar history's big events. The American forces, proceeding unopposed through the beautiful moraine valley that slopes towards Lake Tegern, requisitioned the family home. Ruf removed the floorboards from their house before he relinquished it; the American standard-issue boots might scrape the subfloor, but the parquet would be spared. Their stories also register personal joys and tragedies. In 1958, at the height of his career, Ruf contracted polio. Partial paralysis did not stop him from producing new buildings for nearly two more decades. Although both Notburga and her brother Gregor studied to become architects, a new generation perhaps capable of carrying forward his legacy, neither were in a position to take over Ruf's practice when he retired to Tuscany in the mid-1970s. These stories, the marginalia to academic research, have no corollary in an institutional archive. They are valuable in understanding Ruf's person, whose attributes emerge in his architecture as well. He was an architect who knew his way around construction and building materials. He was an extraordinary manager and a skilled diplomat. He dealt with the limitations under which he operated and acclimated quickly when those limitations were lifted. As Gregor wrote of his father on the first page in *Sep Ruf: Bauten, Wettbewerbsprojekte, Umfeld*, published by the chair of Prof. Uwe Kiessler at the Technische Universität München in 1994, "acknowledging the era and its possibilities, he sought the timelessly valid."

My first visit to the house overlooking the Tegernsee lasted a summer afternoon. Steady rain slipped through weak spots in the roof and fell into pails that Elisabeth had placed with precision around the living room. For hours, I leafed through complete sets of project documents: invoices, sketches in margins, telephone notes, complete working drawings, everything that comprises the life of an architectural project. Reaffirming what the family anecdotes and stories suggested, these documents conveyed how Ruf and his office ran projects: how he adapted what the building industry could offer, why he might decide to construct a portion of a building in wood but the rest in concrete and steel, how he held others to account. The Rufs sat with me, chatting. We interrupted work only once, mid-afternoon, for strong coffee and homemade plum cake.

211

Based upon my own experience managing architecture jobs, I can come up with probable reasons that explain why a well-run office might retain the kinds of documents and drawings still in the Rufs' possession. These records ensure timely and correctly budgeted project completion. They can adjudicate disagreements. They can serve as references for construction details that are required in future projects. But this logic, one of instrumentality, pertains only to an active architecture office. Ruf's office closed decades ago.

During all my many visits, the Rufs remained unfailingly generous with their remarkable collection and with Elisabeth's excellent cooking, while the house around them became increasingly porous to climate. Elisabeth's quarterly trips up to the roof to brush tar-based mastic over emergent leaks could not entirely offset impecunity, even when borne as gracefully as the Rufs have done. The Rufs, their possessions, their home, their kindnesses, the atmosphere in which the remains of Ruf's architectural office can still be found, are integral to an architectural history that still might be written. Too often, such actors and circumstances are omitted from formal writing. Footnotes, bibliographies, acknowledgments, image captions: these will not suffice.

As someone who misses terribly the physicality of construction, handling fragile paper is my compensation for the abstraction of academic research. I favor construction documents because they are legible to me. I have drafted these kinds of details myself. They introduce into history writing the facts of the physical world. By their nature, though, construction drawings are the most expendable, the most instrumental of architectural documents. Because they are subordinate to process, they lose value as soon as the information they communicate has been enacted and the building is complete. Thus, much of the paper I handle as a researcher owes its tenuous survival to someone's disinclination to sort the conventionally valuable from the ephemeral. Often chance is at play. But sometimes, not always, reluctance to discard is an expression of love, an act of collecting as magical thinking. This is true for the Rufs. They care thoroughly for each material witness to their father's life.

Ruf was as prolific as he was exacting. His office oversaw every aspect of his more than 260 projects, as evident in meticulous drawings as in pedantically corrected job site time sheets. Every piece of paper that

Notburga (foreground) and Elisabeth Ruf at home, January 2019

contributed to his realized buildings and unrealized projects is preserved in the two bedrooms overlooking the Tegernsee, perhaps originally intended for Notburga and her brother, the children who grew up to study architecture. Thick rolls of original drawings for all his projects rest in stacks, encased in long corrugated cardboard mailing boxes that, some thirty or more years ago, a helpful employee taped together to accommodate their heft. Leitz-brand ring binders, the hallmark of German bureaucratic efficiency, are exactly as the Ruf office left them.

Part of the awe I feel at seeing precisely lettered vellums from the 1940s spread out on the Ruf's dining table is recompense for my own shortcomings as an archivist. Things that move into my orbit suffer attrition: my beloved but uninventoried books and LPs mailed from Berlin back to New York in 1986 that never arrived; the letter, written by my twenty-seven-year-old father to his younger sister, which my cousin entrusted to me at my father's funeral but which then disappeared during a purge meant to target old bank statements and pay stubs. Lesser and greater tragedies come from the poor archival practices.

Perhaps this also underlies my dedication to architectural ephemera: I am a totemist of sorts, believing that artifacts become, often unpredictably, touchstones of past moments. Here is another reason to favor the unexpectedly preserved construction drawing. Some totems work by convention—the wedding ring, the bronzed baby shoe, the tattoo—but the more attractive proposition is that totemic meaning only emerges over time, of its own accord. Because this emergence offers no dictates to guide the collector, it is the more difficult possibility to nurture. To some eyes, this kind of collecting might be hard to distinguish from an impulse merely to hold onto everything.

To engage with the Ruf archive is to encounter simultaneously order and entropy: with equal rigor, Elisabeth Ruf preserves century-old glass Christmas tree ornaments, organizes her apples in perfect geometric rows, and locates any document I have ever requested. Meanwhile, velum fractures; discarded wood furniture weathers beneath the eaves; hydronic radiators cease to function.

Until relatively recently, Ruf's work received less notice than its prominence within the cultural and political life of West Germany warrants. Although not a candidate for de-Nazification after the war, as were many

214

Drawings for Sep Ruf's Akademie der Bildenden Künste

Diptych, view from the Ruf living room, 2019

217

other prominent architects, the fact that Ruf was able to maintain his architectural practice during the Third Reich was treated as reason for ambivalence in architecture history circles. This has changed with the publication of that long-awaited monograph researched in the closed Technische Universität München archive, the closely watched addition to his beautiful Akademie der Bildenden Künste campus in Nuremberg, and, perhaps most important to his status within the popular imagination, the reconstruction of his 1961 Bonn Chancellor's Bungalow at the 2014 Venice Biennale. While these events brought greater recognition, his papers remain happily unwinnowed; but the house in which his daughters live still, unhappily, needs a new roof.

When I visited the Rufs with my friend the photographer Thad Russell in January 2019, a temporary shelter dominated the house from outside. The regional historic preservation agency had staged an emergency intervention to keep the rain out and the snow off. Seen from outside, the structure overwhelmed the architecture of the house. On the inside, though, the spaces were again dry, including the two small main-floor bedrooms that hold the archive.

Although the purpose of our 2019 visit was to secure images of drawings that appear in this book, Thad and I asked the Ruf daughters' permission to photograph more: not only their possessions but also the traces which their lives leave among them, what Walter Benjamin called the "chaos of memories,"[2] and which inhere to the highest—because least instrumental—form of collection.

---

2 Walter Benjamin, "Unpacking My Library: A Talk about Book Collection," in Hannah Arendt, ed., *Illuminations*, trans. Harry Zohn (New York: Schocken Books, 1968), 59–69, here 59.

Architectures of Greater Means, 1956–1964

Sep Ruf's Hochschule für Verwaltungswissenschaften, Speyer

The glossy blue linoleum floor in Sep Ruf's Hochschule für Verwaltungswissenschaften (College of Public Administration, 1957–1960) has a liquid sheen, regardless of whether the skies above Speyer are occluded or fair. [7.1] Indirect light reflects into the building off the lawn, leaves, and water in the courtyard around which the building is organized. The city has grown to reach the campus, originally set in the empty fields on Speyer's outskirts. Yet the building's interiors remain sensitive to seasonal change: shrubs that flower by trees that blossom, leaf out, then produce pods and berries that hang all winter under the slow-moving middle European skies mirrored in those waxed linoleum floors. To say that the architecture is predicated on proximity to nature, though, would be inaccurate. Its thresholds between inside and outside are thick and definitive; in the classroom wing, the threshold is extended even further by protruding, black-glazed brick walls that effectively double each room's width. In summer when the metal jalousies are let down, the intermediary space thus defined is even harder to attribute to outside or in. Each bit of flora stands more or less isolated, in plant beds or stationed within mown grass. Trees are singular, each a specimen of its kind, not part of a grove or field. The hedges, even where they have been allowed to overgrow, redraw faithfully the lines that the buildings lay out. Lichen adheres precisely to the narrow top edge of the concrete board balustrade on steel offsets just proud of the dormitory facade. [7.2] There are clear rules that govern both the architecture and its grounds, and in each case they are equally abstract. The corridors invert sky and ground: blue under foot, fir slats texturing the plane overhead.

7.1 Sep Ruf, Hochschule für Verwaltungswissenschaften, one of the two primary corridors, 2019

**7.2 Dormitory balustrade detail and
main building, 2019**

**7.3 Courtyard and library, dormitory
in the background, shortly after
completion in 1960**

7.4 Primary entrance plaza on Dudenhoferstrasse, shortly after completion in 1960

Although it is as typologically accurate to call both Ruf's Hochschule für Verwaltungswissenschaften (HfV) and his Akademie der Bildenden Künste campus plans reliant upon courtyard elements, the two building complexes are entirely different in their essence. The firs and birches that thread the surrounding woods through the Nuremberg campus seem, even in historic photos, simultaneous with the buildings: this is a fairy tale landscape populated by coevals and coequals, nature and construction. By contrast, the first photographer to shoot the Hochschule für Verwaltungswissenschaften (HfV) seems to have understood its architect's intention: a bough, a fringe of branches, a tree in every shot as counterpoint. [7.3] [7.4] Plant life is a frame subordinate to the architecture itself, which itself is robust, ordered, its gravitas far outweighing what those limited exemplars of the natural world could bring to bear. [7.5] [7.6]

Of course, the school in Nuremberg was meant for artists, its site literally lost in the woods, whereas the school in Speyer was built to train civil servants for whom the benefits of solid bureaucracy and rule-following would be a professional credo. Their campuses should by all means reflect their different cultures. Yet in the Speyer project, there was more afoot. It was an ideal commission for Ruf at that particular moment. It allowed him to expand upon the means developed for the Brussels World's Fair, through which architecture could express the new democratic consciousness of West Germany. It gave him opportunity to test the spatial and material syntax associated with his close study of SOM. It offered a chance to assemble a palette of materials, semi-products, and design objects that spoke to his facility in construction and to the rapidly increasing capacity of German construction product manufacturers.

Ruf's HfV is a complex of three buildings. Two are lower in height, their facades made up of black-glazed brick and steel shopfront glazing. Of these, the main building houses the instructional and administrative functions; the other substantially smaller one is the cafeteria. Each was originally connected via walkways running below steel canopies to the largest of the buildings, a three-story dormitory, which is faced in matte, light orange brick and striped with smaller steel windows. The main building is a flat, repetitively faced volume, mostly uninflected by the disposition of interior functions. A higher-roofed multipurpose room is the only exception. An early drawing from the design development set shows facades that are reticent, if not mute, about the building's inner life. [7.7] Nothing about it indicates, at least in a conventional manner, that the building is public-facing. Scale is equally difficult to decipher. A few enormous trees, their branches cropped by construction lines that restrict the space each elevation is given on the page, obscure the facade

7.5 One of the main corridors and
courtyard shortly after completion
in 1960

7.6 Dormitory building shortly after
completion in 1960

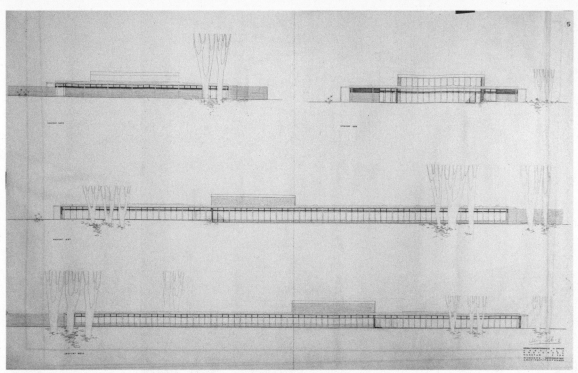

**7.7 Elevations in ink and pencil,
November 1957**

**7.8 Primary entrance plaza on
Dudenhoferstrasse, 2019**

7.9 Interior courtyard adjacent to main entrance, 2019

in the drawing. It is impossible to tell whether the trees stand far in the foreground, which would explain their enormity, or whether the building is particularly low-slung. Either way, neither the trees' shapes nor their positions seem related to the architecture behind them. Likewise, the plant life depicted on the ground plan from the same 1957 set keeps a respectful distance from the building's envelope. Although the instructional building is organized around courtyards and the complex as a whole aligns across the campus grounds, the buildings are aloof from their proximate landscape.

What the drawings belie is the fact that the school's main building, the one that fronts the street and accommodates its most important uses, is not meant to be seen in its entirety as it appears on the sheet of paper, laid out in three neat rows on the velum. Although its short end faces the street, the building is entered on its long side, across a small paved plaza **[7.8]** edged by a black-glazed brick wall parallel to the street, on which the school's name is written in stainless steel letters, for which Ruf's office stipulated the typography. The wall extends the trajectory of an interior wall, behind which the receptionist sits, and its continuity reveals to the visitor the extent to which the experience of the building is predicated on the view-through. Registered on the glazed entry facade, through transparencies and reflection, is a palimpsest of the building's plan. On the right, one sees all the way through the layers of glazing that enclose two smaller courtyards, one on either side of the banked auditorium. **[7.9]** On the left, one can make out the wide primary corridor from which the building's two wings, one for classrooms and one for researcher and professorial offices, extend at right angles. Protruding slightly from the low building is the volume of the multipurpose hall, equal in dimension to the width of the central courtyard. Drawn on the surface of the main facade, legible to the observant visitor, is a map of the building's primary elements, an indication of its hierarchies, a précis of its rules for navigation. What lies behind the repetitive facade is ghosted and reflected within it, allowing Ruf's reticent building to communicate after all.

Although originally planned as a second higher volume in which banked seats would have risen from a ground-level podium, the auditorium was reconceived and realized to step down from grade instead. **[7.10]** For the building's spatial coherence, this change produced a real benefit. Whereas the volume as originally conceived would have obstructed the view upon entry, the down-sloping section allows for windows at the

**7.10 Auditorium, side-lit through
the interior courtyard, 2019**

auditorium's entry level. They sit as a clerestory within the room,
providing glareless ambient light above the heads of audience and
speaker. Window frames and mullions configured as deeper fins double
as baffles. The two transparent short walls of the auditorium face onto
two small flanking courtyards, encircled on their other three sides
by corridors that access offices for the school's upper administration.
From entry, the building is transparent, if not from end to end then from
outside to courtyard to auditorium and again to courtyard. But the
small courtyards serve another purpose besides offering natural light
and a clear shot from outside the entry plaza: they provide for contact
among students and administration by means of cross views that allow
each to observe the other over the course of the day. In the case of the
college, integrating the workings of administration directly into the
school's daily life is beneficial. After all, these students are themselves
learning to become administrators. As the layout makes clear, there
is reciprocity between managing the school's business and engaging in it.

Opposite the long bank of flush wood panels and doors that let
onto the auditorium's upper level is a room even larger in footprint and more
prominent in massing. Unlike the auditorium, the walls of the multipurpose room, the Aula, are opaque upon entering the building. On each side
of the Aula are offsets the width of a single-run stair, where the facade
systems of the long, glazed corridors fold around; through these transparent corners, the visitor catches oblique but limited views of the large
courtyard at the building's center. The Aula, which fronts the courtyard,
is the only space in the building that allows a visitor all the distance and
breadth required to see it as a whole. The courtyard's perimeter is framed
twice: by the building's glass walls in vertical and horizontal, and by an
edging of crushed gray stone onto which expressive roof scuppers drip.
Inside the gravel is lawn, punctuated by two mature trees and stands
of non-native bushes: juniper, rhododendron, blooming perennials. At the
end of the courtyard opposite the Aula, running along the windows
of the library, a linear water basin spans between two stone elements: one
a square basin and the other a bridging sculpture made up of an irregular
granite slab on two solid stone uprights.

The school was formally inaugurated in the Aula. Rows of men in dark
suits, and the few women in attendance who are immediately identifiable
in photos by the way their clothing breaks the pattern of ties and lapels,
watched pensively from chairs lined end to end. Among them was thirty-
year-old Helmut Kohl, future chancellor of reunited Germany, but then
only newly elected as the youngest member of parliament. He appears in
a photo that was shot as he walked the school's hallways. The Aula's long-
span column-free space is resolved in a grid of beams, which, at the glass
facade to the courtyard, rests on a row of cylindrical columns set back
some two meters from the room's edge. [7.11] Although not a curtain wall

in the strictest sense, the courtyard-facing steel mullions are dimensioned not to support the roof's edge from below but rather to secure it against uplift. It is a clever use of materials and static forces, steel performing in tension, as Eiermann and Ruf had already exploited in their Brussels pavilion.

The complex's layout enforces a formality of movement that is utterly unlike the potential for meanders, diagonals, and *Trampelpfade* criss-crossing the grass that characterizes Ruf's Nuremberg campus. From the entry area, as the visitor moves past the auditorium and Aula, there is little choice but to take a sharp left down one of the two long corridors with the glossy blue linoleum floors that run along the courtyard to the library entrance and out to the small rear green behind the main building, where the dormitory and cafeteria stand. Like the auditorium and the Aula, beneath which a reception area with custom-fabricated coat racks and counters is housed, the library has a lower level embedded in the ground: the stacks, upon which the reading room sits. Unlike the other communal spaces in the complex, however, its windows stop short of the ground, ending instead at a knee wall clad in wood paneling that conceals the radiators. **[7.12]** The glass, stretching from wooded slat–clad ceiling to table height, corresponds to the visual dimensions seen by a seated student. Facing south on one side, overlooking the reflective water basin on the other, the library is brilliantly lit, a counterpoint to the sober, north-lit areas through which the building is entered and in which the larger lectures are given.

To the library's south is the one-story cafeteria, which is similar in its architecture to the main building; and the dormitory, which is completely unlike it, at least from the outside. Raised on an inset, glass-enclosed plinth that harbors the common rooms typical of a dormitory, such as lounges,

7.11 Aula and main courtyard, 2019

7.12 Library interior, 2019

meeting spaces, and the like, the building's appearance and meter is entirely determined by the subdivision of rooms on the interior. Perhaps, as can be gathered from the aerial photo taken after the library extension was completed, the pale orange brick and window dimensions were intended to reference the pale orange stucco on the residential buildings along the main street, which predate the school building. **[7.13]**

The cafeteria building and the one remaining walkway, of the two that originally connected to the dormitory before the library was enlarged, are of real interest within the evolution of Ruf's style. **[7.14]** Although its thick eaves clad in aluminum, dark steel-framed windows, and wood slats on soffit and ceiling are all clearly in conformity with the idiom Ruf's office developed for the HfV, the building incorporates motifs lifted directly from the Nuremberg project completed only two years before the Speyer competition was won. The effect here is completely different, however. The first element is the round, thin steel column connected to the cafeteria eave and walkway canopy by a flat stand-off. It is a detail that Ruf used in the Akademie der Bildenden Künste porte-cochère, although it is reintroduced here not to trick the viewer's eye into underestimating the thickness of the roof it holds up or to belie the truth of the materials used to carry loads. Rather, it is yet another addition to the long list of materials and finishes used. In their position at the edge of the eave, which might easily have been made to cantilever without them, the columns hold the building down. Whereas the eaves in the Akademie der Bildenden Künste were set back and profiled multiple times to seem as thin as possible, nonetheless able to self-support, the eaves here are brought back down to the ground, implying that their weight is too great to be borne otherwise. The line of columns redraws the building's edge, this time a couple of meters beyond the glazing, thickening the threshold between inside and out, which Ruf was at such pains to whittle down in his Nuremberg project.

The other detail that quotes directly from the earlier project is the distinctive scupper that protrudes from the face of the roof eave, spewing rainwater in droplets into stone-edged rectangles filled with river rock to break the water's force and set into the lawn. **[7.15]** In the Akademie der Bildenden Künste, the scupper likewise directs its water to a purpose-built drainage area, albeit a circular one, on the grass. **[7.16]** But the effect of the scupper projecting from the top of the thin roofline, set back in multiple recesses like the bed course of a classical architrave to appear even thinner, is quite different: in material and form, it is sculptural, almost figural, against the restrained, thinly dimensioned components of the building. In the HfV, by comparison, the scupper is made of the same material as the eave from which it projects and appears almost equal in dimension to the column near which it protrudes. It is one among a collection of elements, part of an embarrassment of architectural riches, rather than a singular moment of opulence in an otherwise restrained architectural

Hochschule für Verwaltungswissenschaften Speyer

Foto-Fix, Luftbildfreigabe Nr. 2502-7, Bez.-Reg. Rheinh.-Pfalz

7.13 Aerial view of the complex on a promotional card, undated

7.14 Cafeteria and walkway canopy, 2019

landscape. To identify the significant differences in the kind of architecture Ruf was interested in making, the scupper and column offer a one-to-one comparison: same elements, other context, utterly different effect.

> "This hour represents an important incision in the life of the Hochschule für Verwaltungswissenschaften Speyer. May the building that will rise on this site become a happy home for the college. And may it allow a civil service to grow up which, by its selfless service to the community of the state, contributes to the solidification and completion of a democratic social constitutional state in Germany."[01]

Christian-Friedrich Menger, dean of the Speyer College of Public Administration, kept his speech at the cornerstone laying ceremony for the new building brief: November 4, 1958, was a cold, unpleasant day, and no one wanted to spend much time outside, even to celebrate the start of construction. The moment represented a significant ratification of a school whose existence had appeared tenuous from the start. The construction planning process had been set in motion on February 28, 1957, when a competition jury unanimously recommended in favor of Ruf's entry for the new college campus in Speyer. Menger's wish for a "happy home" was understandable, even if its realization was still a long way off. The project's development had been and would continue to be no less fraught than that of the college it was to house.

Even before the competition jury convened, the decision to realize a new building for the college had met with adversity. Since its establishment under French administration in 1947, the college had been housed in a former high school, inadequate to the job of training an entirely new administrative class for a West German government. The city of Speyer first offered sites so unacceptable that public outcry ensued. The school would have moved to a smaller city some twenty-six kilometers away, but for the intervention of the regional government in Mainz. The site finally donated by the city of Speyer was considered far too small for a school that at that point had 250 students, most of whom were meant to live on campus.[02] The formal complaint lodged by a local architect named Gilgenberg, that he had been excluded from the list of invitees, held up the competition until he was placated by inclusion in the jury.[03] The drama was not yet over. Judging of the competition was delayed when four of the five architects invited, including Ruf and his colleague and sometime-collaborator Theo Pabst, refused to submit their work until the Bund Deutscher Architekten had negotiated the architect's fee.[04]

In the end, the jury selected Ruf's compact site plan because of the way it dealt with the site constraints while allowing potential room for future growth.[05] [7.17] Ruf managed this trick by organizing the primary, administrative, and classroom functions around an internal courtyard, then locating only a small cafeteria and a housing block as freestanding buildings on the little remaining land. Even after his project prevailed, Ruf did not submit his first invoice until almost a year later, on January 2, 1958, nearly a year after receiving the commission.[06] By summer 1959, as the topping out ceremony was being planned, relations between Ruf and his client appeared strained. The terse language in which Ruf's invitation to the topping out was framed reflects the tension around escalating costs, which were primarily due to inflation within the construction industry. The invitation letter began by noting that "the timing is not entirely appropriate to the status of work on site [.,.but] on the other hand, with regard to the increasingly reduced labor force on site, this event can no longer be postponed."[07] This clearly was a none-too-subtle complaint about the slow speed of construction. The invitation came on short notice, arriving less than three weeks prior to the event, and informed Ruf that the date could "not be shifted since the college can offer no other possibilities. [...] We close in the expectation that you would like to make arrangements for, and be present on, this date."[08]

Conflict between Ruf and his clients in Speyer, both the college and the municipal building department, continued until the campus opened

01   Christian-Friedrich Menger, cited in Stefan Fisch, "50 Jahre Sep-Ruf-Bau der DHV Speyer" (PowerPoint presentation, Speyer: Deutsche Hochschule für Verwaltungswissenschaften, 2010).
02   Rudolf Morsey, "50 Jahre Hochschule für Verwaltungswissenschaften (1947–1997)," in Klaus Lüder, ed., *Staat und Verwaltung: Fünfzig Jahre Hochschule für Verwaltungswissenschaften Speyer* (Berlin: Duncker & Humblot, 1997), 16–17.
03   Dean Bulla to Dupprè of the city administration, July 30, 1956. Cited in Fisch, "50 Jahre Sep-Ruf-Bau."
04   Meeting notes by Dean Bulla, December 11, 1956, DHV archive.
05   Jury report, February 28, 1957, Collection of Elisabeth and Notburga Ruf, job books 4 and 6.
06   Letters from Dr. W. Schmitt of the Ministry for Finance and Reconstruction, Rhineland-Palatinate, from March 1, 1957, informing Ruf that he had received the commission; and a carbon copy of Ruf's bill dated January 2, 1958, accompanied by a precise accounting of the construction costs associated with the building, which by then had been reduced in size and scope. Collection of Elisabeth and Notburga Ruf.
07   Speyer Department of Building to Sep Ruf, October 16, 1959. Collection of Elisabeth and Notburga Ruf.
08   Speyer Department of Building to Sep Ruf, October 16, 1959.

**7.15 Rain scupper and steel column
with stand-off, 2019**

7.16 Rain scupper at the entry plaza, Akademie der Bildenden Künste, 2019

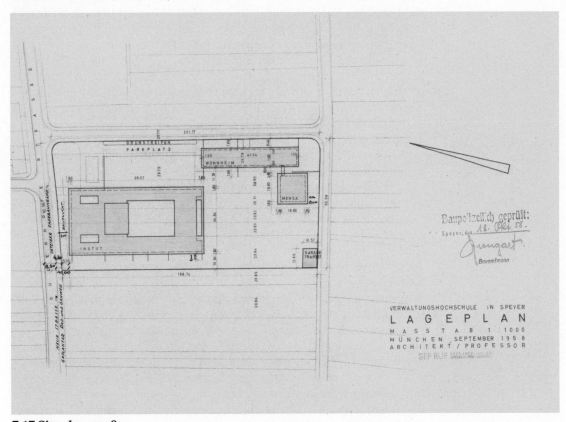

7.17 Site plan, 1958

on September 14, 1960. Construction costs were largely to blame. In the initial competition entry, which included a calculation of construction costs, Ruf's building had appeared to be the least expensive, largely because of its compactness and massing.[09] To save costs, the main building was shortened, the cafeteria reduced by a third, and the library reconfigured while construction was already in process. These changes played havoc with Ruf's planning grids.[10] In spring 1958, there was discussion about simplifying the dormitories by excluding special areas for female professors and students, a decision that was prevented only after intervention by the Speyer Department of Health.[11] The low point for Ruf was likely July 31, 1959, when the formwork supporting a partially poured concrete roof slab collapsed, seriously injuring two construction workers.[12] The construction site was immediately closed, only weeks after the topping out ceremony.

Despite the mishaps, the building was completed in September, in time for a new school year for the incoming class of future public servants. By virtue of the new campus, the college was guaranteed a future. This was significant, considering that the last of the Federal Republic *Bundesländer* had only agreed to co-fund it in 1957. Saarland's acquiescence made federal support for the school unanimous, and secured its status as the location at which all West German civil servants would be educated.[13] Upon the completion of the new campus, the College was also granted the right to offer a *Habilitation* within its curriculum, a right that established its research status in policy and administration beyond its original, much more practically-focused pedagogical purposes.[14]

Unlike the Akademie der Bildenden Künste in Nuremberg, the HfV in Speyer did not enjoy a deep history, rooted in storied German tradition to which its curriculum and architecture could make reference to set it apart from the recent Third Reich past. In fact, the school was established to replace Germany's traditional approach to civil service. The French occupying government, designer of the curriculum, chose its own national tradition as the model for the new system, intended to guarantee democratic practices.

The idea to found the school first arose in the summer of 1946 in Paris as part of the "de-Prussianization" of Germany pledged in a July 20, 1945, policy paper by the Interministerial Committee for Occupation Policy.[15] In opposition to the German civil service tradition, which demanded legal training prior to civil service, the French model proposed offering an admissions exam to students who could have completed degrees in any field. Training would also be offered to higher-ranking civil servants already in government. Finally, a position in government within the French sector would be guaranteed for all those who successfully completed the exit examination. Administrateur Général Émile Laffon signed the school into existence with order number 194 on January 11, 1947. The college administered its first entrance exam on May 15, 1947, and courses began for 49 students, selected from among 190 applicants, several days later in Speyer's city center. Three of those students were women.[16]

The college's French founding and pedagogy were not conducive to its political and financial stability, however, as German sources were loath to make up shortfalls in the French occupying government's allocations. In its early days, funding was so limited that students were asked to contribute a pound of potatoes for each day during which they were housed on campus. The annual budget was shared initially between the French government and Rhineland-Palatinate, the state in which Speyer is located. The two other French-occupied states refused to contribute. At one point German authorities agitated to dissolve the school entirely and incorporate its course of study into the much older University of Mainz. The efforts of a French administrator, Irène Giron, who advocated for the college as a prestige project, kept the HfV in Speyer.[17]

The spring of 1949 marked the first tangible step in the college's transformation from a project of French-initiated reeducation to a German institution. In May 1949, coincident with the founding of the Federal Republic of Germany, all the French-occupied states finally agreed to fund

09   Fisch, "50 Jahre Sep-Ruf-Bau," image 28.
10   The library and lecture hall, intended as higher volumes to frame the courtyard, were reduced to the height of the rest of the building, and the library stacks were resized to accommodate a larger collection. Fisch, "50 Jahre Sep-Ruf-Bau," 34–45.
11   Letter from the Director of the Speyer Health Department to the City of Speyer Administration, dated November 11, 1958. Fisch, "50 Jahre Sep-Ruf-Bau," 50.
12   "Betondecke in Verwaltungshochschule-Neubau eingestürzt," *Die Rheinpfalz*, August 1, 1959. Cited in Fisch, "50 Jahre Sep-Ruf-Bau," 58.
13   Morsey, "50 Jahre HfV," 14–15.
14   Morsey, "50 Jahre HfV," 17.
15   Morsey, "50 Jahre HfV."
16   Morsey, "50 Jahre HfV," 3–9.
17   Morsey, "50 Jahre HfV," 10.

the school. Bavaria, which had no comparable course of study and was already sending prospective civil servants to Speyer, also agreed to contribute. The school was reorganized and re-chartered in August, 1950, under a new, charismatic dean, who understood the political impossibility of asking the German states to adopt a French-chartered institution. Upon the issuance of the new charter, Lower Saxony and Schleswig-Holstein joined the consortium of funders, which by then included the West German federal government as well. This commitment came, however, at the price of a greatly reduced operating budget, to which the dean capitulated. Over the course of the next seven years, all the German states voted to contribute to the school, with West Berlin joining in 1961. The college's existence was thus guaranteed, in terms of both funding and political buy-in.

Throughout its history, the curriculum was based broadly in the humanities, with courses in philosophy, sociology, history, and language, in addition to civil and federal law, theoretical and practical administration, and finance and economics. Its research along with its graduate and postgraduate studies, all established by the mid-1950s, ensured its role in the "old and meaningful German promotion of administrative sciences."[18] The increasing importance of research, in addition to the practical training for which the French had originally intended the college, was evident in the competition brief, which Ruf would have received in July, 1956. For example, the library was to include 350 square meters subdivided into twenty rooms for professors, researchers, assistants, and their secretaries.[19] Ruf's architecture was asked to solidify the college's existing operations as well as to plan for its expansion in research and scholarship. And yet there was nothing in the competition brief to indicate how this new, specifically West German administrative cadre was to represent itself. This was at Ruf's discretion.[20]

Coinciding with the financial, administrative, and curricular transformation of the Hochschule für Verwaltungswissenschaften, Ruf's project defined the image of a new German administrative class. The independence with which he operated was in marked contrast to the multiple collaborations through which the design for the West German Pavilion in Brussels had evolved. There are certain material and construction affinities between the Brussels pavilion and the school building, which overlapped briefly in Ruf's office. It is logical that Ruf would have used his experience with the pavilion to derive an appropriate architectural vocabulary. Other aspects of the project, both its design and realization, point to very different sources.

Ruf's role in Brussels seems to have been a factor in both his invitation to the competition and his first prize. Although the World's Fair is not mentioned in the jury report, a local newspaper identified Ruf as architect "with Egon Eiermann, [of] the German Pavilion for the Brussels World's Fair." The article then lists other, perhaps more comparable projects: "the Bavarian State Bank in Munich, Nuremberg, and Erlangen, the Academy of Fine Arts in Nuremberg, and the Twelve Apostles and Christ the King Churches in Munich were built to his design."[21] Despite his impressive and relevant list of projects, the emphasis was upon his collaboration with Eiermann on behalf of the German Federal Republic. This work justified his authorship of a building that would need to embody the values of the country its students would ultimately serve.

Certainly, the pavilion's programmatic design and highly specialized, speedily realized construction would have been on Ruf's mind. Reflection on his earlier campus project, the Nuremberg Akademie der Bildenden Künste, would also have been natural as Ruf undertook the Speyer competition. The project that resulted is a touchstone, both for Ruf's developing ideas about architectural expression and construction, and for his thinking about the nature of a campus itself, a typology that had become increasingly associated with corporate clients. In their site planning, both the Akademie der Bildenden Künste and the Brussels pavilion evince a similar attitude towards a campus ensemble. Both are

18   Hermann Haußmann, the German commissioned by the French to oversee educational reform in Germany, quoted in Morsey, "50 Jahre HfV," 6.
19   Typescript of competition brief, collection of Elisabeth and Notburga Ruf.
20   Nowhere in the available documentation of meetings between architect and clients is mention made of the aesthetic attributes of the building, with only one minor exception of consternation expressed by the dean about the library in response to a proposal that, to save money, would result in a lower ceiling height for the reading room. One document laconically notes "optimal reasons" for the omission of certain doorways between offices if not functionally required. See Fisch, "50 Jahre Sep-Ruf-Bau," 53.
21   *Speyerer Tagespost* (September 23, 1958), cited in Fisch, "50 Jahre Sep-Ruf-Bau," 30.

22   Immo Boyken et al., *Egon Eiermann/Sep Ruf: Deutsche Pavillons, Brüssel 1958* (Stuttgart: Edition Axel Menges, 2007), 13. Greg Castillo cites Peter Blundell Jones as having provided a similar opinion, which Castillo also seems to accept. Greg Castillo, "Making a Spectacle of Restraint: The Deutschland Pavilion at the 1958 Brussels Exposition," *Journal of Contemporary History* 47, no. 1 (2011), 97–199, here 102.

defined by freestanding pavilions whose relationship to one another, delineated by built walkways, define smaller courtyard-like areas within a larger landscape figure. This parti has been cited in the literature as evidence for the otherwise unsubstantiated but routine claim that Ruf delivered the site design for the Brussels project while Eiermann authored the building design and construction.[22] This simplistic separation of the two collaborators' roles is put in doubt by the way that at Speyer, Ruf handled a material and construction palette related to the pavilion, if to very different spatial ends. The Hochschule für Verwaltungswissenschaften was an opportunity to realign his evolving campus ideas with architectural ideas from other areas of his practice. The result was an architecture appropriate to a new, specifically West German administrative class.

This architecture required calibrations at multiple scales: site planning, landscaping, massing, spatial sequencing, material choices, facade detailing, even the design of office furniture and accouterments. Each aspect is represented in drawings authored by Ruf's office, down to the numerals on wall clocks. The approach to total design displays an affinity with American corporate projects: Eero Saarinen's drawing set for the CBS building included bespoke elevator push-buttons and telephone booth signage. Ruf's analogous desire for tight control was already evident in the way he ran earlier projects, but at Speyer, he also leveraged his status with an increasingly powerful building product industry. The sophistication and variation of facade systems is only one example of how this negotiation played out.

From the start, the project begged questions of representation and referent. A local newspaper report on the competition results compared Ruf's project to a "Roman atrium"

"The 'College Center' with lecture halls, administrative offices and institutes is a new construction organized around landscaped interior courtyards akin to a Roman atrium. This provides a salubrious shelter from street noise. The lecture halls in particular receive light from these interior courtyards. [...] The architectural approach is distinguished by enormous clarity and a salubrious serenity in its

7.18 Site plan, with a smaller auditorium and larger second courtyard, 1957

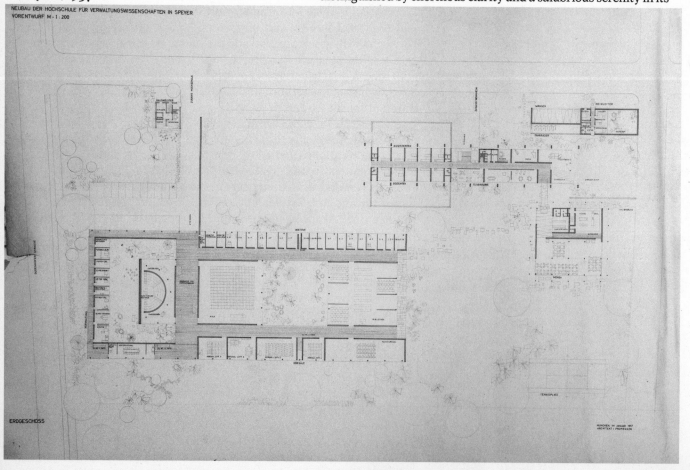

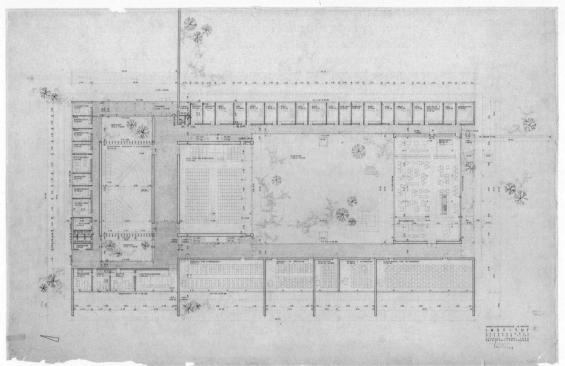

7.19 Plan of the main building as realized, 1958

landscape image. The grouping of buildings has a great deal of appeal and demonstrates a mature design ability."[23] Clarity and serenity were at a premium on a site exposed to a loud, heavily trafficked road on Speyer's outskirts. By proposing a deep, compact building configuration punctuated by interior courtyards in a typology that anticipated what Alison Smithson would later term the "mat-building,"[24] Ruf addressed the challenges of a small, noisy site. The competition jury noted that Ruf's plan allowed for future expansion if needed, while they also praised the organization of the large, central building with respect to the petite glass-and-steel cafeteria and infill masonry dormitory. The compactness of Ruf's scheme also seemed to promise greater economy and speed in construction. **[7.18] [7.19]**

Although they are all nominally courtyard campus types, the similarities among the Akademie der Bildenden Künste, the Brussels pavilion, and the Speyer college are quickly exhausted. As compared with the ambiguous boundaries and continuous landscape ground plane of the other two projects, the interior courtyard at the HfV is unambiguous, its relationship to the spaces outside its walls bounded by heavy window frames, deep wood-clad overhangs, and, in the classrooms, dark glazed brick walls extending perpendicular into the surrounding areas. The way Ruf developed the interior courtyard here marks a new direction, one he would pursue in the early 1960s with his general plan for the Germanisches Nationalmuseum in Nuremberg (1962), the much smaller Olaf Gulbransson Museum in Tegernsee (1962–1966) and perhaps his most well-known building, the Chancellor's Bungalow in Bonn (1963–1964). The small courtyard house integrated into the socle walls at the Brussels pavilion can be seen as the inception of Ruf's work on this type.

The interior spaces, characterized by muted material palettes and limited side-lighting in juxtaposition to open, planted courtyards, invoked an atmosphere of studious quiet and focus. Room heights were relatively generous in the broad corridors along the courtyard perimeter and in the seminar rooms or offices; the same or similar ceiling heights gave larger spaces a sense of modesty. The architecture seemed in this way to elevate the work of small groups by giving the rooms in which it occurred greater presence. In the Aula, the ceiling height was raised only slightly above the rest of the building; above the auditorium it was uninflected. **[7.20] [7.21]** Even among larger gatherings of students focused on a single professor, there was no monumentality, no opportunity for demagoguery. The even-handed massing meant that the college's inner workings remained largely unexpressed to the outside. Only inside the building, as one moved

23   Competition jury report, cited in Fisch, "50 Jahre Sep-Ruf-Bau," 25 and 29.
24   Alison Smithson, "How to Recognize and Read Mat-Building: Mainstream Architecture as It Has Developed Towards the Mat-Building," *Architectural Design* 44, no. 9 (September 1974), 573–90.

25   Ministry of Finance to architects, July 16, 1956, construction planning archive in Fisch, "50 Jahre Sep-Ruf-Bau," 13.
26   Jury report, February 28, 1957, Fisch, "50 Jahre Sep-Ruf-Bau," 23.
27   "Das Lever House in New York," *Werk* 41, no. 2 (February 1954), 49–54; Ernst Zietzschmann, "Neubau der Manufacturers Trust Company, New York," *Bauen + Wohnen: Internationale Zeitschrift* 10, no. 2 (1956), 49–52.
28   The only other corporate project published in German prior to 1956 was the Pan American Life Insurance building in New Orleans, published in fall 1955. It was a bar building similar in scale to the consular projects. See *Bauen + Wohnen: Internationale Zeitschrift* 9, no. 5 (1955), 295–98.

between the bright, side-lit spaces adjacent to the courtyards and the darker seminar rooms, a subtle hierarchy of active and reflective, public and more private spaces was revealed.

Perhaps the initial decision to develop the building around its interior courtyard was a response to site. The original competition brief sent to the four invited competitors noted the nearby road,[25] and the jury advocated for Ruf's submission because of the "particular value [...] attached to the way traffic noise is shielded by inherently architectural means."[26] It is unlikely, however, that this was Ruf's entire motivation. The way in which the courtyards were developed reflects other interests and references appropriate to the emergent German administrative class.

Ruf's familiarity with Skidmore, Owings and Merrill has already been accounted for in the case of the American Consulate in Munich. The HfV owes a clear debt to SOM's corporate campus types realized in collaboration with Isamu Noguchi. The facade detailing, entirely different from projects Ruf completed only a short time before, more closely resembles SOM's Manufacturers Hanover Trust Company Bank (1951–1954) than the Akademie der Bildenden Künste of that same vintage. The two SOM buildings that had been published in Germany prior to the Speyer competition, Lever House in 1954 and Manufacturers Hanover Trust in 1956,[27] are plausible referents for both courtyard and facade. The German publication of Manufacturers Hanover Trust even included a detailed facade section, which Ruf's office would have been particularly well equipped to decode by virtue of the consulate construction documents already in its possession.

The most plausible parti reference for Ruf's project was, however, SOM's suburban corporate campus type. The first of SOM's corporate campuses, the Kimberly Clark complex in Neenah, Wisconsin, would not appear in German-language architecture journals until 1957,[28] and Connecticut General Insurance Company (1954–1957), SOM's quintessential corporate campus project of the mid-1950s, was not published in Germany until well after the Speyer competition. Thus the actual source of Ruf's information on that and other SOM campus projects remains unknown. It is easy to imagine that Otto Apel, SOM's German contact architect, could have been involved; certainly, Apel's contemporary projects for Lufthansa at Frankfurt Airport belonged to an architectural genre, the long-span building, to which SOM was also making important contributions. Nonetheless, there are obvious

7.20 Section through the auditorium and main entrance showing continuous roof height, 1958

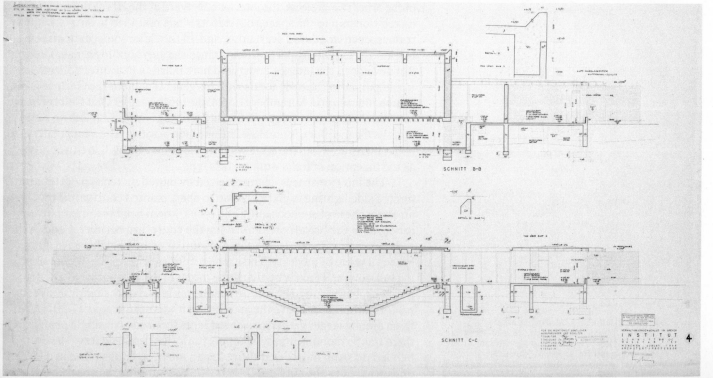

7.21 Auditorium shortly after completion in 1960

correlations between SOM's corporate campus buildings and the HfV, with its deep floorplates punctuated by a formally landscaped courtyard used to introduce side light to the adjacent spaces. Within the milieu for which Ruf was asked to build, this choice of precedent makes considerable sense. Like the College for Public Administration, Connecticut General Insurance had wanted to reinvent itself when it moved out of the city; the architecture designed for it by SOM expressed, literally, the transparence and horizontality of its new corporate structure. What better kind of environment for future government administrators than one internationally recognized as a means to support efficiency, worker productivity, and a culture of contentment with the status quo?[29]

From his earliest drawings as a student of architecture through his late projects in the 1970s, Ruf did not fail to include the plant life that surrounds his buildings. Early plans of the Speyer campus are no exception: along the building's exterior are circles indicating larger trees as well as freehanded patches of leaves in radial organization, stippled areas representing lawn, and irregularly dimensioned rectangular pavers. The main interior courtyard includes a similar array of plantings. Pavers are set individually into a lawn area. Smaller and larger tables with chairs also punctuate the main courtyard, positioned on the edges closest to the west corridor. But unlike the drawings for the Akademie der Bildenden Künste, the drawn vegetation never transgresses the building's perimeter. It also seems more akin to the landscape developed for Brussels in collaboration with Walter Rossow: a composition of framed rectilinear areas for seating, fountains, or ground cover juxtaposed to freeform plantings around larger trees. Rossow's courtyard design for the Academy of Art in Berlin (1957) gives a sense of what Ruf might have envisioned at this early stage: shaggy grasses, water features, and simple, artificial stone pavers or borders.[30]

Neither those early drawings nor Ruf's prior projects presages the landscape design as realized. The informal plantings have vanished. The building's orthogonal geometry registers in the gravel edge and the basin at the southern end of the courtyard. **[7.22]** Water overflows into a basin from a square fountain elevated on a 45-centimeter-high stone pedestal; at the opposite end is a rough-hewn stone bridging element. The naturalistic appearance of the stones in fountain and bridge belies

29   The admiration expressed by German purveyors of the *Bürolandschaft* is discussed in chapter 5. See also Claus William Hess, *Bürobau mit Blick in die Zukunft: Bericht über Connecticut Life Insurance Co., Bloomfield, Conn. USA* (Barmstedt: Schnelle, 1959). The connotations of the American corporate campus and the decision to move top management away from the inner-city skyscraper coincided with suburbanization. The campus, with its references to higher learning, also represented a new corporate managerial structure meant to lionize transparent meritocracy. The campus tradition was linked to the American and English Garden City, which understood the landscape as a tool of social change. See Louise A. Mozingo, *Pastoral Capitalism: A History of Suburban Corporate Landscapes*, Urban and Industrial Environments (Cambridge, MA: MIT Press, 2011).

30   See Hansaviertel Berlin, "Hanseatenweg 10: Akademie der Künste—Werner Düttmann," http://hansaviertel.berlin/en/bauwerke /hanseatenweg-10-akademie-der-kuenste-werner-duettmann/, accessed December 21, 2021; and Winfried Richard, "Immer einen Schritt voraus: Walter Rossow," *Garten + Landschaft* 113, no. 3 (2003).

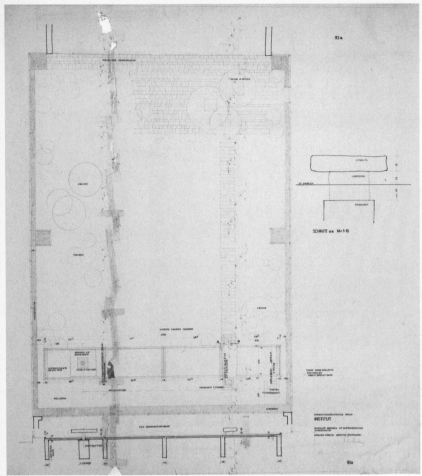

**7.22 Detail drawings of the fountain
in the main courtyard, 1960**

**7.23 Skidmore, Owings and Merrill,
Connecticut General Life
Headquarters, *Life* magazine 1957**

7.24 Fountain in courtyard, 2019

the fact that they were drawn and dimensioned with absolute precision.
[7.23] Labeled "monolith" on the drawing, the bridging element rests
on a stone base that extends a full thirty centimeters below the level of the
ground, where it connected to a concrete foundation. This detail guarantees
that the technical engineering required for its erection is invisible.
Instead, the coarsely chiseled monolith appears to balance with archaic
precision on top of its equally rough plinth. The stone basin at the other
end of the fountain was worked with much more obvious precision. Its narrow
lip barely holds back the water flowing into the shallow basin before
it displaces to the reflecting pool below. The source of its endlessly replen-
ished water, sequestered in its pedestal, is concealed.

    The juxtaposition between rough-chiseled monolith and precise,
highly finished steel facade was no less important at SOM's Connecticut
General Life headquarters. The first realized collaboration between
Gordon Bunshaft and Isamu Noguchi, the campus's four interior courtyards
are edged by a sleek curtain wall perimeter against which are set the
elements that would come to define Noguchi's corporate landscape vocabulary: water, gravel, finished and rough stone, and monolithic rocks all
carefully placed to evoke an idealized Japanese garden tradition.[31] Ruf's
fountain, with its thin, nearly invisible lip and reflecting water surface,
owes more than a passing debt to Noguchi's circular fountains at Connecticut
General Life. In the much smaller space of the Speyer courtyard, the
monolithic bridge is a good translation of Noguchi's stepping stones, which
were so tempting that even a captain of industry would agree to be
photographed while skipping across them.[32] [7.24]

    Unlike the facades in either the Akademie der Bildenden Künste
or the World's Fair pavilion, the exterior glazing systems at the HfV are
heterogeneous, with different construction types ascribed to different
parts of the buildings. The working drawings include aluminum fixed
glazing, operable steel windows, and some glazed wood-framed doors and
windows. In all cases, the dimensions are robust, and the frames are laid
up to emphasize their heaviness. A more complex and varied material

31   For his Chase Manhattan Bank courtyard
(1961–1964), Noguchi traveled to Japan to find
the perfect stone. While the bank was waiting
to approve it, he discovered that the stone
had already been sold and "had been shipped to
the other end of Japan by somebody who had
purchased it. I used every kind of pull I had to get
it back." Martin Friedman, "Noguchi's Imaginary
Landscapes," *Design Quarterly*, no. 106/107
(1978), 3–99, here 61. The idiom of the landscape
garden was quickly appropriated for the new
corporate campus. Kaneji Domoto, another
Japanese American who had been interned
during World War II, spent the second half of his
architectural career in Westchester writing
about bonsai and positioning enormous rocks on
the campuses of corporations.
32   "Symposium in Symbolic Setting: Fine
New Building Meets Challenge of City Crisis,"
Life, October 21, 1957, 50–54.

palette and approach to building physics was taken than had been the case only shortly before: insulation at the junctures between envelope and structural concrete, highly specific instructions for installing heating systems, built-in roller window shades. The wide variety of metal facade components in these drawings also attests to a vastly more sophisticated building industry and construction practice.

Fixed glazing fronts the courtyard running between Aula and library. [7.25] [7.26] It comprises heavy, 70 or 80×50-mm box sections, extrusion sold by Klöckner, the same company that had fabricated the steel doorframes used in the Nuremberg Academy. The sharp edges in the drawings distinguish these extrusions from the rolled steel that would be used in the Aula facade. The double-glazing has been mounted using 15-millimeter aluminum glass stops. Seams at the juncture between the extrusions comprising the frame are overlaid by 25×8-mm flat aluminum, combining the already hefty frames into an even thicker unit. This approach to facade joinery has exactly the opposite effect of the reveals that Ruf had favored everywhere in his details for the Akademie der Bildenden Künste, where shadow lines separate each component of the window frames, making them seem even thinner than they are. The overall 160-millimeter-wide frame at the HfV are a near order of magnitude thicker than the 15- and 20-millimeter thicknesses specified in the drawings for the Akademie der Bildenden Künste. The HfV facade was designed to have only minimal plasticity: absent is any contour among the sharp-edged aluminum rectangular tube frames, joining bars, and glass stops: the offset among elements was also reduced to no more than the thickness of the material, around 2.5 to 3 millimeters. The low, controlled relief was even flatter than Ruf's American Consulate in Munich, which itself had pushed SOM's low-relief detailing further. The facade departs not only from Ruf's earlier work but also from such early aluminum facade products as those developed by companies like Josef Gartner for shop windows and vitrines, all of which had used relief to downplay the thickness of profiles. Rather than emphasize the reciprocity between interior and exterior spaces by painting the frames white to de-materialize them, the black anodized facade elements emphasize and consolidate the line of separation.

The steel facade designed for the tall glazed wall of the Aula required no fewer than eight specifically configured steel channel shapes for its construction. [7.27] [7.28] This high degree of differentiation, however, serves to achieve consistency and homogeneity in appearance. For example, the detailing is finessed so that the hopper-style transom windows and the doors below them appear identical, despite the fact that their motion required very different hinge positions and frame overlays. Like the aluminum facade in the corridors, the steel sections are assembled in low relief, with only minimal offset among components and glass stops. Detailed almost perfectly in plane, the steel frame is a hefty 150 millimeters at the horizontal between door and hopper and 80 millimeters at the jamb and sill. By contrast, the steel windows for the Akademie der Bildenden Künste are 38 millimeters in height and in the horizontal are offset from the 40-millimeter fixed frame to appear even more slender. And unlike many of the elements in the Akademie der Bildenden Künste facades, each of the steel sections used in the Aula facade were purpose-manufactured exclusively for facade construction, including the integrated exterior shades pocketed in the deeply overhanging eave. The presence of integrated drips, overlapping legs, and interlocking components attest to this specificity of manufacture. In the complexity of its components, the Aula facade attests to the significant transformations undergone by the West German facade industry between the early and mid-1950s. Its heaviness corresponds to the adjacent aluminum facade and it likewise is emphasized by a coat of dark paint.

In the library facade, the material choices and detailing are different again, although the results reveal nothing of their differences in construction to the viewer. [7.29] As detailed, these windows were wood casements that opened inwards, although from the outside, their double-paned glazing

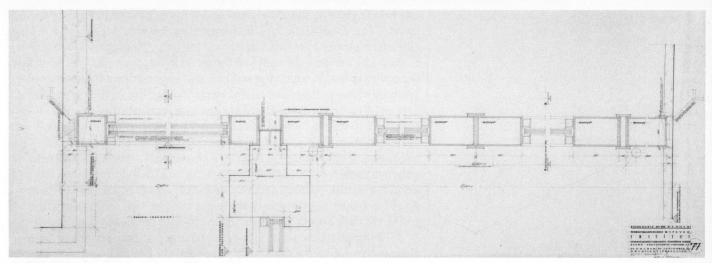

7.25 Horizontal section and corridor
facade, 1959

7.26 Main courtyard, Aula and
corridor facades shortly after
completion in 1960

was held in place by the same aluminum glass stops used in the corridor facade. The sloped exterior sill, a concrete substructure, was clad in an aluminum element provided by a company from Munich. The exterior cladding below the knee wall and the interior sill, deep enough to conceal the cavity below, in which the radiator was located, were both factory-fabricated fiber-reinforced concrete elements specified by their brand name Eternit. As with the Aula, the library facade integrated an exterior sunshade that rose up behind the eave. The fascia of the eave, a full 37 centimeters high, also edged a concealed rain gutter, its contents released along the scuppers described above and through less dramatic although more frequent protruding steel pipes. [7.30] Once painted, the wood frames disappeared entirely: the facade was characterized by its two significant aluminum elements, the fascia and the continuous deep sill, and by the dark Eternit that matched the color of the glazed brick around it.

The emphatic detailing of the plane that separates interior and exterior did much to define the relationship between the building and its proximate landscape, quite unlike the tradition to which Ruf had apparently subscribed earlier, which sought to elide outside and in. The thick, dark lines drawn across the view by the facade and window frames are

7.27 Vertical section of steel facade in the Aula, 1958

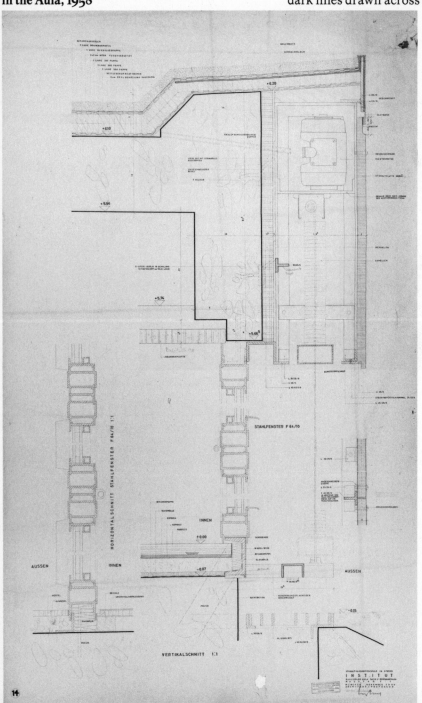

7.28 Aula facade shortly after completion in 1960

intersected by other planes—eaves clad in the same fir slats as the interior ceiling, dark brick-clad walls that extended color and alignment on either side of the glass—which asserted continuity across the building envelope. In the seminar- and classrooms on the building's exterior, those rooms that face outwards rather than towards the courtyard, Ruf devised a gesture that had no precedent in his own earlier institutional work but instead continued some of the ideas he had explored in the small model courtyard house for the World's Fair pavilion as well in his other contemporary residential projects. The demising walls between each of these rooms are extended beyond the plane of enclosure, well past the roof eaves, almost to a depth that equals that of the room indoors. **[7.31] [7.32]** Exterior shades are located at the eave's edge in a clever detail that uses the differential between the roof's structural height and the lower dimension of the integrated shade. The differential here, as in the library detail, conceals a gutter behind the fascia along the roof's edge.

The material palette and fit-out developed by Ruf's office reinforce this atmosphere of decorous, although not explicitly luxurious, everyday design. Except for the waffled ceiling in the auditorium or the exposed beam grid in the Aula, the structural concrete walls and roof slabs are invisible, concealed beneath glazed brick on the walls and spruce strips that cover the underside of the roof slab both indoors and beneath the eaves. The floors are sky blue linoleum installed above a cork underlayment except in the lower-level cloakroom, where black artificial stone was laid on the foundation slab. Wood parquet flooring set in asphalt was originally foreseen for the Aula, but ultimately it, too, was covered with the dark sheet linoleum. In contrast to these sober and unpretentious materials, the partition walls, doors, built-ins, and custom-made furniture were veneered in makore, a reddish wood sourced in West Africa. **[7.33] [7.34]** The veneer represented a careful compromise between the explicit luxury of the extravagantly grained

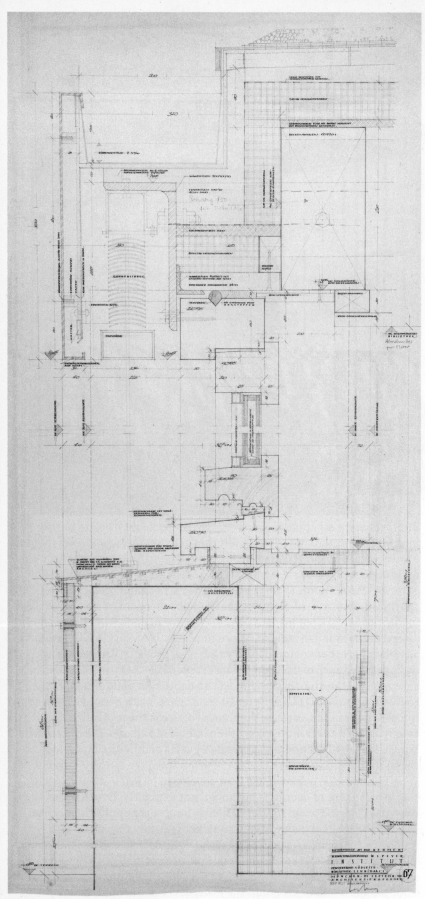

7.29 Vertical wall section of south-facing facade in the library, 1959

7.30 Covered walkway to the dormitory, shortly after completion in 1960

tropical woods favored by Mies van der Rohe and his Chicago acolytes and the demure tones characteristic of European hardwoods. Makore has a relatively ordinary grain so that only its deep, unusual color indicates its exotic origins. Anyone other than a connoisseur would notice the veneer only subliminally; its vaguely rich appearance lent the otherwise quotidian palette an atmosphere of elegance.

The built-ins are spare: floor-to-ceiling-panels of makore for the cafeteria buffet, black-painted steel frames and simple makore-veneered counter and shelves in the cloakroom, partition walls and tall doors also in makore with some furniture in simple maple. In the few instances where doors were lower than ceiling height, black-painted steel frames were used to define transoms, which set a horizon for adjacent built-in cabinetry. Even if this distinction is only apparent upon closer inspection, everything had been designed for the college, from the hooks on which secretaries hung their handbags at their desks to the wall clocks. **[7.35]** By juxtaposing simple forms with a single exotic material, Ruf constructed an environment that was down-to-earth but with a patina of refinement and *Gute Form*. It was the world of the "little man" reconceived for the civil servants who would assure that the little man's world maintained its orderliness.

If, as seems to have been the case during the 1951 Darmstädter Gespräch, the orthodoxy of truth in material no longer governed the tectonics of modern architecture; and if the order of the day was indeed some degree of architectural discretion to the benefit of the "good grid," then Ruf's HfV rightfully demands admiration for the thoroughness with which the facts of construction disappeared beneath a narrative of construction that calibrated the relationship between interior and exterior, natural and built, collective functioning and individual contribution. It is an eloquent narrative, and one that carried forward the ideas first articulated in the program for the West German pavilion at the Brussels World's Fair. It is a chapter in the story of Schwippert's honorable, progressive "little man."

**7.31 Seminar rooms with contiguous
projecting walls, 2019**

**7.32 Seminar room with projecting
wall on interior, 2019**

7.33 Administrative office with makore, spruce, and maple veneer interiors, 2019

7.34 Makore veneer cloakroom tables and black-painted steel uprights, 2019

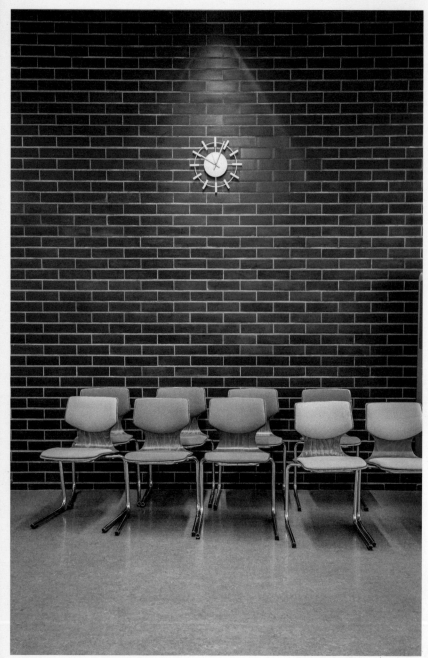

7.35 Bespoke wall clock in a classroom with black glazed brick wall, 2019

There are, of course, always multiple factors at play when any architect breaks with his or her earlier idiom. In Ruf's case, however, the shift that occurred within the few short years between 1951 and 1957 begs the question of what motivated his decisions and how this change was enacted. The impulses deriving from construction practice, including those aspects he encountered through his contact with SOM, resonated with the idea of atmosphere as an overall environment, which Ruf first proposed in the Darmstädter Gespräch. SOM's work was also important because of the way it could express a new genre of administrative culture. Throughout his career, Ruf's construction drawings evidence the intensity of his dialogue with the architectural implications of construction decisions. He always worked closely with the fabricators of his building's facade elements,[33] making him perhaps even more sensitive to changes in available products and practices. The finesse of his construction offers occasion to rethink the German experience of the American Century in its architectural and technological permutations.

33   As evidenced in project files and in conversation with Notburga Ruf, who worked in his office in the 1970s. Notburga Ruf in conversation with the author, July 22, 2012.

The quotation in the chapter title is taken from a lecture given by Hans Schwippert to students at the Düsseldorf Academy of Art in 1965. Courtesy of Horst Peter.

"To Stand for Uncorrupted Form Where Corrupted Form Fills the Market"

Hans Schwippert's Renovation of the Hedwigskathedrale, Berlin

Hard-driving and powerful as head of the German Werkbund, Hans Schwippert approached his architectural practice during the late 1950s and into the 1960s with a much lighter hand. During his postwar German Werkbund tenure, he exercised tight control on publications, exhibitions, and political agendas; but as in his early work of the 1930s, he conceived and realized his architecture in ways that offered license to those charged with its realization. This philosophy was apparent in the way he detailed elements of the Bundeshaus in spite of the accelerated pace of construction. It remained evident a decade later. Schwippert's drawings were only lightly annotated, communicating little more than how a geometry was to be derived or an exterior dimension held. They are instructions for use rather than dictates that produce an inflexible outcome. They communicate Schwippert's knowledge of, and respect for, the act of building as skilled, thoughtful labor. His flexibility and delight in iteration was particularly well suited to the immediate postwar culture of the bricoleur-by-necessity: the lack of standard materials and products could only be overcome by finesse and ingenuity in construction, in the best case, through a collaboration between architect and craftsman. His was an architecture that flourished in a context of lesser means. The reduced reliance on material largesse was compensated by a thorough knowledge of and trust in construction as social practice.

Although he owed the commission to his strong connections to the Catholic Church in the Rhineland, it was his lack of architectural dogmatism that made him the ideal choice for the renovation of Hedwigskathedrale in East Berlin (1956–1963). Working within the fraught climate that resulted in the building of the Berlin Wall in 1961, Schwippert and his Düsseldorf office managed to navigate a host of political constraints, sometimes by skill and other times simply by luck. The East German government's resolution to fund a portion of the project in July 1961 to the amount of 260,000 Mark, and, by extension, to permit its execution, predated the building of the Wall by only a month.[01] Joint funding by the German Democratic and Federal Republics meant that all purchases, contracts, and materials were subject to double scrutiny. [8.1] As such, the shadow economy that might have provided resources otherwise unavailable in East Germany had to be foregone.[02] Another factor mitigating against the allocation of scarce financial and physical resources to the project was East Germany's commitment to new housing construction and, of course, its political aversion to organized religion. As recorded in articles, letters, drawings, visa applications, bills of lading, and varied documents, Schwippert's seven-year undertaking to re-consecrate the Hedwigskathedrale was no less heroic than his completion of the Bundeshaus in less than a single year.

Schwippert's texts make clear that he was most interested in writing about the project's design process and his vision for the space. But with typical self-effacement and collaborative spirit, his text for the self-published brochure on the project begins by acknowledging the three architects who were in his employ for its long duration. He also acknowledged his gratitude to Theodor Blümel, his East German site architect until Blümel's unexpected death late in the course of construction.[03] Well before Schwippert's involvement, Blümel had been involved in the engineering and logistics of building a new dome for the cathedral, which was realized in reinforced concrete between 1951 and '54 to replace an original 1773 wooden dome lost to bombs. Although the building stood more or less empty thereafter, the reconstruction of the dome had been a high-visibility national project, completed by the largest construction combine in East Germany. Because of its central location at the heart of the capital city, the cathedral became a showcase for the country's concrete prefabrication agenda. His affection for the building endured, as is evident in his voluminous correspondence with Schwippert. Moreover, the frequent and often touching correspondence between Blümel and the site foreman, Horst Poller, reflects the intense personal commitment

01   Hans Schwippert, "Bericht über die Architektenarbeit in Skt. Hedwig Berlin Mai 1960 bis heute," November 15, 1961, 1. Archive, St. Hedwigs-Kathedrale, Berlin.
02   From 1994–95, I was project architect for Renzo Vallebuona on the renovation of the Archenhold Planetarium, Berlin. The project involved the restoration of windows, roofing, exterior stairs, and interior woodwork on the building. From conversations with the various craftsmen, it emerged that postwar building construction in East Germany was dependent upon a secondary market of salvaged materials and clever reuse (misuse) of what was available. The only alternatives were black-market materials.
03   Blümel died in 1965, after the consecration ceremony but before the project's ultimate completion. Hans Schwippert, *Ausbau der St.-Hedwigs-Kathedrale zu Berlin 1956–1963* (Düsseldorf: n.p., 1969), 2.

BAUSTEIN
für den Wiederaufbau
der St. Hedwigs-Kathedrale

Umseitig: Die Kathedrale vor der Zerstörung

DER BISCHOF
VON BERLIN

Stadt und Bistum Berlin haben während des Krieges ihre Mutterkirche, die St. Hedwig-Kathedrale, verloren. In der Nacht zum 1. März 1943 brannte sie nieder, und die große Kuppel stürzte zusammen. Nur die Umfassungsmauern blieben stehen.

St. Hedwig war den Berliner Katholiken besonders teuer, und die Nicht-Berliner fühlten sich dort zu Hause. Es war die erste katholische Kirche Berlins nach der Reformation. Vor mehr als 200 Jahren (1746) wurde ihr Bau mit den Opfergaben der Gläubigen Deutschlands, Italiens, Polens, Spaniens begonnen und mit viel Mühe 1773 vollendet.

Seit 1952 bemühen wir uns, die zerstörte Kathedrale wiederherzustellen. Die mächtige Kuppel ist in diesen Jahren wieder aufgebaut, ein Werk, das nicht nur durch die Zeitumstände, sondern auch in technischer Hinsicht sehr schwierig war. Nun müssen wir an die Aufgabe heran, dem Innenraum eine würdige Gestalt zu geben. Auch das ist ein künstlerisch schwieriges und ebenso kostspieliges Werk. Wir haben dazu viele helfende Freunde nötig, die der Kathedrale St. Hedwig innerlich verbunden sind und dies durch ihre Opfer und Spenden bezeugen.

Wir sind dankbar, daß auch Sie zu diesen Freunden von St. Hedwig gehören und sagen Ihnen ein ganz herzliches

„Vergelt's Gott!"

+ Wilhelm Weskamm

Bischof von Berlin

8.1 Acknowledgement from Bishop Weskamm of Berlin to donors of the building stabilization, undated (post-1952)

04   In one of the last letters that Poller wrote to Blümel, Poller notes that another architect had been hired to replace Blümel during his long illness and absence. Poller details how he had cleaned up Blümel's desk and that he borrowed Blümel's ballpoint pen but would be glad to return it. He adds in a postscript that the replacement site architect is only there "on an hourly basis and [...] to bridge the gap." Poller's dedication to Blümel, both personal and professional, is evident. Horst Poller to Theodor Blümel, November 19, 1962. Archive, St. Hedwigs-Kathedrale, Berlin.

05   One such oft-repeated story is that stained glass for the windows was smuggled across the border in a woman's hand bag. Files in the job books include permission for the importation of that glass across more conventional channels. Agatha Buslei-Wuppermann, "Hans Schwippert als Architekt: Seine Pläne zur Umgestaltung der St. Hedwigs-Kathedrale in Berlin," *Das Münster* 67, no. 2 (2014).

06   Schwippert's speech given to seventy guests of the Archbishop of Berlin after the consecration of the cathedral. Schwippert, *Ausbau der St.-Hedwigs-Kathedrale*, 27.

07   Theodor Blümel, "Wiederaufbau der St.-Hedwigs-Kathedrale," *Bauplanung und Bautechnik: Technisch-wissenschaftliche Zeitung für das Bauingenieurwesen* 8, no. 2 (February 1954), 64–67, here 65.

without which the project might never have been realized.[04] Blümel's style, resourceful and persistent, also played well to Schwippert's laconic construction documents. Blümel, Poller, and the architects in Schwippert's employ all changed the trajectory of Schwippert's design process, which was conceived to include a wider scope of authorship. Fantastic stories repeated in oral histories about how materials were procured for the project have to be corroborated by consulting the importation documents, bills of lading, and other documents still extant in the Hedwigskathedrale job books.[05] Still, expressed in each anecdote is the degree to which the material act of construction was inextricable from a unique social moment.

As his successes on behalf of the Werkbund made clear, Schwippert had a sophisticated grasp of how powerfully design could drive consumerism in postwar society. The case of the Hedwigskathedrale was different. As Schwippert averred in his November 1, 1963, speech at the consecration, "I thank my colleagues-at-work. Along with them and on their behalf, I hate the conflation of work and ware."[06] Even as the first large audience convened that day to admire the new building, its architect insisted on distinguishing between the physical outcome they were presently enjoying, and the skill and labor, invisible to them, that had produced it. This was no disingenuous rejection of consumer-oriented design and its objects. Schwippert's words convey his ideal of architecture as social enterprise, within which the construction process was bespoke and deliberate.

In early 1954, Blümel published a highly technical article in the monthly magazine of the German Democratic Republic Ministry for Construction and Residential Economies and its Professional Construction Association. Unlike many of the other featured authors in the magazine, Blümel had no stated affiliation with a central government organization: throughout his professional life, Blümel remained independent of, although in contact with, the large socialist construction combines that dominated the industry. This was, of course, to Schwippert's great advantage. Blümel's article describes precisely the technical and engineering calculations behind the nearly completed segmented concrete dome, referring to "the fabrication facility [...] at the cathedral's portal."[07] His technical language softens only when he describes the circumstances under which the cathedral was damaged and then, after a period of uncertainty, slated for reconstruction.

In the context of the German Democratic Republic's priorities, reconstruction was not at all a foregone conclusion. Although the Staatsoper, the building's immediate neighbor on Bebelplatz, was undergoing restoration around the time that the decision was made in the cathedral's favor, the nearby Berlin Palace was already gone. Other damaged buildings along Unter den Linden were selected to be demolished or reconstructed regardless of architectural merit. In this context, the motivation of an adamantly secular, still-impoverished society to contribute to rebuilding the heavily damaged Catholic cathedral is particularly interesting.

Blümel's article implies that the decision created certain advantages for the East German Ministry for Construction. The Catholic Church considered Berlin a single diocese despite the postwar divisions, although the Catholic provinces that once were associated with it but had been ceded to Poland became part of other jurisdictions. The archbishop's residence was located in Berlin-Charlottenburg in the city's western sector; St. Hedwig's, the cathedral belonging to the episcopal see, was on the other side of the political line and was overseen from the West by Monseigneur Heinz Endres.[08] Blümel explained the political dilemma:

"In the night of March 1, 1943, the building was destroyed by Anglo-American bombs. Following the catastrophic fire, only the cathedral's exterior walls remained. The dome of the venerable crypt was severely damaged by the influx of water.

By means of intervention by forces with a sense of responsibility, expressed in shared efforts to rebuild the cathedral using both state and church means, any further destruction was resisted. The cleanup and re-closing of the crypt vault was completed by volunteers. The order for the reconstruction came from Bishop *Wilhelm Weskamm*."[09]

The text walked a fine and careful line, using active verbs to attribute the church's destruction to the Western Allied forces, typically portrayed in negative terms, but reverting to the passive voice and an abstruse reference to "forces with a sense of responsibility" to characterize the collaboration between the East German state and its ideological and geographic antithesis, the Catholic diocese in West Germany. Bishop Weskamm would later commission Schwippert directly for the project. At the time of the article's writing, however, only the rebuilding of the dome was at stake, although Blümel's words remain ambiguous.

To restore the church fully, including all its liturgical objects, may have been beyond the political capacities of the early 1950s. The restoration of the enormous dome, however, measuring 38.6 meters in diameter, benefited two otherwise unrelated agendas: first, the preservation of the cathedral building, for which the Church and its parishioners in East and West were willing to pay, and second, the demonstration, at a central location in the capital, of the impressive technical and labor potentials of the German Democratic building industry. In technical terms, it was a tour de force. The dome was subdivided geometrically into eighty-four equal segments. An enormous tower 30.7 meters high was built at the church's center to hoist and temporarily support a compression ring upon which these segments would rest. The upper 1.1 meters of original masonry was removed from the exterior drum, which had survived bombing, and replaced by a round, reinforced concrete ring beam, cast in place onto a special double layer of copper flashing. The lower layer prevented water from entering the masonry; the upper layer, separated from the lower layer by a special graphite preparation, allowed the dome to move against the drum, which had not been designed to withstand the new dome's thrust. A crane was built at the primary portal to hoist and position the dome segments with centimeter precision.

It was the production of the eighty-four segments, however, which provided the most attractive opportunity to the German Democratic Republic Ministry of Building. In 1954, when Blümel's article was published, industrialized concrete prefabrication was increasingly promoted within the ministry and its combines, both as a practical solution to speedy building and as an ideological counterpoint to bespoke craft-based

08   The addresses appear on two letters from Schwippert, one from December 14, 1961, to Endres and the other from August 7, 1962, written to Blümel in care of the archbishopric. Blümel lived at Kuglerstrasse 31, Prenzlauer Berg, in East Berlin. A later letter, dated October 17, 1962, is addressed to Blümel in Reinickendorf, in West Berlin. This postdates Blümel's illness, which Schwippert refers to as sepsis. Archive, St. Hedwigs-Kathedrale, Berlin.
09   Blümel, "Wiederaufbau der St.-Hedwigs-Kathedrale," 64.

methods. The article immediately following Blümel's in the newsletter, for example, described a late 1920s case study in concrete prefabrication for housing, completed by a Dutch company in the southeastern Berlin district of Karlshorst. In spring 1955, the first Building Conference of the German Democratic Republic (Baukonferenz der DDR) declared industrialized building "democratic," and shortly thereafter, the German Democratic Republic Ministerial cabinet had translated that declaration into law.[10]

The Hedwigskathedrale construction site was set up as an open-air factory, offering anyone traveling through the center of Berlin a chance to watch concrete prefabrication as it happened. First, four concrete positives or molds were fabricated on site by casting concrete into wooden formworks and polishing the resulting segments to a smooth and precise surface. These molds were then set up in the public plaza in front of the cathedral. Each dome segment was cast onto the positives and then released after curing, using suction mechanisms placed at either end of the components. Images show no fewer than six workers involved in the release process. Each of the four segments had to be positioned on the dome drum, using the crane's gantry arm, before the next segment could be cast. [8.2] It is not hard to imagine how the rhythm of fabrication, release, and placement of these enormous pieces would have dominated the view from Unter den Linden across Bebelplatz for the nearly three years until the work was completed. The activity was a tangible sign of a nation rebuilding itself and of the powerful reconstitution of the building industry.

Since its planning under Friedrich the Great of Prussia in 1745,[11] St. Hedwig's had been a de facto political symbol. As the first Catholic church built in Berlin since the Reformation, its prominent location and royal patron indicated Berlin's policy of religious tolerance. It exalted the faith of largely Catholic Silesia, a newly German territory and the homeland of St. Hedwig herself, at a moment when it was expedient. At the same time, Friedrich the Great's insistence that the building be modeled on the Roman Pantheon aligned it with geometric, technological, and philosophical referents within a architectural tradition symbolic of rationalism. Less fortuitously, the centralized plan also gave rise to liturgical challenges, to which Schwippert also had to respond. In 1955, when Schwippert first visited the cathedral,[12] it was perhaps the most important religious stepchild of the East–West divide at a moment when Catholic Chancellor Adenauer's Christian Democratic Party dominated the Bundestag by a significant majority. The rebuilding of churches throughout West Germany had been a first order of business for reconstruction, indicating the central role played by religion in the war's aftermath. The situation was particularly critical for the cathedral by 1955: as of 1953, the German Democratic Republic had ended mandatory church tithes collected through taxation. Although churches were still allowed to collect tithes independently, any larger plans were made much more difficult without the support of centralized funding.[13]

Monseigneur Endres's strategy was to appeal instead to a broader Catholic network. One letter dated September 10, 1954, refers to a set of plans Endres had procured for the cathedral, indicating that he had already begun considering an interior renovation before the dome was entirely complete.[14] That letter was written by Leonhard Küppers, a cleric and art historian who then was chaplain and professor for Christian art and iconography at the Academy of Art in Düsseldorf, as well as director of the subrectory for art of the *Pax Romana* within the International Movement of Catholic Students.[15] Küppers's letter acknowledges receipt of the drawings from Endres and describes a consultation with "Dr. Weyres," then architect for the Archdiocese of Cologne,[16] the city for which Schwippert's friend and mentor Rudolf Schwarz had served as General Planner until 1952. By 1954, Schwarz was also teaching in Düsseldorf alongside both Küppers and Schwippert. Küppers's letter says little about the plans themselves, however. Instead, he shares two

10   Christine Hannemann, *Die Platte: Industrialisierter Wohnungsbau in der DDR*, 2nd ed. (Berlin: Schelzky & Jeep, 2000), 62.
11   Ronald Rother, " 'Hinter der katholischen Kirche': Zur Bedeutung von St. Hedwig," *Das Münster* 67, no. 2 (2014), 91–107.
12   Agatha Buslei-Wuppermann, "Hans Schwippert als Architekt," 117.
13   Horst Groschopp, "Rasterfahndung nach Kirchensteuerflüchtigen," *Humanistischer Pressedienst* (December 6, 2006), http://hpd.de /node/655, accessed December 16, 2021.
14   Leonhard Küppers to Msg. Heinz Endres, September 10, 1954. Archive, St. Hedwigs-Kathedrale, Berlin.
15   "About: Leonhard Küppers." http:// de.dbpedia.org/page/Leonhard_Küppers, accessed December 21, 2021.
16   J. Hoster and A. Mann, eds., *Festschrift für Willy Weyres zur Vollendung seines 60. Lebensjahres* (Cologne: Greven und Bechtold, 1964).

8.2 Work on the dome's reconstruction using prefabricated concrete segments, undated, around 1953

conversations between Bishop Weskamm of Berlin and himself. In the summer of 1954, he wrote, Weskamm had told him that any plans for the church's interior were still "premature."[17] In a later conversation, however, Küppers reported, "His Eminence suggested that I wait until he was back in Berlin. I myself cannot come before October 18th. [...] I believe I have ascertained that this date would also be suitable to his Excellency."[18] Weskamm's participation in the project, facilitated by Küppers's intervention, would prove decisive: in 1955, upon the twenty-fifth anniversary of the Berlin see, Weskamm announced a significant fundraising effort to support the cathedral's rebuilding.[19]

Küppers did much to move the project ahead. As an art historian with a particular investment in urbanism and architecture, he also ensured himself a role in deciding on the architect and ultimately, the design that would be commissioned. A letter to Küppers dated December 10, 1954, discusses several architects under consideration: Felix Hinssen, a Berlin architect in the *Neues Bauen* mode from Erfurt who had designed the new concrete dome, was already the diocese's house architect[20] and would later be Le Corbusier's contact architect in Berlin;[21] Alfons Leitl, about whom Küppers says only that his St. Carolus was "not extraordinary;"[22] and Paul Meyer-Speer. Küppers appears ambivalent about these architects but does not yet offer suggestions of his own. Nonetheless, to judge from following letters, it seems that he might already have given the matter some thought.

In a letter written on May 18, 1955, to Weskamm and forwarded as a carbon copy to Endres, Küppers describes a weekend visit with Schwippert by plane from Düsseldorf to Berlin. Küppers's letter strikes a familiar tone despite the steep church hierarchy:

17   Küppers to Endres, September 10, 1954.
18   Küppers to Endres, September 10, 1954.
19   Christine Goetz and Victor H. Elbern, eds., *Die St-Hedwigs-Kathedrale zu Berlin* (Regensburg: Schnell + Steiner, 2000), 70.
20   Heinz Endres, *Die St. Hedwigs-Kathedrale in Berlin: Baugeschichte und Wiederaufbau* (Berlin (East): Morus-Verlag, 1963), 28.
21   Schwippert, *Ausbau der St.-Hedwigs-Kathedrale*. Roland Jaeger, *Bauten Theo Kellner und Felix H. Hinssen*, reprint (Berlin: Gebr. Mann, [1930] 2000).
22   Küppers to Endres, September 10, 1954.

23   Leonhard Küppers to Wilhelm
Weskamm, May 18, 1955. Archive, St. Hedwigs-
Kathedrale, Berlin.
24   Konstantin Mathey, "Die Umgestaltung
der St. Hedwigs-Kirche zur Kathedrale des
Bistums Berlin (1930–1932) nach einem Entwurf
von Prof. Clemens Holzmeister (1886–1983)
unter Mitarbeit des Diözesanbaurates Carl Kühn
(1973–1942)," *Das Münster* 67, no. 2 (2014), 107–16.

"During the two-hour flight, I was able to discuss several issues with
Schwippert. By the way, I have the impression that you were not the
only one to find Professor Schwippert sympathetic, but that even
the auxiliary bishop and several gentlemen of the capital found him
sympathetic as well. What pleased me especially was that Professor
Schwippert's suggestion for the interior design of St. Hedwig's was
fundamentally what I had already proposed. An architect—this is
of course ultimately his task and not that of a liturgist—can of
course justify his ideas better."[23]

Küppers's expression of pleasure at finding resonance between his own
and Schwippert's ideas for the church may well have been disingenuous:
as colleagues and travel companions, the two would have had ample
time to discuss the project prior to the visit. Without Küppers's advocacy,
Schwippert might never have received or completed the commission,
especially as other figures challenged Schwippert's design, most prominently Clemens Holzmeister, architect of renovations to St. Hedwig's
prior to the war. Holzmeister's project, completed in 1932, had tempered
the radial symmetry implicit in the circular space by emphasizing the
altar. Two windows on either side of the altar were bricked up and left
as niches. The darker conditions in the sanctuary were then offset
by a new aperture between the main sanctuary and the adjacent chapel
to backlight the altar. Other changes answered functional considerations:
the construction of side altars, new confessionals, and an organ loft.[24]

**8.3 Leonhard Küppers, article
showing one of Schwippert's versions
of the connection between crypt
and main floor, 1957**

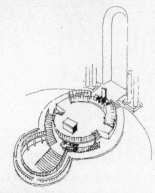

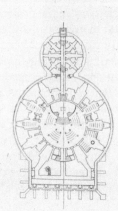

When asked to review Schwippert's design, Holzmeister responded with a scathing review and sent along his own design instead.[25] This conflict was almost inevitable considering the radicality of Schwippert's 1955 proposals.

Küppers most certainly introduced Schwippert in discussions, in lieu of other perhaps better-known or more advantageously positioned architects. But despite Küppers's increasingly close friendship with Endres, whom he addressed with the nickname "Enrico" in both typed and handwritten letters from 1956–57, his role in the project was brief, except in his capacity as a friend and confidant of Endres and Schwippert. Johannes Wagner, director of the Liturgical Institute in Trier and an advocate of the changes in liturgy that would culminate in Vatican II in 1959,[26] replaced him as liturgical consultant to Schwippert's unconventional design. Küppers was disappointed and frustrated by his removal from his semi-official consulting position and even more so because he had not been informed appropriately: he learned of this development only after Schwippert presented work in Berlin in November 1955 without his attendance or knowledge.[27] Schwippert's care and charisma allowed him to navigate this sensitive situation. He met with Wagner officially but informed Küppers regularly about the project's development and continued to integrate Küppers's suggestions into his design development. The project would face much greater internal challenges, not least of them Weskamm's death in the summer of 1956, but Schwippert's handling of this delicate conflict represents his particular approach to interpersonal politics, which ensured his success while earning him a reputation for generosity of spirit. In large part because of his ongoing friendships with Endres and Schwippert, Küppers continued to advocate for the project. His 1957 article published in *Das Münster* offered the public its first view of Schwippert's proposal.[28] **[8.3]**

In his accounts of the project, Schwippert dated the renovation of St. Hedwig's not to 1955, when he first became involved, but to 1951, when "a building was made again out of the remaining raw core, rescued from wartime destruction in accordance with the contemporary rules of historic preservation."[29] It was precisely that wartime destruction that may have inspired Schwippert's innovative decision to resolve the cathedral's design in section rather than plan. The attack that destroyed the dome had also pockmarked the floor, leaving openings between the church sanctuary and its substructure. Whether true or apocryphal, the story persists that this remnant of the bombing inspired him to position the altar within a double-height cutout between the main sanctuary and crypt.[30] But in his self-published 1969 pamphlet about the project, Schwippert instead describes a thorough, iterative design process leading him to his final design parti, which remained controversial until its unmaking in the present.[31]

The project was challenging in many ways, as Schwippert understood even upon his initial visit in 1955: the centralized plan was typologically difficult; the question of whether and how to retain a record of its state of ruin was a concern that Schwippert shared with others, most notably Schwarz;[32] liturgical changes in the celebration of Holy Week beginning in 1955 and the approval of the vulgate in rituals other than Mass were harbingers of the change that would culminate in 1962 with Vatican II, a year before the church's completion; the cathedral's location in East Berlin while the diocese, which did not recognize the city's division, was housed in West Berlin; and finally, given additional urgency by the new, unadorned concrete dome, the question of how modern art and architecture related to Catholic representations of faith. Schwippert reflected upon these challenges in his brief but powerful speech at the cathedral's consecration in 1963:

> "There was a need to consider the use of a respected housing, the bearer of tradition, history, and spirit, for new versions of older contents. There was the need to reconfigure obsolete representation in more stringent, more modest, more discrete forms that would be more relevant today, the need to do without the older and accustomed, the need for courage, sacrifice and diligence in the heads and hands of every assistant. There was a need, simply, to demonstrate

25   Holzmeister's report was delivered on July 3, 1957. Two other critical reviews of Schwippert's design were submitted: one by the art historian Prof. Hubertus Lossow on May 10, 1957, and one by Building Inspector Schädel on August 10, 1957. The reports were sent by Holzmeister's advocate Dr. Georg Banasch, who had been charged with day-to-day oversight of the renovation, to Vice Bishop Tkotsch on October 8, 1957. The controversy around Schwippert's design and the internal strife it caused is one reason for the long delay on the project. When Banasch died in 1960, much of the resistance disappeared.

26   See "Johannes Wagner (Theologe)–Enzyklopädie," *Deutsche Times* (June 18, 2021), https://deutschetimes.com/johannes-wagner-theologe-enzyklopadie, accessed July 1, 2021.

27   Küppers learned of Wagner's selection only after he had been excluded from a series of meetings on the church. He refers to Wagner as "vain [...] because he believes that only he knows what is definitive." Küppers's displeasure at his removal from the project is a topic of a series of letters between February and May, 1956. See Leonhard Küppers to Msg. Heinz Endres, February 23, 1956.

28   Leonhard Küppers, "Die Hedwigs-Kathedrale in Berlin," *Das Münster* 10 (November, 1957).

29   Schwippert, *Ausbau der St.-Hedwigs-Kathedrale*, 2.

30   See, for example, Julia Ricker, "Die St. Hedwigs-Kathedrale in Berlin," *Deutsche Stiftung Denkmalschutz: Monumente Online* (December 2014), https://www.monumente-online.de/de/ausgaben/2014/6/die-st-hedwig-kathedrale.php.

31   The protracted debate about the cathedral's future was ultimately resolved to the detriment of Schwippert's project. See "Landgericht erlaubt Umbau der Berliner Hedwigs-Kathedrale," *rbb24* (July 14, 2020). See also Claudia Keller, "Gott in der Arena," *Der Tagesspiegel* (Berlin, July 2, 2014); Claudia Keller, "Sorge um St. Hedwig," *Der Tagesspiegel* (Berlin, Sept. 2, 2014); Giuseppe Pitronaci, "Kirche zwischen Ost und West: Der geplante Umbau der Hedwigskathedrale wirft Fragen auf," *Herder Korrespondenz* 68 (May 2014).

32   Schwarz developed several architectural strategies for wartime ruin as memento mori, from the use of rubble for rebuilding in St. Anna in Düren (1951–1956) to the literal retention of ruins as part of the Gürzenich complex in Cologne (1949–1955). His many lesser-known projects throughout western Germany for the partial reconstruction of church roofs, clerestories, windows, and portals offer a catalogue of formal and material methods for juxtaposing restoration, remnant, and new construction.

33   Schwippert, *Ausbau der St.-Hedwigs-Kathedrale*, 27.

34   Schwippert, *Ausbau der St.-Hedwigs-Kathedrale*, 4.

35   Schwippert, *Ausbau der St.-Hedwigs-Kathedrale*, 7.

36   Schwippert, *Ausbau der St.-Hedwigs-Kathedrale*, 8.

what the efforts of a community, the achievements of people bound together in work, are. From exactly this bond work arises, and the highest work particularly, as well as political work in the ultimate sense of the word."[33]

The derivation of Schwippert's design is documented in a series of published sketches, which first depict the church before its destruction and then describe the evolution of his strategies. [8.4] Six of those sketches describe the progression from a planimetric to a sectional parti. Schwippert distinguished the Hedwigskathedrale from other centralized churches organized either concentrically—ambulatory, niches, chapels—or radially.[34] On account of the configuration of its perimeter and overall size, the cathedral lacked space for liturgies required for its use as a bishop's church. Schwippert tested, then rejected as arbitrary, his own positionings of altar, choir, and ancillary chapels; his critique of a scheme for the primary altar was particularly harsh: "its position would remain coincidental; it could wander along the wall [...] along the encompassing movement of the wall; it would have no specific place. One could improve this using decoration [...] but that would ruin the space's purity."[35] Schwippert also noted that, "as always in centralized spaces of this kind, the altar tended fundamentally to the space's center. This would be its actual theoretical location. But this is contradicted by many factors. There are not only practical objections. They are augmented by liturgical concerns."[36] Dimension, parti, liturgy, even the state in which Schwippert found the space all argued against his first and most intuitive responses. He found his answer not at his drafting table but in the church itself:

> "The trajectory of these manifold considerations led me to the insight that I should look onsite at the way the base upon which the building stands was configured. Here, now, came surprise and help. Beneath the entire expanse of the rotunda above was a crypt complex. A spur wall and arch system, which carries the church floor, is set in a geometric and spatial order of understandable multiplicity by a wreath of chapel-like chambers, with an ambulatory and a central substructure. And this multiplicity below, long unknown and concealed, carried within it the unity, formed in rational genesis, of the great domed space above! What would it mean, were this condition to be made visible, apparent? The plan immediately

8.4 Hans Schwippert, assessment of the cathedral's condition before and after bomb damage, 1969

Skizzen: Kellergeschoß und Kirchengeschoß vor der Zerstörung.

Aus Skizzen: Raumerweiterungen durch Anbauten?

Wäre die kreisrunde Scheibe des Bodens nun von einer derartigen Größe und Ausdehnung, daß in der großen Weite eines darüber errichteten Gehäuses auf einer faktisch sehr großen Ebene gegen die Raumränder hin die Bildung von Ausstattungs- und Menschengruppen möglich wäre, welche durch wirksamen Abstand, angemessen trennende Entfernung voneinander die jeweils in sich ruhende Selbständigkeit einer Gruppierung erlauben, so könnte es angehen. Doch hat unser Raum solche Ausdehnung nicht.

Was immer in Anlehnung an seine Außenwand rundum aufgestellt, angeordnet oder versammelt würde, käme nicht zum In-sich-selbst-Stehen, würde keinen „Ort" gewinnen, würde beliebig verrückbar und an der Wand entlang im Kreise verschiebbar sein, würde lästige, den Raum störende Zutat oder fragwürdige Dekoration bedeuten. Mit Menschen aber ist der gar nicht so große Raum schnell bis an den Rand gefüllt.

Auch stünde zusätzliches Altarwerk, Bildwerk und Gerät ungut gegen die tief herabreichenden Fenster oder gegen die mächtigen jeweiligen Säulenpaare. Nicht als ob dies praktisch zur Not nicht ginge; doch wäre dieser Fall vergleichsweise ähnlich dürftigen Kirchenräumen, die, zu klein geworden oder aus spärlichen Mitteln entstanden, entlang der Umfassungs-

wände auf jenem schmalen Streifen, den die wachsende Masse der Bänke am Raumrande kümmerlich übrig läßt, jene Dinge notdürftig und zufällig beherbergen. Solcher Mangel ist wesentlicher Art. Der hierarchisch gestaffelte Reichtum des Dienstes, der Sakramente und Sakramentalien prägt sich hier baulich nicht aus. Der gestuften Vielfalt der Verwendung steht verkümmerte Einfalt, der Mehrschichtigkeit des Gebrauchs die Einschichtigkeit des gegebenen Raumes entgegen.

Würde der Hauptaltar wieder der Wand zugeordnet, bliebe er also samt Altarchor und dessen Stufenwerk der Raumwand verhaftet, also angeschoben an das umschließende Wandwerk, so würde auch er das oben angedeutete Schicksal der anderen Plätze teilen: Sein Ort bliebe zufällig, er könnte entlang der Wand wandern. Daß er den Raumeingängen gegenüberläge, ortet ihn nur schwach. Am Umschwung der Wand hätte er im Grunde keinen spezifischen Platz. Man kann das dekorativ verbessern, benachbarte Fensterfelder schließen, ihn mit Aufbauten und Ausbildung des Beiwerks (Bischofssitz, Chorgestühl usw.) betonen. Aber es verdürbe die Reinheit des Raumes. Solange Altar und Chor der Wand, der Peripherie also, verhaftet bleiben, bleibt hier die Gefahr einer dem Raumwesen abträglichen Dekoration, welche dem Raum und

37   Schwippert, *Ausbau der St.-Hedwigs-Kathedrale*, 9–10.

38   Georg Banasch, *Die Sankt-Hedwigs-Kathedrale in Berlin: Nach ihrer baulichen und künstlerischen Neugestaltung im Jahre 1932* (Berlin: Buchverlag Germania, 1933).

39   Hubertus Lossow, "Bericht über den Umbau der Hedwigskathedrale für Dr. Georg Banasch," May 10, 1957, Archive of Sankt-Hedwigs-Kathedrale, 2.

40   Lossow, "Bericht."

41   Lossow, "Bericht," 1–2.

42   Schwippert, *Ausbau der St.-Hedwigs-Kathedrale*, 11.

arose to study how this subterranean space-world could, in a cautious and appropriate manner, be set in connection with the space above, the opposition between 'above' and 'below' could be brought to bear, the desired complexity could be derived from the existing building and, in the end, the essence of building and space could be expressed emphatically."[37] **[8.5] [8.6]**

Although he presented it as a logical conclusion arrived at through careful iteration, Schwippert's design elicited polarized responses from his clients. The most influential opponent was Georg Banasch, the cleric appointed to oversee the process of rebuilding, who had published a book on the cathedral in 1933,[38] after its first modernization by Holzmeister. In response to Schwippert's proposal, Banasch commissioned three separate studies to undermine it. Banasch's minions Holzmeister, Building Commissioner Schädel, and art historian Prof. Hubertus Lossow cited the design's lack of architectural or typological precedent; Lossow argued for abandoning the old church altogether in lieu of a newly built cathedral "on an unrestricted site."[39] Submitted on May 10, 1957,[40] Lossow's report, in its futile search for a precedent, makes clear how radical Schwippert's sectional parti was:

> "Apparently Schwippert is thinking of Maderno's confessio in St. Peter's and the organization of throne, presbyter seats, and altar in an early Christian basilica. Nonetheless, in St. Peter's, the relationships and liturgical demands are entirely different. Communication between the sub-church and primary space would only be achieved here if one were to make the opening significantly larger, so that the upper church became something of a gallery and the lower church, the primary space."[41]

Schwippert, however, never cited a precedent, preferring instead to depict the design process as a collaboration with all those involved and, ultimately, with the building itself. His final design, in which the altar and choir area are elevated on a circular plinth tangent to an opening to the crypt below, ingeniously resolved many of the problems he had diagnosed. The altar, a two-story element that spanned between the upper and lower church to include the tabernacle at the lower level, clearly comprised the church's factual, if not geometric, center, "standing between Bishop and congregation."[42] All other liturgical elements, including baptismal font, secondary altars, and confessionals, were contained in the niches at the

8.5 Hans Schwippert, open floor at the crypt and main floor levels, 1969

Aus Skizzen zur Ausführung:
Die Bodenöffnung ordnet der Oberkirche eine Unterkirche zu.

seiner sparsamen und strengen Festlichkeit zuviel oder falsches zumutet.

Wie immer in zentralen Räumen dieser Art, tendiert im Grunde ein Altar zur Raummitte. Hier wäre sein eigentlicher, wenngleich nicht bis in die Mitte, hereinzuholen, eine Altarinsel, abgelöst von der Anlehnung an die Peripherie freier in den Raum zu stellen, und ihren insularen Charakter tunlichst auszuprägen. Dieser Bereich gewänne so Selbständigkeit und theoretischer Ort. Doch steht dem mancherlei entgegen. Keineswegs sind es nur Einwände praktischer Art. Sie werden ergänzt durch liturgische Bedenken. Die künstlerische, auch denkmalspflegerische Sorge aber war diese: Würde, nicht zuletzt, ein zentraler Altar, mit dem unausbleiblichen Gewicht seiner zentralen Stellung und einer daraufhin ausgeprägten Haltung den Raum durch eine theoretische Konsequenz, die seinen Erfindern fernlag, dahin entstellen, daß er „nur noch" Umraum um eine solche überbetonte Mitte wäre?

Wollte man das nicht, und wollte man aus ebenso gewichtigen Rücksichten auf den großartigen Geist des Raumes ebensowenig eine „Möblierung" an seinen Rändern entlang, so bot es sich an, den Altar samt seinem Chorhügel zunächst einmal abzulösen von der Wand, ihn weit in den Raum, wenngleich nicht bis in die Mitte, hereinzuholen, eine Altarinsel, abgelöst von der Anlehnung an die Peripherie freier in den Raum zu stellen, und ihren insularen Charakter tunlichst auszuprägen. Dieser Bereich gewänne so Selbständigkeit und

ausreichendes exzentrisches Gewicht in einem Raum, der sich ungeschwächt um ihn herum rundet.

So weit, so gut. Doch blieben dann immer noch zu entbehren die angemessenen Orte der Nebenaltäre, der Taufe, der Verehrung, der Andacht. Wohin mit ihnen, sollte die Kraft des Raumes, die Reinheit seiner ursprünglichen Konzeption nicht nur erhalten bleiben, sondern zum Klingen gebracht werden, besser als bisherige Ausstattungen dies bewerkstelligten?

Für den Einbau neuer zusätzlicher räumlicher Vielfalt, denkmalspflegerische und stilistische Bedenken einmal ganz beiseite, ist der Raum einfach faktisch zu klein. Das Ansetzen räumlicher Erweiterungen aber an den in seiner Einfachheit großgearteten Baukörper verbietet der verehrende Respekt vor dem reinen Ausdruck des überlieferten Bauwerks. Es war und wurde in der gegebenen Lage und unter den vorgefundenen Umständen als Baukörper mit allem Recht nach den Regeln angemessener Restauration betreut.

Der Gang der mannigfachen Überlegungen ließ mir einfallen, örtlich zu untersuchen, wie es denn mit dem Sockel bestellt sei, auf dem das Haus steht. Hier nun kam Überraschung und Hilfe. Unter der ganzen Ausdehnung der oberen Rotunde findet sich eine Kryptenraumanlage. Ein Mauerpfeiler- und Gewölbewerk, welches den Kirchenboden trägt, ist mit einem

43   Schwippert, *Ausbau der St.-Hedwigs-Kathedrale*, 11.
44   Leonhard Küppers, "Liturgie und Kirchenbau," typescript, January 28, 1955, 1. Archive, St. Hedwigs-Kathedrale, Berlin.
45   Küppers, "Liturgie und Kirchenbau," 1.

perimeter of the lower church, lending them "their appropriate places, intimate and yet spatially and optically connected to the upper space by the centralized socle and its opening to the upper church."[43]

Schwippert's decision to differentiate the smaller, intimate spaces—the liturgical sites of practices embedded in everyday life such as daily prayer, confession, and the celebration of baptism—from the space's celebratory role as a bishop's cathedral in the divided city reflects the liturgical trends of the late 1950s and 1960s. As the church moved slowly towards Vatican II and the mandate to connect more directly with its congregants, Schwippert found architectural ways to balance quotidian and transcendent. His relationship with Küppers is at least in part to be credited. In two texts written in 1955, Küppers formulated a set of principles on the relationship between contemporary church building, liturgy, and modern art that may well have been the intellectual foundation for Schwippert's design.

Küppers's two texts, both academic lectures given in Düsseldorf and preserved in typescript among the documents in the St. Hedwig's archives, were written at the same time as his anthology of texts on Catholic modern art and architecture, entitled *Kirche und Kunst in zeitgenössischen Dokumenten*, published in Düsseldorf in 1955 by Patmos Verlag. Küppers, a prolific author who published nearly annually during his active career from 1939 into the late 1970s, produced only this one book in the years between 1949 and 1961. Perhaps in response to the many contemporary authors whose writing he had reviewed to prepare his book, Küppers's typescript texts describe his own theories on contemporary Christian art and architecture. His support for modernism as a means to interpret the Church's meaning and practices is clear.

Written in January 1955, "Liturgy and the Church Building" laid out in a brief page and a half his principles for each component of a church: choir, altar, the shape of the church's plan, the ceiling form. Küppers wrote with total certainty, listing requirements and, from the start, warning against "experiments in which the holy yields to the sensationalistic in the foreground."[44] He wrote, "under any circumstances, it is wrong to make the altar the center of the church. The altar is never the center, but is the mediator to God."[45] The altar, he wrote elsewhere,

"must be inaccessible for the people [...] in order to offer the viewers a miraculous theater. [...] The reasons are here given: thus, the

8.6 Hans Schwippert, perspectives of open floor at crypt and main levels, 1969

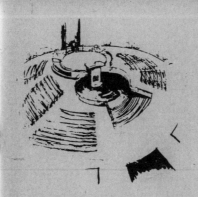

Kranz von kapellenartigen Kammern, mit Umgang und mit einer zentralen Substruktion in der Mitte in eine geometrische wie räumliche Ordnung von übersichtlicher Vielfalt gebracht. Und diese Vielfalt unten, bislang unbekannt und verborgen, trug also die in rationaler Zucht geformte Einfalt des großen Kuppelraumes oben! Wie, wenn es gelänge, dies sichtbar, offenbar zu machen. Sofort entstand der Plan, zu untersuchen, ob diese untere Raumwelt in vorsichtiger und angemessener Weise in Zusammenhang mit dem oberen Raum gebracht werden, die Gegensätze zwischen „unten" und „oben" wirksam gemacht, hier aus dem baulich Gegebenen die erstrebte Vielfalt gewonnen, und, am Ende, das Wesen von Bau und Raum gestärkt ausgedrückt werden könnte.

So wurde der Boden in der Mitte geöffnet mit einem Ausschnitt, der nach dem maßstäblichen Gesetz des Raumes die Kreisform und lediglich die Größe des Oberlichtauges im Scheitel der Kuppel hat. Diese Öffnung nach unten wurde in Beziehung gesetzt zur Chor- und Altarinsel. Die erweiternd angefügte breite Treppenanlage verbindet die Oberkirche verstärkt mit der neu gewonnenen Sockelkirche, die um-

schlossen ist von dem verbliebenen Raumring der eindrucksvollen alten gewölbten Kapellen und Grüfte.

In dem Raumkranz dieser unteren alten Gewölberäume gewinnen die Taufe, die Nebenaltäre, die Beichträume, die private Andacht und Anrufung, die Passion ihre angemessenen Orte, geborgen und doch über die mittige Sockelkirche und ihre Öffnung zur Oberkirche räumlich und optisch dem oberen Raum verbunden.

Nun brauchte diese Unterkirche zunächst einmal ihren eigenen Altar. Er stünde wiederum nicht in der Mitte, sondern wäre sinngemäß, ähnlich wie die obere Altar- und Chorinsel, exzentrisch zu orten. Hier nun setzen weitere Überlegungen ein.

Die sinnvolle Ausbildung der Bischofskirche fordert die Stellung des Bischofssitzes in der Verlängerung der Achse des Altars. Das aber hat zur Folge, daß der Altar, zwischen Bischof und Gemeinde stehend, des Tabernakels entraten muß. Wo aber, erinnert man sich an die Gegebenheiten der Oberkirche, an das strenge Wand- und Fensterrund ihrer Umfassungsmauer, an das Fehlen spezifischer Orte entlang dieser Wand, wo also das Sakrament oben aufbewahren? An irgend-

mysterious character of the sacrifice remains protected; furthermore, the special status of the priest should be demonstrated. He not only serves the congregation but is an intermediary between God and God's congregation."[46]

He was also clear about the meaning of church plan geometries. "As regards the form that the plan of a church should take," he wrote, "so the following should be said: the circle is a symbol of the divine, the rectangle is a symbol of the earthly."[47] For an author whose 1946 book documented medieval and Renaissance churches in Umbria and Tuscany,[48] this statement was strange. Historically, debate on church typologies had juxtaposed the virtues and shortcomings of the cruciform and centralized plans; the circle and rectangle in themselves were not common church plan types.

Küppers's strange assertion is easier to place by reference to St. Hedwig's. His preoccupation with the cathedral early in 1955 makes it seem plausible that he had its plan in mind when he wrote that, in centralized church plans, the circle is a symbol of God. His caveats about positioning the altar in the circle's middle would recur in Schwippert's later admission that "as always in centralized spaces of this kind, the altar tended fundamentally to the center of the space. [...] There are not only practical objections. They are augmented by liturgical concerns."[49] Küppers's recommendations that the choir be separated from the congregation to create a sense of theater, or that an altar should mediate without occupying the church's literal middle, presages the design upon which Schwippert would settle. Perhaps Küppers thus meant quite literally what he wrote to Weskamm, "that Professor Schwippert essentially proposed for the interior design of St. Hedwig's what I had already proposed earlier."[50] Küppers's liturgical underpinning may well have safeguarded the design against the onslaught of attacks solicited by Banasch.[51] The liturgical strength of the foundation Küppers laid for Schwippert's design prevailed, safeguarding Schwippert's radical sectional design, in which the altar, as Küppers had foreseen, was quite literally a "mediator"[52] between upper and lower churches.

"Modern Art in the Space of the Church," the second of Küppers's texts, argues against any specific or singular form, technique, rule set, or purpose for Christian art. He states provocatively: "there is no Christian art. There can fundamentally only be an art of Christians. [...] True art is everything that operates at the level of absolute beauty, Christian longing, and hope."[53] For the creation of Christian art, he explains, "the Christian artist is a prerequisite. In order to depict aspects of Christ, one must know about Christ's life, more still, one must live with Christ. [...] Thus the demand arises that there be no true Christian art without the true and Christian artist."[54] Küppers advocated for church art that emerged in equal parts from the intellect and devotion:

> "The basic error in modern art within the space of the Church to date is certainly that it was produced in the spirit of subjective fervor. The basis for the art of the Christian church must instead be the demand for the objectively divine, which is to say, the words of the Lord must be visible. And a second factor must also be acknowledged, that here, it is a matter of the formless encounter between God and His congregation, in other words, the congregation must be able to pray in the name of God. If these two preconditions are not met, then one must speak of a non-objective manner of work, and through this non-objective work arise mere experiments."[55]

The idea that modern art forms provided an ideal abstract intermediary between God and congregation was advocated too, in a text by Walter Warnach that Küppers included in a 1955 anthology. The passage Küppers selected states that in order to verify art's Christian attributes, "it is enough to ascertain that abstract art evidences a serious will to realize a bright order comprised of the real, in opposition to the downward tendency of the modern world."[56] Schwippert used similar arguments to explain the liturgical objects designed for St. Hedwig's. Many of those artifacts, including the tabernacle, altar cross, tapestry, and stained-glass windows, were made in Cologne or Aachen by long-time collaborators

46   Küppers, "Liturgie und Kirchenbau," 1.
47   Küppers, "Liturgie und Kirchenbau," 2.
48   Leonhard Küppers, *Südliche Stadt— Das Erlebnis von Pisa, Assisi und Florenz* (Düsseldorf: Bastion Verlag, 1946).
49   Schwippert, *Ausbau der St.-Hedwigs-Kathedrale*, 8.
50   Küppers to Weskamm, May 18, 1955.
51   Georg Banasch to Bishop Tkotsch, October 8, 1957. Archive, St. Hedwigs-Kathedrale, Berlin.
52   Küppers, "Liturgie und Kirchenbau," 1.
53   Leonhard Küppers, "Moderne Kunst im Kirchenraum," typescript, February 25, 1955, 1. Archive, St. Hedwigs-Kathedrale, Berlin.
54   Küppers, "Moderne Kunst im Kirchenraum," 1.
55   Küppers, "Moderne Kunst im Kirchenraum," 2.
56   Walter Warnach quoted in Leonhard Küppers, *Kirche und Kunst in zeitgenössischen Dokumenten*, ed. J. Walterscheid and H. Storz, vol. 5, Religiöse Quellenschriften (Düsseldorf: Patmos Verlag, 1955), 18.

8.7 Grete Reichardt, Tapestry of Heavenly Jerusalem, undated postcard

of Schwippert's, including his brother, the sculptor Kurt Schwippert.[57] In a letter to Endres advocating for the commissioning a tapestry, which was ultimately executed by Grete Reichardt, a Bauhaus-trained textile designer living in Halle, he cautiously laid out the three possibilities he foresaw for Christian art:

"Naturally, there is the excellent possibility of the 'pure' and precious tapestry. Here [...] a composition could be generated that, in a different, contemporary manner, could carry as many abstract mysteries as the large oriental carpet has always done. [...] In addition, there remains unchanged the other pathway of a pictorial tapestry with narrative scenes, representative (allegorical) motifs. [...] A third possibility is a monumental textile text across its entirety, the work of letters across the entire surface (including initial and quotation) in consistent scale and rhythm."[58]

Although not completed until 1963, Reichardt's tapestry, which elegantly integrates all three of the options Schwippert outlined, can be said to express the "objectively divine" in abstract motifs that still suggest any encounter with divinity be ungraspable, "formless" for the human subject, to quote Küppers.[59] [8.7] A similarly abstract formal language prevails in Schwippert's own design for a small chest for anointing oils, as well as in the cross, its gold fabricated by Aachen goldsmiths with whom Schwippert had worked since his time in Schwarz's office and its attenuated Christ figure hand-carved from ivory by Kurt Schwippert. [8.8] [8.9] Much like Schwippert's unprecedented parti, they represent a moment in which the possibilities opened by the modernist idiom

57   Hans Schwippert, Die St. Hedwigs Kathedrale in Berlin Information, November 1, 1963, GNM, DKA, NL, Schwippert, Binder for the Hedwigskathedrale.
58   Hans Schwippert to Msg. Heinz Endres, December 14, 1961.
59   Küppers, "Moderne Kunst im Kirchenraum."

60   Küppers, *Kirche und Kunst*, 5.
61   Ulrich Conrads and Peter Neitzke, eds.,
*Mensch und Raum: Das Darmstädter Gespräch
1951* (Braunschweig: Vieweg, 1991), 104–5.
62   Horst Poller to Theodor Blümel,
November 27, 1962, items 2 and 9; Theodor
Blümel to Horst Poller, November 29, 1962; Msg.
Heinz Endres to Fritz Kohlmann, November 27,
1962. Archive, St. Hedwigs-Kathedrale, Berlin.
63   Fachgebiet Heizungstechnik Versorg-
ungskontor für Maschinenbau-Erzeugnisse
to Theodor Blümel, December 5, 1961;
Theodor Blümel to Fachgebiet Heizungstechnik
Versorgungskontor für Maschinenbau-
Erzeugnisse, December 10, 1961. Archive,
St. Hedwigs-Kathedrale, Berlin.

could represent an "opposition to the downward tendency of the modern world."[60] At St. Hedwig's, the "modern" world immediately outside the walls was socialist, a world disinclined to recognize the church hierarchy or to support its congregation, or even the building renovation. It is tempting to draw a parallel between Schwippert's insistence at the 1951 Darmstädter Gespräch that the will to an open architecture transcended a world of existential threat and the way in which the cathedral's modern art communicated with its viewers and users despite a difficult daily reality. By the time of the cathedral's reconsecration in 1963, the "little man" of West Germany was at home in the world but the Catholics of the East German capital, as Schwippert's struggles document, were still forced to realize their *Wohnwollen*[61] amid less materially advantageous conditions.

From the time of his first visit to the delivery of the last elements to the cathedral, well after its consecration on November 1, 1963, Schwippert by his own reckoning spent more than a decade working on the Hedwigskathedrale. The correspondence, invoices, visas, bills of lading, and telegrams preserved in the two job books attest to the enormous logistical machinations the project demanded. A full network of individuals in Berlin and elsewhere in Europe, including the strange bedfellows of clergy, combines, craftsmen, and customs officials, was required to ensure that electrical wiring was copper, not aluminum;[62] that door closers were correctly specified and transported across the German / German border; and even that an oil furnace was delivered not a year after the consecration, but on time.[63] This network was husbanded by a few highly disciplined individuals: Monseigneur Endres, Blümel, and foreman Poller in Berlin, as well as Fritz Kohlmann in Schwippert's office. It was sustained by a postal system that carried letters within the span of a day from Unter den Linden to Düsseldorf. Even in the face of the political developments

**8.8 Hans Schwippert (perhaps Fritz
Kohlmann), construction drawing
for the chest holding sacred oils,
June 1963**

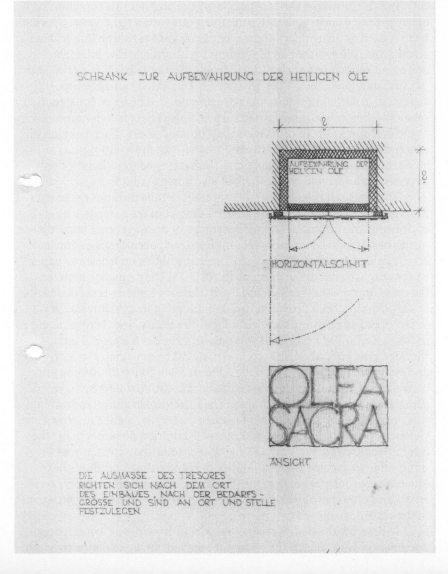

8.9 Kurt Schwippert, Fritz Schwerdt, and Hubertus Förster, altar cross, brochure with sketch, 1963

culminating in the erection of the Berlin Wall, these individuals maintained tight coordination and control.

But the drawings used to determine the architectural outcomes of construction communicated something other than tight control. As had been typical of Schwippert's construction drawings for the Bundeshaus seating and, prior to that, in his designs for affordable furniture, the construction documents for St. Hedwig's offer only basic material and performance guidelines. They are sparsely annotated and dimensioned. In several, a verbal summary of the recommended order of construction, relational dimensions, and desired surface finish effect is communicated as a block of text on an otherwise unannotated sheet. These narrative descriptions served in lieu of the thorough detail drawings typical of construction sets, in which the drawing dictates negotiations not only between architect and craftsman but also among trades.

The unusually vague character of their details does not mean that Schwippert, Kohlmann, and the others did not make extensive use of drawing for this project. The importance of drawing as an immediate means of communication is obvious in numerous pencil sketches drawn on the backs of correspondence, on meeting notes, on whatever paper was readily available at the moment. [8.10] [8.11] The mediation between the many impromptu sketches and the few laconic construction documents could only have been provided through intense personal interactions. In fact, multi-page letters traveled daily within Berlin, and correspondence between Berlin and Düsseldorf was only slightly less frequent. Perhaps the very slow pace of on-site work as dictated by material, product, and labor disruptions was a virtue, since it allowed for discussion and consultation on many items that expedience would otherwise have demanded of a standard drawing set. The final form of almost everything was decided by the availability of needed materials. Unlike in West Germany during this period, as Ruf's construction documents for the Speyer Hochschule für Verwaltungswissenschaften attest, it was impossible to assume the availability of standardized products here. Much was bespoke by necessity. In this respect, the conditions of construction at the Hedwigskathedrale resembled more closely the situation in the early postwar years.

To describe the Hedwigskathedrale detail drawings as "construction documents" is to stretch the term. One such drawing explains the stair

**8.10 Detail and window sketches on
archdiocese letterhead, undated**

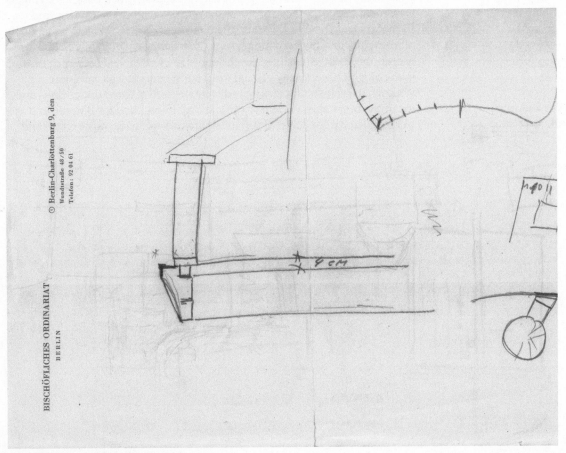

**8.11 Molding profile sketch on
archdiocese letterhead, undated**

64   Sabine Schulte, *Die St.-Hedwigs-Kathedrale als Symbolraum des Aufbruchs*, Architekten- und Ingenieur-Verein zu Berlin (Berlin, September 8, 2015), available at http://www.freunde-hedwigskathedrale.de /dokumente/fachartikel/. Kühn was also in conversation with Egon Eiermann to provide sculptures for the Kaiser-Wilhelm-Gedächtniskirche in West Berlin. Letter from Kühn to Eiermann, February 22, 1961, Egon Eiermann Archive, "Briefe A Projektbezogen," Karlsruhe Institute of Technology.

65   Drawing entitled "St. Hedwig Berlin—Treppenwangen," dated June 14, 1963. Archive, St. Hedwigs-Kathedrale, Berlin.

between the upper and lower church. This single sheet comprising sectional elevation and axonometric at 1:20 scale is all that was provided for the stair's construction. [8.12] Information that would normally have appeared in annotations, such as material designations, relational dimensions that require alignment with other parts of the building, and reveals between finishes, are described instead in a single note. This latitude is even more surprising given that the margin of error on the stair was nevertheless quite tight, accomodating the accurate installation of the crystal and bronze handrail, fabricated by East German artistic metalworker Fritz Kühn, the leading actor in religious art in the German Democratic Republic.[64] [8.13] [8.14] Even as an auxiliary document intended to augment directions given in others, the drawing of the stair is astonishingly understated. It is only viable if one assumes it is being read by responsible, highly invested craftsmen of all associated trades who are able to anticipate and negotiate one another's requirements and tolerances on site, on the sole basis of a sparse depiction of the desired outcome. The block of text in image 8.12, reproduced here in its entirety, describes the alignments and finish surfaces of component elements:

> "The white floor plate will be continued around the stringer to the front for the seventh step. The bearing stringer, like the window embrasures, will be plastered entirely in rough stucco, although the grain of the aggregate should be clearer. The floor plate's surface aligns with the visible base of the stair socle, while the rough stucco is set back the depth of the socle. Socle, rough plaster, and floor plate edge are each separated from one another by a reveal."[65]

Embedded in this text are complex construction negotiations minimally explicated in the drawing. Stucco, floor plate, and socle all had different material depths in rough construction. These differences would have had to be reflected in the work of demolition for the stair opening, in the work of the masons who configured the walls along which the stair stringer was installed, in the work of the stone masons who cut the stairs, and in the work of the metalworkers who fabricated the stringer. Finished alignments, invisible during each of these stages, would have been ascertained using snap lines, levels, and strings stretched between points, some of which were only virtual until construction was complete. Without an architect's drawing to designate each of these dimensions and locations in space, it was up to the site architect, Theodor Blümel, and to the capacity of each craftsman on site to anticipate, respond to, and

8.12 Stair between the crypt and main levels of the cathedral, 1963

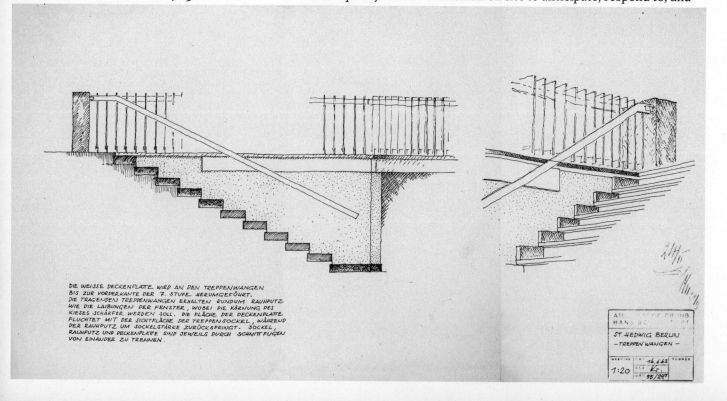

DIE WEISSE DECKENPLATTE WIRD AN DEN TREPPENWANGEN BIS ZUR VORDERKANTE DER 7. STUFE HERUMGEFÜHRT. DIE TRAGENDEN TREPPENWANGEN ERHALTEN RUNDUM RAUHPUTZ WIE DIE LAIBUNGEN DER FENSTER, WOBEI DIE KÖRNUNG DES KIESES SCHÄRFER WERDEN SOLL. DIE FLÄCHE DER DECKENPLATTE FLUCHTET MIT DER SICHTFLÄCHE DES TREPPENSOCKELS, WÄHREND DER RAUHPUTZ UM SOCKELSTÄRKE ZURÜCKSPRINGT. SOCKEL, RAUHPUTZ UND DECKENPLATTE SIND JEWEILS DURCH SCHNITTFUGEN VON EINANDER ZU TRENNEN.

ST. HEDWIG BERLIN
—TREPPEN WANGEN—

1:20

8.13 Fritz Kühn, crystal and bronze
handrail detail, 2014

8.14 Fritz Kühn, crystal and bronze
handrail shortly after completion,
undated

respect the differing margins of errors of each respective trade. It was no wonder that Schwippert thanked them publicly.

Two photographs from Schwippert's archive help to explain the relationship between the stair in process and its completed state. They depict the full three-dimensional development of floor edge, stair, and wall, particularly at the juncture to the tabernacle. The job site photo shows scant implements of work: a wooden ladder, some wooden scaffolding or shoring, and rough boards supporting what appears to be the substructure for the stair. **[8.15]** In the background, at the level of the upper church, is a crew of five or six men, one with a wheelbarrow and another few working at a rough wooden table, which looks as though it has been nailed together on site. This and other construction shots indicate a site in which labor was more plentiful than materials, or at the very least, sophisticated materials. **[8.16]**

Schwippert's drawings for other elements of the interior fit-out, including the entry doors, the main door handle, and the pews, are only slightly more explicit. The metalwork for the main interior doors and door handles was designed to be welded using standard steel rectangular tubing. **[8.17] [8.18]** The handle, a sculptural element ultimately executed only in greatly simplified form, is depicted in flattened, elevational view at full scale, its exterior dimensions given in millimeters. The handle's depth is shown—8 centimeters—only in the accompanying, scaleless axonometric. On closer inspection, the drawing's lines appear to waver slightly, as if traced freehand above millimeter paper or a drafted

8.15 Stair to the crypt under construction,"Mannesmann" pipe filled with concrete as column, undated

8.16 Stair to the crypt, shortly after completion in 1963

66   (See image 8.17) Drawing entitled "St. Hedwig Berlin—Die Innentüren," dated October 22, 1962, scale noted as 1:50, 1:1. Archive, St. Hedwigs-Kathedrale, Berlin, Berlin. The initials KO indicate that Kohlmann may have authored this drawing.
67   Fritz Kohlmann to Msg. Heinz Endres, September 18, 1963, 2.
68   For example, Ernst Kayser, "Berechnung des Nußholzgewichts für Lieferung an die Hedwigskathedrale," July 23, 1963; Msg. Heinz Endres, " 'Zur Klärung der Lage' Nußholz," (July 29, 1963); Msg. Heinz Endres to Fritz Kohlmann, "Caritas Hilfe für Nußholzlieferung nach Ost-Berlin," August 21, 1963. Archive, St. Hedwigs-Kathedrale, Berlin.

underlay. The cultivated imprecision of the lines contrasts with the realistic depiction of the slightly radiused welded and ground corners. The same drawing style was used for the front door drawing: the wavering lines also contrast with the definitive drawing notes, typed on transparent paper and spliced into the drawing before blueprinting. Only one horizontal sectional detail shows the swinging doors. There is no indication of the hinge, how it would be welded to the two frames, or where it should be positioned; the header and threshold details are not even suggested in the drawing. A full-scale detail shows as a hatched block—wood? metal? mastic? masonry?—the element that will mediate between door and column. A tilde and question mark next to that element's specified dimension of 35 millimeters would have told the fabricator that it was his responsibility to verify this dimension on site. The typed text states this unequivocally: "Special attention should be given to a clean connection between fixed frame and wall, with recessed reveal."[66]

There are two drawings for the pews, one which foresaw leather upholstery and one only wood. The former was intended for clergy; the latter for the congregation. Schwippert and his project architect Fritz Kohlmann recommended ash for the furniture, but Endres resisted the choice of a common, inexpensive wood;[67] ultimately, the pews were executed in walnut, imported via West Berlin through the Catholic charity Caritas after no small amount of consternation and delay.[68] The drawing, quite beautifully laid out, uses a 1:1 scale drawing of the pew to frame two 1:10 scale elevations, one lateral and one longitudinal. **[8.19] [8.20]** All dimensions are noted at the 1:10 scale, leaving the 1:1 drawing to serve as a template. The annotations are different in character from those in the other drawings, in that they specify how to affix the wood

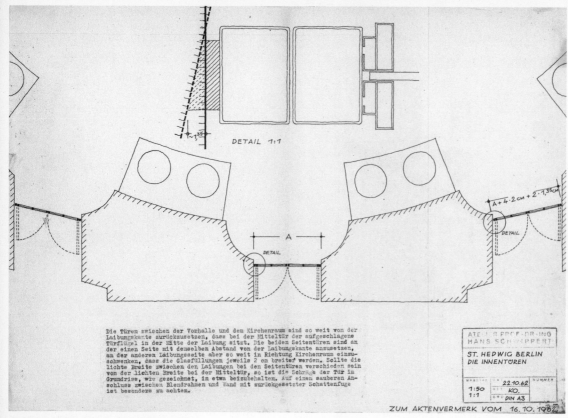

8.17 Interior entry doors from the vestibule to sanctuary, 1962

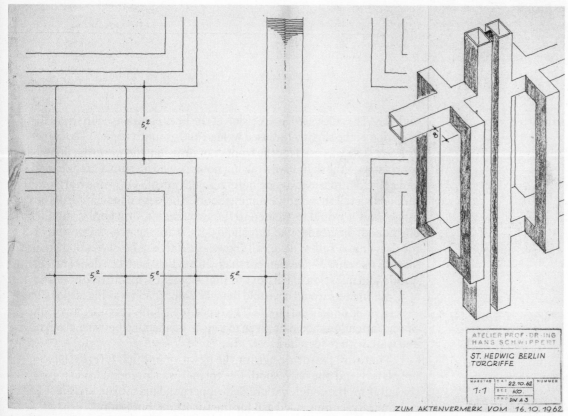

8.18 Entry door handle construction details, 1962

69   Horst Poller to Theodor Blümel, October 2, 1962. Archive, St. Hedwigs-Kathedrale, Berlin.

70   Rothkegel, "Antrag auf Erlaubnis für die Einführung eines Stahlgerüsts," July 28, 1959. Archive, St. Hedwigs-Kathedrale, Berlin.

71   Rothkegel, "Antrag."

72   Rothkegel, "Antrag."

seats and surfaces to the metal frames in a manner that allows the wood to expand and contract with changes in temperature and humidity. This attentiveness to differential material movement demonstrates again a rare investment in the nexus between design and fabrication. Simple and robust in construction but appropriately understated in the space, the pews attest to Schwippert's capacity to find a design that balanced the many rows of seating against the building's dominant circular geometry. [8.21] Here, too, the simple drawing belies the vast undertaking of mobilization and logistics through which solid walnut was imported to East Berlin during fabrication.

In fact, even the most banal of building materials seems to have represented a challenge during the years of active construction at St. Hedwig's. A letter dated October 3, 1962, to Blümel from Poller, the on-site foreman, offers multiple instances of this challenge: the tile-layer was ready to work but had only white tiles; there was no grout for the column bases; three packages of binder were still missing for the painter's spackle.[69] A note written to the magistrate of Greater Berlin in July 1959 evidences the dire limitations on this job site.[70] Following up on a request made a month earlier, the author, secretary in the Hedwigs-kathedrale office, requests permission to import a tubular steel scaffolding from West Berlin in order to "circumvent the shortages in the scaffolding sector."[71] The scaffolding was needed "urgently"[72] to complete work on the cathedral's columns and main portal. As the letter records, a special license had been granted earlier in the year for the scaffolding, which advantageously would remain in East Berlin for use on other sites after the cathedral's completion. There is no record of whether the import

8.19 Pew in steel and walnut, construction detail, 1963

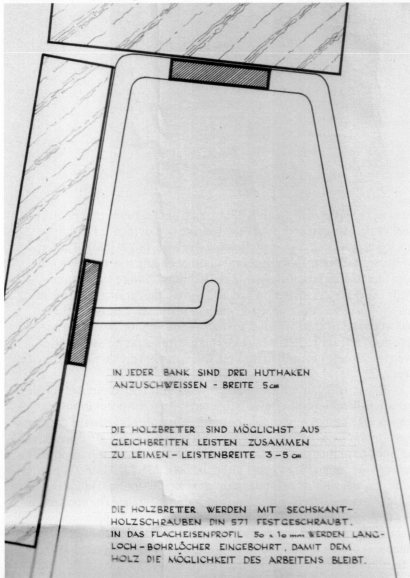

IN JEDER BANK SIND DREI HUTHAKEN
ANZUSCHWEISSEN - BREITE 5 ᴄᴍ

DIE HOLZBRETTER SIND MÖGLICHST AUS
GLEICHBREITEN LEISTEN ZUSAMMEN
ZU LEIMEN - LEISTENBREITE 3-5 ᴄᴍ

DIE HOLZBRETTER WERDEN MIT SECHSKANT-
HOLZSCHRAUBEN DIN 571 FESTGESCHRAUBT.
IN DAS FLACHEISENPROFIL 50 x 10 ᴍᴍ WERDEN LANG-
LOCH-BOHRLÖCHER EINGEBOHRT, DAMIT DEM
HOLZ DIE MÖGLICHKEIT DES ARBEITENS BLEIBT.

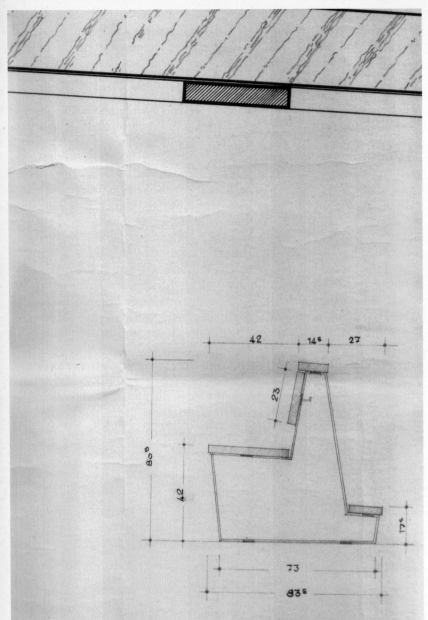

8.20 Pew in steel and walnut, overview elevation, 1963

paperwork was provided, and there are no photographs that depict the steel scaffolding in use, but the extensive deployment of wooden shoring indicates that steel scaffolding was rare. **[8.22] [8.23]** The letter's careful formulation does not reveal whether on-site shortages resulted from material or political conditions: likely, both were significant. While the dome construction had been given high priority and visibility as a showcase for prefabricated concrete technology, a renovation that would allow the cathedral to be used for worship again can hardly have been attractive to the East German bureaucracy, particularly given the diocese's refusal to recognize the political divide within the city it served.

In 1955, the church interior had only recently been cleared of rubble[73] and was still stripped to its bare masonry. At some point in 1956, Schwippert's design was completed for the aperture between the upper and lower church, which enlarged the hole that resulted when, after bombing, the wooden dome was consumed by fire and the cross, mounted at the center of the dome, fell and punctured the floor.[74] **[8.24]** After completing his design, Schwippert, with the support of Berlin Cardinal Julius Döpfner,[75] was able to experiment with wood mock-ups to finalize the connection between crypt and sanctuary. It was this design that Küppers made public at the end of his 1957 article[76] and that Endres deemed a "so-called phantom [...] that allowed for the maturation of the final plan."[77] The use of the job site as a design laboratory enabled involvement of the crafts-men and facilitated an immediate relationship between the architect and

73   The church was not cleared of rubble until 1949/50, and even then only by members of the congregation. Krieger and Kaneko, "Gutachten zur Baugeschichte und Denkmal-substanzerfassung," 74.
74   Endres, *Die St. Hedwigs-Kathedrale*, 22.
75   Endres, *Die St. Hedwigs-Kathedrale*, 32.
76   Illustrations in Küppers, "Die Hedwigs-Kathedrale in Berlin," 430.
77   Endres, *Die St. Hedwigs-Kathedrale*, 32.

8.21a Pews in steel and wood, 2014

8.21b

78   Endres, *Die St. Hedwigs-Kathedrale*, 36.

construction process despite the physical and political distance between Düsseldorf and East Berlin. In this case the act of building was quite literally integral to the design process. **[8.25]**

While even mundane materials from wood to wiring to fasteners presented logistical demands, the provenance of the cathedral's more significant elements allowed for the inclusion of East and West German elements. In his 1963 assessment, Endres attests to the success of Schwippert's design considerations:

> "The form's simplicity should not be underestimated, in that here, the determination to use the best materials and to realize artistic achievement at a high level dominated, and is nowhere lacking in, the configuration of the interior space. Kapfenberg marble from Thuringia was used for the entire floor, a natural stone material generated by the local earth."[78]

The success of the church's powerful, simple formal language, Endres asserted, relied on the use of the best materials, not least among them a marble derived from "the local earth," a term that understands the surrounding space geologically and without respect to politics. The balanced

8.22 Demolition photograph, undated

8.23 Shoring and scaffolding for plasterwork, full-scale mock-up of opening to crypt, ca. 1958

representation of West and East was even more explicit and programmatic for the conception of the artworks that would be integrated into the space. This ambition came not from the client alone but also from the architect.

In June 1961, Schwippert's office issued a twenty-page document entitled "Notizen zur Ausstattung" (notes on the interior fit-out). By then, the difficulties involved in sourcing construction materials would have been obvious. The document therefore begins by recognizing the unusual circumstances and their implications for project and architect:

"The uniqueness of the charge presented by a restoration based in renovation and new design as well as by the given location in East Berlin foregrounds the following:

Inasmuch as artistic and artisanal capacities of the highest artistic quality, if not to say of appropriate European significance, are available in East Berlin and East Germany, then they should be granted priority for appropriate commissions in both design and execution. [...]

Negotiations to that end should therefore be initiated from the outset. I do not doubt that all involved will show understanding for this process given the situation, even in areas where—unlike, for example, window fabrication—it is unusual.

The architect's responsibilities and decisions to assure that details accord with the entire spatial idea are expanded to include the additional responsibility to serve as the connective figure between designer and fabricator.

Fundamentally, the following is noted with the greatest emphasis: the seriousness and international significance of the commission does not tolerate any artistic half-measures."[79]

Demonstrating how seriously Schwippert's office took its role, an attached inventory covers every possible instance, including altar utensils,

79   Hans Schwippert to Msg. Heinz Endres and Theodor Blümel, "Notizen zur Ausstattung," June 19, 1961, 1. Archive, St. Hedwigs-Kathedrale, Berlin.

80   Schwippert to Endres and Blümel, "Notizen zur Ausstattung."
81   Schwippert to Endres and Blümel, "Fenster Unterkirche," n.p.
82   Schwippert to Endres and Blümel, "Fenster Oberkirche," n.p.
83   Annemarie Richter, "Gottfried Heinersdorff (1883–1941): Ein Reformer der deutschen Glasbildkunst" (Berlin: Diss. Technische Universität Berlin, 1983), 134.

wall painting and graphics, tapestries, sculptures, and windows, to which alone one-fifth of the document is dedicated. Echoing the cover letter, the itemized list not only proposed a number of designers and fabricators—ranging from Schwippert's brother Kurt to Marc Chagall—but also noted possibilities for collaboration and fabrication in the eastern part of Germany. Among the items listed, the windows in the upper and lower church as well as in the lantern of the dome were perhaps most fundamental to the church's spatial integrity. By any standards, these would have demanded the architect's attention. Even so, Schwippert could hardly have imagined the way in which their design and execution would "expand" his role as a "connective figure between designer and fabricator."[80]

There were three sets of windows to be designed and fabricated, one at each level of the church: crypt, upper church, and dome lantern. For each, Schwippert produced a sheet that described his design idea: for the lower church, "strongly colored although bright (in order to allow light to enter)"[81] and for the upper church, "light glazing, 'cool,' no coloration, sober, based upon classicist ornamentation (geometry)."[82] [8.26] He also provided a few prospective designers and a fabricator, noted in handwriting as Puhl and Wagner in Berlin-Treptow in the city's southeast. In fact, Puhl and Wagner, founded in the nineteenth century, was not in Treptow at all, but in Neukölln, in the West. Schwippert's mistaken assumption derived from the company's recent work: after furnishing glass mosaic and other decorative glazing for public works during the Third Reich, the company had launched its postwar business in 1946 by completing the commission for the Soviet memorial in Treptow Park.[83] There is no evidence that Puhl and Wagner ever bid work for the Hedwigskathedrale.

There was significant effort invested in finding a fabricator in the East. The struggle to source and deliver decorative glazing began in late 1961 and continued through 1964. In addition to a brochure from the Glaswerkstätten Rudolf Beier in Dresden and Pillnitz, this section of the job book includes an older letter dated 1954, likely re-filed for reference from an earlier phase of renovation, from Richard Eitel and Tomee in Berlin Mitte. The letter reports that two specific shades of green were no longer

8.24 Opening to crypt during the youth Mass "Christ the King," October 28, 1962

84   Hans Schwippert, notes dated August 7, 1962. Archive, St. Hedwigs-Kathedrale, Berlin.
85   Heinz Endres to Fritz Kohlmann, October 9, 1962. Archive, St. Hedwigs-Kathedrale, Berlin.
86   Schwippert had also commissioned Wendling to design a tapestry for the back wall of the Bundeshaus plenary. Letter from Schwippert to Minister Director Wandersleb, September 22, 1949, AM TUM, schwi-92-09.

available and asks whether this might cost the company the commission for the windows. A letter from Schwippert to Endres and Blümel in August 1962 conveyed that "unfortunately the large and long-standing glass workshop and factory in Pirna,"[84] Saxony, would not be able to provide the glass. Shortly thereafter, in a note to Kohlmann dated October 9, 1962, Endres described a visit from Glaswerkstätten Potsdam to discuss the glazing in the lantern, during which he sought to procure color samples.[85]

The failure to find a source in East Germany for the glazing might explain the choice of Anton Wendling[86] to design the windows. The Aachen artist delivered samples to Schwippert's office in summer of 1962, which were to be matched on site. It was unlikely that an East German company would have been able to access exactly the same colors and produce the same glass specifications. Ultimately, the commission went to Derix Glasstudio in Darmstadt. The solution of one problem produced a new one: how to organize the transport of the leaded glass across the border.

Although Wendling's glass samples date to 1962, the design for the windows was slow in development. Kohlmann's meeting minutes from a three-day site visit in October 1962 capture the decision to ask Wendling to revise his design to include the entire window, not only its top half. At the cathedral consecration in 1963, the windows were all still filled with clear *Rohglas.* **[8.27] [8.28]** According to Heinz Endres, the designs were not finalized until later. Endres's description of the importance of the windows to the rest of the building reveals just how strongly he supported Schwippert's concept. It also reflects the degree to which the architectural agenda was inextricable from the program for the art:

> "For the windows, the cartoons based upon designs by Professor Anton Wendling, Aachen, are complete. The artistic glazing of the eight windows, still filled with rough glazing, will do justice to the essence of the church building. The windows should neither serve the purpose of looking out, nor bring the world into the church. They are a continuation of the walls, and the structure of their glazing must be like tapestries, which are intended to diffuse, screen, and transform earthly light. Therefore, the walls' geometric figures and tones transition to the windows. Made of delicately hued glass

8.25 Arched doorway in the crypt during construction, undated

87   Endres, *Die St. Hedwigs-Kathedrale*, 42.
88   Fritz Kohlmann to Heinz Endres, February 13, 1964.
89   Agatha Buslei-Wuppermann, "Hans Schwippert als Architekt: Seine Pläne zur Umgestaltung der St. Hedwigs-Kathedrale in Berlin," *Das Münster* 67, no. 2 (2014), 117–22, here 120.
90   Schwippert to Endres and Blümel, "Notizen zur Ausstattung."

in grey, green, and reflective silver-yellow, they will create a graphic curtain like a mesh."[87]

The description evokes the light colors and geometric motif conveyed in Schwippert's initial suggestion from 1961, a suggestion reinforced in numerous sketches from Schwippert's own hand over the years between conception and completion. As correspondence demonstrates, the architects were no less tenacious in retaining responsibility for the design execution than they had been for its conception.

By February 1964, Derix Glasstudio was ready to furnish samples of no fewer than ten variations of each shade of glass. Kohlmann, writing to Endres, argued that the final selection could only be made on site. He instructed Endres to have the on-site glazer, Rabach,

"remove around 9–12 horizontally and vertically adjacent fields from windows that are already installed. We will then insert pieces of sample glass into different areas of the edge glazing, return the windows to their installed locations, and then decide which of the two hues we wish to use additionally for the edge glazing. This is the only way to enable a perfect decision process. I would therefore appreciate a visa to permit the transport of around 10 sample panes."[88]

Endres requested the visa on February 18 and, in an unusual example of logistical efficiency, it was granted to Kohlmann on February 25. It was in this way—and sadly, not as legend has it, in the handbag of a willing female companion[89]—that the glass was brought to the site. The painstaking process of filling sample glass into the steel frames was executed over the course of Kohlmann's multi-day site visit. Indeed, the architect played a greatly expanded role as "connective figure."[90]

As careful and complex a process as it had been to select and procure the stained-glass panes, the window frames into which they were inserted could hardly have been more straightforward: the portion of the frame facing outwards was made of welded steel T-sections, into which

8.26 Study for stained glass window, undated

**8.27 Stained glass windows
in the vestibule, with trough for
condensation, 2014**

steel glass stops were caulked from the inside. Tabs at the meeting
of each panel permitted the removal of the glass stops as needed. **[8.28]**
Finesse was a matter of careful assembly: the slight shift in plane
from the surface of the T-section to the glass stops produced a reveal;
the alignment of the steel tabs created a pinwheel pattern. This capacity
to make architecture from the careful modulation of minimal difference
was nowhere more apparent, however, than in the wall surfaces. The highly
differentiated, meticulously specified plasterwork was realized using common components treated with particular precision and skill. The wall
plaster represents Schwippert at his most ingenious; but given the
building's uncertain future fate, it was also the most fragile part of the
architectural effect, the one most easily destroyed.

In his description of the building, Heinz Endres dedicated several
paragraphs to the interior plaster and its effects. He wrote:
"Upon observing the simplified classical space, we become aware
that the inside wall of the cylindrical walls bears a particularly
interesting finish plaster. To ensure an appropriate surface effect,
the remains of the pilasters behind each of the twelve columns
were removed. The checkerboard-like plaster texture applied to the
exterior walls was installed by hand and proves to be a good solution
for both scale and craftsmanship. It also improves the acoustics.
The window embrasures were treated with a smooth plaster.
The tonality of the ring beam, which is visible behind the architrave
and supports the ribbed dome, approximates the wall surface.
We note a desired connection among wall, marble floor, and dome
interior, created through coloration and structure. The fine,
quadratic structure of the wall plaster is echoed in the acoustic panels
inserted between the dome's ribs. The domes' subdivision into segments finds its correspondence in the radially patterned marble floor.
Standing in front of the interior wall are the twelve paired
columns and architrave, with simplified profile, in light plaster.
In the search for the best way to clad the columns, a prefabricated

91   Endres, *Die St. Hedwigs-Kathedrale*, 36–39.
92   Schwippert, "Bericht," 2.
93   Schwippert, "Bericht."
94   Theodor Blümel, "Für die Besprechung
am 23. und 24.5.1961 bei Herrn Prof. Schwippert,
Düsseldorf," May 20, 1961. Archive,
St. Hedwigs-Kathedrale, Berlin.

plaster shell was chosen. Since the remaining masonry column cores were partially in front of the architrave, their complete diameter could only be restored through addition and the fabrication of the plaster shells already mentioned. [...]

The columns and the architrave they support were colored titanium white. A narrow encircling profile on the cornice was gilded. The coloration expresses clearly the static function of each building element. Above the cylindrical wall sits the ring beam, upon which the ribbed dome rises. All three elements are colored grey-green. The column group and the architrave with the dome's ringed base, all luminous white, contrast. The decorative significance of the columnar elements is obvious; the columns do not pretend to carry the dome."[91]

This painstaking render evolved over several months, using on-site samples reviewed during meetings at which all participants, from the highest ranking to the most hands-on, were assembled on site in East Berlin, no mean feat given the challenges of procuring entry permission for those from West Germany and West Berlin, for whom different rules and border crossings applied. In his eight-page recapitulation of the progress on site from 1960 to November 1961, Schwippert referenced a site meeting in January 1961 at which the decision to mock-up various plaster treatments on site was made by a smaller group of clerics involved at the church on a daily basis, among them Endres, Blümel, and Kohlmann, visiting from Düsseldorf.[92] Schwippert explained the architectural thinking behind the plastering:

"It had become clear that, as we had long argued, the building's nobility demands this wall treatment, appropriate in terms of both scale and material value, and in harmony with floor, columns, and ceiling. All wall surface treatments attempted until then at the clients' behest, regardless of type or color, were seen to be inadequate and inappropriate with regard to their combinatory potential."[93]

Half a year later, in early June, the decision-makers re-assembled: Cardinal Döpfner from West Berlin, Endres and Weber from the church, Blümel, Kohlmann, and Schwippert, as well as the artist Fritz Kühn, who had already been commissioned to design and fabricate the balustrade between upper and lower churches. A week earlier, Blümel had visited Schwippert's Düsseldorf office to discuss progress on site. Part of his meeting agenda had been the plaster samples, which he had supervised and described as having a "true" plasterer's surface texture.[94] The scene was set for the decision that Schwippert favored. Much of what Endres would later describe in his book is reflected in Schwippert's meeting notes:

"The space's wall is to be covered with the plaster surface treatment represented in the sample with the small format. To achieve the greatest surface effect, the pilasters behind the columns will

8.28 Detail of steel glass stop tabs, stained glass windows, 2014

be removed. Because the window embrasures will have smooth plaster because of their surface area, the smooth plaster fascia in the wall must be appropriately dimensioned. At the top, the plaster texture meets the ceiling directly; at the bottom, it will transition to a smooth strip still to be dimensioned. The plaster will be white. [...] The columns will be extremely smoothly plastered (stucco) and finished with wax. They will remain pure white. [...] The upper architrave will be pure white, perhaps with a narrow gold band."[95] This decision must have been a comparative relief to Blümel, leaving him only to ensure the procurement of the plaster and add-ins, which seems from later correspondence to have been quite straightforward, and to solicit acceptable bids from the trade. A letter from Schwippert shows that Blümel did his work well, soliciting estimates that compared in situ stucco with applied gypsum pre-casts for both walls and columns. For the walls, the cost of prefabricated panels was more than one and one-half times the cost of in situ stucco: this argument resolved Schwippert's concern that the prefabricated elements could result in "significant lack of vitality" in the finished surface.[96] For the columns, the prefabricated column cladding was the only practicable option, since the distance between the columns and wall was too narrow to run a jig or plaster comb. This, too, was a good practical argument for the smooth finish, which Schwippert preferred. At the bottom of the letter was a handwritten note from Kohlmann to Blümel, asking that Blümel send along sketches for the junctures between the walls and adjacent planes, most of which were resolved in deep reveals (*Schattenfuge*) simply and without fanfare.

The synergy between practical concerns and design preference produced a situation in which traditional construction methods and materials were the means of a radically modernist take on a fundamentally classical building. This recalls the ideas expressed by Schwippert's contemporary Rudolf Steinbach at the Darmstädter Gespräch of 1951:

"Whoever enters [...] finds himself face to face with a wall that is a *pure plane*, a solid masonry wall. [...] The wall seems to vibrate on account of the workmanship of the plaster, which contains irregularities. Immediately, for us, we sense the entire world as it is present, but also as it might entirely be imagined."[97]

With the simplest means, textured plasterwork, Schwippert's renovation celebrated an traditional architectural quality that retained its fascination within modernist contexts: the "pure plane."

Because of its implicit immediacy, the "pure plane" was a natural locus of commonality not only for the architect and the construction worker, but also for the architecture and its audience. Following consecration, the building's early reception in international press coverage attests to the appeal of the modest, stringent reconstruction. Articles describing the struggle to rebuild the church and the efforts to resume its use as a cathedral appeared in no fewer than four languages. The texts focused on aspects as varied as liturgical meaning, geopolitical symbolism, architecture, and popular appeal. Dieter Hildebrandt, writing in the *Frankfurter Allgemeine*, praised the allegiance among these various aspects:

"Even at the Heinrich-Heine-Straße border crossing, the church bells can be heard. The crowd of West Germans who want to go to East Berlin is particularly large this morning. It is All Saints' Day; many have come to Berlin for a long weekend to see family. The Berlin event of All Saints' Day 1963, the altar consecration of St. Hedwig's Cathedral in East Berlin, is already making itself known in the barracks: three clerics with suitcases marked in block letters with the airport name 'Rome' are lined up for a day pass. However, one hour later they are sitting, now in their red garments, on a bench in the broad rotunda of the reconstruction church, in a space characterized by sobriety and clarity, by nearly Protestant modesty (if such characterizations can still hold). The colors are grey-white in this church rotunda, the twelve pairs of columns rise in their whiteness to the dome, which in turn consists of 84 steel ribs. Dark grey marble comprises the floor; in the center of the church, a stair leads

95   Schwippert, "Bericht," 3.
96   Hans Schwippert to Dean of the Cathedral Weber, November 17, 1961. Archive, St. Hedwigs-Kathedrale, Berlin.
97   Otto Bartning, ed., *Mensch und Raum: Das Darmstädter Gespräch 1951* (Darmstadt: Neue Darmstädter Verlagsanstalt, 1951), 250.

98   Dieter Hildebrandt, "Damals wie heute ein kirchenpolitischer Akt," *Frankfurter Allgemeine* (November 1, 1963).
99   Endres, *Die St. Hedwigs-Kathedrale*, 44.

to the lower church from which the altar, again in grey marble, rises into the upper space. [...] There are moments on this Friday morning in 1963 when the past and the present seem to become identical. [...] Is this not the meeting at this moment of two reconciliatory tendencies in church history: then, Prussia's first step away from the totalitarian implementation of Reformation principles; today, the conciliatory and insightful words of Pope Paul to the Council to which Archbishop Bengsch will return after the consecration? 'The House will remain,' sings the congregation with the clergy. The first mass is celebrated at the newly consecrated altar and in prayer, even those who have only a day pass think deeply about God."[98]

Hildebrandt's article reflects familiar tropes that aligned architectural modesty with community strength and political reconciliation. It also suggests that, with architecture as symbol and vehicle, two significant liberalizing moments in German religious history had been evoked and associated. As a shared, tangible artifact, the cathedral represented collaborative potential, which carried significant weight in a physically divided city increasingly understood as a geopolitical flashpoint.

Writing around the same time, Endres averred that the cathedral embodied, rather than merely symbolized, collaboration. At the end of his short book, he acknowledged the effort that had been invested in reconstruction and speculated on what it meant. "Particular recognition should also go to the many craftsmen who served the project loyally and reliably," he wrote. "However, the devout of the entire Bishopric, who always contributed their willing self-sacrifice to the cathedral, have the right to claim: this is *our* St. Hedwig's Church."[99] For Schwippert, the production of a work that could elicit loyalty and reconcile political division was the greatest possible achievement.

CONSTRUCTION DRAWINGS

Once during the spring of my return to New York after a six years' absence, I biked across Central Park to visit my parents. At Fifth Avenue I hit a nail and my front tire went flat. I bought a vulcanization kit in a Second Avenue bike store, borrowed a wrench to remove the wheel, and went upstairs. My father watched silently as I filled the kitchen sink, submerged the inner tube to find the puncture, then sanded it and applied the rubber patch. "How," he asked, "did you learn to do that?" It was a question he hadn't asked of the projects I'd produced in architecture school, the articles I'd published as editor for a quarterly in Berlin, or the buildings I'd helped to realize. My intellectual life never gave him pause; patching an inner tube was different.

I was taught early that physical labor meant hardship. My parents, raised during the Depression in immigrant families, eschewed it. My mother made two exceptions in her general aversion to labor: she kept a spotless home and she loved to garden on the weekends. Like her father, admired for his Bronx victory garden, she tended her plants with the special ambition Germans call *Ehrgeiz*, a compound built on the words for honor and parsimony. My father did little in the garden except to kill weeds on the brick patio each spring by applying gasoline with a paint roller while we cowered indoors. He preferred sport fishing, bluefish, which we rarely ate. As my parents enjoyed them, neither gardening nor fishing count as manual labor. Practiced by choice at substantial cost, what could be a greater luxury than labor become leisure?

My parents' deep respect for craft was no contradiction. My mother named me for her maiden aunt Lydia, seamstress and milliner. Magical thinking aside, however, dexterity and manual skill cannot be inherited. No one taught me to darn, patch, reweave, tat, or block, and I never asked to be. The craft revival of the 1970s notwithstanding, traditional women's work had little appeal to a girl growing up in the era of bra-burning. That did not diminish the appeal of my mother's stories about Lydia's uncanny ability to reblock the same hat each season to near-unrecognizability, remaining at the height of fashion solely through her own efforts. My mother stayed at the height of fashion by purchasing selectively. She certainly had an eye. After her death, her immaculate Geoffrey Beene, Seymour Fox, Yves Saint Laurent, and Koos van den Akker were acquisitioned by a museum. I inherited her chic no more than I inherited Lydia's way with felt. My relationship to fashion came instead through boys who befriended me in clubs, each devoted to constructing clothes for imagined women: Daniel Eltinge's hand-hemmed black taffeta hobble skirts; or David Young's communion dress, a white sateen sheath with a huge lace ruff. The drag queen who runwayed it at the club where I worked coat check made him sew her in. She wanted as tight as it would go. I still have that dress, far too narrow for my female hips.

Two years after the communion dress debuted, I took my first college architecture course.

From that first course onwards, we were offered countless versions of architecture's well-documented and fraught relationship with manual labor. That relationship is central to the origin stories architecture has proliferated from its earliest written records. Despite variations, the stories agree: once we outgrew the found spaces of caves or groves, a first act of architecture occurred. There is disagreement about its means, whether felled and intercut branches, woven and knotted grasses, or compacted and burnished earth. But there is even greater uncertainty about whether architecture happened first in the mind's eye or in the hand. Someone had to imagine it. Someone had to make it. Which is act is architecture?

And yet no one in the 1980s, during my studies or after, foresaw what was about to happen: that digital technology would subsume elaborating and fabricating anyway. Instead, we indulged an opposition framed a century earlier. Some of my professors advocated for abstraction, insisting that architecture worked linguistically. Its purpose was to communicate meaning through a semiotic system inherent to forms and their syntax. The materials from which those forms were made and the methods used were footnotes. Others insisted that architecture was especially real, distinguished by its relationship with the physical world. It embodied the haptic, the innately sensual, the genuine. Class consciousness was stood on its head: the advocates for semiotic theory thought of themselves as populists, enamored of billboards and highway truck stops, while the appropriators of phenomenology, the advocates of craft and labor, acted the part of the mystics and mandarins, speaking in inscrutable poetics. This was a strange, solipsistic debate, so easy to puncture at three decades' remove. I learned elsewhere how architecture was made.

284

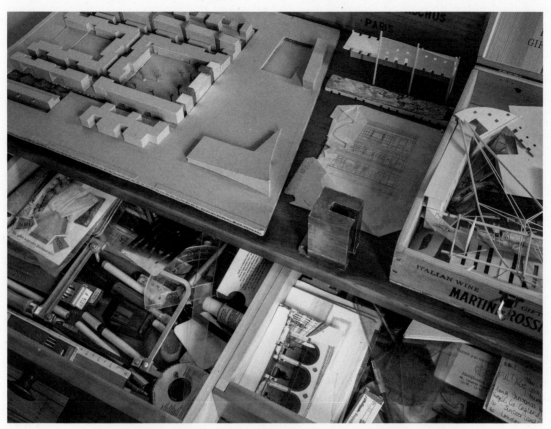

Drafting supplies, models, and photographs, 2013

The distinction between labor and craft is obvious to the eye, incremental for the hand. In junior high school we were taken to a recreated eighteenth-century town, where we helped card wool and cooper barrels. With yarn I spun myself, I handloomed a short piece of fabric, hopelessly hourglassed. Its imprecision was a harbinger, at least in retrospect. It is hard to turn an idea into a real thing, even a simple thing, of any worth.

Most professions delegate their lesser-skilled tasks. Architects instead delegate tasks requiring skill in building that exceeds their own. Although fabrication lies outside the remit of most architects, they are called upon to envision and describe construction processes of which they themselves have never been capable. I did not learn this in school. It is, in a certain sense, unteachable in an academic context. When I, as a professor of architecture, had to try, I reverted to a work-around. I sent my students to draw the framing in their attics and the stonework in their basements, to knock on horsehair-reinforced plaster and lathe, then to try to put onto paper what they thought they'd seen. They backed into their first construction drawings. To manage the other way around, from drawing to assembly, is much more elusive.

I began to grasp the construction drawing in the mid-90s when I was hired to work on the renovation of an East Berlin planetarium. I worked for a gifted Northern Italian architect, Renza Pitton, who had grown up in a family of furniture makers. From the time she was sixteen, she had worked in the family shop as draftsman. Were she to look up from her drawings, she would have seen things being fabricated all around her.

Because of that, she knew how to ensure that the built thing was no less perfect than the imagined. Of course that required expertise. More importantly, it demanded the strategy and insight derived from comprehensive knowledge of how people who make things think. The results were remarkable. We had designed a large pivot window with double-paned glass—a massive thing—to be milled from solid, aged wood. She insisted on the narrowest possible molding to hold the glass in place. "Draw it at seventeen millimeters," she directed, anticipating that the cabinetmaker would balk at restraining so much glass behind such a flimsy dimension. Because she knew precisely what was possible, she could gauge her bargaining power perfectly. "Twenty-five millimeters," insisted the *Tischler* at the meeting to review the drawings. He sat at our office

286

table in the periwinkle blue overall that all German tradesmen wear, the originary blue collar; promptly at ten o'clock he removed a paper-packaged bread and butter from his overall pocket and began to eat, his *Brotzeit*, the traditional German workman's mid-morning meal. But only shortly after he crammed the used bread-and-butter paper back into his overall, a compromise was found: twenty-one millimeters for the molding. Twenty-one matched perfectly the details of the adjacent original nineteenth-century window frames. It was what she had intended from the start.

She demanded that details be drawn at life-size. Misconceptions and mistakes appeared on paper, where they were corrected, rather than on site, where it was too late. The principles she applied were logical, not academic: Draw from the bottom up to mimic the way gravity will act upon the elements you're depicting. Draw elements in order of their assembly. Imagine what would be put in place first, what would happen thereafter as a laborer builds. Draw each component as a discrete, closed figure, especially where elements touch. The tiny gap between the lines defining each component means that you never forget: everything we make in the world is assembled from smaller pieces. Know where components are fastened to one another but also know the direction from which a nail or screw is driven. If there is no place in the drawing for a hammer to swing or a screwdriver to twist, then no one will be able to build what you draw.

Learning to exercise these principles took many unhappy months. What training such as this yields, though, is the capacity to see a time machine in every construction drawing, one that tracks from a desired outcome to its genesis in material and know-how.

In the process of making a building, authorship passes through many hands. It includes the more general—products specified, details mandated, building codes maintained—as well as the singular and the particular—the worker in the field, the worker at a desk, the inhabitant of what results from their labors. Historically, however, architects have preferred to tell a more glorified story about their practice, one indulged by architectural history. This story insists on the heroic individual, whether virtuoso designer or unnamed master craftsman. It is an inherently classist story, dismissive of "unskilled" labor or standardized components.

In this version of the story, intention is valued above realization. The drawings used to envision a design—the rendered views, the measured

Dollhouse as literal cross-section, 2013

288

Women's work as fabrication:
handmade sweaters, blouses, blankets, 2013

orthographic, the persuasive sketch addressed to a client—are the ones that are cared for in libraries, archives, and museums. But the purposeful construction document, the annotated take-off, the catalogue cut sheet, the down-and-dirty on-site scribble? These exist for the lowly purpose of communication between white and blue collared. They bridge the gap between what is imagined and what is made; to undervalue them is to misunderstand what is at stake. Construction drawings vanish over time. No one bothers with them once their work is done.

Construction drawings are, moreover, inherently unlike other architectural drawings. Perspectives, plans, cross-sections, and frontal elevations all have referents in a layperson's life: we can recognize the spaces we inhabit in these drawings. We have all navigated cities using a map or looked into the rooms of a dollhouse whose facade has been lopped off. Because they have no such corollaries, construction details and drawings are much harder to enter. They are instructions for use. They negotiate the juncture among different trades, each of which works with a different margin of error. They suggest a finished state while they describe all the steps required to get there. In the absence of special training, they are illegible. Their authority to coordinate labor and assemble materials should command respect anyway.

As an architectural historian who more rarely practices as an architect, I project my own experience with construction drawings onto ones completed by the architects I study. This act of speculative empathy allows me to see through each drawing. I read the degree of trust transferred to the workers on site, the affection for specific materials or products, the dedication to ensuring precise execution of what is on the paper. Each architect has a tendency, and each draftsman who works within his office learns to follow his example. Both, in the late 1940s and '50s, were likely men. The dearth of construction drawings from the period I study increases exponentially if I search for drawings made for the job site by women.

Hans Schwippert and his office produced construction drawings that offer leeway; or so it seems from the few that survived as yellowed diazo prints in the looseleaf binders archived at St. Hedwig's Cathedral in Berlin. The drawings presume that workers on site make good decisions. Details note finish dimensions and overall geometries but give few indications of

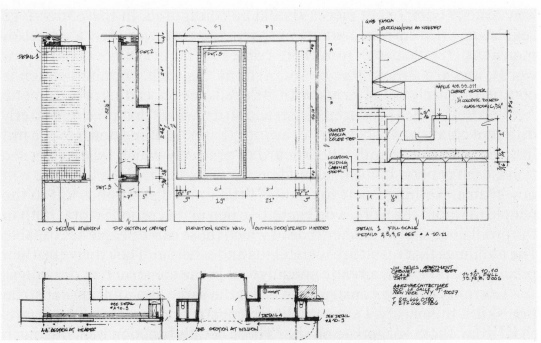

Cabinetry construction drawing, JS Apartment, New York 2005

Self-portrait, Lurie House under construction, 2015

how exactly component pieces should be configured. In these drawings, regulating lines correlate points in space; there are very few absolute dimensions free-floating from their context. The drawings contain few words, and are almost free of annotations. As such, communication is couched in purely visual terms, with little reliance on reading or arithmetic.

Sep Ruf's office produced construction drawings that presume utterly different conditions. These are drawings that determine down to the millimeter how wide to mill a floorboard or precisely which rolled steel sections, each generic in itself, should be combined to make a bespoke window frame. Nothing is left to chance; little or no discretion is left to the people to whom the work is delegated. In lieu of discretion is total faith in the prodigious skill and exactitude of which those same people are capable. The buildings that result are meticulous and ethereal. They thrive on their precision, a precision already unequivocal in the construction drawings.

Learning to draw construction is not the same as acquiring construction skills. In honesty, I am a mediocre construction worker. The details that I draw, those I negotiate on site? Those details function well. But much as I've tried, I lack capacity for the skilled manual labor my drawings demand. Over the past several years I learned how to tape and spackle, to plaster an edge bead, to align and grout tile, to frame a wall (albeit with screws, not framing nails) precisely enough for the tolerances of precision cabinetry. But I am slow, compelled by my errors to undo and redo each step. I feel, each time, as though I am doing penance for my parents' aversion. Despite the reference to craft that my mother embedded in my name, I struggle to approximate what the first generation was able to make. Despite my coveted education, I struggle to equal what the second was able to achieve. I work to outrun the prophecy that haunted my father: from rags to riches to rags in three generations. The manual and the intellectual, the blue collared and the white: the construction drawing, a touchstone between the two.

01   See the eloquent argument made by Tony Judt, *Ill Fares the Land* (New York: Penguin Press, 2010), on the nature of that success and what it has meant progressively to dismantle its structures and mechanisms. What Judt writes about the mission of the emergent social welfare state in the postwar United Kingdom and the implications of its subsequent dismemberment holds true in many ways for continental Europe, too.

02   See Gerhard Besier, "Ökumenische Mission in Nachkriegsdeutschland: Die Berichte von Stewart W. Herman über die Verhältnisse in der evangelischen Kirche 1945/46. 2. Teil," *Kirchliche Zeitgeschichte* 1, no. 2, Theologie und Politik (October 1988), 316–52, here 333.

03   Heike Springhart, "'Dass es eine Hoffnung gibt für Deutschland [...]' Religion und Kirchen im Nachkriegsdeutschland als gesellschaftliche Institutionen der Reeducation," in Hans Braun, Uta Gerhardt, and Everhard Holtmann, eds., *Die lange Stunde null: Gelenkter sozialer Wandel in Westdeutschland nach 1945* (Baden-Baden: Nomos, 2007), 95.

04   American pastor and Office of Strategic Services operative Stewart Herman wrote in a September 1945 report: "The Russian attitude toward the church work seems to be quite free and reasonable, except perhaps in the matter of Christian organizations for the youth, which go beyond catechetical instruction." It is strange that religious instruction was allowed but civil instruction restricted. As quoted in Besier, "Ökumenische Mission," 336.

9.1 Max Taut,
Berlin im Aufbau 1946

Year Zero, Verso

The experiment of rebuilding Germany at the end of World War II had its darker consequences, not least of them unaddressed trauma and ongoing proxy conflicts. But in many regards, it was a remarkable success.[01] Almost miraculously, an entire country was "reeducated," the term applied by the occupying forces, amidst the ruins of a generation-old Fascist lifeworld; within a decade, it was made able to construct an economically thriving, participatory democracy.[02] [9.1] To address this transformation with sufficient nuance would be to launch an entirely new, and probably unresolvable, project at the close of this one. But it would be wrong to end this book without an attempt to connect its narrative to the larger story of its place and era. The ideas posited, the buildings constructed, and the lifestyle celebrated by Hans Schwippert, Sep Ruf, and their cohort existed in reciprocity with the country's projects of civil society, individual ethics, and institutional restructuring. These architects recast the legacy of *Neues Bauen* to comport with the realism and political incrementalism of the new social market economy. Their buildings navigated material conditions of both privation and industrialization. They recalibrated the balance of individual and public realms in philosophical and physical terms. What, then, were the terms of the society in which they operated?

Christian identity, expressed early in Christian Democratic politics, was woven through the social fabric of West Germany in the late 1940s and 1950s. In 1946, 96 percent of all Germans identified as practicing Protestants or Catholics.[03] No other element of society was so widely shared or respected, despite the acknowledged moral failings of both churches under the National Socialist regime. The Allied occupying forces recognized that religious institutions were the only intact structures with which to partner in rebuilding. Even in the Soviet-occupied sector, at least initially and in contravention of anti-religious Communist tenets, the two major confessions enjoyed support.[04] But in the American and British zones, support for both Protestant and Catholic clergy was inscribed in official policy. Through churches and clergy, the occupying forces could distribute aid, track a populace in motion, and begin stabilizing efforts, which included moral reeducation. "Democracy [...] lives from Christianity and alone protects law and liberty. It is the responsibility, therefore, of the church to foster democracy," stated Pastor Martin

BETRACHTUNGEN UND BILDER DES ARCHITEKTEN MAX TAUT

Niemöller at the Treysa Conference of August 1945, convened in a small Hessian town with support from the occupying forces to address the future of the Protestant church.[05] Niemöller's words were repeated to significant effect in a report for the Office of Strategic Services by Stewart W. Herman, who had been pastor at the American Church in Berlin during the 1930s. Churches needed intact spaces for their work, and this need offered a much-desired opportunity for architects who aspired to express in built terms the conditions of a new vision for German society. "The existential had precedence; no one wanted to live in cellars," as Ulrich Conrads explained. By contrast, "churches were comparatively free of purpose, therefore spatial building was only possible in church building."[06] The impulse that Hans Schwippert followed when he transposed Rudolf Schwarz's typologies of liturgical space to the new Bundeshaus attests to this confluence of organized religion, architectural design, and statecraft.

Both Protestant and Catholic churches embraced their role in this realpolitik. A 1949 text by Protestant ethicist Friedrich Karrenberg, to cite one prominent example, cast religious tradition as uniquely and inherently equipped to address the blind spots of political structures:

> "It is clear that an optimistic conception of humankind, as it has been and still is found widely in the doctrines of idealism, liberalism and socialism, leads to entirely different conclusions about what the human is capable of and what he may be entrusted with over time in terms of freedom or compunction, than the conclusions to which a realistic interpretation, such as that based in the Holy Scriptures and the Reformation, must arrive. It is also clear, however, that such a realistic view of humankind is much more circumspect with regard to constructions, much less believing in development, much less dogmatic about systems. In the end, all systems must deal with the same, corruptible humans who tend toward the lapsed."[07]

Religion was clearly more than a delivery system for rebuilding efforts: it was inherently suited to accomplish an ethical balance for which politics had fallen short. Karrenberg was editor and co-author of the *Evangelisches Soziallexikon* (1953/54), a practical Protestant guidebook to problems of everyday life. Organized as a dictionary of terms for reference, it covered activities that ranged from union membership to the domestic sphere. Karrenberg's perspective, shared by the mainstream of early West German political life and the Allies who oversaw it, distanced itself from the belief systems that had guided Weimar politics. Neither proletariat revolution nor top-down social reform could inspire any faith. This shift from political to religio-social emphasis would also affect the way architects defined their roles.

Whether Marxists or more incrementalist reformers, the best-known architects of the interwar avant-garde had aligned their professional efforts with the promise of a strong state, if not with wholesale revolution. The connections between the Bauhaus directorship of the Marxist Hannes Meyer and building culture in the Soviet Union are well documented;[08] but even Ernst May, who was more a reformer than a revolutionary during his time as head of Frankfurt's housing authority, authored the plans for Soviet mining cities in Siberia during the early part of his exile during the National Socialist regime.[09] A state in full control of all means of production, to architects across the political Left, must have seemed a perfect mechanism for transforming everyday life. In this they differed from their contemporaries who would hold sway in West Germany after the War, where a wholesale centralized takeover of the construction industry remained unthinkable despite the horrendous housing shortage. For the postwar architects who defined the discourse, housing was a philosophical and spiritual concern; know-how and logistics, in many cases borrowed from Weimar experimentation, were treated as non-ideological and therefore not central to discourse.

Eclipsed in the writing of architectural history, whether justly or not, the ideas these architects articulated well before the war presaged those they advocated thereafter in a new society founded upon a *Soziale*

05   Besier, "Ökumenische Mission," 320.
06   Ulrich Conrads in conversation with the author, February 3, 2004, Berlin.
07   Friedrich Karrenberg, "Liberales und kollektivistisches Eigentumsverständnis als soziologisches und ethisches Problem (mit Einschluß der heutigen Parteiprogramme)," in *Das Eigentum als Problem evangelischer Sozialethik* (1949), 7–59, here 58, cited in Jörg Hübner, "Protestantische Wirtschaftsethik und Soziale Marktwirtschaft: Verbindungslinien und Zusammenhänge zwischen 1937 und 1954," *Zeitschrift für Theologie und Kirche* 109, no. 2 (June 2012), 235–69, here 262.
08   See, for example, William Richardson, "Architecture, Urban Planning, and Housing During the First Five Year Plans: Hannes Meyer in the USSR, 1930–1936," *Urban Studies* 26, no. 1 (January 2, 1989), 155–63.
09   Thomas Flierl, *Standardstädte: Ernst May in der Sowjetunion 1930–1933. Texte und Dokumente* (Berlin: Suhrkamp, 2012). Also see Bernhard Schulz, "Gescheitert, aber doch gewonnen: Die Protagonisten des Neuen Bauens in der Sowjetunion," *Osteuropa* 66 no. 11/12, Die Ordnung der Dinge: Qualitative Analysen zum Osten Europas (2016), 169–80.

9.2 Advertisement, *What to Do with Germany* by Louis Nizer, 1944

Marktwirtschaft. Within the new Werkbund, reestablished in 1950 under Schwippert's leadership, their beliefs were consolidated in an agenda for architecture and design that could contend with new facts on the ground. Gone was the belief in resolving social need through a central government. The country's strong industrial history, underpinned by domestic coal and iron ore, would give rise again to a manufacturing economy. Architecture and design were well-positioned to help find new outlets for manufacturing capacity, first in buildings and spaces, and then in objects of daily life. Architects designed consumer goods and the contexts that made them desirable: shop windows, aluminum-framed vitrines, trade shows at home and abroad, department stores, showrooms, and ultimately, the average home. Because the social market economy depended upon participation by a new, "reeducated" German citizenry, home and workplace were understood as incubators of robust democracy. "Good form" was meant to provide contentment and quiet joy in both places. So close was the presumed alignment between moral education and economic health, between private ethics and the public exercise of buying power, that commerce in the world of the "little man" transcended mere satisfaction of desire. The label "Made in West Germany" as it was represented in Schwippert's curation for the 1958 Brussels World's Fair was itself tantamount to the country's "return to the peaceful garden of Europe's children."[10]

From the beginning, British, American, and Soviet occupying forces in Germany—more so than French[11]—treated what remained of church infrastructure as an effective partner in stabilizing a population subject

10   *Le Figaro*, as cited in Hans Schwippert, "Notizen zur deutschen Beteiligung an der Weltausstellung Brüssel 1958," undated manuscript, GNM, DKA, NL, Schwippert, 11.
11   Besier, "Ökumenische Mission," 336, 331.

to displacement, trauma, and starvation. Their decisions, codified in policy that led to longer-term American government collaboration with Protestant and Catholic churches in West Germany, were guided by both more and less conventional concerns. Émigré theologians in the United States, such as Paul Tillich, who broadcast in German for Voice of America in the 1940s, advocated strongly for the churches. They, Tillich claimed, could "restore the virtues upon which democratic society is carried."[12] Carl J. Friedrich, another émigré who served as chief advisor to US military governor in Germany General Lucius Clay, argued that the basis for democracy lay not in the Enlightenment but rather in seventeenth-century Protestant theology.[13] Such ideas were welcome at a moment when the United States was inclined towards greater public religiosity: only in 1955 was the phrase "under God" added by law to the US Pledge of Allegiance, with which schoolchildren began their days.[14]

This advocacy was reinforced by the new field of social psychology. Columbia University clinical psychiatrist Richard Brickner's 1943 book *Is Germany Incurable?* popularized a psychoanalytic characterization of German history and national character.[15] The book was widely reviewed in outlets as varied as *Foreign Affairs*, *Bulletin of the History of Medicine*, *The New York Times*, and the popular Canadian magazine *McClean's*. Before the book's publication, Brickner had written shorter articles on the topic, including one that Emil Ludwig clipped and mailed to Franklin D. Roosevelt in 1942.[16] Brickner's "diagnosis" was further circulated in 1945, after he hosted a conference of thirty scientists and scholars to discuss the psychology of the German character.[17] [9.2] Among them was anthropologist Margaret Mead, who wrote the foreword to Brickner's book and would soon embark on work at the RAND corporation to provide the Department of State with psychological portraits of national characters to serve as the basis for foreign policy.[18] Brickner argued that the "psychocultural aggressiveness"[19] of the German nation and its citizenry alike could only be transformed within "clear areas" for democracy. The churches offered precisely such "clear areas." No one seemed to mind that scientific—or pseudoscientific—authority had become an advocate for religion, its old nemesis.[20]

American policy formally integrated church structures into its governance logistics. "Religious institutions are recognized as a significant element in the social structure of Germany," stated the Military Government Regulations issued on September 22, 1948. "The values inherent in the moral and spiritual resources of the German people are recognized as essential to the realization of the program [of Democratization]."[21] Religion allowed Germany to return to international circles even before the country's sovereignty was restored. Stewart Herman, the diplomat and clergyman whose reports on church activity were included in official policy discussion, advocated strongly for the German Evangelical Church to rejoin the World Council of Churches as early as 1945.[22] An operative who reported both to George Kennan and John Foster Dulles, Herman argued that international exchange, and the support it might solicit from other European churches, would strengthen the role played by "the Christian forces in Germany [...which are] probably the strongest single agency for rehabilitation that the bankrupt nation possesses."[23] At a moment in which social, familial, and historic ties were deeply ruptured, the church represented historical continuity, institutional universalism, and for the individual, a locus of meaning and grace.

The American tenet of separation between church and state was satisfied, at least nominally, by distinguishing between 'clerical' and 'secular' roles. While American documents express conviction that the clerical functions would contribute to moral reeducation, the occupying forces did not fund these functions specifically. They instead supported the "secular" presence of religion in daily life through youth and women's groups, charity, schooling, and food distribution. In a 1945 report issued on behalf of the Department of Reconstruction and Inter-Church Aid, Herman affirmed the success of this strategy. He also described the early

12   Springhart, "'Dass es eine Hoffnung gibt'," 913.
13   Paul Betts, *Ruin and Renewal: Civilizing Europe after World War II* (New York: Basic Books, 2020), 155–564.
14   Betts, *Ruin and Renewal*, 135.
15   Brickner, Richard M. *Is Germany Incurable?* Philadelphia: J. B. Lippincott, 1943.
16   Springhart, "'Dass es eine Hoffnung gibt'," 95.
17   "Science: Prescription for Germany," *Time* (Monday, May 14, 1945), http://content .time.com/time/subscriber/article/0,33009 ,792120-1,00.html, accessed March 23, 2021.
18   On Mead's work at RAND, see Pamela M. Lee, *Think Tank Aesthetics: Midcentury Modernism, the Cold War and the Neoliberal Present* (Cambridge, MA: MIT Press, 2020), chapter 2, "Pattern Recognition circa 1947," 87–128.
19   "Science: Prescription."
20   Springhart, "'Dass es eine Hoffnung gibt'," 94.
21   Springhart, "'Dass es eine Hoffnung gibt'," 95.
22   Besier, "Ökumenische Mission," 330.
23   Besier, "Ökumenische Mission," 329.

days of what would become the era's dominant political party, in which religious values could register while clergy, at least on the surface, remained uninvolved:

> "For the first time there seems to be a strong reaction away from German nationalism—as a political faith—toward a sense of international responsibility. There is a new party appearing, especially in Berlin but also in other sections of the country, called the Christian-Democratic Union, which constitutes a deliberate attempt to combine both Catholic and Protestant elements into a political organization. Many ministers are following the development of this party with lively interest and, although most of them abstain from overt participation, they are invariably encouraging their members who become interested in it to transmute their Christian interest into political practice."[24]

The idea of "transmuting" Christian faith into its political corollary was an important one. As Herman explained in his report, "no guidance" should be offered by any individual clergy member "for connecting the moral responsibility of the Christian with his political responsibility as a citizen." Instead, guidance was to come in the form of concerted, coherent guidelines issued by both Protestant and Catholic churches for the country's citizenry, an undertaking that extended far beyond the scope of any one clergy member.

Wordsmith of the term *Soziale Marktwirtschaft* Alfred Müller-Armack, looking back across his career as a statesman, called the particular economic model he helped to establish an *irenische Formel*, a peaceable formula, whose calculus drew in equal measure from economic liberalism, Catholicism, and Protestantism.[25] The formula was predicated on the integration into secular society of ethical tenets that were delineated and propagated by the two Christian confessions and framed so as to suit the needs of each everyday citizen as she or he navigated the new West German lifeworld. The authors of these codes and guidebooks were the same men, Protestant and Catholic, who defined Christian socialism within the Christian Democratic Union: Evangelical politician Joachim Tiburtius, pastor Hans Lutz, and Jesuit economist Oswald von Nell-Breuning, to name only a few.[26] Von Nell-Breuning, author of the first practical Catholic guidebook, served as advisor to the Ministry of Economics (1948–1965) and as chairman of the Council on Housing. Tiburtius led the Deutsches Institut für Wirtschaftsforschung, contributing actively to national economic policy, and was a senator in West Berlin from 1951 to 1963.

The first four volumes of von Nell-Breuning's *Wörterbuch der Politik*, published between 1947 and 1949, provided guidelines concurrent with Catholic belief for navigating the state, social relations, and economic order. Shortly thereafter, between 1951 and 1958, came Dominican economist Eberhard Welty's three-volume *Herders Sozialkatechismus*.[27] Welty set the standard for such guidebooks with his three pragmatic rules: his books' content had to be "correct" rather than open-ended or debatable; comprehensive, omitting none of the questions that might arise in everyday life; and written in language easily understood. In 1954, responding to von Nell-Breuning's and Welty's books, came the *Evangelisches Soziallexikon*, edited by Karrenberg.[28] With these titles—dictionary, lexicon—the books presented themselves as no different from the dictionaries or encyclopedias found in middle-class homes by mid-century. The first two of Welty's volumes were translated into English in 1960 and 1963. The jacket text summarizes both scope and intent:

> "There has long been a need for a work in which the burning problems of modern society, such as marriage, divorce, education, the just wage, the rights to live and to work, are treated with clarity and in the light of Christian moral and religious principles.
>
> The advantages of this book are in its lucid and practical approach and in its question-and-answer form. [...] All questions are prefaced by ample and relevant quotations from the encyclicals and other papal documents, so that the reader is spared the time-consuming

24   Besier, "Ökumenische Mission," 335.
25   Alfred Müller-Armack, "Soziale Irenik" in *Religion und Wirtschaft: Geistesgeschichtliche Hintergründe unserer europäischen Lebensform Wirtschaftspolitik* (Stuttgart: Kohlhammer, 1959), cited in Hübner, "Protestantische Wirtschaftsethik," 235.
26   Hübner, "Protestantische Wirtschaftsethik," 235, 237 n.17, 241ff.
27   Hübner, "Protestantische Wirtschaftsethik," 238.
28   Friedrich Karrenberg, ed. *Evangelisches Soziallexikon*. (Stuttgart: Kreuz, 1954). See also Sabrina Hoppe, " 'The Strength of Weak Ties'—Protestantische Netzwerke in der frühen Bundesrepublik," *Mitteilungen zur Kirchlichen Zeitgeschichte* 9 (2015),165–172, here 168, https://mkiz.ub.uni-muenchen.de/mkiz/article/view/54/47.

effort of looking up references. [...] Father Eberhard Welty OP [...] has here provided an excellent, comprehensive work, which aims at the translation of principles into practice."[29]

These books did not avoid uncomfortable questions but they also did not offer pat answers. The goal was not to offer directives for unthinking execution. Especially in a German context, there was much at stake in the appropriate balance between individual judgment and consensus through social cohesion, as there was between independent entrepreneurship and the role of government intervention to ensure the survival of small businesses. Equally significant were the inclusion of workers in equitable managerial policies, the ascendancy of home ownership, and a framework that would never allow market profit-taking to mislead society into accepting useless nonsense meant for mindless consumers.[30] None of these objectives could be guaranteed without a thoughtful, adjudicating populace. Karrenberg's writing in particular considered the appropriate scale at which society should be organized, neither large and anonymous nor individuated and atomized. Just as Catholic and Protestant belief guided federal and state policies, individual ethical action should likewise be cultivated in daily life. Consider the entry in the *Evangelisches Soziallexikon* for "market economy": "If people do not allow themselves to be guided by basic moral principles, then that which one expects of a market economy cannot come into existence."[31] The essential fallibility of the individual, a core tenet in Christian faith, could be countered by these lexicons, dictionaries, and encyclopedias. Both Marxism and Fascism, according to Karrenberg, exploited this fallibility by promising the apotheosis of a particular idealized type of human being. Christian democracy, made up of individuals exercising "basic moral principles," could instead consistently self-correct. Karrenberg's premise that "all systems must deal with the same, corruptible humans who tends towards the wrongful,"[32] meant that the success of the Bundesrepublik relied upon the "deep interpenetration of liberal orientation in the economy and social reform of the citizenry as foreseen in religious praxis and theology."[33]

Hans Schwippert, Rudolf Schwarz, Sep Ruf, Alfons Leitl, and Otto Bartning were all church builders and religious men, each committed to his faith. But the importance of religion for these architects and their profession exceeds questions of their clientele or their personal faith, practice, and philosophy. The equilibrium between private and public life, between scales of intimacy and those of quorum, between personal ownership and common use was meant to be held in the spaces of architecture and translated through the semantics of objects. Moral education was to be inscribed in home, workplace, and community. It suffused all aspects of West German society in the decade after capitulation. Understood in this context, the emphasis on lifestyle and product, on spatial transparency and material modesty framed by Schwippert for the West German pavilion of 1958, for example, had spiritual and philosophical dimensions.

There are many similarities between West German modern architecture and its Weimar antecedents: white walls, flowing spaces, glazed expanses, flat roofs, the other hallmarks of *Neues Bauen*. The formal differences are nuanced, although the values and aspirations they embodied diverged more starkly. As the photographic juxtaposition in *Baukunst und Werkform* made clear (see image 4.4), two contemporaneous works by Walter Gropius and Rudolf Schwarz shared formal characteristics even as the two architects' stances diverged. The success of a strategy that repressed nuance in the interest of presenting a unified modernist style, epitomized by the redrawing of Mies van der Rohe's floorplans for Hitchcock and Johnson's 1932 *International Style* exhibition at the Museum of Modern Art,[34] exacerbated the tendency to repress difference. An early tactic in the effort to configure a coherent modern architecture at an international scale, this tendency became a blind spot only much later addressed by historiography.

29   Eberhard Welty, *A Handbook of Christian Social Ethics* (New York: Herder and Herder, 1960), cover overleaf.
30   Hübner, "Protestantische Wirtschaftsethik," 247–48 and 265.
31   E. Schuster, "Marktwirtschaft" in *Evangelisches Soziallexikon*, 696, cited in Hübner, "Protestantische Wirtschaftsethik," 244.
32   Karrenberg, "Liberales und kollektivistisches Eigentumsverständnis" in *Das Eigentum* 7–59, 58, cited in Hübner, "Protestantische Wirtschaftsethik," 261.
33   Hübner, "Protestantische Wirtschaftsethik," 257.
34   Barry Bergdoll, "The Nature of Mies's Space," in Terence Riley et al., *Mies in Berlin* (New York: Museum of Modern Art, 2001), 67, 374 n.1.

Just as formal nuance was erased, the better-known narrative of the interwar German avant-garde eclipsed important intellectual and theoretical distinctions. Two instances of particular note are Bartning's schemes for progressive arts education and Schwarz's theories of technology. Both Bartning and Schwarz were closely associated with the interwar avant-garde: Bartning with the architecture collective Der Ring and the Arbeitsrat für Kunst; Schwarz with Mies van der Rohe and Romano Guardini. But the fact that even now neither Bartning's nor Schwarz's contributions are widely known indicates how fully the story of modern architecture remains dominated by Bauhaus-dictated historiography.

After forcing the Bauhaus to leave in 1925, the city of Weimar recruited Bartning to establish a new art and architecture school. Bartning's Staatliche Bauhochschule survived only four years. The school, which architectural historian Julius Posner called the "other Bauhaus,"[35] was also designed to offer an alternative to traditional arts education. Its curriculum was organized in three successive phases, beginning in workshops that taught basic fabrication skills, in many ways comparable to the Bauhaus foundation year and workshop structure. Unlike the Bauhaus, however, the Staatliche Bauhochschule culminated in a phase of what Bartning called higher-level schooling ("höhere Ausbildung"). Lectures, readings, and seminars during the students' final year would prompt "shared exchange in auditoria and laboratories between artists and architects."[36] This culminating intellectual exchange, which was distinct from the kinds of practical interactions the students would have shared in the workshops, reinstated what Gropius's Bauhaus program systematically expunged: the teaching of history, law, mathematics, and professional skills. Gropius claimed that eliminating traditional, humanist subjects would destroy the "class-dividing assumptions that intend to erect a wall of condescension between craftsmen and artists."[37] Bartning's proposals for the Bauhochschule made no reference to socioeconomic class. But his omission was not merely a strategy to appease Weimar's conservative government. It expressed a long-held conviction that knowledge that is derived from training hand and eye, which Gropius's Bauhaus curriculum intended to celebrate, should be counterbalanced by knowledge that is earned by training the intellect. In 1918–19, as colleagues in the Arbeitsrat für Kunst, Gropius and Bartning had written the speculative curriculum to which they both referred in establishing their respective schools. That curriculum included the disciplines that, unlike Gropius, Bartning, the primary author of the Arbeitsrat proposal, chose not to eliminate: history, law, economics, and of course, architecture. Intellectual work, Bartning believed, "crowned" the years in the workshop and made the "master." In 1953, this fundamental disagreement dating to the 1910s would resurface in the Bauhaus Debate.

Modernist rhetoric was often quite literal in the way it conceived technology: as engineering capacity and as new materials. Rudolf Schwarz's *Wegweisung der Technik*, published in 1928, attempted a much more expansive definition.[38] It is unlike any other work of its moment. A collaboration with the photographer Alfred Renger-Patzsch, the publication is both austerely beautiful and unmistakably declarative in its appearance. Its typeface, designed and set by Ernst Birkner, a faculty member at the Aachen art school Schwarz directed, is tightly kerned, boldface and sans serif. Set in justified blocks, the lines are a challenge to read. Schwarz's writing, full of invented compound words, is no less of a challenge to follow. Renger-Patzsch's photos, one to a page, end the book, preceded in overleaf by a key Schwarz wrote. This key lists the photos' subjects, often difficult to decipher, and the concepts each was meant to communicate. More than illustrations, according to Schwarz, these photos were "*variatio* on the same theme."[39] Interpaginated views of tightly-cropped plant life, architectural close-ups and large-scale machinery reiterated Schwarz's assertion: that technology was a force that clothed itself in forms. But technology also gave rise to those forms, Schwarz argued dialectically, according to principles that presented "astonishing similarities between natural-organic and technical-mechanical examples."[40] As readers have

35   Otto Bartning et al., *Das andere Bauhaus: Otto Bartning und die Staatliche Bauhochschule Weimar 1926–1930* (Berlin: Bauhaus-Archiv, 1996), 7.
36   Bartning, *Das andere Bauhaus*, 18.
37   Bartning, *Das andere Bauhaus*, 19.
38   Rudolf Schwarz, *Wegweisung der Technik*: Part 1 (Potsdam: Müller & Kiepenheuer, 1928).
39   Wolfgang Pehnt, "Kalte Hochglut: Entstehung und Botschaft des Buches 'Wegweisung der Technik'," in Maria Schwarz and Ann and Jürge Wilde, eds. *Rudolf Schwarz: Wegweisung der Technik* (Cologne: Walther König, 2008), i–xi, here viii.

73
GOTISCHE FENSTERREIHEN AN DER INNENFRONT DES
HOLSTENTORES, LÜBECK.
Serie als reines Kunstprinzip, äußerster Gegensatz
zum ökonomischen Prinzip.
Steigerung des Einzelbogens durch Reihung zu einer
höheren künstlerischen Wirklichkeit: Reihe ist mehr
als Zusammenzählung von Einzelnem.

74
SÄULENVORHALLE DES ALTEN MUSEUMS, BERLIN.
ARCHITEKT: SCHINKEL.
Mehrfach übereinandergeschaltete Seriensysteme
Kannelierungen der Einzelsäulen und Reihung der
Säulen.
Übereinanderschaltung des technischen und des
formalen Serienprinzips in der gleichen Form.
Höchste Möglichkeit des Prinzips:
Mehrfach zu sein und doch edel;
aus gleichen Gliedern einen einmaligen
Sinn aufzubauen.

60   61

9.3 Plant structures as morphological referent, Rudolf Schwarz, *Wegweisung der Technik*, 1928

remarked since the text first appeared, Schwarz drew heavily upon philosophical texts of its moment: Oswald Spengler and Friedrich Dessauer on technology, Ferdinand Tönnies on social relations, Max Scheler on phenomenology.[41] Or, as architect Hans Bernoulli complained in a 1928 review for *Das Werk: Architektur und Kunst*, "the text is a playground for fashionable intellectual words [...] from the *Gehäuse* of Heidelberg philosopher Karl Jaspers to the impressions left by Max Scheler or Ludwig Klages, with hardly a component of current jargon missing."[42] **[9.3]**

Playground or no, Schwarz's concerns are utterly different from the more practical and instrumental approaches typical in those architectural texts associated with the *Neues Bauen*, which argue that new materials and calculation methods inexorably result in modern architecture. In the same magazine issue, Bernoulli highly praised one such book, by Julius Vischer and Ludwig Hilberseimer, on the transformative formal powers of reinforced concrete.[43] The idea of technology as stylistic helpmate to architecture was certainly easier to conceive and more immediately useful than Schwarz's abstract thoughts. In Schwarz's account, however, technology is not a means to an end, a determinant of architectural style; it is a force that clothes itself in form in order to be apprehended. The relationship between technology and form is subject to change:

"When, for the first time around the mid-nineteenth century, technical forms and methods were applied with a certain pride, it was not much different than as if the Gothic imagination had slumbered two hundred years and again come to life. For one, the understanding of 'material' appeared to be the same: one once again saw material as threaded with a linear system of forces, once again collected those lines in a work of sinews and eliminated the remaining mass as valueless. [...This understanding] seems directly carried forward in the forming of iron bars to iron profiles or rail sections, and the new regulating work of spider-web-fine bars gave glass palaces and bridges their scaffolding and form. [...] But something new has entered: the increasing tension of form is freeing itself to become perfect movement. At first slow and clumsy, these 'machines' continue to move on their own, in forms of embryonic ugliness. [...] The purpose concealed in the whole effect [...] is achieved and shows itself; a new form of existence is archived. Volume, subjected to immeasurable stress, condenses and compresses. [...] The cage of bars disappears in favor of a fully mural construction [...] all this indicates the tendency of the technical towards bodily existence. If one follows the formal development of a technical construct from its

40   Hans Bernoulli, "Philosophische Bemühungen: Rudolf Schwarz, Wegweisung der Technik," *Das Werk: Architektur und Kunst* 15, no. 12 (1928), 394.
41   Panos Mantziaras, "Perspectives of Technology: Rudolf Schwarz on the Artifice and Its Reproducability," *Thresholds* no. 24, Reproduction and Production (Spring 2002), 6–10.
42   Bernoulli, "Philosophische Bemühungen," 394.
43   Hans Bernoulli, "Die Gesetze des Materials: Julius Vischer und Ludwig Hilberseimer: Beton," *Das Werk: Architektur und Kunst* 15, no. 12 (1928), 394–95.

invention to its new form, plane and volume begin to be more important than the thin-lined tensile network. Material comes to be seen less as a bearer of a system of force lines (which of course was largely a *conceptual crutch* not grounded in the material, in other words, it was merely the result of *Weltanschauung*) and instead, as mass and 'resistant volume.'"[44]

Technology not only acts upon matter; it is revealed through matter, with increasing articulateness. Through its "force and greatness,"[45] it can transform human capacity and human perception. Comparable to the divine and the natural, the technical is simply the newest force to make itself known to mankind, and the human experience is triangulated through interaction with all three. The human desire to make form is a way to contend with these incommensurable forces. And yet it can never achieve their "heroic" scale, which is left to God. Like the natural and the divine, technology inspires man to edge towards the heroic, regardless of its impossibility. Although incommensurate with these forces, humankind is compelled to engage with them and, in the process, continues to strive ahead:

> "The human being is not made for the one or the other [...]: nature and spirit. Humankind's situation in nature was always endangered, because this nature is a dark thing, its progress [...] proceeding in abstract and consequently incommensurate measure, loveless and violent. By contrast, the human being is bound to concrete measurement; if he approaches its limits, he is endangering himself. [...] Human form resists simultaneously nature's tendency toward force and equilibration, and spirit's tendency toward insight, illumination, and eternity. Human measure is fluid in its image."[46]

The heroic capacity of technology, in a narrower sense, was often cited as an inspiration for *Neues Bauen*: Robert Maillart's bridges, Eugène Freyssinet's shell structures. **[9.4]** Its scale and form provided precedents even before architecture had caught up with engineering. Schwarz advocated something quite different, however. To his eyes, engineering forms captured technology in a merely provisional way. Segmented, crudely geometric, divisible into components: the technological forms delivered by engineering, far from being aspirations, were for Schwarz "forms of embryonic ugliness."[47]

In contrast to much modernist rhetoric, Schwarz's version of technology is not a means by which either to reform social ills or to effect revolution. It is an aspiration, like the divine or the natural: measureless and embodied through progress and noble failure. Only an ideal architectural response—"mural" and "corporeal" in Schwarz's words, a "resistant volume"—could tame technology, internalize it in smooth planes and clear volumes, if only provisionally. These formal affinities, and more importantly, this fascination with abstract rather than instrumental concepts, was fully evident at the 1951 Darmstädter Gespräch. It was a difficult way of thinking and, ultimately, a vision no more widely adopted in the 1940s and 1950s than it had been in the 1920s. Schwippert, Schwarz's acolyte and friend, was remarkable in his ability to accommodate this expansive scale of thought along with more pragmatic approaches. On the one hand, his efforts on behalf of the postwar German Werkbund leveraged the potentials of the social market economy, providing design goods that spurred economic growth while also conveying the core values of workmanship, quality, and modernity. On the other hand, in his architectural work, Schwippert cultivated ideals and practices affiliated with those of Schwarz.

Throughout its discussion of labor, material production, authorship, and public debate, this book skirts another, perhaps unanswerable question that lies beneath the surface of the transformations that occurred in West German architecture during the first decade after the war: What were the effects of the experience of ruin and privation? As the child of Depression-era American parents and the friend of many Germans whose parents were children during the war, I can speculate on two associated but distinct responses. The first could be a longstanding and

44   Rudolf Schwarz, *Wegweisung der Technik und andere Schriften zum Neuen Bauen, 1926–1961*, ed. Maria Schwarz and Ulrich Conrads, Bauwelt Fundamente (Braunschweig: Vieweg, 1979), 20.
45   Schwarz, *Wegweisung der Technik*, 12.
46   Schwarz, *Wegweisung der Technik*, 12.
47   Schwarz, *Wegweisung der Technik*.

9.4 Formal analogies, Ulrich Conrads, "Material Euphoria and Play," 1953

inextinguishable respect for the intrinsic value of goods and materials. I recall, in the mid-1990s, traveling by car across Germany with a friend and his mother, who had survived the war in Hamburg and then, in the more easy-going 1960s, worked as a stewardess for *Lufthansa*. She had packed our lunch for the trip, *Butterbrot,* and as the time to eat approached, she passed around our sandwiches, wrapped in rubber-banded plastic and mylar foil liners saved from cereal boxes or cracker packages. It had never occurred to me that such things could be reused. The care that this frugality expresses seems again relevant in the context of increasing concerns for resource flows and waste. A second, very different response is one I learned at home in the United States. During the energy crisis of the 1970s, I had been instructed at school on how to save heating fuel. I turned down the thermostat in my parents' house and closed the doors to the bedrooms, which we would not use during the day. "Don't do me any favors," my father said, resetting the thermostat to 73 degrees. "I don't need to recreate the Depression. It was horrible the first time." Comfort, if not excess, marked an achievement to be celebrated.

The bright lines that I have drawn between Schwippert and Ruf, between architectures of lesser and greater means, may be either too blithe or too heavy handed for some. Schwippert of course built large, material-intensive projects, including his housing projects in Berlin and Sweden. Ruf's careful and exacting construction practice never excluded simple traditional materials couched in pure, powerful forms. But there is a spectrum between frugality and largesse, or, perhaps more accurately, the two can co-exist in one constellation of possibilities. As my own position has shifted within the field of architecture, my sense of its benefits and challenges has become more differentiated and more deeply embedded in practice—for example, in my attempt to renovate a mid-century house without the use of power tools, just as it had been built, just as my concerns for resource husbandry would have dictated. That lasted fewer than two days. I chose largesse over the frugality I otherwise idealize. I would therefore offer the following speculation: this same sense of constellation, of varying possibilities and combinations at the scales of personal, social, ethical, and ultimately, economic activity held true throughout the unique architectural moment that occurred at the beginnings of West German life.

Adorno, Theodor W., and Theodor W. Adorno Archiv. *Adorno: Eine Bildmonographie*, 2nd ed. Frankfurt am Main: Suhrkamp Verlag, 2003.

"Amerikanische Generalkonsulate in Bremen, Düsseldorf, Frankfurt und Stuttgart." *Bauen + Wohnen Internationale Zeitschrift* 10, no. 4 (1956), 113–18.

"Architektur der USA seit 1947." Exhibition catalogue. Stuttgart: Dr. Cantz-sche Druckerei, 1950.

Banasch, Georg. *Die Sankt-Hedwigs-Kathedrale in Berlin: Nach ihrer baulichen und künstlerischen Neugestaltung im Jahre 1932*. Berlin: Buchverlag Germania, 1933.

Barnstone, Deborah Ascher. *The Transparent State: Architecture and Politics in Postwar Germany*. London: Routledge, 2005.

Bartning, Otto, Dörte Nicolaisen, and Christian Wolsdorff. *Das andere Bauhaus: Otto Bartning und die Staatliche Bauhochschule Weimar 1926–1930*. Berlin: Bauhaus-Archiv, 1996.

Bartning, Otto. *Spannweite: Aus Schriften und Reden, Ausgewählt und Eingeleitet von Alfred Siemon*. Bramsche bei Osnabrück: Rasch, 1958.

Bartning, Otto, ed. *Mensch und Raum: Das Darmstädter Gespräch 1951*. Darmstadt: Neue Darmstädter Verlagsanstalt, 1951.

Bender, Michael, Roland May, and Kunsthalle Darmstadt. *Architektur der fünfziger Jahre: Die Darmstädter Meisterbauten*. Stuttgart: K. Krämer, 1998.

Bergdoll, Barry. "The Nature of Mies's Space." In Barry Bergdoll and Terence Riley, eds. *Mies in Berlin*. New York: Museum of Modern Art, 2001, 66–105.

"Bericht für General Lucius D. Clay, den Militärgouverneur für Deutschland (U.S. Zone)." *Baurundschau* 9 / 10 (1948), 76–78.

Bernoulli, Hans. "Die Gesetze des Materials. Julius Vischer und Ludwig Hilberseimer: Beton," *Das Werk: Architektur und Kunst* 15, no. 12 (1928), 394.

Bernoulli, Hans. "Philosophische Bemühungen: Rudolf Schwarz, Wegweisung der Technik," *Das Werk: Architektur und Kunst* 15, no. 12 (1928), 392.

Besier, Gerhard. "Ökumenische Mission in Nachkriegsdeutschland: Die Berichte von Stewart W. Herman über die Verhältnisse in der evangelischen Kirche 1945 / 46. 2 Teil," *Kirchliche Zeitgeschichte* 1, no. 2, Theologie und Politik (October 1988), 316–52.

Betts, Paul. *Ruin and Renewal: Civilizing Europe after World War II*. New York: Basic Books, 2020.

Betts, Paul. *The Authority of Everyday Objects: A Cultural History of West German Industrial Design, Weimar and Now*. Berkeley: University of California Press, 2004.

Betts, Paul. "The Bauhaus as Cold-War Legend: West German Modernism Revisited," *German Politics and Society* 14, no. 2 (Summer 1996), 75–100.

Blaser, Werner. "Mies van der Rohe, Chicago School, 1938–56," *Bauen + Wohnen* 10, no. 7 (1956), 217–27.

Blümel, Theodor. "Wiederaufbau der St.-Hedwigs-Kathedrale," *Bauplanung und Bautechnik: Technisch-wissenschaftliche Zeitung für das Bauingenieurwesen* 8, no. 2 (February 1954), 64–67.

Bonatz, Karl. "Anmerkungen zu den Presseinterviews mit Professor Gropius und zu seinem Vortrag im Titania-Palast am 22 August 1947," *Neue Bauwelt* 11 / 12 (November / December, 1947), 550.

Boyken, Immo. "Ludwig Mies van der Rohe and Egon Eiermann: The Dictate of Order," *Journal of the Society of Architectural Historians* 49, no. 2 (June 1990).

Boyken, Immo, Heinrich Heidersberger, Georg Pollich, and Eberhard Tröger. *Egon Eiermann/ Sep Ruf: Deutsche Pavillons, Brüssel 1958*. Stuttgart: Edition Axel Menges, 2007.

Breitenstein, Mikel. "Global Unity: Otto Neurath and the International Encyclopedia of Unified Science." In Gerhard Budin, Christian Swertz, and Konstantin Mitgutsch, eds. Proceedings of the Ninth International ISKO Conference "Knowledge Organization for a Global Learning Society." Würzburg: Ergon, 2006, 93–100. https:// www.ergon-verlag.de/isko_ko /downloads/aikovol102006.pdf (accessed February 9, 2022).

Breuer, Gerda, ed. *Das gute Leben: Der Deutsche Werkbund nach 1945*. Tübingen: Wasmuth, 2006.

Breuer, Gerda. *Hans Schwippert. Bonner Bundeshaus 1949*. Tübingen: Wasmuth, 2009.

Breuer, Gerda, Pia Mingels, and Christopher Oestereich, eds. *Hans Schwippert 1899–1973: Moderation des Wiederaufbaus*. Berlin: Jovis, 2010.

Brickner, Richard M. *Is Germany Incurable?* Philadelphia: J. B. Lippincott, 1943.

Bührer, Werner. *Ruhrstahl und Europa: Die Wirtschaftsvereinigung Eisen- und Stahlindustrie und die Anfänge der europäischen Integration, 1945–1952*, Schriftenreihe der Vierteljahrshefte für Zeitgeschichte. Munich: R. Oldenbourg, 1986.

Bungenstab, Karl-Ernst. "Entstehung, Bedeutungs- und Funktionswandel der Amerika-Häuser. Ein Beitrag zur Geschichte der amerikanischen Auslands-information nach dem 2 Weltkrieg," *Jahrbuch für Amerikastudien* 16 (1971), 189.

Buslei-Wuppermann, Agatha. "Hans Schwippert 1899–1973: Von der Werkkunst zum Design." Diss., Bergische Universität Wuppertal, 2006, Utz Verlag, 2007.

Buslei-Wuppermann, Agatha. "Hans Schwippert als Architekt: Seine Pläne zur Umgestaltung der St. Hedwigs-Kathedrale in Berlin," *Das Münster* 67, no. 2 (2014), 117–22.

Buslei-Wuppermann, Agatha, and Andreas Zeising, eds. *Das Bundeshaus von Hans Schwippert in Bonn: Architektonische Moderne und demokratischer Geist*, 1st ed. Düsseldorf: Grupello, 2009.

Busmann, Johannes. *Die revidierte Moderne: Der Architekt Alfons Leitl 1909–1975*. Wuppertal: Müller und Busmann, 1995.

Cadwell, Mike. *Strange Details, Writing Architecture*. Cambridge, MA: MIT Press, 2007.

Carlin, Wendy. "West German Growth and Institutions, 1945–1900," London: Centre for Economic Policy Research, University College London 1994, 29. https://www.ucl.ac.uk/~uctpa36/west%20germany%20in%20crafts%20toniolo.pdf (accessed December 19, 2021).

Carnap, Rudolf. *Der logische Aufbau der Welt*. Hamburg: F. Meiner, 1998.

Castillo, Greg. "Domesticating the Cold War: Household Consumption as Propaganda in Marshall Plan Germany," *Journal of Contemporary History* 40, no. 2 (2005), 261–88. https://doi.org/10.2307/30036324.

Castillo, Greg. "Making a Spectacle of Restraint: The Deutschland Pavilion at the 1958 Brussels Exposition," *Journal of Contemporary History* 47, no. 1 (2011), 261–88.

Cedro, Rico. "Restoring Mies van der Rohe's 860–880 Lake Shore Drive: When Less Is Not Enough," *CTBUH Journal* 1 (2009), 38–43.

Colomina, Beatriz. *Privacy and Publicity: Modern Architecture as Mass Media*. Cambridge, MA: MIT Press, 1994.

Conrads, Ulrich. "Materialrausch und Spiel: Notizen zur Situation des neuen Bauens," *Baukunst und Werkform* 7, no. 8 (1953), 392–407.

Conrads, Ulrich. *Die Städte himmeloffen: Reden und Reflexionen über den Wiederaufbau des Untergegangenen und die Wiederkehr des Neuen Bauens 1948/49*, Bauwelt Fundamente. Basel: Birkhäuser, 2003.

Conrads, Ulrich, Magdalena Droste, Winfried Nerdinger, and Hilde Strohl, eds. *Die Bauhaus-Debatte 1953: Dokumente einer verdrängten Kontroverse*, Bauwelt Fundamente. Braunschweig: Vieweg, 1994.

Conrads, Ulrich, and Peter Neitzke, eds. *Mensch und Raum: Das Darmstädter Gespräch 1951* Braunschweig: Vieweg, 1991.

Crowley, David. "From Homelessness to Homelessness." In Robin Schuldenfrei, ed. *Atomic Dwelling: Anxiety, Domesticity, and Postwar Architecture*. Abingdon: Routledge, 2012.

Cunha, Ivan F. da. "Utopias and Forms of Life: Carnap's Bauhaus Conferences," *Princípios revista de filosofia* 24, no. 45 (Winter 2017), 121–48.

"Das Bundeshaus in Bonn." *Handelsblatt: Deutschlands Wirtschafts- und Finanzzeitung, Die technische Linie* 3, no. 13 (Friday, July 14, 1950), 1–2.

"Das Lever House in New York." *[Das] Werk* 41, no. 2 (February 1954), 49–54.

"Der Kaufhof-Hauptsitz." *Bauen und Wohnen* 9, no. 4 (1955), 252.

Dillon, Brian. *Ruins, Whitechapel: Documents of Contemporary Art*. London/Cambridge, MA: Whitechapel Gallery/MIT Press, 2011.

Döllgast, Hans. *Journal Retour*. Salzburg: Anton Pustet, 2003.

Dorsemagen, Dirk. "Büro und Geschäftshäuser der 50er Jahre konservatorische Probleme am Beispiel West-Berlin." Diss., Technische Universität Berlin, 2004.

Durth, Werner. *Deutsche Architekten: Biographische Verflechtungen 1900–1970*. Schriften des Deutschen Architekturmuseums zur Architekturgeschichte und Architekturtheorie. Braunschweig: Vieweg, 1986.

Durth, Werner. *Deutsche Architekten: Biographische Verflechtungen 1900–1970*, rev. ed. Stuttgart: K. Krämer, 2001.

Durth, Werner, and Paul Sigel. *Baukultur: Spiegel gesellschaftlichen Wandels*. Berlin: Jovis, 2010.

Eckstein, Hans. "Ist das Bonner Bundeshaus zu schlecht gebaut? Zu den Angriffen gegen die Schlichtheit der neuen Architektur," *Die Neue Zeitung* (August 19, 1950).

Endres, Heinz. *Die St. Hedwigs-Kathedrale in Berlin: Baugeschichte und Wiederaufbau*. Berlin (East): Morus-Verlag, 1963.

Fischer, Wend, and Generalkommisar der Bundesrepublik Deutschland bei der Weltausstellung Brüssel 1958, eds., *Deutschlands Beitrag zur Weltausstellung Brüssel 1958. Ein Bericht*. Düsseldorf: A. Bagel, 1958.

Flierl, Thomas. *Standardstädte: Ernst May in der Sowjetunion 1930–1933. Texte und Dokumente*. Berlin: Suhrkamp, 2012.

Frank, Hartmut. "Dächerkrieg?" In Barbara Burren, Martin Tschanz, and Christa Vogt, eds. *Das schräge Dach: Ein Architekturhandbuch*. Sulgen: Niggli, 2008.

Friedman, Martin. "Noguchi's Imaginary Landscapes," *Design Quarterly* 106/107 (1978), 13–99.

Friedrich, Thomas. *Hitler and Berlin: Abused City*. New Haven: Yale University Press, 2012.

Frisch, Max. *Tagebuch, 1946–1949*. Frankfurt am Main: Suhrkamp Verlag, 1965.

Frybergh, Frank. "Materials," *Journal of Architectural Education (1947–1974)* 16, no. 2 (1961). https://doi.org/10.2307/1424151.

Geiser, Reto. *Giedion and America: Repositioning the History of Modern Architecture.* Zurich: gta Verlag, 2018.

George, Christian. "Studieren in Ruinen: Die Studenten der Universität Bonn in Der Nachkriegszeit (1945–1955)." Diss., University of Bonn, 2008–2009, V&R unipress, 2010.

Giedion, Sigfried. "Der moralische Einfluss der Architektur Mies van der Rohes," *Bauen + Wohnen: Internationale Zeitschrift* 10, no. 7 (1956), 227–29.

Giedion, Sigfried. *Space, Time and Architecture: The Growth of a New Tradition.* Cambridge, MA: Harvard University Press, 1941.

Goetz, Christine, and Victor H. Elbern, eds. *Die St-Hedwigs-Kathedrale zu Berlin.* Regensburg: Schnell + Steiner, 2000.

Gold, John R. *The Experience of Modernism: Modern Architects and the Future City 1928–53.* London: E & FN Spon, 1997.

Grimm, Hans. *Volk ohne Raum.* Munich: Langen-Müller, 1926.

Gropius, Walter. *Apollo in the Democracy: The Cultural Obligation of the Architect.* [Articles and lectures selected, translated, and edited by Ise Gropius.] New York: McGraw-Hill, 1968.

Gropius, Walter. *Bauhausbauten Dessau,* Bauhausbücher. Munich: Albert Langen Verlag, 1930.

Hannemann, Christine. *Die Platte: Industrialisierter Wohnungsbau in der DDR,* 2nd ed. Berlin: Schelzky & Jeep, 2000.

Hasler, Thomas. *Architektur als Ausdruck—Rudolf Schwarz, Studien und Texte zur Geschichte der Architekturtheorie.* Zurich: gta Verlag, 2000.

Häupl, Nadja. *Münchner Nachkriegs-architektinnen: Bea Betz und Edith Horny; Sieben Beiträge zu Leben und Werk nach Begegnungen im Winter 2010.* Munich: Institut für Entwerfen Stadt und Landschaft, Technische Universität München, 2010.

Heidegger, Martin. *Basic Writings.* Edited by David Farrell Krell. San Francisco: Harper Collins, 1977.

Heidegger, Martin. "Building Dwelling Thinking." In *Poetry, Language, Thought,* translated by Albert Hofstadter. New York: Harper Colophon, 1971.

Hein, Carola. "The New York Museum of Modern Art: Engagement in Housing, Planning and Neighbourhood Design." In Robert Freestone and Marco Amati, eds. *Exhibitions and the Development of Modern Planning Culture.* Surrey: Ashgate, 2014, 243–260.

Herbert, Gilbert. *The Dream of the Factory Built House: Walter Gropius and Konrad Wachsmann.* Cambridge, MA: MIT Press, 1984.

Hérvas y Heras, Josenia. "Eine Bauhaus-Architekt in der BRD: Wera Meyer-Waldeck / A Bauhaus Architect in West Germany: Wera Meyer-Waldeck." In Mary Pepchinski, Christina Budde, Wolfgang Voigt, and Peter Cachola Schmal, eds. *Frau Architekt. Seit mehr als 100 Jahren: Frauen im Architekturberuf.* Tübingen: Wasmuth, 2017, 167–296.

Hess, Claus William. *Bürobau mit Blick in die Zukunft: Bericht über Connecticut Life Insurance Co., Bloomfield, Conn. USA.* Barmstedt: Schnelle, 1959.

Hillmann, Roland. *Die Erste Nachkriegsmoderne: Ästhetik und Wahrnehmung der westdeutschen Architektur 1945–63.* Petersberg: Michael Imhof Verlag, 2011.

Hitchcock, Henry-Russell. "The Evolution of Wright, Mies & Le Corbusier," *Perspecta* 1 (1952), 8–15.

Hitchcock, Henry-Russell, and Philip Johnson. *The International Style: Architecture since 1922,* 1st ed. New York: W. W. Norton, 1932.

Hatje, Gerd, and Hubert Hoffmann. *Neue Deutsche Architektur.* Stuttgart: Verlag Gerd Hatje, 1956.

Hoppe, Sabrina. " 'The Strength of Weak Ties'—Protestantische Netzwerke in der frühen Bundes-republik," *Mitteilungen zur Kirchlichen Zeitgeschichte* 9 (2015), 165–172.

Hoster, J., and A. Mann, eds. *Festschrift für Willy Weyres zur Vollendung seines 60 Lebensjahres.* Cologne: Greven und Bechtold, 1964.

Hübner, Jörg. "Protestantische Wirtschaftsethik und Soziale Marktwirtschaft: Verbindungs-linien und Zusammenhänge zwischen 1937 und 1954," *Zeitschrift für Theologie und Kirche* 109, no. 2 (June 2012), 235–269.

Iverson, Margaret. *Alois Riegl: Art History and Theory.* Cambridge, MA: MIT Press, 1993.

Jester, Thomas C., ed. *Twentieth-Century Building Materials: History and Conservation.* New York: McGraw-Hill, 1995.

Johan, Ernst. "Haltung der Zurückhaltung," *Werk und Zeit* (June 1958), 3–6.

Jucho, C. H. "Jucho-Kupferstahl-Fenster für Büro-, Geschäfts- und Wohnhäuser und Siedlungsbauten," industry pamphlet (Dortmund, 1931).

Judt, Tony. *Ill Fares the Land.* New York: Penguin Press, 2010.

Jung, Hyun Tae. "Organization and Abstraction: The Architecture of Skidmore, Owings & Merrill from 1936 to 1956." PhD Diss., Columbia University, 2011.

Karrenberg, Friedrich, ed. *Evangelisches Soziallexikon.* Stuttgart: Kreuz, 1954.

Kleeberg, Martin John. "The Disconto-Gesellschaft and German Industrialization: A Critical Reexamination of the Career of a German Universal Bank, 1851–1914." Diss., St. Catherine's College, University of Oxford, 1988.

Kleinman, Kent, and Leslie Van Duzer. *Mies Van Der Rohe: The Krefeld Villas.* New York: Princeton Architectural Press, 2005.

Köhler, Bettina. "Architecture History as the History of Spatial Experience," *Daidalos: Berlin Architectural Journal* 67 (1998), 36–43.

Krieger, Jan, and Yuima Oliver Kaneko. "St. Hedwig-Kathedrale, Bebelplatz, Berlin-Mitte: Gutachten zur Baugeschichte und Denkmalsubstranzerfassung," Erzbistum Berlin, Erzbischöfliches Ordinariat. Berlin: July, 2013.

Kroll, Benno. "Aufstieg und Fall der Gebrüder Schnelle," *Manager Magazin* (1972), 67–69.

Küppers, Leonhard. "Die Hedwigs-Kathedrale in Berlin," *Das Münster* 10 (November, 1957), 424–30.

Küppers, Leonhard. *Kirche und Kunst in zeitgenössischen Dokumenten.* Edited by J. Walterscheid and H. Storz, vol. 5, Religiöse Quellenschriften. Düsseldorf: Patmos Verlag, 1955.

Küppers, Leonhard. *Südliche Stadt—Das Erlebnis von Pisa, Assisi und Florenz.* Düsseldorf: Bastion Verlag, 1946.

Laws, Christopher. "Art and Architecture Towards Political Crises: The 1937 Paris International Exposition in Context." https://culturedarm.com/1937-Paris-International-Exposition/ (accessed December 16, 2021).

Lee, Pamela M. *Think Tank Aesthetics: Midcentury Modernism, the Cold War and the Neoliberal Present.* Cambridge, MA: MIT Press, 2020.

Leitl, Alfons. "… keine Zeit, eine verlorene Generation zu sein," *Baukunst und Werkform* 11, nr. 4 (1958).

Leitl, Alfons. "Anmerkungen," *Baukunst und Werkform* 5 (May 1951).

Logemann, Jan. *Designed to Sell: European Emigrees and the Making of Consumer Capitalism.* Chicago: University of Chicago Press, 2020.

Lukács, Georg. *The Theory of the Novel: A Historico-Philosophical Essay on the Forms of Great Epic Literature.* Cambridge, MA: MIT Press, 1973.

MacCarthy, Fiona. *Walter Gropius: The Man Who Built the Bauhaus.* Cambridge, MA: Harvard University Press, 2019.

Mäckler, Hermann. "Praeceptor Germaniae et Europae?" *Baukunst und Werkform* 6, no. 2/3 (February/March 1953).

Mantziaras, Panos. "Perspectives of Technology: Rudolf Schwarz on the Artifice and its Reproducability," *Thresholds* 24, Reproduction and Production (Spring 2002), 6–11.

Marcuse, Ludwig. "European Anti-Americanism," *Partisan Review* (May–June 1953), 314–320.

Martin, Reinhold. "The Bunshaft Tapes: A Preliminary Report," *Journal of Architectural Education* 54, no. 2 (2000), 80–87. https://www.jstor.org/stable/1425594.

Mathey, Konstantin. "Die Umgestaltung der St. Hedwigs-Kirche zur Kathedrale des Bistums Berlin (1930–1932) nach einem Entwurf von Prof. Clemens Holzmeister (1886–1983) unter Mitarbeit des Diözesanbaurates Carl Kühn (1973–1942)," *Das Münster* 67, no. 2 (2014), 107–116.

Meissner, Irene. *Sep Ruf 1908–1982, Kunstwissenschaftliche Studien.* Berlin: Deutscher Kunstverlag, 2013.

Metschke, Walter G. "Memoirs of Walter G. Metschke / Compiled under the Auspices of the Chicago Architects Oral History Project, the Ernest R. Graham Study Center for Architectural Drawings, Department of Architecture, the Art Institute of Chicago," in *Chicago Architects Oral History Project.* Chicago: The Art Institute of Chicago, 1998.

Meyer-Waldeck, Wera. "Das Bundesparlament in Bonn," *Architektur und Wohnform* 58, no. 5 (1950), 99–109.

Mitchell, Timothy. *Carbon Democracy: Political Power in the Age of Oil.* London: Verso Books, 2011.

Morsey, Rudolf. "50 Jahre Hochschule für Verwaltungswissenschaften (1947–1997)." In Klaus Lüder, ed. *Staat und Verwaltung: Fünfzig Jahre Hochschule für Verwaltungswissenschaften Speyer.* Berlin: Duncker & Humblot, 1997.

Mozingo, Louise A. *Pastoral Capitalism: A History of Suburban Corporate Landscapes, Urban and Industrial Environments.* Cambridge, MA: MIT Press, 2011.

Müller-Armack, Alfred. "Soziale Irenik" in *Religion und Wirtschaft: Geistesgeschichtliche Hintergründe unserer europäischen Lebensform Wirtschaftspolitik.* Stuttgart: Kohlhammer, 1959.

Nell-Breuning, Oswald von, ed. *Wörterbuch der Politik*, vols. 1–4. Freiburg i. Br.: Herder, 1947–1949.

Neumann, Dietrich, and Juergen Schulz. "Johnson's Grid," *AA Files: Annals of the Architectural Association School of Architecture* 70 (Spring 2015), 60–69.

Oechslin, Werner. *Otto Wagner, Adolf Loos, and the Road to Modern Architecture*, translated by Lynnette Widder. Cambridge: Cambridge University Press, 2002.

Oestereich, Christopher. "Umstrittene Selbstdarstellung: Der Deutsche Beitrag Zur Weltausstellung in Brüssel 1958," *Vierteljahrshefte für Zeitgeschichte* 48, no. 1 (2000), 127–53.

Otero-Pailos, Jorge. *A Polygraph of Architectural Phenomenology: Architecture's Historical Turn.* Minneapolis: University of Minnesota, 2010.

Otto, Elizabeth, and Patrick Rössler. *Bauhaus Women: A Global Perspective.* New York: Bloomsbury, 2019.

Paulmann, Johannes. "Representation without Emulation: German Cultural Diplomacy in Search of Integration and Self-Assurance during the Adenauer Era," *German Politics and Society* 25, no. 2 (83) (2007), 168–200.

Pehnt, Wolfgang. *Die Regel und die Ausnahme: Essays zu Bauen, Planen und Ähnlichem*. Ostfildern: Hatje Cantz Verlag, 2001.

Pehnt, Wolfgang. Epilogue to *Rudolf Schwarz: Wegweisung der Technik*. Edited by Maria Schwarz, Ann Wilde, and Jürge Wilde. Cologne: Walther König, 2008.

Pehnt, Wolfgang, and Hilde Strohl. *Rudolf Schwarz, 1897–1961: Architekt einer anderen Moderne, Bewohnte Bilder*. Ostfildern-Ruit: Hatje Cantz, 1997.

Pommerin, Reiner, ed. *Bonn zwischen Kriegsende und Währungsreform: Erinnerungsberichte von Zeitzeugen*. Bonn: Bouvier, 1991.

"Professor Gropius gibt gute Ratschläge." *Baumeister* (November / December 1947), 389–91.

Ratzel, Friedrich. "Der Lebensraum. Eine biogeographische Studie." In *Festgaben für Albert Schäffle zur siebzigsten Wiederkehr seines Geburtstages am 24 Februar 1901*. Tübingen: H. Laupp, 1901, 101–189.

Reichel, Alexander, and Henning Baumann. *Tragen und Materialisieren / Scale: Stützen, Wände, Decken*. Basel: Birkhäuser, 2013.

Richardson, William. "Architecture, Urban Planning, and Housing During the First Five Year Plans: Hannes Meyer in the USSR, 1930–1936," *Urban Studies* 26, no. 1 (January 2, 1989), 155–63.

Richter, Annemarie. "Gottfried Heinersdorff (1883–1941): Ein Reformer der deutschen Glasbildkunst." Diss., Technische Universität Berlin, 1983.

Ricker, Julia. "Die St. Hedwigs-Kathedrale in Berlin," *Deutsche Stiftung Denkmalschutz: Monumente Online* (December 2014). https://www.monumente-online.de/de/ausgaben/2014/6/die-st-hedwig-kathedrale.php (accessed February 9, 2022).

Riegl, Alois. *Stilfragen: Grundlegungen zu einer Geschichte der Ornamentik*. Berlin: n.p., 1893.

Rössler, Patrick. *Bauhausmädels: A Tribute to the Bauhaus's Women Artists*. Cologne: Taschen, 2019.

Rössler, Patrick, Miriam Krautwurst, and Elizabeth Otto. *4 "Bauhausmädels": Getrud Arndt, Marianne Brandt, Margarete Heymann, Margaretha Reichardt*. Dresden: Sandstein, 2019.

Rother, Ronald. " 'Hinter der katholischen Kirche': Zur Bedeutung von St. Hedwig," *Das Münster* 67, no. 2 (2014), 91–107.

Rowell, Roger M. *Handbook of Wood Chemistry and Wood Composites*, 2nd ed. Boca Raton: CRC Press, 2013.

Schäfer, Hermann. "Kulturelle Wiederbelebung: Ausstellungen in Westdeutschland von Kriegsende 1945 bis in die 1960er Jahre." In Klaus Hildebrand et al., eds. *Geschichtswissenschaft und Zeiterkenntnis. Von der Aufklärung bis zur Gegenwart: Festschrift zum 65. Geburtstag von Horst Möller*. Munich: Oldenbourg, 2008.

"Science: Prescription for Germany." *Time* (Monday, May 14, 1945). http://content.time.com/time/subscriber/article/0,33009,792120-1,00.html (accessed March 23, 2021).

Schmidt, Walther. "Rasteritis," *Bauen und Wohnen* 2 (December 1947), 290–92.

Schmitthenner, Paul. *Baugestaltung: Erste Folge, Das Deutsche Wohnhaus*, 3rd. ed., repr. Stuttgart: Deutsche Verlags-Anstalt, 1984.

Schneck, Adolf G. *Die Bauelemente*, Volumes I and II: *Fenster* and *Türen*. Stuttgart: Julius Hoffmann, 1932/3.

Schöttler, Sonja. *Funktionale Eloquenz: Das Kölner Amerika-Haus und die Kulturinstitute der Vereinigten Staaten von Amerika in Deutschland*. Worms: Wernersche Verlagsgesellschaft, 2011.

Schulte, Sabine. "Die St.-Hedwigs-Kathedrale als Symbolraum des Aufbruchs, Architekten- und Ingenieur-Verein zu Berlin." Presentation to the Architekten- und Ingenieurverein zu Berlin-Brandenburg e.V. September 8, 2015. http://www.freunde-hedwigskathedrale.de/dokumente/fachartikel/ (accessed February 9, 2022).

Schulz, Bernhard. "Gescheitert, aber doch gewonnen: Die Protagonisten des Neuen Bauens in der Sowjetunion," *Osteuropa* 66, no. 11/12: *Die Ordnung der Dinge: Qualitative Analysen zum Osten Europas* (November 2016), 169–80.

Schulz, Walter. "Über den philosophiegeschichtlichen Ort Martin Heideggers," *Philosophische Rundschau* 1, no 4 (1953/54), 211–32.

Schwartz, Frederic J. "The Disappearing Bauhaus." In Jeffrey Saletnik and Robin Schuldenfrei, eds. *Bauhaus Construct: Fashioning Identity, Discourse and Modernism*. London: Routledge, 2009, 61–82.

Schwarz, Rudolf. "Das Unplanbare." In Ulrich Conrads and Peter Neitzke, eds. *Mensch und Raum: Das Darmstädter Gespräch 1951*. Braunschweig: Vieweg, 1991.

Schwarz, Rudolf. *The Church Incarnate: The Sacred Function of Christian Architecture*. Chicago: H. Regnery, 1958.

Schwarz, Rudolf. *Vom Bau der Kirche*, 2nd ed. Heidelberg: L. Schneider, 1947.

Schwarz, Rudolf. "Was dennoch besprochen werden muss," *Baukunst und Werkform* 7, no. 4 (1953), 191–99.

Schwarz, Rudolf. *Wegweisung der Technik: Part 1*. Potsdam: Müller & Kiepenheuer, 1928.

Schwarz, Rudolf. *Wegweisung der Technik und andere Schriften zum Neuen Bauen, 1926–1961*, Bauwelt Fundamente, ed. Maria Schwarz and Ulrich Conrads. Braunschweig: Vieweg, 1979.

Schwippert, Hans. *Denken Lehren Bauen*. Düsseldorf and Vienna: Econ, 1982.

Schwippert, Hans. *Neuer Hausrat*. Aachen: Kunstgewerbeschule, 1932.

Semper, Gottfried. *Die vier Elemente der Baukunst: Ein Beitrag zur vergleichenden Baukunde*. Braunschweig: Friedrich Vieweg und Sohn, 1851.

Singh, Patwant. "Design in Deutschland," in *Design* 4, no. 2 (February, 1960).

"Skidmore, Owings & Merrill." *The Bulletin of the Museum of Modern Art* 18, no. 1 (1950), 4–21. https://doi.org/10.2307/4058240.

Smith, Woodruff D. "Friedrich Ratzel and the Origins of Lebensraum," *German Studies Review* 3 (1980).

Smithson, Alison. "How to Recognize and Read Mat-Building: Mainstream Architecture as It Has Developed Towards the Mat-Building," *Architectural Design* 44, no. 9 (September 1974), 573–90.

Smolian, Alexander Henning. "Serie oder Persönlichkeit—zum Technikverständnis von Rudolf Schwarz," *Wolkenkuckucksheim/Cloud-Cuckoo-Land* 19, no. 33 (2014), 193–209, cloud-cuckoo.net /fileadmin/issues_en/issue_33 /article_smolian.pdf (accessed December 16, 2021).

Solsten, Eric. "Germany: A Country Study." Washington: GPO for the Library of Congress, 1995. http:// countrystudies.us/germany /and http://countrystudies.us /germany/84.htm (accessed February 9, 2022).

Springhart, Heike. " 'Dass es eine Hoffnung gibt für Deutschland ...' Religion und Kirchen im Nachkriegsdeutschland als gesellschaftliche Institutionen der Reeducation." In Hans Braun, ed. *Die lange Stunde null: Gelenkter sozialer Wandel in Westdeutschland nach 1945*. Uta Gerhardt, and Everhard Holtmann. Baden-Baden: Nomos, 2007, 91–114.

Staub, Alexandra. *Conflicted Identities: Housing and the Politics of Cultural Representation*, Routledge Research in Architecture. New York: Routledge, Taylor & Francis Group, 2016.

Stephan, Alexander. *"Communazis": FBI Surveillance of German Émigré Writers*. New Haven: Yale University Press, 2000.

Stern, Robert A. M., Thomas Mellins, and David Fishman. *New York 1960: Architecture and Urbanism between the Second World War and the Bicentennial*. New York: Monacelli Press, 1995.

"Symposium in Symbolic Setting: Fine New Building Meets Challenge of City Crisis." *Life* (October 21, 1957), 49–52.

Tamms, Friedrich. "Düsseldorf, eine neue Stadt," *Der Architekt BDA* IV (1955), 421–25.

Taut, Bruno. *Die neue Wohnung: Die Frau als Schöpferin*, 2nd ed. Leipzig: Klinkhardt & Biermann, 1924.

Taut, Bruno, Walter Gropius, and Adolf Behne. "New Ideas on Architecture." In Ulrich Conrads, ed. *Programs and Manifestoes on 20th-Century Architecture*. Cambridge, MA: MIT Press, 1971.

Thöner, Wolfgang. "Bauhaus in der DDR: Im Schatten der Parteiideologie." *Der Spiegel* (April 1, 2019), https://www.tagesspiegel.de /kultur/bauhaus-in-der-ddr-im-schatten-der-parteiideologie /24157522.html (accessed November 13, 2020).

Truman, Harry. "Program for US Aid for European Recovery, December 19, 1947." Reprinted in "In der Vergangenheit nach Zukunftsperspektiven Ausschau halten: Die Vereinigten Staaten von Amerika und Deutschland 1945–1950 und danach," *Zeitschrift für Kulturaustausch* (1987).

Turner Construction Company. *A Record of War Activities*. New York: Turner Construction Co., 1918.

Vallye, Anna. "Design and the Politics of Knowledge in America, 1937–67: Walter Gropius, Gyorgy Kepes." PhD diss., Columbia University, 2011.

Völkel, Hellmuth. "Mantelwände bei Skelettbauten," *Bauwelt* 16 (1958), 366–67.

Vonyó, Tamás. "The Wartime Origins of the Wirtschaftstwunder: The Growth of West German Industry, 1938–55," *Jahrbuch für Wirtschaftsgeschichte* 55, no. 2 (2014).

Vossoughian, Nader. *Otto Neurath: The Language of the Global Polis*. Rotterdam: NAi, 2008.

Wagnleitner, Reinhold. "Propagating the American Dream: Cultural Policies as Means of Integration," *American Studies International* 24, no. 1 (1986). https://doi.org /10.2307/41278824.

Welty, Eberhard. *A Handbook of Christian Social Ethics*. New York: Herder and Herder, 1960.

Welty, Eberhard. *Herders Sozialkathechismus: Ein Werkbuch der katholischen Sozialethik in Frage und Antwort*. 3 vols. Freiburg i. Br.: Herder, 1951–1958.

Widder, Lynnette. "Ist damit räumliches Bauen zu Ende? Hans Schwippert, Sep Ruf and the Culture of Building in German Modern Architecture 1949–59." Diss., ETH Zurich, 2016.

Widder, Lynnette, and John Caserta. *Ira Rakatansky: As Modern as Tomorrow*. San Francisco: William Stout Books, 2010.

Wintgens, Benedikt. "Neues Parlament, neue Bilder? Die Fotografin Erna Wagner-Hehmke und ihr Blick auf den Bundestag." In Marij Leenders and Andreas Biefang, eds. *Das ideale Parlament: Erich Salomon als Fotograf in Berlin und Den Haag, 1928–1940*. Düsseldorf: Droste Verlag, 2014, 293–314.

Zietzschmann, Ernst. "Neubau der Manufacturers Trust Company, New York," *Bauen + Wohnen: Internationale Zeitschrift* 10, no. 2 (1956), 49–52.

Zietzschmann, Ernst. " 'Teamwork': Eine Architekturfirma mit 322 Mitarbeitern," *Bauen + Wohnen: Internationale Zeitschrift* 6, no. 3 (June 1952), 139–45.

Zietzschmann, Ernst. "Wäscherei in Kalifornien," *Bauen + Wohnen: Internationale Zeitschrift* 6, no. 5 (October 1952), 264–67.

Zimmerman, Claire. *Photographic Architecture in the Twentieth Century*. Minneapolis: University of Minnesota Press, 2014.

"Zum fünfzigjährigen Bestehen der Firma C.H. Jucho in Dortmund." *Die Bautechnik* 5, no. 31 (July 15, 1927).

Abbreviations

AM TUM
Architekturmuseum der
Technischen Universität München

BDA
Bund deutscher Architektinnen
und Architekten

CIAM
Congrès internationaux
d'architecture moderne

GNM, DKA, NL
Germanisches Nationalmuseum,
Deutsches Kunstarchiv, Nachlass

HICOG
United States High Commissioner
on Germany

SOM
Skidmore, Owings and Merrill

HfV
Hochschule für Verwaltungswissenschaften, Speyer

HfG
Hochschule für Gestaltung, Ulm

Image Credits

Photographs of drawings from the collection of Elisabeth and Notburga Ruf by Thad Russell.

0.1: GNM, DKA, NL, Schwippert, Hans, 49
0.2: Baukunst und Werkform B4, 1958. AM TUM, ruf-121-1013
0.3: AM TUM, Schwi-92-30
0.4: Stadtarchiv München, FS-STR-1397-1
0.5: Courtesy of the Universität für Verwaltungswissenschaften Speyer Archive
0.6: GNM, DKA, NL Schwippert, Hans,158
1.1: *Der Bau*, July 1950. GNM, DKA, NL Schwippert, Hans, 117
1.2: Hugo Schmölz. AM TUM, schwi-92-3
1.3: Erna Wagner-Hehmke. Stiftung Haus der Geschichte der Bundesrepublik Deutschland Nr. 1987/1/32.1486
1.5: Adolf G. Schneck, *Fenster aus Holz und Metall- Konstruktion und Maueranschlag: Ein Überblick über das Gesamtgebiet* (Stuttgart: Hoffmann, 1942), 134–35
1.6: Associated Press. AM TUM, schwi-92-49
1.7–1.13: AM TUM, schwi-92-54, 41, 52, 53, 55, 43, 56, 47, 34, 48, and 32
1.14: Rudolf Schwarz, *The Church Incarnate: The Sacred Function of Christian Architecture* (Chicago: Henry Regnery Company, 1958) 12–13, 114–15, 194–95; American translation of Rudolf Schwarz, *Vom Bau der Kirche* (Heidelberg: Schneider, 1947)
1.15–1.17: AM TUM, schwi-92-14, 32, 50, and 51
1.18–1.22: GNM, DKA, NL Schwippert, Hans, 122-0029, 0004, 0047, 0053, 0057, and 0026
2.1: Thad Russell
2.2–2.6: Collection of Elisabeth and Notburga Ruf
2.7: Thad Russell
2.8: Collection of Elisabeth and Notburga Ruf
2.9–2.19: Thad Russell
2.20–2.21: Collection of Elisabeth and Notburga Ruf
2.22–2.23: Thad Russell
2.24–2.28: Collection of Elisabeth and Notburga Ruf
2.29: Thad Russell
2.30–2.31: Collection of Elisabeth and Notburga Ruf
2.32: Thad Russell

2.33–2.34: Collection of Elisabeth and Notburga Ruf
2.35: Thad Russell
2.36–2.38: Collection of Elisabeth and Notburga Ruf
2.39: Thad Russell
"Job Books": Job Book for the Akademie der Bildenden Künste in Nuremberg photograph by Thad Russell; Hedwigskathedrale job book photographs by the author; Archive, St. Hedwigs-Kathedrale Berlin and collection of Elisabeth and Notburga Ruf
3.1: Denkmalarchiv Wissenschafts-stadt Darmstadt
3.2–3.3: *Mensch und Raum* exhibition catalogue, Berlin 1951, 3, 4, last page, and overleaf
3.4: Rudolf Schwarz and Albert Renger-Patzsch, *Wegweisung der Technik* (Potsdam: Müller & Kiepenheuer, 1928), 68–69, 72–73
3.5: Otto Bartning, ed. *Mensch und Raum: Därmstädter Gespräch 1951* (Darmstadt: Neue Darmstädter Verlagsanstalt, 1951), 187
4.2–4.5: *Baukunst und Werkform*, 1951–53 covers no. 2/3 (1953), 66–67; no. 8 (1953), 402–403; no. 2/3 (1953), 80–83
"UC": *Programs and Manifestoes* photograph by Thad Russell, books collection of Mary McLeod; Ulrich Conrads, "Material Euphoria and Play," from *Baukunst und Werkform* 7, no. 8, (1953), 392–407, here 392–93; Ulrich Conrads at home in Berlin, Photograph by Wolfgang Reuss, courtesy Redaktion Bauwelt
5.1: saai Archiv für Architektur und Ingenieurbau, Karlsruhe Institute of Technology, Werkarchiv Egon Eiermann, EE_137_N_0071
5.2–5.10: Wend Fischer and Generalkommisar der Bundes-republik Deutschland bei der Weltausstellung Brüssel 1958, eds., *Deutschlands Beitrag zur Weltaus-stellung Brüssel 1958. Ein Bericht.*, (Düsseldorf: A. Bagel, 1958), appendix, 20–21, 110–11, 138–39, 108–9, 110, 106, 70–73
5.11: Werner Blaser, "Mies van der Rohe, Chicago School, 1938–56," *Bauen + Wohnen Internationale Zeitschrift* 10, no. 7 (1956), 218–19
6.1: "So wohnt Amerika," *Information Bulletin* (December 1949), 63 and 67, University of Wisconsin Digital Collections
6.2: *The Bulletin of the Museum of Modern Art*, "Skidmore, Owings

and Merrill Architects, USA," vol. 18, no. 1, fall 1950. Digital image ©Museum of Modern Art/Licensed by SCALA/Art Resource NY.

6.3: Claus William Hess, *Bürobau mit Blick in die Zukunft*, (Barmstedt: Schnelle, 1959), 16–17

6.4: Hubert Hoffman, ed., *Neue deutsche Architektur*, (Stuttgart: Hatje, 1956), 156–57

6.5: Josef Gartner GmbH, promotional calendar, May and June 1952

6.6–6.9: *Bauen und Wohnen*: vol. 9, February 1954; vol. 9, April 1954; vol. 11, April 1956; vol. 12, January 1957

6.10: Photographs and notes by Natalie de Blois, collection of the author

6.11: *Bauwelt* 47, no. 11, March 12, 1956, 246–47

6.12: Morley Baer, photograph of United States Consulate in Düsseldorf, Box 3, Folder 29, Gordon Bunshaft architectural drawings and papers, 1909–1990, Drawings and Archives, Avery Architectural & Fine Arts Library, Columbia University

6.13: *Bauwelt* 47, no. 11, March 12, 1956, 248–49

6.14–6.16: Construction documents A-007, A-008, and A-14, courtesy of Skidmore, Owings and Merrill New York Office

6.17: Collection of Elisabeth und Notburga Ruf

"Ruf Family Archive": Photographs by Thad Russell

7.1–7.2: Thad Russell

7.3–7.6: Photographer unknown; courtesy of the Deutsche Universität für Verwaltungswissenschaften Speyer

7.7: Collection of Elisabeth und Notburga Ruf

7.8–7.12: Thad Russell

7.13: Courtesy of the Deutsche Universität für Verwaltungswissenschaften

7.14–7.16: Thad Russell

7.17: Courtesy of the Deutsche Universität für Verwaltungswissenschaften and the Hochbauamt Speyer

7.18: Collection of Elisabeth und Notburga Ruf

7.19: AM TUM, ruf-53-2

7.20: Collection of Elisabeth und Notburga Ruf

7.21: Courtesy of the Universität für Verwaltungswissenschaften; published in the Speyer *Tagespiegel*, September 14, 1960

7.22: Collection of Elisabeth und Notburga Ruf

7.23: *Life* Magazine, October 21, 1957, collection of the author

7.24: Thad Russell

7.25: Collection of Elisabeth und Notburga Ruf

7.26: Courtesy of the Universität für Verwaltungswissenschaften

7.27: Collection of Elisabeth und Notburga Ruf

7.28: Courtesy of the Universität für Verwaltungswissenschaften

7.29: Collection of Elisabeth und Notburga Ruf

7.30: Courtesy of the Universität für Verwaltungswissenschaften

7.31–7.35: Thad Russell

8.1–8.2: Archive, St. Hedwigs-Kathedrale Berlin

8.3: Leonhard Küppers, "Die St. Hedwigskathedrale," *Das Münster* 10, November 1957, 430

8.4–8.6: Hans Schwippert, *Ausbau der St.-Hedwigs-Kathedrale zu Berlin 1956–1963*, self-published brochure, 1969, 6–11

8.7–8.12: Archive, St. Hedwigs-Kathedrale Berlin

8.13: Photograph by the author

8.14–8.16: GNM, DKA, NL Schwippert, Hans,122-0031a, 158-1963-05-31a, and 158-001a

8.17–8.20: Archive, St. Hedwigs-Kathedrale Berlin

8.21: Photograph by the author

8.22–8.26: GNM, DKA, NL Schwippert, Hans 158-0006, 158-0002a, 158-1962-10-28a, 158-0004a, 158-0003a

8.27–8.28: Photograph by the author

"Construction Documents": Photographs of drafting supplies, dollhouse, and "women's work" by Walter Mair, 2013; cabinetry construction drawing and self-portrait by the author

9.1: Max Taut, *Berlin im Aufbau* (Potsdam: Müller & Kiepenheuer, 1946), cover

9.2: *Saturday Review*, January 29, 1944, centerfold

9.3: Rudolf Schwarz, *Wegweisung der Technik*, part 1 (Potsdam: Müller & Kiepenheuer, 1928), 60–61

9.4: Ulrich Conrads, "Materialrausch und Spiel," *Baukunst und Werkform* 7, no. 8 (1953), 404

About the Author

Lynnette Widder was educated as both an architect and architectural historian. Raised and schooled in New York City, she has practiced architecture in New York, Berlin, Basel, and Zurich; and has taught at universities in the United States, Canada, and Switzerland. She is currently Associate Professor of Professional Practice at Columbia University, where she teaches courses on the sustainable built environment and has conducted collaborative research, including most recently a project funded by the United Nations Development Program in Guinea on community-based environmental impact tracking. She is the co-author of two books on architecture and architectural education, as well as author of numerous journal articles and book chapters on architectural history and sustainable building practices. In 2020–2022, she was a fellow at the Institute for Ideas and Imagination at Reid Hall in Paris and, in 2022, a MacDowell fellow.

Acknowledgements

As the culmination of more than two decades of on- and off-again work, this book has drawn upon more conversations, exchanges and opportunities afforded than I was able to document along the way. Were my record-keeping more consistent, I would use this space to list all the friends, colleagues, family members, and students who have listened for years now as I went on about construction details drawn two-thirds of a century earlier. I'll name Thomas Gardner, Brian Goldberg, Joseph Imorde, Kathrin Stengel, and Evita Yumul here, hoping that all the many others will know how much I valued their thoughts and attention.

Thanks to its long timeline, the project could benefit greatly from the mentorship of Barry Bergdoll, Mary McLeod, Dietrich Neumann, Andreas Huyssen, Eeva-Liisa Pelkonen, Ute Poerschke, and Philip Ursprung, each of whom provided different perspectives on the material and my approach to it. Without the enormous generosity and trust offered to me by the heirs and arbiters of the archival material at stake, there would be no project at all: Elisabeth and Notburga Ruf; Horst Peter; the Skidmore, Owings and Merrill New York Office; Prof. Stefan Fisch of the Universität für Verwaltungswissenschaften; Dr. Claudia Laurien-Kehnen and Thorsten Schenk of the Hedwigskathedrale Berlin; Dr. Anja Schmidt at the Technical University of Munich; the staff of the Deutsches Kunstarchiv at the Germanisches Nationalmuseum in Nuremberg; and the staff of Avery Library at Columbia University.

As I finished the manuscript amidst statutory confinement in Paris at the beginning of 2021, the daily conversations with the other fellows and staff at Columbia's Institute for Ideas and Imagination—in particular Abounadara Collective, Anuk Arudpragassam, Lamia Joreige, Sky Macklay, Mark Mazower, João Pina, Ersi Sotiropoulos, Mila Turajlić, Clair Wills, Marie d'Ornigny, and James Allen—provided unexpected and new ways to think about material I thought that I had already understood. Lorin Stein brilliantly edited the non-academic texts and encouraged me with long, decisive conversations from various far-flung pandemic hideaways. Thad Russell, a beloved friend and collaborator, tramped through snow, complicated train connections, and a bad back for ten intensive days in Germany to make the wonderful contemporary photos to which I wrote. I am also indebted to Dr. Irene Meissner, Kaye Geipel, Sebastian Redecke, and Prof. Lars Blunck for their timely answers and generosity. I also wish to thank Dr. Steve Cohen, founder and head of Columbia's Masters of Sustainability Management, where I hold my faculty position, for his support in all things academic.

And finally, of course, I want to thank my two families, the one which I helped to make and the one into which I was born.

The publication project received financial support from an Arnold W. Brunner Grant from the Center for Architecture; Columbia University School of Professional Studies Dean's Applied Research Award, 2018; Columbia Institute for Ideas and Imagination; Graham Foundation for Advanced Studies in the Fine Arts; and DAAD (German Academic Exchange Service).

Project assistance: Regan Mies, Jamie Hardy, Gabi Levy
Photography: Thad Russell
Copyediting: Elizabeth Tucker
Project management and proofreading: Jennifer Bartmess
Graphic concept, typesetting & design: Dan Solbach, Hjördis Lyn Behncken
Production: DZA Druckerei zu Altenburg GmbH
Typeface: Magister (Source Type)
Paper: Holmen TRND; ProfiSilk (cover); Pop'Set Californian Blue (endpaper)

Cover images: Erna Wagner-Hehmke, Stiftung Haus der Geschichte der Bundesrepublik Deutschland Nr. 1987/1/32.1486 (front);
Albert Renger-Patzsch, Architekturmuseum der Technischen Universität München (back)

© 2022
gta Verlag, ETH Zurich
Institute for the History and Theory of Architecture
Department of Architecture
8093 Zurich, Switzerland
www.verlag.gta.arch.ethz.ch

Bibliographic information published by the Deutsche Nationalbibliothek The Deutsche Nationalbibliothek lists this publication in the Deutsche Nationalbibliografie; detailed bibliographic data are available on the Internet under http://dnb.dnb.de.

ISBN 978-3-85676-427-2